Pragmatism, Neo-Pragmatism, and Religion

American Liberal Religious Thought

Donald A. Crosby and W. Creighton Peden
General Editors

Vol. 6

PETER LANG
New York • Washington, D.C./Baltimore • Boston
Bern • Frankfurt am Main • Berlin • Vienna • Paris

Pragmatism, Neo-Pragmatism, and Religion

Conversations
with Richard Rorty

Edited by
Charley D. Hardwick
& Donald A. Crosby

PETER LANG
New York • Washington, D.C./Baltimore • Boston
Bern • Frankfurt am Main • Berlin • Vienna • Paris

B
832
.P765
1997

Library of Congress Cataloging-in-Publication Data

Pragmatism, neo-pragmatism, and religion: conversations with Richard Rorty /
Charley D. Hardwick and Donald A. Crosby, editors.
  p. cm. — (American liberal religious thought; vol. 6)
"Essays ... selected from those presented at a Highlands Institute
  for American Religious Thought conference in June 1995
  in Highlands, North Carolina"—Pref.
Includes bibliographical references.
1. Pragmatism—Congresses. 2. Rorty, Richard—Congresses. 3. Religious
thought—United States—Congresses. 4. Religion—Philosophy—Congresses.
5. Liberalism (Religion)—Congresses. 6. United States—Religion—19th
century—Congresses. 7. United States—Religion—20th century—
Congresses. I. Hardwick, Charley D. II. Crosby, Donald A. III. Series.
   B832.P765   144'.3—DC21   97-12507
              ISBN 0-8204-3730-1
              ISSN 1080-5389

Die Deutsche Bibliothek-CIP-Einheitsaufnahme

Pragmatism, neo-pragmatism, and religion: conversations with Richard Rorty /
Charley D. Hardwick and Donald A. Crosby, eds. –New York;
Washington, D.C./Baltimore; Boston; Bern; Frankfurt am Main;
Berlin; Vienna; Paris: Lang.
(American liberal religious thought; 6)
ISBN 0-8204-3730-1

The paper in this book meets the guidelines for permanence and durability
of the Committee on Production Guidelines for Book Longevity
of the Council of Library Resources.

© 1997 Peter Lang Publishing, Inc., New York

All rights reserved.
Reprint or reproduction, even partially, in all forms such as microfilm,
xerography, microfiche, microcard, and offset strictly prohibited.

Printed in the United States of America.

CONTENTS

Preface — ix

I. Keynote Address

Religious Faith, Intellectual Responsibility, and Romance — 3
Richard Rorty

II. Plenary Addresses

Rorty, Diggins, and the Promise of Pragmatism — 25
Henry S. Levinson

A Paleopragmatic Philosophy of History of Philosophy — 43
Robert C. Neville

Religion and Inquiry in William James — 61
Wayne Proudfoot

Religious Naturalism: Humanistic versus Theistic — 75
J. Wesley Robbins

III. Rorty, Pragmatism, and Historicism

The Pragmatic Secularization of Theology — 99
Victor Anderson

Habet Dewey Animam? — 113
J. Harley Chapman

Judging Theologies: Truth in an Historicist Perspective   129
Sheila G. Davaney

Pragmatism, Postmodernism, and Politics   149
Mary Doak

Minds, Bodies, Experience, Nature: Is Panpsychism Really Dead?   163
Warren G. Frisina

From Loneliness to Solitude: The Pragmatist's Path to Salvation   187
David L. Hall

Correspondence, Coherence, Satisfaction, Power: 205
The Four Elements of James's Pragmatic Theory of Truth
Fred W. Hallberg

Pragmatism, Philosophical Respectability,   223
and the Meaning of Life
Yeager Hudson

Radical Empiricism and the Holographic Model of Reality   239
Jennifer G. Jesse

Rorty's Neopragmatism and the Religious Humanist Option   253
Mason Olds

Rorty among the Theologians: 273
The Possibility of Theology after the New Historicism
Hendrik R. Pieterse

Rorty's Final Vocabularies and the Possibility of a   293
Historicist Metaphysics
Jerome P. Soneson

Richard Rorty and the Possibility of Theology   309
Everett J. Tarbox, Jr.

The Function of Religion in Culture: 337
A Hiatus in the Liberal Pragmatic View of Culture and Religion
Henk M. Vroom

IV. Other Themes

Finite is All Right! Confessions of a Slow Learner Donald A. Crosby	357
The Place of the "Sacred": *A Critical Response to Edward Farley's Good and Evil* Charley D. Hardwick	383
The Minimalist Critique of Radical Monotheism: *A Reconsideration of Transcendence* Thomas D. Parker	403
On Listening to Indigenous Peoples and Neo-Pagans: *Obstacles to Appropriating the Older Ways* Jerome A. Stone	421
Gordon Kaufman as a Liberal Theologian: *An Aesthetic Appraisal* Edgar A. Towne	437
Why Do We Make Those Choices? Some Reflections on Faith, *Pluralism, and Commitment* J. Wentzel van Huyssteen	453
About the Authors	469

PREFACE

The essays in this volume were selected from those presented at a Highlands Institute for American Religious Thought conference in June 1995 in Highlands, North Carolina. The conference was on the theme "Pragmatism (Paleo- and Neo-) and American Religious Thought" and featured Richard Rorty as the keynote speaker and focus of discussion. The Highlands Institute wishes to thank Professor Rorty for his attendance and his contribution to this conference. Papers were welcomed on other themes as well, and a selection from these has been included in Part IV. Though most of the essays printed here reflect the scholarly outlook of the Highlands Institute, some articulate different perspectives.

The Highlands Institute is a community of productive scholars with diverse theological and philosophical perspectives. The Institute contributes to the academic study of religion through interpretive, critical, and constructive reflection, the principal focus of which is on distinctively American religious thought. It fosters broad discussion of relevant options through its sponsorship of conferences, seminars, workshops, and publications.

The work of the Institute emphasizes:
- the interface between theology and philosophy, especially where theological efforts have utilized the American religious tradition;
- the history and development of liberal religious thought in America;
- themes pertinent to the "Chicago School" of theology; and
- naturalism in American theology and philosophy.

The editors wish to thank Jane Auhl for her invaluable assistance in the editing and production of this volume.

Charley D. Hardwick and Donald A. Crosby
Highlands, North Carolina
February 1997

I. Keynote Address

RELIGIOUS FAITH, INTELLECTUAL RESPONSIBILITY, AND ROMANCE

Richard Rorty

I.

In thinking about William James, it helps to remember that James not only dedicated *Pragmatism* to John Stuart Mill, but reiterated some of Mill's most controversial claims. In "The Moral Philosopher and the Moral Life," James says that "The only possible reason there can be why any phenomenon ought to exist is that such a phenomenon actually is desired" (WB, p. 149). This echo of the most ridiculed sentence in Mill's *Utilitarianism* is, I suspect, deliberate. One of James' most heartfelt convictions was that to know whether a claim should be met, we need *only* ask which other claims—"claims actually made by some concrete person"—it runs athwart. We need not also ask whether it is a "valid" claim. He deplored the fact that philosophers still followed Kant rather than Mill, still thought of validity as raining down upon a claim "from some sublime dimension of being, which the moral law inhabits, much as upon the steel of the compass-needle the influence of the Pole rains down from out of the starry heavens" (WB, p. 148).

The view that there is no source of obligation save the claims of individual sentient beings entails that we have no responsibility to anything other than such beings. Most of the relevant sentient individuals are our fellow humans. So talk about our responsibility to Truth, or to Reason, must be replaced by talk about our responsibility to our fellow human beings. James' account of truth and knowledge is a utilitarian ethics of belief, designed to facilitate such replacement.[1] Its point of departure is Peirce's treatment of a belief as a habit of action, rather than as a representation. A utilitarian philosophy of religion must treat being religious as a habit of action. So its principal concern must be the extent to which the actions of religious believers frustrate the needs of other

---

This essay will appear in the forthcoming *The Cambridge Companion to William James* to be published by Cambridge University Press.

human beings, rather than the extent to which religion gets something right.

Our responsibility to Truth is not, for James, a responsibility to get things right. Rather, it is a responsibility to ourselves to make our beliefs cohere with one another, and to our fellow humans to make them cohere with theirs. As in Habermas' account of "communicative rationality," our obligation to be rational is exhausted by our obligation to take account of other people's doubts and objections to our beliefs.[2] This view of rationality makes it natural to say, as James does, that the true is "what would be better for us to believe" (P, p. 42).

But of course what is good for one person or group to believe will not be good for another person or group. James never was sure how to avoid the counter-intuitive consequence that what is true for one person or group may not be true for another. He fluctuated between Peirce's identification of truth with what will be believed under ideal conditions, and Dewey's strategy of avoiding the topic of truth and talking instead about justification. But for my present purpose—evaluating James' argument in "The Will to Believe"—it is not necessary to decide between these strategies.[3] For that purpose, I can duck questions about what pragmatists should say about truth. I need consider only the question of whether the religious believer has a right to her faith—whether this faith conflicts with her intellectual responsibilities.

It is a consequence of James' utilitarian view of the nature of obligation that *the obligation to justify one's beliefs arises only when one's habits of action interfere with the fulfillment of others' needs*. Insofar as one is engaged in a private project, that obligation lapses. The underlying strategy of James' utilitarian/pragmatist philosophy of religion is to *privatize* religion. This privatization allows him to construe the supposed tension between Science and Religion as the illusion of opposition between cooperative endeavours and private projects.[4] On a pragmatist account, scientific inquiry is best viewed as the attempt to find a single, unified, coherent, description of the world—the description which makes it easiest to predict the consequences of events and actions, and thus easiest to gratify certain human desires. When pragmatists say that "creationist science" is *bad* science their point is that it subordinates these desires to other, less widespread, desires. But since religion has aims other than gratification of our need to predict and control, it is not clear that there need be a quarrel between religion and orthodox, atoms-and-void, science, any more than between literature and science. Further, if a private relation to God is not accompanied with the claim to knowledge of the Divine Will, there may be no conflict between religion and utilitarian ethics. A suitably privatized form of religious belief might dictate neither one's scientific beliefs nor anybody's moral choices save one's own. That form of belief would be able to gratify a need without threatening to thwart any needs of any others, and would thus meet the utilitarian test.

W.K. Clifford, James' chosen opponent in "The Will to Believe," thinks that we have a duty to seek the truth, distinct from our duty to seek happiness. His way of describing this duty is not as a duty to get reality right, but rather as a duty not to believe without evidence. James quotes him as saying "if a belief has been accepted on insufficient evidence, the pleasure is a stolen one . . . It is sinful, because it is stolen in defiance of our duty to mankind . . . It is wrong always, everywhere, and for anyone to believe anything upon insufficient evidence" (WB, p. 18). Clifford asks us to be responsive to "evidence," as well as to human needs. So the question between James and Clifford comes down to: is evidence something which floats free of human projects, or is the demand for evidence simply a demand from other human beings for cooperation on such projects?

The view that evidential relations have a kind of existence independent of human projects takes various forms, of which the most prominent are realism and foundationalism. Realist philosophers say that the only true source of evidence is the world as it is in itself.[5] The pragmatist objections to realism start from the claim that ". . . it is impossible to strip the human element from even our most abstract theorizing. All our mental categories without exception have been evolved because of their fruitfulness for life, and owe their being to historic circumstances, just as much as do the nouns and verbs and adjectives in which our languages clothe them" (ECR, p. 552).[6] If pragmatists are right about this, the only question at issue between them and realists is whether the notion of "the world as it is in itself" can be made fruitful for life. James' criticism of correspondence theories of truth boil down to the argument that a belief's purported "fit" with the intrinsic nature of reality adds nothing which makes any practical difference to the fact that it is universally agreed to lead to successful action.

Foundationalism is an epistemological view which can be adopted by those who suspend judgment on the realist's claim that reality has an intrinsic nature. A foundationalist need only claim that every belief occupies a place in a natural, transcultural, transhistorical order of reasons—an order which leads the inquirer back, eventually, to one or another "ultimate source of evidence."[7] Different foundationalists offer different candidates for such sources: for example, Scripture, tradition, clear and distinct ideas, sense-experience, and common sense. Pragmatists object to foundationalism for the same reasons as they object to realism. They think that the question of whether my inquiries trace a natural order of reasons or merely respond to the demands for justification prevalent in my culture is, like the question whether the physical world is found or made, one to which the answer can make no practical difference.

Clifford's demand for evidence can, however, be put in a minimalist form—one which avoids both realism and foundationalism, and which concedes to James that intellectual responsibility is no more and no less than responsibility to people with whom one is joined in a shared endeavour. In its minimalist form, this demand presupposes only that the meaning of a statement consists in the inferential relations which it bears to other statements. To use the language in which the sentence is phrased commits one, on this view, to believing that a statement S is true if and only if one also believes that certain other statements which permit an inference to S, and still others which can be inferred from S, are true. The wrongness of believing without evidence is, therefore, the wrongness of pretending to participate in a common project while refusing to play by the rules.

This view of language was encapsulated in the positivist slogan that the meaning of a statement is its method of verification. The positivists argued that the sentences used to express religious belief are typically not hooked up to the rest of the language in the right inferential way, and hence can express only pseudo-beliefs. The positivists, being empiricist foundationalists, equated "the right inferential way" with eventual appeal to sense experience. But a non-foundationalist neo-positivist might still put forward the following dilemma: If there are inferential connections, then there is a duty to argue; if there are not, then we are not dealing with a belief at all.

So even if we drop the foundationalist notion of "evidence," Clifford's point can still be restated in terms of the responsibility to *argue*. A minimal Clifford-like view can be summed up in the claim that, although your emotions are your own business, your beliefs are everybody's business. There is no way in which the religious person can claim a right to believe as part of an over-all right to privacy. For believing is inherently a public project: all us language-users are in it together. We all have a responsibility to each other not to believe anything which cannot be justified to the rest of us. To be rational is to submit one's beliefs—all one's beliefs—to the judgment of one's peers.

James resists this view. In "The Will to Believe" he argues that there are live, momentous and forced options which cannot be decided by evidence—cannot, as James put it, "be decided on intellectual grounds." But people who side with Clifford typically rejoin that, where evidence and argument are unavailable, intellectual responsibility requires that options *cease* to be either live or forced. The responsible inquirer, they say, does not *let* herself be confronted by options of the sort James describes. When evidence and argument are unavailable, so, they think, is belief, or at least *responsible* belief. Desire, hope, and other non-cognitive states can legitimately be had without evidence—can legitimately be turned over to what James calls "our passional nature"—but *belief* cannot. In the realm of belief, which options are live and forced is not a private matter. The same options face us all; the same truth-candidates are proposed to everyone. It is intellectually irresponsible either to disregard these options, or to decide between these truth-candidates except by argument from the sort of evidence which the very meanings of our words tell us is required for their support.

This nice sharp distinction between the cognitive and the non-cognitive, between belief and desire, is, however just the sort of dualism which James needs to blur. On the traditional account, desire should play no role in the fixation of belief. On a pragmatist account, the only point of having beliefs in the first place is to gratify desires. James' claim that thinking is "only there for behavior's sake" (WB, p. 92) is his version of Hume's claim that "reason is, and ought to be, the slave of the passions."

If one accepts either claim, one will have reason to be as dubious as James was of the purportedly necessary antagonism between science and religion. For, as I said earlier, these two areas of culture seem to fulfill two different sets of desires. Science enables us to predict and control, whereas religion offers us a larger hope, and thereby something to live for. To ask "which of their two accounts of the universe is true?" may be as pointless as asking "is the carpenter's or the particle physicist's account of tables the true one?" For neither question needs to be answered if we can figure out a strategy for keeping the two accounts from getting in each other's way.[8]

Consider James' characterization of the "religious hypothesis" as that (1) "the best things are the more eternal things . . ." and (2) "that we are better even now if we believe [1]" (WB, pp. 29–30).[9] Many people have said, when they reached this point in "The Will to Believe," that if that hypothesis exhausts what James means by "religion," then he is not talking about what they, or Clifford, are interested in. I shall return to this objection shortly. For now I merely remark that if you had asked James to specify the difference between accepting this hypothesis (a "cognitive" state) and simply trusting the larger hope (a "non-cognitive" state)—or the difference between believing that the best things are the eternal things and relishing the thought that they are—he might well have replied that such differences do not make much difference.[10] What does it matter, one can imagine him asking, whether you call it a belief, a desire, or a hope, a mood, or some complex of these, so long as it has the same cash value in directing action? We know what religious faith is, we know what it does for people. People have a right to have such faith, just as they have a right to fall in love, to marry in haste, and to persist in love despite endless sorrow and disappointment. In all such cases, "our passional nature" asserts its rights.

I suggested earlier that an utilitarian ethics of belief will reinterpret James' intellect-passion distinction so as to make it coincide with a distinction between what needs justification to other human beings and what does not. A business proposal, for example, needs such justification, but a marriage proposal (in our romantic and democratic culture) does not. Such an ethics will defend religious belief by saying, with Mill, that our right to happiness is limited only by others' rights not to have their own pursuits of happiness interfered with. This right to happiness includes the rights to faith, hope, and love—intentional states which can rarely be justified, and typically should not have to be justified, to our peers. Our intellectual responsibilities are responsibilities to cooperate with others on common projects designed to promote the general welfare (projects such as constructing a unified science, or a uniform commercial code), and not to interfere with their private projects. For the latter—projects such as getting married or getting religion—the question of intellectual responsibility does not arise.

James' critics will hear this riposte as an admission that religion is not a cognitive matter, and that his "right to believe" is a misnomer for "the right to yearn" or "the right to hope" or "the right to take comfort in the thought that . . ." But James is not making, and should not make, such an admission. He is, rather, insisting that the impulse to draw a sharp line between the cognitive and the non-cognitive, and between beliefs and desires, even when this explanation is relevant neither to the explanation or the justification of behavior, is a residue of the false (because useless) belief that we should engage in two distinct quests—one for truth and the other for happiness. Only that belief could persuade us to say *amici socii, sed magis amica veritas*.

II.

The philosophy of religion I have just sketched is one which is shadowed forth in much of James' work, and is the one he *should* have invoked when replying to Clifford. Unfortunately in "The Will to Believe" he attempts a different strategy, and gets off on the wrong foot. Rather than fuzzing up the distinction between the cognitive and the non-cognitive, as he should have, James here takes it for granted, and thus yields the crucial terrain to his opponent. The italicized thesis of "The Will to Believe" reads: "Our passional nature not only lawfully may, but must, decide an option between propositions, whenever it is a genuine option that cannot by its nature be decided on intellectual grounds . . ." (WB, p. 20). Here, as in his highly unpragmatic claim that "in our dealings with objective nature we obviously are recorders, not makers of the truth" (WB, p. 26),[11] James accepts exactly what he should reject: the idea the mind is divided neatly down the middle into intellect and passion, and the idea that possible topics of discussion are divided neatly into the cognitive and the non-cognitive ones.

When philosophy goes antifoundationalist, the notion of "source of evidence" gets replaced by that of "consensus about what would count as evidence." So objectivity as intersubjectivity replaces objectivity as fidelity to something non-human. The question "is there any evidence for *p*?" gets replaced by the question "is there any way of getting a consensus on what would count in favor of *p*?" The distinction between settling the question of *p* on intellectual grounds and turning it over to one's passional nature thus turns into the question: am I going to be able to justify *p* to other people? So James should have rephrased the issue between Clifford and himself as "What sort of belief, if any, can I have in good conscience, even after I realize that I cannot justify this belief to others?" The stark Cliffordian position says: no beliefs, only hopes, desires, yearnings, and the like. The quasi-Jamesian position I want to defend says: do not worry too much about whether what you have is a belief, a desire, or a mood. Just insofar as such states as hope, love, and faith promote only such private projects, you need not worry about whether you have a right to have them.

To suggest that the tension between science and religion can be resolved merely by saying that the two serve different purposes may sound absurd. But it is no more nor less absurd than the attempt of liberal (mostly Protestant) theologians to de-mythologize Christianity, and more generally to immunize religious belief from criticism based on accounts of the universe which trace the origin of human beings, and of their intellectual faculties, to the unplanned movements of elementary particles.[12] For some people, such as Alasdair MacIntyre, the effect of this latter attempt is to drain all the interest out of religion. Theologies which require no *sacrificium intellectus* are, these people think, hardly worth discussing. MacIntyre disdainfully remarks of Tillich that his "definition of God in terms of ultimate human concern in effect makes of God no more than an interest of human nature."[13] A pragmatist however, can reply that Tillich did nothing worse to God than pragmatist philosophy of science had already done to the elementary particles. Pragmatists think that those particles are not the very joints at which things as they are in themselves divide, but are objects which we should not have come across unless we had devoted ourself to one of the many interests of human nature—the interest in predicting and controlling our environment.

Pragmatists are not instrumentalists, in the sense of people who believe that quarks are "mere heuristic fictions." They think that quarks are as real as tables, but that quark-talk and table-talk need not get in each other's way, since they need not compete for the role of What Is There Anyway, apart from human needs and interests. Similarly, pragmatist theists are not anthropocentrists, in the sense of believing that God is a "mere posit." They believe that God is as real as sense-impressions, tables, quarks, and human rights. But, they add, stories about our relations to God do not necessarily run athwart stories about our relations to these other things.

Pragmatist theists, however, do have to get along without Personal Immortality, Providential Intervention, the efficacy of sacraments, the Virgin Birth, the Risen Christ, the Covenant with Abraham, the authority of the Koran, and a lot of other things which many theists are loath to do without. Or, if they want them, they will have to interpret them "symbolically" in a way which MacIntyre will regard as disingenuous, for they must prevent them from providing premises for practical reasoning. But de-mythologizing is, pragmatist theists think, a small price to pay for insulating these doctrines from "scientific" criticism. De-mythologizing amounts to saying that, whatever theism is good for, it is not a device for predicting or controlling our environment. Or, to put it another way: whatever God is good for, he is not, like our earthly fathers, a powerful controlling force. He is not somebody we are trying to get on the right side of in order to prosper.

From a utilitarian point of view, both MacIntyre and "scientific realists" (philosophers who insist that, in Sellars' words, "science is the measure of the things that are, that they are") are unfairly privileging some human interests, and therefore some areas of culture, over others.[14] To insist on the "literal reality" of the Resurrection is of a piece with insisting, in the manner of David Lewis, that the only non-"gerrymandered" objects in the universe—the only objects that have not been shaped by human interests—are those of which particle physics speaks.[15] Pragmatists think that we shall only see religion and science as in conflict if we are unwilling to admit that each is just one more attempt to gratify human needs, and to admit also that there is no way to gratify both sets of needs simultaneously.

Scientific realism and religious fundamentalism are products of the same urge. The attempt to convince people that they have a duty to develop what Bernard Williams calls an "absolute conception of reality" is, from a Tillichian or Jamesian point of view, of a piece with the attempt to live "for God only," and to insist that others do so also. Both scientific realism and religious fundamentalism are private projects which have gotten out of hand. They are attempts to make one's own private way of giving meaning to one's life—a way which romanticizes one's relation to something starkly and magnificently non-human, something Ultimately True and Real—obligatory for the general public.

III.

I said earlier that many readers of "The Will to Believe" feel let down when they discover that the only sort of religion James has been discussing is something as wimpy as the belief that "perfection is eternal." They have a point. For when Clifford raged against the intellectual irresponsibility of the theists, what he really had in mind was the moral irresponsibility of fundamentalists—the people who burnt people at the stake, forbade divorce and dancing, and found various other ways of making their neighbors miserable for the greater glory of God.[16] Once "the religious hypothesis" is disengaged from the opportunity to inflict humiliation and pain on people who do not profess the correct creed, it loses interest for many people. It loses interest for many more once it is disengaged from the promise that we shall see our loved ones after death. Similarly, once science is disengaged from the claim to know reality as it is in itself it loses its appeal for the sort of person who sees pragmatism as a frivolous, or treasonous, dereliction of our duty to Truth.

A pragmatist philosophy of religion must follow Tillich and others in distinguishing quite sharply between faith and belief. Liberal Protestants to whom Tillich sounds plausible are quite willing to talk about their faith in God, but demur at spelling out just what beliefs that faith includes. Fundamentalist Catholics to whom Tillich sounds blasphemous are happy to enumerate their beliefs by reciting the Creed, and to identify their faith with those beliefs. The reason the Tillichians think they can get along either without creeds, or with a blessedly vague symbolic interpretation of credal statements, is that they think that the point of religion is not to produce any *specific* habit of action, but rather to make the sort of difference to a human life which is made by the presence or absence of love.

The best way to make Tillich and fuzziness look good, and to make creeds look bad, is to emphasize the similarity between having faith in God and being in love with another human being. People often say that they would not be able to go on if it were not for their love for their spouse or their children. This love is often not capable of being spelled out in beliefs about the character, or the actions, of these beloved people. Further, this love often seems inexplicable to people acquainted with those spouses and children—just as inexplicable as faith in God seems to those who contemplate the extent of seemingly unnecessary human misery. But we do not mock a mother who believes in her sociopathic child's essential goodness, even when that goodness is visible to no one else. James urges us not to mock those who accept what he calls "the religious hypothesis"—the hypothesis that says "the best things are the more eternal things" (WB, p. 29)—merely because we see no evidence for this hypothesis, and a lot of evidence against it.

The loving mother is not attempting to predict and control the behavior of her child, and James' ascent to the religious hypothesis is not part of an attempt to predict and control anything at all. Concentration on the latter attempt, the attempt to which most of common sense and science is devoted, gives rise to the idea that all intentional states are either beliefs or desires, for the actions we take on the basis of prediction and in the hope of control are the results of practical syllogisms, and such syllogisms must include both a desire that a given state of affairs obtain and the belief that a certain action will help it do so. The same concentration gives rise to the idea that anything that counts as a belief—as a cognitive state—must be capable of being cashed out in terms of specific practical consequences, and to the related idea that we must be able to spell out the inferential relations between any belief and other beliefs in considerable, and quite specific, detail.

These two ideas have often led commentators to see a tension between James' pragmatism and his trust in his own religious experiences, and between the Dewey of *Reconstruction in Philosophy* and the Dewey of *A Common Faith*. The question of whether the tension seen in James and Dewey's work is real or apparent boils down to the question: can we disengage religious belief from inferential links with other beliefs by making them too vague to be caught in a creed—by fuzzing them up in Tillichian ways—and still be faithful to the familiar pragmatist doctrine that beliefs have content only by virtue of inferential relations to other beliefs?[17]

To give up this latter claim would be to be abandon the heart of both classical and contemporary pragmatism, for it would be to abandon the holistic view of intentional content which permits pragmatists to substitute objectivity as intersubjectivity for objectivity as correspondence to the intrinsic nature of reality. But what becomes of intersubjectivity once we admit that there is no communal practice of justification—no shared language-game—which gives religious statements their content? The question of whether James and Dewey are inconsistent now becomes the question: is there some practice other than justification of beliefs by beliefs which can give content to utterances?

I think that this question should be answered by reminding the questioner that the only point in attributing beliefs to other people, and in asking about whether our or their beliefs cohere in such a way as to be justified, is to understand and explain human actions. Contemporary externalists in the philosophy of mind insist, and James and Dewey could heartily agree, that the only reason we attribute intentional states to human beings at all is that doing so enables us to coordinate our actions with theirs. When we encounter paradigmatic cases of unjustifiable beliefs—Kierkegaard's belief in the Incarnation, the mother's belief in the essential goodness of her sociopathic child—we can still use the attribution of such beliefs to explain what is going on: why Kierkegaard, or the mother, is doing what she is doing. We can give content to an utterance like "I love him" or "I have faith in Him" by correlating such utterances with patterns of behavior, even when we cannot do so by fixing the place of such utterances in a network of inferential relations. For such utterances do help us figure out what the utterers are likely to do in various situations, and thus help us figure out how to coordinate our own actions with theirs.

The fact that Kierkegaard is not about to explain how Christ can be both mortal and immortal, nor the mother to say how a good person could have done what her child is done, is irrelevant to the utility of ascribing those beliefs to them. Just as we can often answer the question "Why did she do that?" by attributing a practical syllogism to the agent, so we can often answer it simply by saying "She loves him" or "She hopes against hope that he . . ." or "She has faith in him." The "him" here may be either her son, her lover, or her God. We thereby give an explanation of action which is not capable of being broken down into beliefs and desires—into individual sentential attitudes connected with other such attitudes by familiar inferential links—but which is nonetheless genuinely explanatory.

IV.

So far I have been content to accept James' own description of the religious hypothesis. But it is, I think, an unfortunate one. Just as I think James took the wrong tack, and partially betrayed his own pragmatism, in his reply to Clifford, so I think that he betrayed his own better instincts when he chose this definition of religion.[18] For that definition associates religion with the conviction that a power not ourselves will do unimaginably vast good rather than with the hope that we ourselves will do such good. Such a definition of religion stays at the second of Dewey's three stages of the development of the religious consciousness—the one Dewey called "the point now reached by religious theologians"—by retaining the notion of something non-human which is nevertheless on the side of human beings.[19]

The kind of religious faith which seems to me to lie behind the attractions of both utilitarianism and pragmatism is, instead, a faith in the future possibilities of mortal humans, a faith which is hard to distinguish from love for, and hope for, the human community. I shall call this fuzzy overlap of faith, hope and love "romance." Romance, in this sense, may crystallize around a labor union as easily as around a congregation, around a novel as easily as around a sacrament, around a God as easily as around a child.

There is a passage in the work of the contemporary novelist Dorothy Allison which may help explain what I have in mind. Toward the beginning of a remarkable essay called "Believing in Literature," Allison says that "literature, and my own dream of writing, has shaped my own system of belief—a kind of atheist's religion . . . the backbone of my convictions has been a belief in the progress of human society as demonstrated in its fiction."[20] She ends the essay as follows:

> There is a place where we are always alone with our own mortality, where we must simply have something greater than ourselves to hold onto—God or history or politics or literature or a belief in the healing

power of love, or even righteous anger. Sometimes I think they are all the same. A reason to believe, a way to take the world by the throat and insist that there is more to this life than we have ever imagined.[21]

What I like best about this passage is Allison's suggestion that all these may be the same, that it does not greatly matter whether we state our reason to believe—our insistence that some or all finite, mortal, humans can be far more than they have yet become—in religious, political, philosophical, literary, sexual, or familial terms. What matters is the insistence itself—the romance, the ability to experience overpowering hope, or faith, or love (or, sometimes, rage).

What is distinctive about this state is that it carries us beyond argument, because beyond presently used language. It thereby carries us beyond the imagination of the present age of the world. I take this state to be the one described (in italics) by James as "a positive content of experience which is literally and objectively true as far as it goes": namely, "the fact that the conscious person is continuous with a wider self through which saving experiences come" (VRE, p. 405). The images and tropes which connect one with this wider self may be, as Allison suggests, political or familial, literary or credal. I think James would have liked Allison's pluralism, and would have thought that what she says in the above passage harmonizes with his own praise of polytheism in the final pages of *Varieties*, and with his insistence that "The divine can mean no single quality, it must mean a group of qualities, by being champions of which in alternation, different men may all find worthy missions" (VRE, p. 384).

In past ages of the world, things were so bad that "a reason to believe, a way to take the world by the throat" was hard to get except by looking to a power not ourselves. In those days, there was little choice but to sacrifice the intellect in order to grasp hold of the premises of practical syllogisms—premises concerning the after-death consequences of baptism, pilgrimage, or participation in holy wars. To be imaginative and to be religious, in those dark times, came to almost the same thing—for this world was too wretched to lift up the heart. But things are different now, because of human beings' gradual success in making their lives, and their world, less wretched. Non-religious forms of romance have flourished—if only in those lucky parts of the world where wealth, leisure, literacy and democracy have worked together to prolong our lives and fill our libraries.[22] Now the things of this world are, for some lucky people, so welcome that they do not have to look beyond nature to the supernatural, and beyond life to an after-life, but only beyond the human past to the human future.

I have to admit, however, that James fluctuated between two states of mind, two ways of dealing with the panic which both he and his father had experienced, and the return of which he always dreaded.[23] In one of these the Whitmanesque dream of plural, democratic vistas stretching far away into the future was enough.[24] Then he would respond to the possibility of panic by saying, as in the quotation from Fitzjames Stephen which ends "The Will to Believe": "Act for the best, hope for the best, and take what comes. . . . If death ends all, we cannot meet death better" (WB, p. 33). In those moods, James could find this bravura as appropriate for the death of the species as for that of an individual.

But in other moods James was unable to shrug off panic in the name of healthy-mindedness, unable to rid himself of a panic-inducing picture of mankind as

> in a position similar to that of a set of people living on a frozen lake, surrounded by cliffs over which there is no escape, yet knowing that little by little the ice is melting, and the inevitable day drawing near when the last film of it will disappear, and to be drowned ignominiously will be the human creature's portion (VRE, p. 120).

In such moods he is driven to adopt the "religious hypothesis" that somewhere, somehow, perfection is eternal, and to identify "the notion of God" with the "guarantee" of "an ideal order that shall be permanently preserved" (P, p. 55). In such moods he demanded, at a minimum, what Whitehead called objective immortality—the memory of human achievements in the mind of a "fellow-sufferer who understands."[25] He hoped that in his own best moments he had made contact with that mind. At other moments, he hoped that that mind was actively intervening in the history of the universe—that that mind was a power not ourselves that made for righteousness. These were, in his terms "overbeliefs," and he fluctuated at various times in his life between a minimal Whitmanesque identification of the divine with a future human community, a middling identification of it with Whitehead's Consequent Nature of God, and a maximal identification of it with a powerful force for good.

All of us, I think, fluctuate between such overbeliefs. We fluctuate between God as a perhaps obsolete name for a possible human future, and God as an external guarantor of some such future. Those who, like Dewey, would like to link their days each to each by transmuting their early religious belief into a belief in the human future, come to think of God as Friend rather than as Judge and Savior. Those who, like me, were raised atheist and now find it merely confusing to talk about God, nevertheless fluctuate between moods in which we are content with utility and moods in which we hanker after validity as well. So we waver between what I have called "romance" and needy, chastened, humility. Sometimes it suffices to trust the human community, thought of as part of what Dewey called "the community of causes and consequences in which we, together with those not born, are enmeshed . . . the widest and deepest symbol of the mysterious totality of being the imagination calls the universe."[26] Sometimes it does not.

James was not always content to identify the "wider self through which saving experiences come" with Dewey's "widest and deepest symbol" of the universe. In Whitmanesque moods he could identify this wider self with an Americanized humanity at the farthest reach of the democratic vistas. Then he could (to paraphrase the title of his father's book) think of Democracy as the Redeemed Form of God. But in Wordsworthian moods his "over-belief" was in something far more deeply interfused with Nature than the transitory glory of democratic fellowship. Then he thought of the self from which saving experiences come as standing to even a utopian human community as the latter stands to the consciousness of our dogs and cats (VRE, pp. 518–519).

We can, I think, learn two lessons from recapitulating what Henry Levinson calls "the religious investigations of William James." The first is that we latest heirs of time are lucky enough to have considerable discretion about which options will be live for us and which will not. Unlike our less fortunate ancestors, we are in a position to put aside the unromantic, foundationalist, view that all the truth-candidates, and thus all the momentous options, have always already been available, live, and forced—because they are built into a language always and inevitably spoken by common sense. We can, with James, relish the thought that our descendants may face live and forced options which we shall never imagine. The second lesson is that letting his liveliest option be the choice between Whitman and Wordsworth—between two romantic poets rather than between an atheistic creed and a theistic one—was enough to satisfy William James' own religious needs.

James combined, to an extent of which most of us are incapable, honesty about his own needs with concern for those of others. So the upshot of his investigations is worth bearing in mind.

NOTES

The following abbreviations are used for references to William James in parentheses in the text:

ECR *Essays Comments and Reviews.* Vol. 17 of *The Works of William James* (Cambridge: Harvard University Press, 1987).
P *Pragmatism and The Meaning of Truth.* Vol. 1 of *The Works of William James* (Cambridge: Harvard University Press, 1976).
VRE *Varieties of Religious Experience.* Vol. 15 of *The Works of William James* (Cambridge: Harvard University Press, 1985).
WB *The Will to Believe and Other Essay in Popular Philosophy.* Vol. 6 of *The Works of William James* (Cambridge: Harvard University Press, 1979).

1. Ruth-Anna Putnam has suggested that I might wish to use "consequentialist" in place of "utilitarian" in this description of James. On reflection, I have retained the latter term. This is because I think that, for James, J. S. Mill was the paradigm utilitarian, and that that Mill was as aware as James and Dewey that there can be no Benthamite measuring of context-free quantities of need-satisfaction, and that consequently there will always be agonizing moral dilemmas. I find "consequentialist" a rather flexible and pallid term, whereas "utilitarian" has a sharp-edged polemical force, thanks to its associations with the tough-minded Huxleyite suggestion that human beings be thought of as complex, needy, animals. There seem to me to be Huxleyite overtones throughout James' work, and my use of "utilitarian" is intended to bring these out.

2. But Habermas, unlike James and Dewey, still believes in a "transcendent moment of universal validity." I have argued against Habermas' retention of this Kantian doctrine in "Sind Aussagen Universelle Geltungsansprueche?," *Deutsche Zeitschrift für Philosophie*, Spring 1995.

3. In fact I prefer a third strategy, that of Davidson, who cuts truth off from justification by making it a non-epistemic notion. I defend the counter-intuitive implications of this strategy in "Is Truth a Goal of Inquiry?: Davidson vs. Wright," *Philosophical Quarterly*, v. 45, no. 180 (July 1995), pp. 281–300.

4. Many people would agree with Stephen Carter's claim that this reduces religion to a "hobby," and would accept his invidious contrast between a mere "individual metaphysic" and a "tradition of group worship." (See his *The Culture of Disbelief: How American Law*

and Politics Trivialize Religious Devotion (New York: Basic Books, 1993), esp. c. 2). I argue against Carter's views in "Religion as Conversation-Stopper," *Common Knowledge*, vol. 3 (Spring 1994), pp. 1–6.

5. See, for example, John McDowell's claim that without "direct confrontation by a worldly state of affairs itself" thought's "bearing on the world" will remain inexplicable (*Mind and World* (Cambridge, MA: Harvard University Press, 1994), pp. 142–143).

6. Compare Nietzsche, *The Will to Power*, sec. 514.

7. See Michael Williams, *Unnatural Doubts* (Oxford: Blackwell, 1993), p. 116: ". . . we can characterize foundationalism as the view that our beliefs, simply in virtue of certain elements in their contents, stand in *natural epistemological relations* and thus fall into *natural epistemological kinds*."

8. Although I have no proof text to cite, I am convinced that James' theory of truth as "the good in the way of belief" originated in the need to reconcile his admiration for his father with his admiration for such scientific friends as Peirce and Chauncey Wright.

9. Note that for a pragmatist (2) is superfluous. "P" and "we are better off even now if we believe p" come pretty close, for pragmatists, to saying the same thing.

10. Pragmatists can, of course, make a distinction between hope and knowledge in cases where knowledge of causal mechanisms is available. The quack hopes, but the medical scientist knows, that the pills will cure. But in other cases, such as marriage, the distinction often cannot usefully be drawn. Does the groom know, or merely hope, that he is marrying the right person? Either description will explain his actions equally well.

11. Here James buys in on a dualism between objective nature (The Way the World Is) and something else—a dualism which critics of the correspondence theory of truth, such as the future author of *Pragmatism*, must eventually abjure.

12. Paul Tillich claimed that his existentialist, symbolic, theology was an expression of "the Protestant Principle"—the impulse that led Luther to despise scholastic proofs of God existence and to label Reason "a whore." James said that "as, to papal minds, protestantism has often seemed a mere mess of anarchy and confusion, such, no doubt will pragmatism often seem to ultra-rationalist minds in philosophy" (P, p. 62; see also VRE, p. 396).

13. Alasdair MacIntyre and Paul Ricoeur, *The Religious Significance of Atheism* (New York: Columbia University Press, 1969), p. 53.

14. In his "Atheism, Relativism, Enlightenment and Truth" (forthcoming in *Studies in Religion*), my fellow-pragmatist Barry Allen remarks that Hume saw no need to proclaim himself an atheist. Holbach and Diderot, by contrast, did see a need, for, unlike Hume, they substituted a duty to Truth for a duty to God, a duty explained in terms of what Allen elsewhere (in his *Truth in Philosophy*) has called an "onto-logical," specifically anti-pragmatic, account of truth. Holbach would, today, proclaim himself a scientific realist, and *therefore* an atheist. Hume would proclaim himself neither.

15. See David Lewis, "Putnam's Paradox," *Australasian Journal of Philosophy*, 1983, pp. 226–228.

16. See, for example, Clifford's "The Influence Upon Morality of a Decline in Religious Belief" in his *Lectures and Essays*, vol. II (London: Macmillan, 1879), pp. 244–252.

17. Davidson and other externalists have emphasized that this claim is compatible with saying that we can attribute content to intentional states only if we are able to correlate utterances with their extra-mental causes. They have, I think, thereby shown us how to be radically holistic and coherentist without running the danger of "losing touch" with the world. Realist philosophers such as McDowell, however, have doubted whether Davidson's view allows "cognitive" as opposed to merely "causal" connections with the world. I attempt to reply to these doubts in "McDowell, Davidson and Spontaneity," forthcoming in *Philosophy and Phenomenological Research*.

18. Acceptance of the claim that "perfection is eternal" was not, of course James' only definition of religion. He had as many conflicting quasi-definitory things to say about religions as he did about truth.

19. See John Dewey, *A Common Faith* (New Haven: Yale University Press, 1934), p. 73. Dewey's own conception of the "the human abode" is not of something non-human but friendly, but rather of a Wordsworthian community with non-human nature—something like Spinoza's "face of the whole universe."

20. Dorothy Allison, *Skin: Talking about Sex, Class and Literature* (Ithaca, NY: Firebrand Books, 1994), p. 166.

21. *Ibid.*, p. 181.

22. James said that there is reason to think that "the coarser religions, revivalistic, orgiastic, with blood and miracles and supernatural operations, may possibly never be displaced. Some constitutions need them too much" (VRE, p. 136). He could have added that people placed in some circumstances (no wealth, no literacy, no luck) also need them too much.

23. "Not the conception or intellectual perception of evil, but the grisly blood-freezing heart-palsying sensation of it close upon one. . . . How irrelevantly remote seem all our usual refined optimisms and intellectual and moral consolations in presence of a need of help like this! Here is the real core of the religious problem: Help! help!" (VRE, p. 135).

24. See James' "pluralistic way of interpreting" Whitman's "To You" (P, p. 133), and his account of the "the great religious difference," the one "between the men who insist that world *must and shall be*, and those who are contented with believing that the world *may be*, saved" (P, p. 135).

25. A.N. Whitehead, *Process and Reality* (New York: Macmillan, 1929), pp. 532–533.

26. *A Common Faith*, p. 85.

II. Plenary Addresses

RORTY, DIGGINS, AND THE PROMISE OF PRAGMATISM

Henry Samuel Levinson

My aim in this essay is to discuss how promising pragmatism is for my own festive Jewish American naturalism. In particular, I want to consider how promising pragmatism is when it comes to pursuing some large religious, ethical, and political ideas. Even more specifically, I want to pursue two topics that link up my own thinking to classical pragmatists like James, Dewey, and Santayana, along with current ones, especially Richard Rorty. These are the large ideas of joy and responsibility. In this regard, I'll be trying to push and pull my current preoccupations with religion, Judaism, and liberalism in directions that some of us pragmatic naturalists have taken lately at Rorty's instruction and advice.

If these plans of mine make much sense, however, then the thrust of John Patrick Diggins's recent book, *The Promise of Pragmatism*, should provoke me to scratch my head a little. This is so because, in Diggins's view, pragmatism isn't much of a live option for intellectuals these days interested in pursuing public issues in public ways. Why? Because, to use its own measure of assessment, pragmatism has not worked the way it claimed it could and would. Diggins's point is this: Whatever its fortunes might turn out to be in the academy—which, as an institution, isn't cashing out all that well these days—pragmatism surely hasn't panned out as a resource for public intellectuals, either for policy formulation, or for moral education, or for the celebration of our collective memories, practices, and hopes for the future.

Certainly, Diggins's account of pragmatism leaves the tradition of little or no use to public intellectuals who identify their efforts with some religious tradition or other. This is so because, as he narrates its story anyhow, when it comes to religion, pragmatism was, and is, caught between two dead options. On the one hand, William James gave us his romantic will-to-believe doctrine, all too subject to self-deception and self-fulfillment. On the other, John Dewey commended, first, displacement of religious criticism by a reliance on scientific method, progressive education, and democracy; and second, reduction of the diversity of religious traditions to a—finally vacuous—celebration of "experience."

These paltry options, Diggins claims, undercut the realistically sick-souled role that religion, specifically Christianity, used to play in America. In his view, Christianity had lent America spiritual weight, for example, when Calvinists issued their jeremiads on election days. It continued to do so when James Madison and John Adams championed the separation of powers and built up road blocks to various threats of tyranny that majoritarian democracy might muster. These American patriarchs, indeed, developed their proposals in light of biting Christian intuitions and criticisms, especially about the sins of pride and greed. Diggins argues that Christianity then lent ballast to American culture again when, in Dewey's heyday, the Niebuhr brothers gave Neo-Orthodoxy something public and intellectual to do in a vital liberal democracy. The Niebuhrs showed how Augustinian analyses of desire and guilt, along with more-or-less Lutheran accounts of power and responsibility, could be deployed to criticize presumably pansy liberals like Dewey and former fellow-travellers like Sidney Hook.

On Diggins's view, Reinhold Niebuhr, not Dewey and his crowd, is the real hero of mid-Century America that public intellectuals ought to extol these days. This is so because Reinie, by combining essentialism with an acute analysis of power, group-egotism, and justice, gave America a backbone that the pragmatists never managed to provide, as it encountered and fought off horrifying totalitarian threats in Western Europe and further East. So, finally, on his view, we'd be far better off returning to Niebuhr's *Moral Man and Immoral Society*, and away from, say, Dewey's *Problems of Men*, to deal with the "negations of modernism" that caused the "crisis of knowledge and authority" that we have faced, ever since Darwin. For it was Darwin, Diggins reminds us, who gave us pragmatic naturalists the tools we think we need to reject and abandon, without exactly refuting, essentialisms, foundationalisms, eternalisms, totalisms, and supernaturalisms, whether religious or theological or not.

And what is the modern "crisis of knowledge and authority," more exactly, according to Diggins? It is the predicament, he suggests, we experience when we live in a bunch of cognitive and conative ditches or gaps. These fissures separate what we know we are from what we desire to be. They leave us suffering a series of "felt absences," most significantly "knowledge without truth, power without authority, society without spirit, self without identity, politics without virtue, existence without purpose, and history without meaning" (p. 8). In sum, they gut both responsibility *and* joy.

"To the pragmatist," Diggins further claims, these "discrepancies and contingencies of the universe should not provoke meaninglessness and anxiety. On the contrary, life must be seen as a challenge and an adventure, and a universe that is potential and 'unfinished' presents abundant opportunities to create meaning through the use of creative intelligence" (p. 34). But far from delivering the character-building therapy it promises, Diggins's pragmatism appears to continue causing the very disabilities of aimlessness and apprehension it had set out to overcome. Put another way, according to Diggins, pragmatism pledged, but failed to provide, practical clarification, guidance, and instruction in the just and humane uses of power—in uses of power that permit and perhaps even foster *more* joy and responsibility in a fragile and death-haunted world. Moreover, Diggins suggests, clarification, guidance and instruction in the equitable and humane uses of power for us sinful and mortal critters is just what the Christian realists, Reinhold Niebuhr first among them, bequeathed.

As Diggins sees it, there are four keys to understanding the pragmatists' failure to deal effectively with the crisis of knowledge and authority caused by the fissures of modern life. The first is their misconstrual of science as experimental inquiry; the second is their naive or uncritical endorsement of democracy; the third is their understanding of progressive education, which is method-obsessed in the same way their "science" or "experimental inquiry" is, leaving our young people supposedly ready to change, and for change, but not knowing *what* to believe, that is, forsaking the cultural literacy our kids require to get along prudently, morally, and spiritually; and the fourth is their belittling of religion, pictured as a cultural system which causes superstition and fanaticism, but provides little benefit in a liberal, democratic, federal republican culture like ours.

The first thing to keep in mind as we come more closely to grips with these four complaints that Diggins charges against pragmatism is this: at least as most pragmatists see themselves, there will be, and should always be, conflicting narratives about pragmatism as a movement. This conflict of narratives, indeed, *makes up* or reflects a good deal of pragmatism's liveliness. So the thing we pragmatists should *never* want to do is to settle into some supposedly definitive story about our movement. In the end, we'll have to ask *what good* this or that narrative does.

Indeed, according to *my* narrative of pragmatism, at any rate, at the heart of its history lies James's reflection that philosophy condemned itself to absent-mindedness at its beginning, when Socrates and Plato taught

> that what a thing really is told us by its *definition*. Ever since Socrates we have been taught that reality consists of essences, not of appearances, and that the essences of things are known to us by their definitions. So far we identify the thing with a concept, and then we identify the concept with a definition, and only then, inasmuch as the thing is whatever the definition expresses, are we sure of apprehending the real essence of it or the full truth about it. [This is] but the old story, of a useful practice first becoming a method, then a habit, and finally a tyranny that defeats the end it was used for. Concepts, first employed to make things intelligible, are clung to even when they make them unintelligible (*Pluralistic Universe*: p. 99).

According to histories like mine—accounts that make a lot of this Jamesean diagnosis of philosophy's first false step, for instance—the originating pragmatists characterized science as experimental inquiry in order to give it the sort of face lift it required to smooth away the creases and folds of essentialism that disfigured reflection, and to get on with its interest in issuing accurate predictions and enabling effective control of particular conditions. In Darwin's wake, they found it timely and good to dump every aspect of science that left it part of a grand Platonic quest to establish how fixed mind knows fixed nature[s] according to fixed principles of knowledge or understanding. They did so because Darwin had taught them that the incisive question for people in quest of more joyful lives was how variable and changing minds know variable and changing circumstances according to variable and changing principles of knowledge and understanding. Darwin, in other words. showed by example how and why science is not a natural kind—any more than anything else is a natural kind—but rather a bunch of disciplines or skills letting people cope better by predicting and controlling certain parts of a world subject not only to variation and change, but also to second-order change and variation—to changes and variations in the ways that things vary and change. The pragmatists learned the Darwinian lesson, in still other words, that even evolution evolves. That lesson, indeed, stands behind James's memorable diagnosis of Socrates's and Plato's philosophical disease.

Diggins thinks, I gather, that this Darwinian account leaves us suffering from "knowledge without truth." He chides pragmatism for this, as well as for failing to come up with effective criticisms of science's dark sides, in particular, the bureaucratic sides Max Weber isolated in his theory of rationalization and the technocratic, and commodifying sides Henry Adams uncovered in his theory of acceleration, and the madness-and-wonder-suppressing sides ridiculed by Nietzsche's ever-more prescient challenge to the nerds and nabobs of Kuhnian normal science.

But gosh! Apart from the deserved criticism that Dewey and his most influential—pre-Rortyan—disciples, e.g., Hook and Joseph Ratner, get from Diggins on a misplaced sense of trust in some distinguishable scientific *method*, this sort of criticism seems to suffer from shell-game syndrome. I mean that if we look under other entries besides "science" in the indexes of the pragmatists' best books and essays, we'll find criticisms galore of mindless bureaucracy, spiritless technocracy, rapacious capitalism, and robotic intelligence, wherever these things contribute to the sneaking suspicion that our lives, as Nietzsche suggested and Milan Kundera has put it, are unbearably light—without truth or power, authority, spirit, personal identity, virtue, purpose, or meaning! Moreover, we are likely to find criticisms of "truth," where, or because, the term is so closely tied to old Platonic games, that its use—to borrow James's metaphor—has become tyrannous. So saying that pragmatism gives us knowledge without truth is a lot like saying it gives us room for everything we used to rely on or look for in truth except old Platonic games, which falsify our situation!

Other shell-games may be going on when we turn from Diggins's criticism that pragmatists tended to engage in something close to thoughtless boosterism for American democracy. I give Diggins this: surely the pragmatists failed to fight the ideological, much less military, revolution of the 1770's over again or to slog through the issues confronting the Constitutional Convention in the 1780's and 90's once more. But did they actually fail to come to grips with American democracy's pitfalls, at least with the subtlety that Henry Adams or, later, Walter Lippman brought to bear? I think the answer to that question boils down to a judgment call, especially when we remember that, at least up through the time Lippman wrote his seminal works, Santayana—who shared a lot of Adams's judgments and prejudices, and whose work inspired Lippman's timocratic views on government—continued to count, for influential proponents and critics alike, among pragmatist voices. Diggins pictures Santayana as one of pragmatism's sharpest critics, especially as regards the worthiness of democracy. I agree. But, in my narrative anyhow, Santayana's criticisms of democracy and pragmatism itself were pragmatic and naturalist. They were internal to pragmatism. He commended a government more timocratic than many more romantically-inclined, or even theistic, democrats thought proper, because he predicted that skills in the arts, sciences, and engineering, would work out better than the old Christian republican doctrine of the *Vox Populi*, or charismatic leaders, or popularity contests, or tyrannous majorities.

Moreover, by voicing these suggestions, Santayana was simply deepening the criticisms that James had made around the time of the Haymarket Square riots, and then again during the Philippine Tangle. James surely paved the way for Santayana then, when he read about mob violence in the newspapers, pronounced the death of the doctrine of *Vox Populi*, and urged *Les Intellectuels* to begin a long, hard campaign against the "human blindness" of 19th century Weathermen and imperialist "parties of red-blood." Was James any less critical of democracy's pitfalls or affirming of timocracy than Santayana—or Adams or Lippman—when he celebrated "the social value of the college bred" and called for political and social leaders disciplined by the liberal arts and sciences? Was his account of group egotism any less incisive than Niebuhr's, when he developed his doctrine of human blindness and called on those enlightened by it to become, among other things, practically *irresponsible* enough to open themselves up to a world of "impersonal worths"? Was that doctrine of human blindness, or James's "Moral Philosopher and Moral Life," or Santayana's *Life of Reason*, each of which offered recommendations, if not blueprints, for self-critical democratic culture, any less aware of democracy's dark sides than Neo-orthodox Christian theologians? I really think not, but I'll assert at least this: here we have another judgment call.

To be sure, in the face and wake, first of the Civil War, then of the Great War, then of the Great Depression, and finally of Studs Terkel's "Good War," Dewey's crowd sometimes let democratic hopes get the better of their capacity to evaluate American—not to mention Soviet— actualities. But, again, I believe it requires pretty close calls to decide, on balance, whether secular pragmatists or Christian realists offered the public better advice about how best to stay an American democratic course during these years. Diggins claims that Adams and Weber and then the Niebuhrs "met one of the central challenges of modernism, the problem of meaning. . . .[and] also remained skeptical of science as a means to social reconstruction. . . . For both . . . the real problem was reality itself, the world of power as opposed to the realm of value" (pp. 29–31).

But did the pragmatists' rendition of democracy leave us without any capacity to manage problems of meaning or to explain power—and its links to the problems and promise of meaning—to ourselves? Did pragmatists like James, Santayana, and Dewey leave us with a picture of raw power without authority, politics without virtue, and individual life without ballast? Were Christian realists or Adams's medievalists or Lippman's timocrats any more instructive than James and Santayana and Dewey about political life together? *None* of these parties suggested very effective ways to handle the all-too-apparent problems of greed and shortsightedness that have plagued the rich North Atlantic democracies since birth. But *all* of them brought these problems to the attention of the American public. None, certainly, were prescient enough to do much, and surely not enough, to wake people up to the humiliations and hypocrisy of pigmentocracy or patriarchy or rural and urban varieties of nativism at home; or to the "bright, shining lies" at the heart of North Atlantic imperialist expansion abroad, especially in poor nations dotting the southern hemisphere. But, to take an example shamefully underplayed in our histories of philosophy in the U.S., Horace Kallen's pragmatic cultural pluralism, inspired by James's doctrine of human blindness and Santayana's *Life of Reason*, predicted core mid-to-late 20th century problems of meaning and ways to manage them a lot more instructively than, say, Adams's *Virgin and Dynamo*, or Lippman's *Preface to Morals*, or Niebuhr's [or is it Alan Heimert's] *Irony of American History*. Kallen's prophetic voice calling on America to realize the promise of *e pluribus unum* was all but drowned out by Niebuhr's. Niebuhr's response to the Nazi war against Western civilization was surely militant enough in its opposition to the *Führer* and his machine. But how did alien others fit into his scheme of things? When it came to drumming up some enthusiasm for stopping the Nazi war against the Jews, in particular, Niebuhr's rhetoric relied on his invention of a triumphalist Christian fantasy about the glories of—what he was among the first to call—our "Judeo-Christian civilization." Niebuhr gave us a picture of our culture that melted Jews and Judaism into Christianity; indeed, a view that turned out to be Christian in every vital respect, and blind, at least, to Jews as "a people" living anything like a distinctive way of life. The very idea of Judeo-Christianity was first deployed by Niebuhr as a gimmick to persuade American Christian leaders to feel some sympathy for European Jews when the trains were running to Auschwitz. As it was normalized, though, it became yet another way for Christian theologians to sweep *live* Judaism out of their sacred canopy in much the same passive-aggressive mood of final judgment they had presented in their appropriation of a reorganized *Tanakh*.

But if there are forceful alternative narratives to Diggins's account of the promise of pragmatic interpretations of democracy, especially when compared to Christian realism, how about the pragmatist development of the program in progressive education? Did it contribute to that unbearable lightness which seems to characterize life in the West since . . . since when? since Darwin? the Gilded Age? the Great War? The Roaring Twenties? The Great Depression? The decade of Dachau, Dresden, and Hiroshima? Eden? Pick your favorite mythic marker eponymous with the emergence of modern acedia. Did Dewey's Lab schools actually leave its charges that way, over-methodized, automatized, and culturally illiterate? Or was it more, say, our love of the market and our chronic cultural unwillingness to delay certain gratifications? No very forceful inquiry has been mounted in this regard. Surely test scores suggest that, currently, students in the United States are comparably neither very methodical nor culturally literate and do their best, which is still comparably worse, on multiple choice tests which suppress active inquiry and suggest automatons. Is that because Dewey's revolution succeeded or failed, or because of issues randomly related to Dewey's program?

Whatever brought present day America to life—the America that, as Neil Postman has put it, is "amusing itself to death," Dewey was surely no Mr. Mardi Gras, and his own deep distrust of any scheme/content dualism in schooling, or any other intellectual practice, highlighted the necessity of traditional literacy, or the literacy of traditions, at every level (not to mention numeracy wherever it could help us cope). So, too, did James's principle of conservatism in inquiry—the principle which called for "a minimum of jolt and a maximum of continuity" in *what* we desire, believe, and do. So, too, did the complex analysis of cultural continuity and coherence in *The Life of Reason,* summed up in Santayana's quip about the catastrophes incumbent on not remembering the past. All these pragmatic messages championed the importance of putting a pedagogy of beliefs and desires and informed performance first and foremost. They did so with a commitment to telling the bald and often disturbing truth about our past and present life together that could and should put to shame, say, the Christian Coalition's jibes at Dewey which accompany their contract *on* the American family. So where's the beef? Where, more precisely, are

Rorty, Diggins, and the Promise of Pragmatism 33

the pragmatist miscues in pedagogy that led to knowledge without truths, societies without spirit, or selves without identity?

Well, Diggins might suggest, if not in our schools, then surely we will find these pragmatist *faux pas* outside, if not in, our houses of worship. If we didn't know his *corpus* better, we could almost draw the inference from Diggins's jabs at pragmatist accounts of religion that—in the golden days when essentialists and supernaturalists and full-blooded *worshippers* roamed the world and called all the shots—churches and synagogues used to guard us from pagans and goyim by equipping us with true knowledge, authoritative power, spirited societies, authentic individuals, lives with purpose, and a "whole" history virtually dripping in the blood of "meaning." But we do know better. We know that Diggins is no Norman Rockwell groupie, and we know that he knows that the felt absences attributed to modernism go as deep in American psyches as they go far back in Western history.

In this regard, however, Diggins argues, pragmatism simply mirrors the most irresponsible and anxious fissures—dumping truth, authority, spirit, identity, purpose and meaning—without offering much, if any, effective candle power to help light up any path to move us toward the just and humane uses of power most of us say we'd adore. Remember: on Diggins's account, this was the case when James made religion first a slick do-it-yourself project, and then a kind of pluralistic, panpsychic, pantheistic "model of and for"—as Clifford Geertz would put it—a Polish Diet. It remained the case when Dewey made "art as an experience" something close to salvific. It was, again, the case when Dewey urged people to stop worshipping some pater-monarchial Other, and to start working to construct and maintain a democratic culture. For rather than celebrating a *kingdom of God*, Dewey championed a just and humane life *with* others, *e pluribus unum*, chartered and charted by citizens themselves, using their own, recognizably and admittedly human, fallible, corrigible voices.

Here, I find myself half agreeing with Diggins, but only half. I pretty much fully embrace James's doctrine of human blindness and Dewey's commitment to strong liberal democracy. But I don't find James's or Dewey's pragmatisms, at least all by themselves, all that promising for the sort of Jewish naturalism in which I've declared an interest. On my narrative, James started with a religious will-to-believe that turned out to be pretty strictly anthropological, or at least was theological only by way of ventriloquy. But he ended up, in his effort to salvage an "intimate" theology of some sort, confusing causes with consequences and, so, ultimately suffering from the very "vicious intellectualism" he had done so much to uncover. Dewey, in the story I tell, lost his religious audiences by suggesting that, when it came to religious inspiration, democratic or socialist party politics, county fairs, and either doing or contemplating arts and crafts ought to fill the bill.

But, as I read the record, neither James nor Dewey had any patience for the rituals and canonical scrolls or books or orally presented legends that anchor the thick stuff of on-going religious life the way most of us bourgeois Americans live it. Indeed, they implied (without actually showing) that this stuff was responsible for religion's twin demons, superstition and fanaticism.

Unsatisfied with this impatience, I recently turned, in *Santayana, Pragmatism, and the Spiritual Life*, to highlighting another option in the pragmatic fold on this score. Santayana introduced a religious naturalism that was just as opposed to James's crass supernaturalism and Dewey's aesthetic-political displacement of thick religious life, as it was to Josiah Royce's "Absolute Pragmatism." He characterized religion, you may recall, as "another world in live in" (*Life of Reason*: 3:p. 5), another world that was cultural, not parapsychological, theological, or postmortem—a *festive* world where diverse peoples learned, by way of unforgettable stories and performances, disciplines it took to "love life in the consciousness of impotence" (WD, p. 43). In other words, Santayana began with an interest in salvaging thick religious life—I mean the poetry and the poetry in motion that shape calendars of festive activities as much as it does consciences. He began with activities and narratives geared to shape up moral and spiritual character or personality while they stabilize identities by extending memory as far backward as they stretch hopes forward.

In other words, Santayana identified management of the problems of meaning—suffering, absurdity, and evil—as religion's distinctive cultural task a half century before Geertz did again. Then he showed how religious stories and rituals helped to enable such management. For example, he showed how religious festivities and rituals helped to render suffering sufferable. And then he argued that supernaturalism—or the will to show that the world is rigged intentionally with hardwired purposes which, lo and behold, turn out to coincide with our own understanding of our best purposes—is far more to blame for superstition ("the confusion of ideals and powers") and fanaticism ("the redoubling of our efforts after we forget our aim") than religious stories and performances *per se* ever were, or now have to be. Santayana argued for keeping our religious festivities and consciences as thick as—actually thicker than—ever while dumping the supernaturalisms responsible for, or rationalizing, wishful thinking and ethnic cleansing. He suggested that bringing this cultural change to pass would clear up "the natural but hopeless misunderstanding of imagining that poetry in order to be religion, in order to be the inspiration of life, must first deny that it is poetry and deceive us about the facts with which we have to deal" (IPR, pp. 71–72).

That philosophical prescription for therapy found theological cures—including, for example, Niebuhrian neo-orthodoxy and Chicago's religious empiricisms—themselves diseased. Santayana's suggestion, that we accept poetry for what it is—seemed obvious to some of us in the generations succeeding his; it went without saying, anyhow, to those of us whose character formation happily, if critically, depended on nourishment provided by their religious school stories and plays *and* by their Western Civ courses including Darwin, Freud, and Nietzsche, *and* by their American Civ courses including Emerson, Thoreau and Dickinson, Jefferson, Madison, and Adams, *and* by the rich diversity of African, Asian, East European, Latin American, Middle-Eastern, and other until-recently-suppressed literatures that now instruct and inspire us. But for *worshippers*—that is, for people who still piously imagine that "the deepest powers" in the universe are, intentionally or not, friendly, and coincide with their highest ideals and zaniest dreams—the very idea of Santayana's poetic religion still appears to cause nausea; or it gives them vertigo; or it leaves them stone cold.

This brings me to Diggins and Levinson on Rorty. This is so because, at least as both Diggins and Levinson read him, Rorty urges us to consider imagining what it would be like to help constitute a liberal democratic culture that demanded justice and permitted joy *without worshipping anything at all.* It is just that Rorty leaves Diggins shivering and Levinson mildly warm.

On Diggins's view, wittingly or not, Rorty inherits pragmatism's preoccupations with salvation and social responsibility. But Rorty, so the argument goes, privatizes salvation in the direction of aestheticism in much the same lame way that Dewey had. Then he characterizes social responsibility as solidarity in an epoch pocked by memories and media events highlighting the slummy sides of total communities that have placed "solidarity" on their banners and tanks. What are these dark characteristics of total communities? They are the tabloids and radio shows, schools, political conventions and movements, commercials and diverse other venues, where individuals are violated, critics are silenced and hunted, minorities are humiliated and exiled, and social and physical misfits are scheduled for one form of elimination or another, all while the mainstream—whatever "total" nation we look at—celebrates its own heartland and self-righteously delivers light to other nations.

Diggins complains that Rorty's aesthetic private good and communitarian public good, combined like water and oil, do little to dispel the acedia, the anxiety of meaninglessness, that is etched into our century's, if not our species', grisly headstone. In Rorty's conceptual world *worshipping* has lost its *raison d'etre* and its emotional punch, as have metaphysical questions—questions like "What is the meaning of the whole of history?" and "What is the purpose of existence?" and "What is the really real and the truly true and the essentially essential?" For Rorty, questions like these have lost their power to provoke much else besides the kind of laughs that Woody Allen's comedies or John Callahan's cartoons might provide—the kind people like me get when we read spoofs like Allen's "Mr. Big." Allen's piece, found in *Getting Even*, transforms the history of Western thought into a Raymond Chandleresque murder mystery that turns on revealing who killed God. In "Mr. Big," Heather Butkiss, aka Ellen Shepherd, Barnard physics professor, is God's stunningly svelte murderess. In the midst of trying, unsuccessfully, to seduce Lupowitz, a frumpy Jewish p.i., she begs him "not to go ontological on me—not now. Anything but *that.*"

But Diggins's sense of humor appears to stop short of such punch lines. He approaches Rorty with the same sort of "brimstone mentality" Santayana chided James and Royce for seventy-five years ago in *Character and Opinion in the United States*, as he turned to his own variety of festive criticism. In effect, Diggins faults Rorty for failing to reveal how we Americans could or will win a new heaven and a new earth. While he intends to give Rorty's pragmatic naturalism a just hearing, he thinks Rorty fails, like his pragmatist heroes, to deliver an account of just and joyful uses of power, and he criticizes Rorty's work for continuing to let us suffer the felt absences of modernism. This is the case, he claims firstly, because Rorty's "solidarity" converts private vices into collective virtues the way alchemists tried to convert gunk to gold, by sleight of mind. It is the case, secondly, because Rorty's aestheticism is nothing but amusing, and carries with it neither guilt, nor responsibility, nor burden of truth, nor burden of self, nor divine authority, nor any other dependable friendly rational beings besides ourselves to constrain the various irrational powers that will not only kill us in the end but, odds are, will do so in some cruel way, whether pedestrian or titillating.

I don't read Rorty the same way Diggins does. He sees the alchemy of guiltless, but all-too-destructive, solidarity on the social responsibility side of Rorty's cultural agenda. I see something pretty close to George Kateb's analysis of democratic individualism which, if modest in its proposals, is telling and workable. Rorty's account of responsibility doesn't transform private vices into public virtues. Very much like, say, Spinoza's or Hegel's or Emerson's or James's, it subordinates some natural desires to others, analyzing virtues as shared intentions.

Diggins sees Rorty commending spiritual suicide by urging us to amuse ourselves to death. I see him quite properly suggesting that private—meaning *voluntary* and (only) sometimes solitary—festive creativity breathes fresh life into our democratic culture. In sum, I see very promising intellectual moves helping to inform my own Jewish American essays on joy and responsibility. In other words, where Diggins sees liberal *false* consciousness, I see a liberal artist engaged in an intellectual carnival celebrating something pretty close to what Santayana would have called a *severely honest* love of life in the consciousness of impotence.

Construed this way, from one angle, I read or misread Rorty's interest in private and public goods against the backdrop of an American aesthetic tradition of spirituality. In other words, I read him, perhaps ironically and parodically, as an inheritor, sometimes witting and sometimes not, of a tradition moved by an intuition that beauty is to duty as grace is to law, an intellectual movement articulated by Peirce, James, Santayana and Dewey in a time with other problems and difficulties before ours, and then again by the likes of Jonathan Edwards and Ralph Waldo Emerson in times with still other problems and difficulties even before theirs.

From another angle, like Richard Bernstein, I see Rorty giving us the most telling narrative linking post-War American philosophers—as intellectually powerful as Quine, Sellars, Goodman, Putnam, Davidson and himself—to a pragmatic tradition shaped by the preoccupations of these predecessors, mentors and contemporaries. For these are the voices of persuasion that Rorty orchestrates in support of the no-longer-new pragmatism for which he is eponymous. They are the champions of knowledge as interested inquiry; of reason as immanent criticism; of language as expressive or poetic; of every part of existence as historical and contingent; and finally, of philosophy understood as reflection on problems of human finitude rather than as a search for first principles or the really real, truly true, or essentially essential.

Read this way, Rorty is a philosopher seeking to hang together the ways in which we hang things together in a democratic individualist way. For me, anyhow, he is a leading figure—maybe *the* leading intellectual—provoking crucial conversations, especially, for those of us self-critical *democratic individualists* who repudiate searches for final solutions, but are nonetheless committed to managing, suitably if piecemeal, both large and little things impeding public and private goods characterizing mortal human joy. He is especially helpful for suggesting good ways to recover from Deweyan diseases that Diggins himself diagnoses. He shows us how to dump Dewey's apparent preoccupation with scientific method. He suggests better ways to inform progressive pedagogy with cultural literacy. He gives us even better ways to understand how the rules of thumb at work in scientific inquiry overlap with the virtues exhibited in democratic consensus-building.

Rorty, like Kateb after reading the Emersonians, opposes individualisms that, under banners of existential or romantic *authenticity* or theological *worship*, smell of aristocratic or monarchial pretensions and give cultural greed and resentment a new lease on life. That's one reason why he has no use for "truth-to-self" or "loyalty-to-God" talk. And like Kateb, he is equally opposed to democratic movements so majoritarian or *solid* that they carry the stench of mass or bulk life, as they vaporize or tyrannize individuals and voluntary association. That's one reason why he urges us to giggle, as the better part of wisdom, in the face of this or that metanarrative spelling out the *Meaning of History* or the *Purpose of Existence*.

This is where I jump in with my Jewish American sensibilities. Rorty's account of bad individualisms, bad communities, and howling revelations of the really real, provides a lot of insight about a variety of idolatries that currently plague our culture. I emphasize *idolatries* because, if deep concern for establishing conditions of joy and responsibility make up the positive center of my *Festive Jewish American* perspective, surely such idolatries stand out among the powers impeding them. This is why I have no more use than Rorty does for existential authenticity, theological worship, or hegemonic stories about the one and only meaning of history or the one and only purpose of existence. Like him, I see the will to authenticity, to worship, and to metaphysical hegemony impeding joy and responsibility all too often. So these idols of self and idols of community and idols of metaphysical presence give me, alternatively, the heebeegeebees, for the fanaticisms they can muster, and the giggles, for the sick jokes they can provide.

My effort, much indebted to Rorty among others, is to celebrate joy without transcendence, responsibility without theology or existentialism, science without scientism, coherence and clarity without essentialism, inquiry without foundationalism, reason without representationalism, chance without chaos, sufficiency without certainty and, all the way up through wit's end, the love of life in the consciousness of impotence.

It is just that where any religious tradition appears to Rorty to be more trouble than it is worth, or what James would have called a dead option, Jewish American festivities—Jewish American memories, practices, and hopes—move me. My Judaism qualifies or informs my American democratic individualism and vice-versa. They are my threads, my weave, the ropes that rig me and, so, that characterize or qualify whatever imprint I make on things. They make up the horse power that pushes and pulls my heart and my soul and my might. Take away the relevant chunks of my Jewish American repertoire, and my spirit runs still. Put another way, take away either 1-800-JUDAISM or the Library of America or the new editions of Dewey, James, Peirce, and Santayana, and I'd be deprived of the greater bulk of my cultural nourishment. As James would put it, I'd suffer a maximum of jolts and a minimum of continuity.

To my own mind, that makes my investigations in Jewish American naturalism mainly a matter of self-understanding and further identity formation, not primarily or intentionally some big bone of metaphysical or epistemological contention. The very ideas of *persuading* somebody to become Jewish American like me, much less *showing why and how* everybody ought to pledge my allegiances, are howlers. They are veritable pieces of obscene humor. They propose activities, indeed, that turn my liberal Jewish American stuffing inside out.

Here Woody Allen's "Mr. Big" is instructive again: looking for Mr. Big, a small time Italian hood asks a local Jewish cleric how much it costs to belong to the Children of Israel. The rabbi responds laconically but profoundly: "Don't ask." A Jewish American repertoire of bittersweet memories, beliefs and desires is who *I* am and aim to continue becoming. It provides the sites where I turn my spades. It motivates my priorities and organizes what I do and what I say. If forced, I suppose, I'd defend it, or give witness to it, to my death.

But does that mean that my Jewish American beliefs and desires are emotivist commitments that stand somehow outside critical jeopardy? No. They—*I*—invite such trials and, often enough, demand them. Their—*My*—liveliness exacts critical jeopardy. Their vitality makes them indefinite, subject to modification and change, as James would put it, when the world of which we are part boils over; or, as midrash suggests, whenever creation goes on. In my Jewish American culture, when beliefs and desires go *literal*, it is time to say kaddish because they have died. That is the occasion either, honorably, to bury them or, more hopefully, to try resurrecting them through some strong misreading or other or, disreputably, to idolize them. Here it always helps to remember James on Socrates's *faux pas* and the tyranny of essential definitions.

So let me end this meditation on the promise of pragmatism for my *festive Jewish American* sensibilities, if for nothing else, on a comic—if not exactly ribald—note. Let me propose a scheme for my pragmatic essays toward a festive Jewish American naturalism.

By "comic" I mean, following Rob Polhemus, a view that takes joy as seriously as it does meanness. Comedy, as I understand it, doesn't blink when it encounters suffering, absurdity, and evil. To the contrary, it insists on highlighting them. But it doesn't lend these things any romantic grandeur. Instead, it finds ways to celebrate "passing joys and victories in the world." Rather than revealing, or pretending to reveal, ways to triumph *over* finitude in some fantasy world of transcendent and eternal bliss, comic vision makes suffering, absurdity, and evil mean and tries to find festive ways to cope with them, ways geared to foster "more joyful life in a lasting world."

That, it turns out, is the sort of divine comedy I think I learned from *Tanakh* or the Hebrew Bible as a Jewish American kid. *Tanakh*, in my Jewish American world, functioned to shape up and continually refine moral and spiritual virtues for Jewish Americans. As a kid, I was bred to honor and adore its messages along with other profundities, like Jefferson's Declaration and the good parts of the debates leading to the United States Constitution. I began learning its lessons about the same time I was introduced to Washington's cherry tree, Henry's liberty, Jefferson's black mistress, Abe Lincoln's Other Mother, the Cherokee's Trial of Tears, Sojourner Truth, and the Woman called Moses.

I learned not only *Tanakh*, but also that *Tanakh* doesn't end the way my neighbor's Christian Old Testament does, much less the way my neighbor's whole Christian Bible does. Indeed, eventually I learned that the editors of my *Tanakh* compiled it in the order *Torah, Prophets, Wisdom Literature*, whereas the editors of the Christian *Old Testament* assembled that book, as prequel to presumptively better news, in the order *Torah, Wisdom Literature, Prophets*.

Read as *Tanakh*, the bible stories and aphorisms I began studying as a Jewish American kid eventually provide comic relief for us earth-bound humans. I mean that, in its endings, *Tanakh* undermines the early and mounting transcendent thrusts of its first stories: Its protagonist, God, neither talks nor acts after Job. There is nothing left for him to say or do after he comes to realize that people like the gentle gentile live by his best lessons better than he does. Indeed, after Job, *Tanakh* barely mentions God save in—or as—history. It undercuts the out-of-this world kinds of flight that inform a lot of *Prophets*. Indeed, it ends with a soft and comic landing, a landing that takes joy as seriously as meanness and disrobes suffering, absurdity and evil of any glory. Equipping its cultures with fables and legends that are decidedly this-worldly, *Tanakh* finally informs its people with the counsel of Psalms and the homilies of Proverbs, the impatient integrity of Job and the equanimity of Koheleth; the passionate affection of the Song of Songs; the resilience, loyalty, and appreciation for alien others found in the character of Ruth; the trickster qualities of Esther; the severe self-criticism of Lamentations; the consoling and inspiring day-dreams of Daniel; the prudent or responsible community-building of Nehemiah; and the historical lessons we better not forget of Chronicles. The sense of its multiple endings reframes the point of *Tanakh's* many beginnings. It underscores the immanent character of its Passover message of liberation from oppression. It highlights the actual-space, actual-time horizon for its Sinai covenant. Its clarifies the finitude of its marvelous agreement proposing pathways for the just and humane uses of power along with festivities fostering a love of life in the consciousness of impotence. Indeed, and finally, I'd venture to say, the sense of its endings enables its readers eventually to take Santayana's advice and recognize that Judaism, among other religions, becomes better, as Judaism, when we take it for the interventionist poetry that it is.

WORKS CITED

Allen, Woody. *Getting Even*, Vintage Books (New York, 1978).

Clebsch, William A. *American Religious Thought*, University of Chicago Press (Chicago, 1973)

Diggins, John Patrick. *The Promise of Pragmatism*, University of Chicago Press (Chicago, 1995).

Geertz, Clifford. *The Interpretation of Cultures*, Basic Books (New York, 1972).

James, William. *A Pluralistic Universe*, Harvard University Press (Cambridge, 1977).

———. *Pragmatism*, Harvard University Press (Cambridge, 1975).

Kallen, Horace. "Democracy Versus the Melting Pot," *Nation*, February 25, 1915.

Kateb, George. *The Inner Ocean*, Princeton University Press (Princeton, 1993).

Levinson, Henry Samuel. *Santayana, Pragmatism, and the Spiritual Life*, University of North Carolina Press (Chapel Hill, 1992).

Miles, Jack. *God: A Biography*, Knopf (New York, 1995).

Polhemus, Robert. *Comic Faith*, University of Chicago Press (Chicago, 1980).

Postman, Neil. *Amusing Ourselves to Death*, Penguin Books (New York, 1985).

Santayana, George. *Character and Opinion in the United States*, Scribner's (New York, 1920).

———. *Interpretations of Poetry and Religion*, MIT Press (Cambridge, 1989).

———. *Winds of Doctrine*, Scribner's (New York, 1913).

———. *Reason in Religion*, Scribner's (New York, 1905).

Silk, Mark. *Spiritual Politics*, Simon & Schuster (New York, 1989).

A PALEOPRAGMATIC PHILOSOPHY OF HISTORY OF PHILOSOPHY

Robert C. Neville

Among the most important contributions of Richard Rorty to the revival and extension of pragmatism is a philosophy of the history of philosophy. Peirce, James, and Dewey had all commented on historical philosophers, often with great insight. They also had important points to make about the history of philosophy. One thinks of Peirce's complaint that modernity has been a long decline into nominalism, and of Dewey's point about the deformation of philosophy into academic epistemological irrelevance.[1] But none of the great pragmatists dwelt at length on the philosophic nature of the history of philosophy as such. Richard Rorty has done that, and it is one of the main themes of David Hall's recent book on him.[2]

Rorty's Neopragmatic philosophy of the history of philosophy is that it is a narrative, and it is as parts of narratives, or of a grand narrative, that his discussions of readings and misreadings are to be understood. His philosophy of the history of philosophy as having narrative structure is also closely allied with his view of philosophical conversation. The general view that the history of philosophy is a narrative, of course, is Hegelian, and it has come to seem natural to us in the West. Hegel had a philosophic theory about the narrative structure of the unfolding of philosophy's history, and also an historical account of that history in the form of a narrative.[3] Wilhelm Windelband, the Hegelian historian of philosophy put it in narrative form, and so has nearly every other historian, even non-Hegelians such as Copleston, Reale, and, most influential of all, Will Durant.[4] Although Hegel was the great master of the history of philosophy as narrative, he surely was not the first to think of it that way. I suppose that, with a generous enough understanding of what counts as philosophy, one that plays better in East and South Asia than in West Asia or its European extensions, the sermons of St. Peter and St. Stephen as recorded in Acts 2 and 7 present the history of philosophy as having a narrative form. Like Hegel, but probably not like Rorty, the Saints had reason to think of philosophy's history as a narrative because they believed that there was a single main agent of history, God, and that philosophy as well as everything else is God's story.

Natural to us as it seems, narrative is not the only form philosophers have defended for the history of philosophy. Aristotle (*Metaphysics* A) structured the history of philosophy according to a classification of ideas, not a narrative. Richard McKeon has given this classificatory approach as much sophistication in our time as the narrative approach enjoys.[5] Walter Watson and David Dilworth have continued the extension of this work, the latter dealing with the history of world philosophies, not merely Western ones, although we should note that Hegel himself dealt with the philosophies of South and East Asia, and with unusual insight for his time, especially if we count his treatment of religious ideas as part of philosophy (as would make sense in most cultures).[6]

To take the history of philosophy to be either a narrative or a process of filling in possible types of ideas is not satisfactory, however. Much can be learned from both approaches. But to take the history of philosophy to be the development of examples of types of ideas treats it as merely possible, never actual except in accidental ways. According to Watson and Dilworth, for example, what is important about a philosophy is its locations in grids and matrices of possible ideas, and the structure of those ideas can be known from the classificatory scheme. That a philosopher's philosophy actualizes a position in the scheme provides flavor, but nothing really new. The drama of narrative is far truer to the struggles to build an actual philosophy. On the other hand, to conceive of the history of philosophy as a narrative has its own limitations, however pungent and seductive its drama. The principle limitation is that the narrative form, any narrative form, imposes a story on the material that trivializes and dismisses all the positions that do not fit that story. A good historian would try to tell as fair and inclusive a story as possible, but the narrative form carries with it its own principles of what counts in the story and what does not. As postmoderns would say, this is to do violence to those positions that are marginalized or trivialized by the logocentric story.[7] Or as Hegel said, in defending the thesis that the rational is the real and the real is the rational, all those things that exist but do not fit in to the dialectical narrative form of Reason are *as if* they had not existed, were only mere possibilities.[8] Whereas the classificatory approach treats history's philosophies as possible positions, the narrative approach treats them as actual only insofar as they play roles in the narrative. My title word, "Paleopragmatic," reflects my own pique that the Neopragmatic grand narrative trivializes Peirce because it can relate to him only as someone not quite liberated from classical epistemological concerns; it therefore misses his main contributions in speculative philosophy and semiotics. Similarly, the Neopragmatic narrative truncates Dewey to dismiss his metaphysics for which it has no role, and it trivializes Whitehead, Weiss, Hartshorne, and others whose work has little bearing on what Neopragmatism says is important to the conversation.[9] This violence is not refutation, which is respectful, but delegitimation made possible by control of the concepts that say what is important.

My purpose in this paper is not to consider the narrative or classificatory approaches to the philosophy of the history of philosophy at greater length but to develop a third alternative, one deriving from ideas of Peirce, the Paleopragmatist. My philosophy of the history of philosophy is guided by Peirce's theory of categories and signs. I shall discuss, first, philosophies as signs themselves, then as signs in reference to reality, and finally as signs under interpretation, each as paradigmatic for some dimension of the study of the history of philosophy. To consider philosophies as signs is to treat them as firsts; to consider them in their modes of reference is to treat them as seconds; to consider them as under interpretation is to treat them as thirds. With firsts, seconds, and thirds, and Peirce's theory of signs, the paleopragmatic wagon lumbers along at a remarkable clip.[10]

I.

Signs. According to Peirce, the fundamental classification of phenomena is as Firsts, Seconds, and Thirds. Firsts are things in themselves without reference to any other thing; Seconds are things that are what they are in reference to other things; and Thirds are things that are what they are by virtue of connecting two other things. Signs as phenomena thus can be considered in themselves, in comparison with one another, and in terms of their influence on one another.

i. This scheme causes us to note first that philosophies have a character of their own, prescinding from their relation to one another, to reality, or to a subsequent tradition of interpretations. This character is what it is regardless of the roles the philosophy might play in some larger narrative or the positions it might occupy in a larger typology of philosophic ideas. The character of a philosophy is the philosophic identity of the philosopher, however borrowed or novel the ideas and their connections.

The outer bounds of a phenomenon might very well be fixed arbitrarily. So, by *a philosophy* in this sense might be meant the entire corpus of a philosopher, or a single work, or a period in the philosopher's development, or a school or tradition of philosophy. The point is that, however the boundaries are set, what is within them has a character.

The writing of a history of philosopher, therefore, needs to begin with an articulation of all the philosophies, however bounded, on their own terms. New terms and perspectives of analysis might be required to make the philosophy clear on its own terms, but the intent of this dimension of a historical analysis of philosophy is to acknowledge and lift up what the philosophies do and assert. This is a powerful heuristic corrective to both narrative and typological approaches to the history of philosophy. Whereas both of those approaches come to a philosophy with biases to relate it to a larger story or fit it in to predetermined categoreal types, this first Peircean point stresses what might be called a phenomenology of philosophy.

Phenomenology of philosophy is not likely to be the most congenial approach for philosophers to engage historical figures. Even if we are not trying to understand philosophers in terms of larger narratives or typologies, we usually are interested in them because of some point of our own work. Most active philosophers approach its history reconstructively, bending interpretations so as to be helpful in current work, or to provide dialectical foils. This is well and good for philosophy, but it is not as such responsible history of philosophy. History of philosophy ought to have a strong phenomenological beginning, a resolute attempt at non-biased piety.

ii. To articulate philosophies phenomenologically on their own terms is not to understand much about them. Serious understanding requires noting the boundaries of philosophies and how they differ from one another, their Secondness. Regardless of whether a philosophy represents its own differences from other philosophies within itself, it is different, according to its character and the characters of others. Even philosophies within the same school, or that use the same terms, have unique identities over against each other. Despite their school ties, Plato and Aristotle were very different in their philosophies. That difference consists in lifting up different things as important, treating different things as focus and background, taking different things to require explanation, shaping conceptual representations differently, and plainly asserting different things, each asserting some things the other denied. The history of philosophy is not merely a bunch of philosophies, but philosophies that differ from one another in important respects.

Therefore, the writing of a history of philosophy needs to be comparative. Comparison by itself can be rather dull; teachers pray to be delivered from "compare and contrast" term papers. Nevertheless, a philosophy cannot be understood fully on its own terms alone. It needs to be understood from the outside, in terms of its differences from other philosophies. It needs to be understood in terms of how its forms, and the components it seeks to integrate, look when registered within other philosophies. This is precisely where both narratives and typologies give helpful guidance for studying the history of philosophy. Of course there are other points of comparison as well, such as themes, ways of handling ancient motifs and older philosophies, interests, audiences, and so forth. A faithful historian of philosophy will not limit comparisons to ready-made strategies but will look at the philosophies' own characters to determine interesting points of comparison and contrast. Comparison requires what Peirce would have called Thirds, namely "respects of comparison." Even the phenomenology of philosophy calls for the use of Thirds in description. The Secondness I am emphasizing now is the real differences between philosophies and how the study of the history of philosophy needs to mark these differences in describing that history.

iii. The Thirdness at this point in a Paleopragmatic philosophy of history consists in the fact that philosophies have influence in other philosophies. They are connected by influence, sometimes mutual influence in the case of contemporaries but most often by historical influence. Philosophers rework their antecedents' ideas, reshaping, affirming or denying, and generally forming their own philosophies so as to be able to retain the good and get away without the bad in their predecessors. Sometimes philosophical influence is not very conscious. Sometimes it is ironic, as when a philosopher in haste to deny some predecessor's point presupposes the predecessor's way of setting up the problem.

A third dimension of the study of the history of philosophy thus is the tracing of influences. Some thinkers might over-value this kind of understanding through influences: How much do you understand when you know Thomas Aquinas was an Aristotelian or Whitehead was a Platonist? Not much, unless you know in exactly what respects the influences held and how they were carried down. You would need to know in what respects Aquinas was *not* an Aristotelian and Whitehead *not* a Platonist, and why. Narrative has an important place in the tracing of influences. This is especially so if attention is given to the career of the influential idea and its adventures in affecting this or that philosophy. If one starts from a given philosopher, however, and asks what diverse things from the past have functioned influentially, that study might be far more neatly organized by structural considerations within the philosophy itself. Typology is important in the tracing of influences because structural connections of ideas affect how influences are possible and impossible, and how ideas have to change as they get carried along. A good historian's subtle detective work in identifying influences, and following out the influences of a philosophy on subsequent philosophies, is not to be limited to either narrative or typological forms but needs to take conceptual causation or influence to be a philosophical problem in itself for each kind of philosophy. When we contemplate the ways Peirce, James, and Dewey related to the history of philosophy, the very meaning of "being influenced" is different in each case.

Treating the history of philosophy as a set of complex signs, to be studied phenomenologically, comparatively, and in terms of historical influences, is intellectual history, the history of ideas. Intellectual history without careful phenomenology of philosophy falls into ideology. Without careful comparison it can lose the richness of its topic. Without tracing historical influences it can lose the real connections among philosophies that allow us to speak of *a history* of philosophy. All three are necessary and together they point to the objective reality of philosophy's history and to the natural piety or faithfulness appropriate to its study.

As a topic in intellectual history, every philosophy is important and due its day. Even if seriously influenced by philosophic or scientific or religious ideas that later turn out to be wrong, and even if totally neglected by subsequent philosophers, or so seriously misunderstood as to have trivial real influence, every philosophy deserves study. Or, put more cautiously in respect of demands on time and interest, no philosophy should be judged or forgotten without careful study. This is the moment in the study of the history of philosophy that guards against reductionism. The creative appropriation of elements from the history of philosophy might legitimately be reductive, if there is no suggestion that it is a true representation of history. But historical commentary that presents itself as doing justice to the subject matter needs first of all to be respectable as history of ideas, with these three Peircean moments.

II.

Philosophies as Referents. Peirce claimed there are three kinds of reference that signs might have to their objects, namely as icons, as indices, and as symbols. An icon refers by saying that reality is something like the sign's character. An index refers by pointing out something in the object that otherwise would not be represented. A symbol refers by means of a complex of conventional connections in a semiotic system. Each of these kinds of reference lifts up an important dimension of philosophy and its history, and the study of its history.

i. The conceptual structure of a philosophy is a putative icon of reality, or of that portion of reality to which the conceptual structure refers. This is most obvious in the case of systems. Leibniz said the best way to conceive of reality is that it is like an infinite plenum of monads described as in the *Monadology*. Hegel's logic is an icon of the rational structure of reality. Whitehead asserted that what reality is most like at its most general is a bunch of actual entities defined and related according to the category of the ultimate, the categories of existence, the principles of explanation, and the categoreal obligations. Justus Buchler said that reality is like a complicated set of natural complexes. Of course, every systematic philosopher knows reality is more than what is modeled in these categories, but hopes that everything else can be represented as illustrations of the categories.

Not all philosophies are systematic, and perhaps none is wholly that. Most philosophies are indexical in the sense of pointing out things other philosophies had missed. But most philosophies have conceptual structures of one sort or another and part of their claim to truth and importance is the implicit or explicit assertion that reality is like that conceptual structure.

An icon, of course, needs to be interpreted; philosophic icons are turned into complex symbols when interpreted, as I shall discuss shortly. As interpreted, an icon is taken to be like reality, or reality is asserted to be like it, in a certain respect. Taking the icon itself to be a sign and referring it to reality is to construe it as standing for reality in a certain respect. Thus, philosophies as icons can be distinguished in part by the respects in which they assert reality is like their conceptual structure. Two quite different iconic philosophies might be compatible if they are like reality in quite different respects.

Like myths, philosophies as icons can be inhabited. Without much consciousness that one's philosophy is a sign, one simply works with it to engage life, sharpening and correcting it and living life according to it, learning the while. Only when someone points out that this philosophy is a complex representation, a kind of life-world shaping perception, thought, and practice, would a philosophers insist, "O, yes, and reality is like this philosophical structure." Mythopoeic thought tends to collapse with the realization that there is a distinction between the myth as icon and the reality of which it is an icon; before the breakdown, the mythopoeic person simply takes reality to be the way the myth says. Philosophy survives that breakdown, or perhaps actually was born of it, by virtue of being able to understand the icon of the philosophic world of representations as distinct from the reality of which it is a putative icon.

Some contemporary philosophers forget this distinction, and assume that the references within the icon, of one sign to another, are the only references there are. They miss the point that philosophers, or at least most of them, assume that the structure of intra-systemic interpretations is an icon of reality, and that if it is not, the system ought to be changed to be more like reality. The internal interpretive structure of a philosophy contains extensional references and interpretations of its signs; but the actual interpretation of reality by means of constructing and inhabiting a philosophy involves the intentional referent of the system as an icon, as well as the existential interpretations of the system for relating people to reality. A philosophy is an icon that can be referred to reality, with the interpretation that reality is like the philosophy.[11]

ii. Most philosophies are also indices, pointing to parts or aspects of reality that might not otherwise be noticed. Philosophies in contrast to most other forms of thought call attention to things both larger and smaller than the usual human scale, and also to origins and destinies, and to extremely general or universal traits. Philosophies differ from one another by their indexical references. Kierkegaard, for instance, dramatically called attention to particularity, individuality, and subjectivity, in contrast to the palette of indexical references in Hegel's philosophy. Hegel's thought itself was the development and extension of a line of thinking in European modernity that emphasized the universal, the whole, and the objective. Of course Hegel recognized Kierkegaard's topics, and even said about them much the same things that Kierkegaard said; but his overall philosophy deflected attention from them and trivialized them, represented them as things to be overcome and made part of something else. Kierkegaard showed their irreducible importance. Marx showed the importance of economic determinants of culture, Freud of the unconscious. Nietzsche, Heidegger, and Derrida have pointed out the marginalizing effects of systematic representations of the world.

Whitehead and Weiss have pointed out the dogmatic violence of unsystematic philosophies based on biased evidence. Weiss points out continuities that Whitehead barely recognizes.

The conceptual devices by which a philosophy exercises indexical reference might be parts of an overall system, as is typical with Weiss and Whitehead. In these cases, the iconic structure of the philosophy allows for pointing to things that other iconic structures obscure; they give those otherwise obscured things prominence and articulation. But many devices of indexical reference in philosophy are demonstrations by indirection. Kierkegaard is the obvious example of this, but it is as old as Socratic irony. Points made by silence, humor, double entendre, and other forms of indirection are indexical in their reference. Systematic philosophers of an idealistic persuasion, bent on being faithful to coherence, often have neglected the importance of indexical reference and thus have not appreciated what might be learned from that which cannot be made coherent with a system.[12]

Part of understanding the history of philosophy is discerning the kinds of things philosophies lift up for attention and the kinds of things they obscure. Furthermore, philosophies are helpfully compared with respect to their indexical references. Among the most interesting questions of comparative philosophy, in fact, is whether the philosophies, say, of China, point up an extremely different set of elements of reality from those to which West Asian philosophies point. Do they emphasize the metaphysics of morals, for instance, to the neglect of the metaphysics of cosmology, as is sometimes suggested? Do the indirections of Zhuangzi about knowledge point up characteristics of language and communicative behavior that are found in Chinese but do not occur in Western languages, as Chad Hansen s argues?[13] Answers to the questions about what things are real and important are given through indexical references as well as through iconic references that say the real and important are "like this."

iii. In addition to iconic and indexical reference, philosophies have symbolic reference, by which I mean that they present a fabric of conventions about how to behave in the world. This includes not only overt behavior for which questions about ethics arise, but also intellectual and emotional behavior. A philosophy articulates what is important to know, and why, what is important to appreciate and why, what is important to feel deeply, to take to heart, to mould oneself and one's society around, and why. One of the most important cultural functions of philosophy is to provide orientation. A society such as ours has many philosophies, and hence many orientations. So far our problems are still insufficient orientation, not too many conflicting ones, and thus the more orienting philosophies the better.

Philosophies can perform the orienting function only so long as they are expressed in conventions that connect up with the other elements of life. Philosophies need to address ethical, artistic, economic, domestic, political and all other dimensions of life, or at least employ signs that allow for these connections to be made. For this reason philosophies do not employ a language private to philosophy, not for iconic, indexical, or symbolic orienting reference. Philosophies might get technical, but they cease to be symbolic ways of taking the world if there is no way to make connections between the philosophies and other affairs.

The symbolic reference of a philosophy, relative to its iconic and indexical references, has to do with how it refers the civilization's cultural world to reality. The philosophy is a symbolic sign mediating between the culturally formed signs of life and the subject matter of philosophy. A philosophy does this, of course, only insofar as it is a sign in living interpretation, and intepretation is the topic of my next set of points concerning a paleopragmatic philosophy of the history of philosophy. Let me stress at the conclusion to this discussion of the ways philosophies refer, however, an indexical point. Intellectual history of philosophy examines and compares philosophies as artifacts, as I mentioned earlier. It does not ask whether those philosophies are true, although it might well discriminate among them on grounds of coherence, elegance, and so forth. Existential history of philosophy is something in addition to mere intellectual history; it has to do with the ways by which philosophies refer, and the nature of the realities imaged, pointed to, or taken into orientation by philosophies. Existential history of philosophy has often been missed in thinking about the elements of the discipline of history of philosophy.

III.

Philosophies as Interpretive Engagements. The third main dimension of history of philosophy to which a paleopragmatic theory calls attention concerns philosophies as under interpretation. When philosophies are used to interpret the world, they are to be judged according to their normative qualities, as true or false, accurate or confused, alert to what is important or trivializing. The vast array of elements that enter into what makes a philosophy good or bad cannot be the topic of my remarks here, except in a summary way. For the sake of convenience, we can speak of a philosophy's virtues as truth and its faults as falsity or error.

There are three principal elements to be discussed concerning philosophies under interpretation, namely, their relative truths and falsities, their potential contributions to our own development of true philosophies, and their corrective powers for philosophy more generally. Both narrative and typological philosophies of the history of philosophy are concerned to assess what is good or bad in the philosophies studied. Hegel, like Aristotle before him, wanted to show what is true in each philosophy, and also what its limitations are. Moreover, each as a philosopher himself constructed a philosophy that aimed to incorporate all the truths without the limitations to which the historical conceptualities were bound. On behalf of a paleopragmatic philosophy of the history of philosophy, I want to sort the normative interpretations of philosophies into three questions.

i. The first question inquires about the truth of a philosophy in its own context. This is a meaningful question, in contrast to what might be taken to be the more natural question about a philosophy's truth as such and in general. The contextual truth of a philosophy has to do with whether the philosophy carries over what is important and real into the philosophic interpreters who are themselves contextually defined. Their context includes their science and religions, their political and historical situation, their arts and economies. Plato and Aristotle are contextually true and false in the ways they relate to their own culture, and we can understand that easily as we understand the differences between their science and religions and ours. As I argued above, philosophies refer as symbols with conventional connections to many other cultural symbol systems. For a philosophy to provide good orientation to reality for a culture, it must symbolically connect with that culture.

Western philosophers by habit make allowances for the cultural contextualization of their historical precedents. Whitehead, for instance, did not hold Greek science against Plato but quickly translated the implications of Plato's physical philosophy into relevance for quantum mechanics and relativity theory. Similarly, he decried the slavery Plato seemed to countenance but argued that the real implications of Plato's views unfolded in the adventure of liberation through two thousand years of European institutional development. This was generous and acceptable from the standpoint of the development of a twentieth century philosophy. But it obscures the question of historical truth on Plato's own terms, namely, in addressing the world as Plato could know it. Part of the history of philosophy is the worth of philosophies in their own contexts.

The complexity of this issue is heightened by the fact that philosophies assert on so many levels. Some are highly contextualizable to historical conditions, such as science, religion, politics, and art, and other levels of philosophic assertion seem to be more general across cultural contexts. A paleopragmatist would point out that generalities are not ontologically imposed abstractions but rather are growths and extensions of historical contexts. Our own philosophic context is every bit as historically contextual as Plato's, and if there are levels of reality where the differences between his context and ours are irrelevant, as in discussions of being, sameness, and difference, that is because we share a large historical context with him in those respects. It is not because the topics, either the representations or the realities represented, are wholly transcendent of culture.

This point is particularly important in comparative history of philosophy in which the philosophies of South and East Asia are brought into conversation with those of the West. In these instances the historical contexts might be far more different from one another than appears on the surface. So it is especially important to pause in the study of history of philosophy to analyze the context in which a philosophy is framed as an interpretation of reality, and to be explicit about the salient features of that context. For, a philosophy that is true in one context, carrying over the values resident in real things into the interpretive conclusions with accurate representations, might be quite false in another context. This is to say, the conceptual forms of a philosophy might mediate one thing in one context, and quite a different thing in another context. A strong sovereign with unlimited powers looks far more attractive in a violent state of nature than in a working democracy. A proper history of philosophy ought to make appropriate contextual assessments.

ii. On the other hand, history of philosophy is interesting not only as history but as important material for the development of our own philosophy. The senses in which this is so are commonplaces among philosophers. First, understanding the history of philosophy is essential to understanding our own situation as the present part of that history. Second, the philosophies in history are extraordinary achievements of intellectual invention, providing conceptual elements crucial for civilization, and our own philosophies should not begin with less. Third, by examining the structures and mutual criticisms of historical positions we can tell where the main ideas lead and what their limitations are. In developing our own philosophies we try to preserve their strengths and avoid their limitations. Fourth, we can conceive the fallibility and contextuality of our own philosophies by seeing them in continuity and conversation with history.

Generalizing these points, we can see that the history of philosophy is both the substance with which we philosophers begin and also a lesson for us, or many lessons. Contemporary philosophy is always reconstructive of the history of philosophy. Dewey's brilliant *Reconstruction in Philosophy* is only one of the more honest recognitions of this point. Any attempt to construct a philosophy needs to reinterpret the history of philosophy critically, learning which projects to abandon as well as which to carry on. Furthermore, although historical philosophies might have all sorts of values on their own, of the sort I have already mentioned and more, those philosophies have special values for what they can contribute, positively or negatively, to our own philosophic work. In this context, special readings, even strong misreadings, of the history of philosophy are in order, so long as they are not presented as if they were phenomenologies of those philosophies, or existential analyses of that to which those philosophies point. The epistemological tradition of which Dewey and Rorty have been so rightly critical likes to sort modern philosophers into rationalists and empiricists, with Kant mediating the two. Whitehead, by contrast, claimed that Descartes, the arch rationalist, was the great philosopher of subjective experience, whereas Locke, he said, had the best metaphysical ideas.[14] Given the empiricist and the process philosophy projects, both of those reconstructions make sense, respectively. Neither are faithful historical accounts in the senses I discussed earlier.

Many elements enter into the situation in which philosophy is a creative enterprise, such as our own. The reason that historical philosophies expressed many truths but with crippling limitations is that their conceptual structures entailed the bad parts while embodying the good. Usually the first impetus to creative philosophy is the attempt to find a novel conceptual structure that would preserve some prized truth while avoiding the disastrous implications of the way some previous philosopher expressed it. So, Paul Weiss, for instance, admired Whitehead's reinvigoration of physical cosmology in the age of late modern science, especially with its emphasis on the dynamism of creativity; but he lamented the inability of process philosophy to acknowledge continuities of personal identity in serious ways. Weiss's philosophy, which looks so different from Whitehead's in its conceptual structure, is an attempt to make Whitehead's good points without being stuck with the bad ones. The imaginative side of philosophical creativity is important for precisely this reason—philosophy in this respect is an imaginative dance.

Another crucial element of the situation for creative philosophy is the shifting character of the public. Western philosophy, beginning in ancient Greece, has gone through several major upheavals of publics. The encounter with Christian theology in late antiquity, with Islamic philosophy in the high middle ages, and with science in the modern period are all crisis points. Our present time is characterized by the interaction of West Asian civilizations with East and South Asian, and that means the relevant philosophic public includes the Indian and Chinese philosophic traditions. Dewey, Whitehead, and Rorty are surely right in playing down the importance of Kant and the epistemological project of foundationalist modernity. But their critiques have been internal to the Western tradition. As the conversation emerges employing the histories of East and South Asian philosophies as well as our West Asian ones, Kantian modernism looks even less important, and postmodernism as a reaction against that seems merely unnecessary.[15] The conversation has not progressed enough yet to establish a new pantheon of philosophic heros, or to discard previous heroes to long range obscurity. But we can be sure that the reconstructive histories of philosophy for creative 21st century philosophy will be quite different from what we Westerners inherited from Windelband and McKeon.

The paleopragmatic philosophy of history of philosophy underscores the importance of noting the difference between appropriating elements in the history of philosophy for one's own philosophic projects and understanding those historical philosophies on their own, in relation to one another, and in terms of their own contextual worth.

iii. The last point in the paleopragmatic philosophy of the history of philosophy is to emphasize the importance of making our own philosophies vulnerable to correction by rereading the history of philosophy. This is pragmatism's general philosophy of fallibilism as applied to the use of the history of philosophy to interpret reality. The history of philosophy should correct our creative mistakes.

Pragmatism says that philosophy is less knowledge than learning, to use Dewey's play on words. In contrast to foundationalisms, pragmatism says we are in the middle of knowing, and learn by correcting what we've got wrong, insofar as we can find that out. Therefore, considerations of the form of a philosophy ought to include those elements that set a philosophy up for being corrected. A good philosophy is not well entrenched but vulnerable to correction. Philosophies should present their hypotheses boldly so that they can be grasped and criticized, not surrounded with such hedges that they could not conceivably be shown wrong.

Among the devices of making a philosophy vulnerable is the reconsideration of it in the history of philosophy. This has many dimensions. One is to understand a philosophy as the outcome of historical trajectories. Another is to compare it to similar and different philosophies to see whether it does as well or better, and at what prices. Yet another dimension is to test a philosophy's depth, subtlety, and penetration by comparison with a great historical philosophy. There are few limits to what can be known about a contemporary philosophy, for instance one's own, by reading it through the knowledge of the history of philosophy as I have laid it out here.

IV.

Summary. In this paleopragmatic philosophy of the history of philosophy, based on Peirce's categories and theory of signs, I have tried to indicate complexities in the study of philosophy's history that might get short shrift as registered by the narrative and the typological philosophies. Peirce's categories are abstract and wooden, but they make us look for what we might otherwise miss.

I divided history of philosophy into its firstness, secondness, and thirdness. The firstness of the history of philosophy is intellectual history; its secondness is in the ways philosophies refer to reality, which I called existential history of philosophy, and its thirdness is in the roles historical philosophies play in interpretation. The firstness of the firstness is the character philosophies have on their own, and the exposition of this. The secondness of the firstness is the relations and comparisons of these characters. The thirdness of the firstness is the causal connections of ideas from one philosophy to another and the tracing of these connections. The firstness, secondness, and thirdness of firstness in history of philosophy make up intellectual history.

The firstness of secondness is the iconic character of philosophies; the secondness of secondness is their indexical characters; and the thirdness of secondness is their symbolic characters in which philosophies are parts of cultures. Because reference has to do with how philosophies engage reality, I call this existential history of philosophy.

The firstness of thirdness is the assessment of philosophies in their own historical contexts. The secondness of thirdness is the critical appropriation of elements from the history of philosophy for our own philosophy, with a resultant reconstruction of the history of philosophy according to what is important in our own schemes. The thirdness of thirdness is making our own philosophies vulnerable to correction by the history of philosophy so that that history is extended and, hopefully, increased in value and relevance for our situation by our work. These three degrees of thirdness can be called the normative element in the history of philosophy. In discussing the intellectual, existential, and normative dimensions of the history of philosophy, I have been careful to refer both to philosophy's own historical course and to our writings and other representations about that historical course.

Now, we need to cultivate a sense of humor about this kind of schematic philosophy. I have treated Peirce's categories and theory of signs not as icons, the way he thought of them, but as indices, pointing us to elements in the history of philosophy that easily might be neglected. To press beyond this point to iconic and serious symbolic reference would require an actual representation of the history of philosophy. Although my prejudices are only thinly disguised, I have not attempted to defend them. My concluding point is illustrated, however, by the fact that the paleopragmatic philosophy of the history of philosophy I have sketched here is vulnerable to further correction by an actual interpretation of philosophy's history and current situation.[16]

NOTES

1. See, for instance, Peirce's *Collected Papers*, volume 5, edited by Charles Hartshorne and Paul Weiss (Cambridge: Harvard University Press, 1934), CP. 5.61. See Dewey's *Reconstruction in Philosophy* (New York: Henry Holt, 1920).

2. This is the main burden of Rorty's theory of philosophy as conversation, developed in Part 3 of *Philosophy and the Mirror of Nature* (Princeton: Princeton University Press, 1979) and elsewhere. See Hall's *Richard Rorty: Prophet and Poet of the New Pragmatism* (Albany: State University of New York Press, 1994) especially chapter 1, "Holding One's Time in Thought."

3. See Hegel's *The Philosophy of History*, translated by J. Sibree (New York: Dover, 1956) and his *Lectures on the History of Philosophy*, translated by E. S. Haldane (New York: Humanities, 1953) in three volumes. Hegel is very clear that he means a *philosophical* narrative, not a plain one, whatever that might be.

A Paleopragmatic Philosophy 59

4. See Windelband's *A History of Philosophy*, translated by James H. Tufts (New York: Macmillan, 1901) in two volumes. See Frederick Copleston, S.J., *A History of Philosophy* (Westminster, MD: Newman, 1959), in five volumes. See Giovanni Reale's *Storia della filosofia antica*, 5 volumes (Milan: Vita e Pensiero, various dates and editions); these volumes are being translated by John Caton and published by State University of New York Press, beginning in 1985. Will Durant's *The Story of Philosophy* can be found in most yard sales.

5. David Dilworth cites McKeon's "voluminous career-text" on this point. See Dilworth's *Philosophy in World Perspective: A Comparative Hermeneutic of the Major Theories* (New Haven: Yale University Press, 1989), p. 213.

6. See Walter Watson's *The Architectonics of Meaning: Foundations of the New Pluralism* (Albany: State University of New York Press, 1985); for Dilworth, see the previous note. Hegel begins his *History of Philosophy* with a discussion of the *I Ching*, Confucius, and Laozi.

7. See Hall, *op. cit.* chapter 1 and also chapter 3, "Irony's Master, Irony's Slave."

8. Hegel treated this theme in the introductions to the *Lesser Logic* and *The Philosophy of Right*. I discuss the texts at some length in my *Highroad around Modernism* (Albany: State University of New York Press, 1992), pp. 177 ff.

9. See the Introduction to *The Highroad around Modernism*.

10. The theory of signs is detailed throughout the first two volumes of Hartshorne and Weiss's *Collected Papers of Charles Sanders Peirce* (Cambridge: Harvard University Press, 1931–32). I have discussed many of the relevant texts, for my present purposes, in chapter 1 of *The Highroad around Modernism*.

11. Perhaps one of the reasons that Derrida falls into error of universal textuality (or idealism), taking so many others with him, is that he misconstrues iconic references as symbolic conventions for mapping one thing onto another.

12. Some of us remember Brand Blanshard saying that Kierkegaard's philosophy was like a sickroom whose windows needed to be opened so that the airs of reason might blow through.

13. Chad Hansen, *Language and Logic in Ancient China* (Ann Arbor: University of Michigan Press, 1983).

14. In *Process and Reality*, corrected edition by David Ray Griffin and Donald Sherburne (New York: Macmillan/Free Press, 1978), part 2.

15. This is a main thesis of my *Highroad around Modernism*.

16. At the end, let me remind the reader that "paleopragmatism" is a joke. Either we are talking about Peirce, or we are talking about what we think is philosophically true ourselves, perhaps using Peirce. As for labels, we really have no right to choose our own but get stuck with what history gives us, if we are so lucky as to be remembered and labeled. If I were to choose my own, however, I would want to be called a "paleogalactic philosopher," remembered as a primitive anticipation of the galactic-wide public for philosophy. We won't get anywhere by wanting to be "post" or "neo" something.

RELIGION AND INQUIRY IN WILLIAM JAMES

Wayne Proudfoot

The concept of inquiry is central to the work of the classical pragmatists. Charles Peirce and John Dewey both developed elaborate theories of inquiry. William James did not, but his attempt in *Pragmatism* to discriminate between real disputes and purely verbal ones is continuous with their concern to distinguish between genuine and spurious inquiry. It came as something of a surprise, then, when Rorty, in the course of retrieving the pragmatist tradition, replaced the term "inquiry" with "conversation," alluding to Oakeshott's phrase "the conversation of mankind."[1]

This substitution was motivated in part by Rorty's rejection of the distinction between the natural and human sciences, and of the idea that one could identify distinguishing marks of scientific inquiry. The three classical pragmatists also rejected that distinction, but inquiry remained central. Science served for them as a paradigm of inquiry, but they had a very broad notion of science, viewing it as continuous with, if more deliberate than, the inquiry that informs everyday life and practice.

One might say of much contemporary religious thought that there has been very little inquiry going on. By that I don't mean that there is no distinctive method, or that it is not empirical or scientific, but only that there seems to be nothing at stake. The conversation is often one in which there is little expectation, on the part of either author or reader, that some gain might be made toward solving a problem or resolving a dispute.

I want to examine several of James's writings on religion with an eye to the kind of inquiry with which he was engaged. That will lead me to a reading of *The Varieties of Religious Experience* that differs from the way it has generally been received, and to some critical comments on its legacy.

Varieties is usually read as a classic study of "the problem of religious experience," a problem that had not been identified in quite that way previously. In part as a result of James's book, and in part because of the work of his students and others on mysticism, religious experience quickly became a topic in the psychology and philosophy of religion, generating an extensive literature that continues to the present.[2]

The common element in much of that literature is a comparison between religious experience and sense perception, with attention to the similarities and differences and their epistemic implications. At several points in *Varieties* James draws attention to that comparison. Early in the book he gives a general characterization of religion as a sense of an unseen order, and suggests a parallel with the other senses. In the chapter on mysticism, he addresses the cognitive status of religious experience, an issue he has explicitly deferred at several points, and evaluates that status with reference to the parallel with ordinary sense perception. Examples quoted throughout the book to illustrate what James calls the ripe fruits of religious experience are often ecstatic moments or Pauline-like crossroads or turning points, brief in duration and cast in the language of perception.

But many of the examples are not of this sort. And a reading of James's work both earlier and later would dispel any temptation to read him as a classical empiricist who privileges sense perception. He is certainly not a foundationalist. *The Principles of Psychology* includes detailed and devastating criticisms of British empiricism, with its impressions or sense data, and James carefully lays out the distortions to which that approach leads. He shows that the categories and interests of the mind shape perception at its most basic levels. The idea of selective attention, and the ways in which it constitutes experience, is the chief theme of that twelve hundred page book. Later, in his essays on radical empiricism, he argues that consciousness is itself a construct, and not something given, to which we can have access by introspection.

I.

The chief question that informs James's writing on religion is that of whether there is an unseen order in the world, a moral order that is shaped to human interests, and to which humans can shape themselves.

In the first pages of *The Principles of Psychology* James writes: "Is the Kosmos an expression of intelligence rational in its inward nature, or a brute external fact pure and simple? If we find ourselves, in contemplating it, unable to banish the impression that it is a realm of final purposes, that it exists for the sake of something, we place intelligence at the heart of it, and have a religion. If, on the contrary, in surveying its irremediable flux, we can think of the present only as so much mere mechanical sprouting from the past, occurring with no reference to the future, we are atheists and materialists."[3] Twelve years later, in

Varieties, he writes, less anthropomorphically: "Were one to characterize the life of religion in the broadest and most general terms possible, one might say that it consists in the belief that there is an unseen order, and that our supreme good lies in harmoniously adjusting ourselves thereto. This belief and this adjustment are the religious attitude in the soul."[4]

If this question is a pressing one, as it was for James both as a person and as a philosopher, how would one go about trying to settle it? What kind of inquiry would be appropriate? Traditional appeals to scripture, to ecclesiastical authority, and to metaphysical argument were not available to him, having been rendered problematic by Enlightenment and historicist critiques.

James had thought extensively about inquiry in science and philosophy, especially in connection with the writing of his *Psychology*. In 1877 Peirce had begun his series of "Illustrations in the logic of science" with an essay on "The fixation of belief," in which he recommended that the kind of inquiry that had been successful in the sciences ought to be adopted by philosophers.[5]

Peirce argues in that essay that the practices most often employed for settling opinion and assessing one's beliefs, including those employed by philosophers, are inadequate. People tenaciously hold on to current beliefs while ignoring evidence to the contrary, or they appeal to traditional authorities. Philosophers have set out to improve on these practices, but the *a priori* methods they have employed amount finally to an appeal to intuition. Philosophers as different as Plato, Descartes, Kant, and Hegel adopt beliefs that, after careful reflection, seem to them to be the case.

The method of science, according to Peirce, is a disciplined extension of a more effective way of settling disputes that we employ in everyday matters. We try, he says, to put ourselves in such a position that doubt will be settled by something outside our minds, "by something on which our thinking has no effect."[6] A scientist with a new hypothesis does not just think hard about it and see whether, on reflection, it seems to her to be true. She clarifies her idea by considering what practical effects it might have, and designs an experiment to see whether or not those effects obtain. Peirce argues that, suitably modified, something like this ought to be adopted for any inquiry.

II.

James's lecture entitled "The will to believe," delivered in 1896 and published that year as the lead essay in a book of the same title, is usually taken to be addressed to the opponents he cites in the text: the British agnostics William Clifford and Thomas Huxley. But the volume of which this is the title essay is dedicated to "my old friend, Charles Sanders Peirce, to whose philosophical comradeship in old times and to whose writings in more recent years I owe more incitement and help than I can express or repay."[7] The essay is at least as much a response to Peirce's article on fixing belief as it is to Clifford, as are many of the articles included in the volume. James describes this essay as "a defense of our right to adopt a believing attitude in religious matters, in spite of the fact that our merely logical intellect may not have been coerced."[8] This constitutes a direct response to "The fixation of belief."

James agrees with Peirce that all beliefs are corrigible, that the origin of an hypothesis is unimportant, and that it is to be judged by its outcome. He also makes two points that bear directly on the claim that opinions ought to be settled by putting oneself in a situation in which belief can be fixed "by something on which our thinking has no effect."

His first point is that this is a fantasy. Belief can never be settled by making contact with something that is independent of the self and its interests. Those interests always enter into the way in which a question is framed, and the categories with which we think. It is not only objects of inquiry like the Renaissance and the Big Dipper that are products of selective attention and interest, but also tables and chairs and electrons. There are many beliefs over which I have no voluntary control. I cannot decide either to believe or to disbelieve that today is Wednesday, for example, or that Newt Gingrich is the Speaker of the House. But that is not because those facts are independent of human interests. It is because the categories by which they are constituted, categories that are the products of those interests, are well entrenched and not open to doubt.

His second point is that there are some questions that cannot be settled on intellectual grounds, either by logical analysis or empirical evidence, but are such that we are unable to withhold assent and remain neutral. When both options are motivated for us, and the question cannot be settled intellectually, the matter will be determined by non-intellectual factors. This conclusion follows from the way James has framed the issue, and initially his point is a descriptive one. If neutrality is impossible, and the matter cannot be settled by appeal to evidence or logic, then other interests, or what James calls "our passionate nature" or willing nature, will determine our response.

A paradigm of this sort of question for James is the problem of free will and determinism. In the *Psychology* he had tried to clarify the issue, identifying freedom of the will with the freedom to attend selectively, and arguing that neither logical nor evidential considerations could settle the matter. Yet he held that our interests come down firmly on one side. In "The dilemma of determinism" he argues that the "block universe" of determinism leads to either a Schopenhauerian pessimism or a theological optimism, either of which belies our experience and makes a mockery of some of our deepest interests and emotions.[9] If I regret the Oklahoma City bombing, or that Gingrich is Speaker, and think the world would be better off without them, then I have to reject the whole universe, because it all comes together as one package. Or I can relinquish my regrets, assuming that from God's point of view these things are all for the best. Neither option permits me to appropriate my experience. The problem of free will, for James, is closely connected with that of theism, and he sometimes identifies them.[10] Both have to do with whether or not the world is hospitable to the moral life.

James uses the terms "we" and "our" throughout, as I have. But he is not appealing to some pure interest of practical reason that holds for all rational beings. He does not think that transcendental arguments are valid, or that one can identify any pure universal interests. The interests he refers to are products of social and historical forces. By "willing nature," he writes, "I mean all such factors of belief as fear and hope, prejudice and passion, imitation and partisanship, the circumpressure of our caste and set."[11] These are the factors that tip the scales and settle belief when neutrality is not an option and the issue is underdetermined by logic and evidence.

James is describing what he calls the actual psychology of belief. But when one consciously deliberates in such a situation, how does she assess the options? In the early essay "The sentiment of rationality," James asks: "If, then, there were several systems excogitated, equally satisfying to our purely logical needs, they would still have to be passed in review, and approved or rejected by our aesthetic and practical nature. Can we define the tests of rationality which these parts of our nature would use?"[12] He considers ways of fixing belief that don't claim some touchstone outside the mind, and that can operate when logical and evidential considerations have no purchase. At this point he suggests that to be rational an idea must define the future in such a way as to banish uncertainty and be congruous with our spontaneous powers. All great periods of revival, he says, have "said to the human being: 'The inmost nature of reality is congenial to *powers* which you possess.'"[13] That is to say, reality is shaped to human interests.

In "The dilemma of determinism," published in 1884, James says that the achievements of mathematics and science proceed from the desire to cast the world into a rational shape, and we can't know in advance how amenable it is to this demand for rationality. "Our only means of finding out is to try; and I, for one, feel as free to try conceptions of moral as of mechanical or logical rationality. If a certain formula for expressing the nature of the world violates my moral demand, I shall feel as free to throw it overboard, or at least to doubt it, as if it disappointed my demand for uniformity of sequence, for example; the one being, so far as I can see, quite as subjective and emotional as the other is."[14] How does one try conceptions of moral rationality? We have no moral absolutes, any more than we have them in other areas of knowledge. We have to begin where we are, and revise our conceptions from day to day. But, James writes, ". . . the stable and systematic moral universe for which the ethical philosopher asks is fully possible only in a world where there is a divine thinker with all-enveloping demands."[15] In several essays in the volume, he says that the idea of God is the only natural object of belief, representing as it does a universe accessible to our understanding and shaped to our moral interests. And he thinks that religious faith gives rise to the strenuous mood, providing energy, courage, and a capacity for life's trials that is, practically, the deepest difference between individuals with regard to the moral life.[16]

III.

The Will to Believe was published in 1896. In the summer of 1898, in Berkeley, James delivered the lecture "Philosophical conceptions and practical results," which was the first public use of the term "pragmatism." He gave full credit in the lecture to Peirce for both the name and the doctrine. In a letter to his son that spring, James described the Berkeley lecture as a rehearsal for the Gifford lectures in Edinburgh, which were to become *Varieties*, and for which he had been formally invited in January.[17] Both in the lecture and in *Pragmatism*, published in 1907, James's chief application of the new method is to the issue of theism versus materialism. In the lecture, he paraphrases Peirce's pragmatic criterion for clarifying the meaning of a concept: "To attain perfect clearness in our thoughts of an object, then, we need only consider what effects of a conceivably practical kind the object may involve—what sensations we are to expect from it, and what reactions we must prepare."[18] James adds: "I think myself that it should be expressed more broadly than Mr. Peirce expresses it. . . . the effective meaning of any philosophic proposition can always be brought down to some particular consequence, in our future practical experience, whether active or passive; the point lying rather in the fact that the experience must be particular, than in the fact that it must be active."[19]

We can now see that this broadening of the principle of pragmatism to include not only perceptual effects and reactions to them, but other consequences for future practical experience, including passions, is not a misunderstanding of Peirce, but something that James has been preparing for some time. Practical consequences for one's hopes and regrets and moods, in short moral consequences, enter into the meaning of a proposition.

Applying this principle, James says that if there were no future experience, there would be no difference between materialism and theism. Both explain the past equally well. "Theism and materialism, so indifferent when taken retrospectively, point, when we take them prospectively, to wholly different practical consequences, to opposite outlooks of experience."[20] Theism, he says, is the affirmation of an eternal moral order, materialism its denial.[21] This is an idea that makes a difference in our experience. The metaphysical attributes of God, and related doctrines, James concludes, make no practical difference, but the moral attributes do. Even these doctrines are secondary accretions on concrete religious experiences that are connected with feeling and conduct. These "direct experiences of a wider spiritual life with which our superficial consciousness is continuous" are the originals of the God-idea, and theology is the translation.[22] We can see here much of the outline of *Varieties*.

IV.

Varieties appeared in 1902. Coming to it from this background, we can see that it looks slightly different. It is not a work on the problem of religious experience, as that phrase would later be understood, but a study of the experience of the religious life, or of the variety of religious attitudes toward life, where those attitudes are identified most generally by a sense of an unseen order.

The bipartite typology James introduces at the outset, healthy-mindedness and the sick soul, has nothing to do with analogies to perception, or with experiences of brief duration. It portrays two religious attitudes, one in which a person sees herself as basically in tune with an unseen order, so that she can affirm that everything that is is good, and another in which she views her life as divided, alienated, estranged, or somehow wrong with respect to that order, and longs for a transformation that will turn her around. James had first identified these two forms of religious life almost twenty years earlier, in his introduction to his father's literary remains.[23]

From this perspective, the well known definition with which James begins *Varieties* takes on a different aspect. "Religion," he writes, "as I now ask you arbitrarily to take it, shall mean for us the feelings, acts, and experiences of individual men in their solitude, so far as they apprehend themselves to stand in relation to whatever they may consider the divine."[24] This does not pick out discrete experiences analogous to perceptions, of the sort one finds discussed in the subsequent literature on religious experience. It is about the different ways in which individuals find, feel, or experience themselves to stand in relation to whatever they consider divine. Even "in their solitude" does not necessarily refer to a mystical moment or conversion experience, but to the standpoint of an individual, in contrast to the doctrine of church or theologians.

In the opening chapter of *Varieties*, referring to "recent books on logic," by which he means chiefly Peirce's series on the logic of science, James distinguishes two modes of inquiry concerning anything: (1) What is its nature, constitution, origin, and history? (2) What is its importance, value, or significance? These judgments, he says, are independent of one another. Some try to discriminate true beliefs from false by attention to their origin: origin in intuition, revelation, or ecclesiastical authority, for instance. But the origin of a belief or experience is irrelevant for a judgment of its value. "Not its origin, but the way it works on the whole," he writes, "is our own empiricist criterion; and this criterion the stoutest insisters on supernatural origin have also been forced to use in the end . . . In the end it had to come to our empiricist criterion: By their fruits ye shall know them, not by their roots."[25]

In "The fixation of belief" Peirce proposed to reform philosophy by bringing scientific inquiry to bear on philosophical problems. James, however, views his task chiefly as descriptive, identifying tacit criteria already at work. The subtitle of *Pragmatism* is "a new name for some old ways of thinking." Even those who claim to be settling belief by appeal to intuition, the Bible, or traditional authority, he says, are actually selecting only those beliefs that work, and satisfy their interests. For instance, the greater part of Jonathan Edwards's *Religious Affections* consists of appeals to the authority of scripture and the exegesis of biblical texts. But the selection of those texts and their interpretation are governed by careful and critical reflection on moral discourse, and on criteria for the ascription of virtues and other traits of character. Those who sincerely claim to derive their morality directly from the Hebrew Bible or the New Testament choose some prescriptions and paradigms from the text and ignore others. They pick those that work best, and interpret them in the light of the assumptions and values they bring to the text.

We take certain experiences, or states of mind, to be superior to others, James says, not because of their organic or neurological antecedents, but "because we take an immediate delight in them, or because we believe them to bring us good consequential fruits for life."[26] He then elaborates the fruits as moral helpfulness and philosophical reasonableness. The book is structured as a description and an assessment. After a description of his method and criteria for assessment, and an identification of the religious question as the question of an unseen order, James sketches the two main types of religious stance toward the world and this order. He judges the second type, the sick soul, to be more comprehensive than the first because it acknowledges estrangement and melancholy as well as joy and happiness. The divided self and conversion are topics that must be addressed in order to complete the portrayal of this second type. The resulting picture of the religious life is described in a "composite photograph" that centers on "a feeling of being in a wider life than that of this world's selfish little interests" and a sensible conviction of the existence of an ideal power.[27]

This description is followed by what James takes to be the proper pragmatic approach, an examination of the fruits or consequences of this life. First, the moral consequences; James offers a frankly utilitarian assessment of whether the life he has described is, on the whole, beneficial or detrimental to the well being of those who live it and those they affect. Second, he considers the epistemic implications of this sense of an unseen order. Under the topic "mysticism," James discusses the sense of insight, revelation, or access to some deeper knowledge of reality that is often part of the religious life. And he goes on to give a pragmatic assessment of religious doctrine, concluding as he did in "Philosophical Conceptions and Practical Results" that the moral attributes of God have a practical effect on the religious life, but the strictly metaphysical ones do not.

This separation between mysticism on the one hand, identified as a momentary experience of insight, and the rich moral texture of the religious life on the other, has had a debilitating effect on much subsequent literature. Philosophers of religion and others have searched through mystical texts, or translations of those texts, looking for the few places in which they could find descriptions of ecstatic experiences or revelatory moments, and lifted them out of the broader literary, social, and cultural contexts in which they have their meaning. They then consider to what extent they are similar to and different from paradigmatic examples of sense perception, and what epistemic implications follow. The result has been the construction of the somewhat artificial topics of religious experience and mysticism.

How does one assess the moral consequences of belief in an unseen order and attempt to bring one's life in accord with it? James is explicit about his method. Here, as in any other area of inquiry, we have no access to absolutes. "We have merely to collect things together without any special *a priori* theological system, and out of an aggregate of piecemeal judgments as to the value of this and that experience—judgments in which our general philosophic prejudices, our instincts, and our common sense are our only guides—decide that *on the whole* one type of religion is approved by its fruits, and another type condemned."[28] These prejudices, instincts, and common sense are the fruit of an empirical evolution. Today, he says, claims for a deity who demanded blood sacrifices would not be taken seriously, but there was a time when such cruel appetites were themselves credentials. Different deities are deemed useful in different cultures.

James judges that, on the whole, the practical consequences of a religious attitude are positive: zest, a strenuous mood, and increase of charity. The sense of insight or revelation is analogous to the deliverances of our other sense, he thinks, and thus cannot be refuted, but carries no authority for one who does not have it. The moral attributes of God and related doctrines do have practical implications, but abstract metaphysical doctrines do not.

I have selected a certain strand running through *Varieties* in order to bring out the continuity with James's earlier work on religion. The idea of an unseen order, a moral order, with which one can get in touch, is central. James takes the idea of such an order to be sufficiently in accord with human interests that it commends itself, as long as it does not conflict with other considered beliefs or experience. He also takes the material he has gathered in *Varieties* as evidence that in different times and places, across cultures and doctrinal traditions, people have claimed experience of some such moral order, or as he puts it in his conclusion, some More that is continuous with the higher parts of the self.

V.

Within three years of James's death, Durkheim had published *The Elementary Forms of Religious Life* and Freud *Totem and Taboo*, each with a very different explanation of how an unseen moral order might come into being.[29] From very early on, James had recognized that the world we try to understand and are engaged with is in part the result of our own beliefs and actions. To that extent, the work of Durkheim and Freud ought to be assimilable, even though his own speculation ran in the direction of panpsychism, and he suggests an order that is not completely man-made.

But something else distinguishes their work from his. Each engages in an hermeneutic of suspicion. James's approach is intentionally ahistorical, and even though he describes "willing nature" as "fear and hope, prejudice and passion, the circumpressures of caste and set," there is no suggestion of a critical examination of this evolution of values and prejudices, or a Nietzschean genealogy. More surprisingly, James never seriously considers issues of self-deception, and the layers of construction of self that constitute the fears, hopes, desires, and regrets that inform the religious life.

This is suprizing, first, because in his *Psychology* he is extremely successful in detecting the layers of construction and reification that lie behind such allegedly primitive notions as the ideas and impressions of the empiricists. Second, because the Puritan tradition had developed and refined a rigorous regimen of moral and spiritual self-scrutiny, which is central, for instance, to Edwards's *Religious Affections*. That book is a treatise about love and the assessment of loves.[30] By attending to the practice of moral inquiry and to the ways in which we attribute character traits to others and to ourselves, Edwards captures and contributes to the complex reflective self-consciousness, with attention to various forms of self-deception and subtle changes in the moral will, that is often constitutive of religious life.

James's resolute turn away from causal explanation, articulated in the sharp distinction between existential and spiritual judgment in the first chapter of *Varieties* precludes attention to the kind of consideration that informs the suspicious scrutiny of affections, values, and desires in thinkers as different as Edwards, Nietzsche, and Freud.

Bernard Williams has argued that ethical insight into institutions and practices comes in part "through explanations of how they work and, in particular, of how they generate belief in themselves. . . . Ethical thought should stand up to reflection, and its institutions and practices should be capable of becoming transparent."[31] Not all at once and never with total explicitness, but an understanding of the ways in which our institutions and practices generate and shape belief, and of the causes of our perceptions and affections, ought to be compatible with those perceptions and affections, and with our engagement in those institutions and practices. This is a point that is central to Spinoza's *Ethics*. If ethical insight requires coming to understand the institutions and practices in which one is engaged and the experiences one undergoes in such a way as to be able to explain them and how they exert their authority, the kinds of inquiry pursued by Durkheim and Freud ought to be encouraged.

NOTES

1. Richard Rorty, *Philosophy and the Mirror of Nature* (Princeton: Princeton University Press, 1980), p. 318.

2. In the introduction to the Harvard edition, John Smith writes: "James for some time to come established 'religious experience,' both in name and substance, as the central focus for the philosophical interpretation of religion." John E. Smith, "Introduction," in William James, *Varieties of Religious Experience* (Cambridge: Harvard University Press, 1985), p. xiii.

3. William James, *The Principles of Psychology* (Cambridge: Harvard University Press, 1981, 1983), p. 21.

4. William James, *Varieties*, p. 51.

5. Charles S. Peirce, "The fixation of belief," in *Writings of Charles S. Peirce: a Chronological Edition, Vol 3 (1872–1878)*, ed. C. J. W. Kloesel (Bloomington: Indiana University Press, 1986), pp. 242–257.

6. Peirce, "The fixation of belief," p. 253.

7. William James, *The Will to Believe* (Cambridge: Harvard University Press, 1979), p. 3.

8. James, *The Will to Believe*, p. 13.

9. William James, "The dilemma of determinism," in *The Will to Believe*, pp. 114–140.

10. See, for example, William James, *The Meaning of Truth* (Cambridge: Harvard University Press, 1975), pp. 5–6.

11. James, *The Will to Believe*, p. 18.

12. James, *The Will to Believe*, p. 73.

13. James, *The Will to Believe*, p. 73.

14. James, *The Will to Believe*, pp. 115–116.

15. James, *The Will to Believe*, p. 161.

16. James, *The Will to Believe*, pp. 159–161.

17. James, *Varieties*, p. 523.

18. William James, "Philosophical conceptions and practical results," in *Pragmatism* (Cambridge: Harvard University Press, 1979), p. 259.

19. James, *Pragmatism*, p. 259.

20. James, *Pragmatism*, p. 263.

21. James, *Pragmatism*, p. 264.

22. James, *Pragmatism*, p. 266.

23. William James, "Introduction to *The Literary Remains of the Late Henry James*," in *Essays in Religion and Morality* (Cambridge: Harvard University Press, 1982), p. 62.

24. James, *Varieties*, p. 34.

25. James, *Varieties*, pp. 24–25.

26. James, *Varieties*, p. 21.

27. James, *Varieties*, pp. 219–220.

28. James, *Varieties*, p. 263.

29. Emile Durkheim, *The Elementary Forms of Religious Life*, tr. Karen Fields (New York: The Free Press, 1995); and Sigmund Freud, *Totem and Taboo*, tr. James Strachey (New York: W. W. Norton, 1950).

30. See my "Perception and love in *Religious Affections*," in *Jonathan Edwards's Writings: Text, Context, Interpretation*, ed. Stephen J. Stein (forthcoming, Indiana University Press).

31. Bernard Williams, *Ethics and the Limits of Philosophy* (Cambridge: Harvard University Press, 1985), p. 199.

RELIGIOUS NATURALISM:
Humanistic versus Theistic

J. Wesley Robbins

We Americans put a lot of stock in ingenuity. We admire people who come up with better mousetraps or with better ways to predict economic cycles. William James, in his early essay "Great Men and Their Environment," was the first American pragmatist to suggest that there are interesting analogies between the roles that ingenious people play in social change and bearers of genetic variations play in biological evolution.[1] He proposed that the categories in terms of which we conduct various cultural activities start as idiosyncratic "brainstorms" in the heads of individual human beings, much as Darwin theorized that species start as genetic variations in ancestral organisms. When these mental variations occur in a suitable environment, they may end as new forms of science, morality, art, or religion. Such new ideas enable their bearers to cope with the world differently, and perhaps more profitably, than their ancestors did before them. Social progress when it occurs is a function of the meliorative power of this fortuitous human creativity, not of anything preprogrammed with its own logic or method.

John Dewey made a religion out of the ingenuity that Americans prize and this Jamesian account of it. He described human creativity as part of an ongoing process that does endlessly what the God of classical theism supposedly did once and for all, bring ideal values and actuality together.[2] This artistic reworking of existing conditions for the sake of imagined and hoped for futures is Dewey's functional replacement for the God who eternally unites Being and value. The operations of this unifying religious function have all of the iffiness and chanciness that are hallmarks of Darwinian evolution. Intellectual progress, says Dewey, is a function of the "sheer abandonment" of old questions and their replacement with new ones.[3] The resolution of old questions by "getting over them" reflects changes in interests and preferences, not the methodical exploration and systematic elimination of alternatives within a fixed set of logical possibilities. The history of Western science, for instance, is not the story of successive approximations to the formal structure that governs the world. It is a chapter in the story of human creativity. People like Galileo, Newton, and Darwin are "artists" whose new interests and preferences move them to rework the questions and categories of their scientific predecessors into new questions and new categories previously unimagined.

Richard Rorty calls Dewey's religious function "poetry." Both of them locate this creativity, once thought to be the prerogative of the gods, in human communities rather than in extra-human nature. That makes them humanists. They also recognize that the natural world is the place in which the values associated with human creativity are embedded. For, although art or poetry has a "human abode," this abode itself occurs in a larger environment that produced it and sustains the creativity occurring there. This connection of human creativity with its surrounding world is what natural piety celebrates.

Rorty is a proponent of the Jamesian view of social change and of the role of human creativity in it.[4] In his neo-pragmatist version, James's great men are "poets" whose variant linguistic behaviors are the stuff of scientific, moral, and other sorts of cultural revolutions and progress. Like Dewey, Rorty recommends that we rely on this human creativity for our betterment rather than looking to "higher powers" for salvation or for the legitimation of our activities. Ideally, American society would understand itself in these terms. The liberal utopia, Rorty says, is a society

> whose hero is the strong poet and the revolutionary because it recognizes that it is what it is, has the morality it has, speaks the language it does, not because it approximates the will of God or the nature of man but because certain poets and revolutionaries of the past spoke as they did.[5]

The human self-reliance that Dewey and Rorty advocate is not a self-centered stance, excluding the rest of the world in which we are located. As Rorty describes it, we should couple reliance on our own poetic powers with gratitude based on our awareness of the contingency of the practices that get produced in the way that James described. The awareness that there are ways to talk and to act other than our own fortuitously produced linguistic practices enables us, says Rorty, to "feel *gratitude* for and to those words, those practices, and the beings they disclose."[6] This acceptance of our existence in the natural world as a gift, rather than as "an occasion for the exercise of power," is Rorty's version of natural piety. Unlike traditional theistic piety, it is not thankfulness to the Supreme Creator for the stars and the trees, for instance.

It is rather a matter of being grateful to the stars and trees themselves—
to the beings that were disclosed by our linguistic practices. Or, if you
prefer, it means being grateful for the existence of *ourselves,* for our
ability to disclose the beings we have disclosed, for the embodied
languages we are, but not grateful to anybody or anything.[7]

Rorty describes himself as an atheist. However, his atheism is not
the "militant" variety that Dewey criticized, along with supernaturalism,
for being preoccupied with "man in isolation." To the contrary, Rorty
explicitly endorses the key elements of Deweyan religious humanism.
These are (i) reliance on the religious function, conceived of as linguistic
creativity, in its human abode and (ii) celebration of the connection of
human life with the larger natural world.

Rorty's most extended discussion of religion, to date, occurs in
"Pragmatism Without Method," a piece in honor of Sidney Hook that first
appeared in print in 1983.[8] There he tells of preparing a philosophy of
religion course in which he was going to lecture on Dewey's *A Common
Faith* and Tillich's *Dynamics of Faith,* among other books. He says that,
when it came down to it, he didn't see any great difference between the
pragmatist Dewey and the existentialist Tillich. So he ended up telling his
students that when Tillich talked about the God beyond the God of theism
and Dewey talked about the active relation between ideal and actual, they
were "saying the same things to different audiences."[9] Both were talking
in novel ways about the connection of human life and the things we prize
with the rest of the world, a connection that traditional theists speak of in
terms of our being creatures of God.

When Dewey and Tillich recast the notion of God in their respective
ways they were functioning as "poets," creatively reworking their system
of beliefs. Speaking of *A Common Faith,* Rorty says that Dewey was
there "doing just the sort of creative problem-solving that he thought was
illustrated by both scientific and moral progress."[10] In this instance,
Dewey and Tillich were experimenting with which of the old beliefs
associated with the word "God" could remain in their belief system when
they converted from classical theism, or Hegelian idealism, to naturalism.
As James put it, we are "extreme conservatives" when it comes to
incorporating new elements into our belief systems. We try to leave as
many of our old beliefs undisturbed as we can. The creative process is the
same as when scientists try to square old theories with unanticipated
observations. Regarding this creative reworking of our belief systems,

there is no difference in "method" or "logic" between scientific and religious inquiry.

Dewey's and Tillich's theological innovations serve a purpose that the natural sciences do not. They are ways to "envisage" our connection with the natural world that protect us, in Dewey's words, "from a sense of isolation and from consequent despair or defiance."[11] Certain forms of art serve this purpose, says Rorty, "when not construed romantically and transcendentally as a peep into another world," as do certain forms of religion, "when not construed as an encounter with a preexisting power that will rescue us." Such artistic and religious forms of discourse, he says, are "necessary for our lives" even though they do not contain "the sort of proposition that can be tested against explicitly formulated public criteria."[12] Rorty, thus, agrees with James that we are not able to live our lives just in terms of the natural sciences and the descriptions of the world that they provide.

These non-scientific forms of discourse by which we make ourselves at home in the natural world are not intellectually second-rate because they fail to meet the standards typical of scientific discourse. Artistic and religious "envisagings" of our connection with the enveloping world, like scientific innovations, are products of the same creative process in which mental/linguistic variations fuel social change. All are examples of "human beings doing much the same sort of problem-solving across the whole spectrum of their activities." Art and religion take their cultural place alongside physics and biology as part of "a single, continuous, seamless activity in which the divisions are merely institutional and pedagogical."[13]

Rorty's brief discussion of religious discourse in terms of the creative process that forms and reworks our cultural practices over time needs to be placed in the context of his non-reductive physicalism.[14] Rorty links non-reductive physicalism to Donald Davidson's philosophy of language. In this view, the different purposes that sentences of a language serve distinguish them from one another. These various purposes are, as such, on a par. There is no ranking them in terms of some prior, non-purpose serving relationship between language and the world in virtue of which the world itself makes those sentences that enjoy it true. There is no difference to be found between sentences that are robustly true because they have that relationship to the rest of the world and sentences that are "true" only in some attenuated sense because they do not.

Physicalists, according to Rorty's definition of them, are committed to the proposition that "every event can be described in micro-structural

Religious Naturalism 79

terms, a description which mentions only elementary particles, and can be explained by reference to other events so described."[15] Anti-reductionist physicalists, in turn, are committed to the proposition that "'reduction' is a relation merely between linguistic items, not among ontological categories."[16]

The failure to couple sentences of folk psychology about beliefs and desires with sentences about brain states, for example, says nothing about the truth of Cartesian dualism or the falsity of physicalism. Nor does it say anything about the deficiencies of folk psychological vocabulary for stating facts when compared with the vocabularies of subatomic physics. It does tell us something about the respective usefulness of folk psychology and physics, about different purposes that these vocabularies serve. Thus, to cite Rorty's example, the language of current microphysics serves better than any other "to describe any portion of space-time, no matter how small or large."[17] Folk psychological vocabulary is better for "predicting what our friends and acquaintances will do next."[18]

Likewise, failure to couple religious discourse about our connections with the larger world with any sentences of micro-physics says nothing about the natural world having mysterious depths to it that have no physical description. Nor does it say anything about the fact-stating deficiencies of religious language. It does tell us something about the respective usefulness of religion and physics, about different purposes that these vocabularies serve. Talk such as Dewey's, about the active relation between ideal and actual, is of no use for describing any and all portions of space-time. It is, however, better suited than current microphysical vocabularies to articulate our connection with the natural world in ways that support our moral efforts. Thus, it is quite unlikely that anyone will show that since we can talk about subatomic particles we don't need to talk about any such thing as Dewey's God. This is so, as Rorty explains, because,

> any tool which has been used for some time is likely to continue to have a use The cases in which a tool can be discarded will be recognized as such only after a new tool has been devised and has been employed for some time. E.g., after a hundred years of experience with Newtonian language we may all come to agree that we no longer need Aristotelian language. ... In such cases, X-talk just fades away, not because someone has made a philosophical or scientific discovery that there are no X's, but because nobody any longer has a use for this sort of talk.[19]

Similarly, being a non-reductive physicalist is quite compatible with saying that in all likelihood we will continue to talk about such things as God, the ground of Being, the active relation between the ideal and actual, for the foreseeable future. To make this prediction is to say that language of this sort is as good as any we are likely to come up with for enabling us to keep faith with the ideals we hope to realize in this world.

I will call Rorty's position "pragmatic humanism" to indicate that it consists of two distinct components, an intellectual self-image and a religious stance. The pragmatic intellectual self-image derives from James's account of the role of human creativity in social change and of the adaptation of our thoughts and words to the environment. The humanist religious stance derives from Dewey's reworking of Christian faith into a reliance on our own creative powers in pious recognition that they and we are in a larger environment on which we depend for support of our efforts to realize ideal values. As James once noted, pragmatism is theologically neutral. There is nothing about the pragmatic intellectual self-image that automatically rules theistic religion out as nonsense or that leaves humanism as the only reasonable religious alternative.

Having said that, I hasten to add that the combination of pragmatism and humanism has at least one advantage to it. That is its harmony with the natural sciences. As noted earlier, pragmatists see the sciences, morality, the arts, and religion as products of the same creative process that forms and reforms all cultural practices *vis a vis* the natural environment. Both human creativity and its connections with rest of the natural world arc physically describable. They have other descriptions as well. So, the power on which humanists would have us rely is not something that the natural sciences call into question. It is not something that transcends their descriptions.

This advantage aside, many otherwise sympathetic readers of James, Dewey, and Rorty in particular, take exception to pragmatic humanism. There is a split among religious naturalists who trace their intellectual lineage back through James and Dewey. There are for my purposes two parties to this family quarrel: pragmatic humanists and more nearly theistic radical empiricists. In the remainder of what I have to say I want to discuss this disagreement and advocate pragmatic humanism.

I will take William Dean as my example of theistic radical empiricism. Dean makes a worthwhile effort in his work to connect the classic versions of radical empiricist theology with important contemporary intellectual positions. He, more than any other contemporary advocate of radical empiricist theology of whom I am aware, tries to make his own version of that theology conversant with Rorty's pragmatic humanism.

Pragmatic humanists see the natural world, excepting living things on earth, as indifferent to considerations of value. Take, for example, the ingenuity that Americans prize. Doubtless, over time the natural world produces new things. However, it seems not to care one way or another about its own creative powers. Nor does it look to direct those powers toward the enhancement of values. Despite this indifference, the natural world is a place in which there is room in our lives for "fruits of the spirit" like love, joy, peace, and hope that are reflections of human creativity operating in its natural setting.

Dean disagrees with this. He contends that Dewey's "art" and Rorty's "poetry" are part of a broader worldly creativity that is not merely human. The natural world, so he says, does in fact direct its seemingly profligate creativity with respect to values. It tends to create ever more complicated, that is to say, ever more beautiful things. Biblical theists are correct in this respect. Human creativity images a greater creative power that is not our own. Creativity is not just a local, Yankee, virtue. It is a universal, natural, virtue. It is important for those of us who prize ingenuity in humans to understand this connection between our creative power and that of the natural world as a whole. Otherwise, we are liable to be isolated and demoralized, losing the very sense of connection with the larger natural world that pragmatic humanists agree it is the purpose of religious discourse to foster and to celebrate.

Dean's radical empiricist theism differs from the pragmatic humanism that I advocate in five areas: theological, metaphysical, epistemological, sociological, and scientific. Theologically, as I have just said, Dean proposes that we should rely on a value oriented creative power not just our own that operates throughout the natural world. Metaphysically, he contends that this ascription of value oriented creativity to the natural world as a whole makes sense because of its panpsychic character. Epistemologically, he cites as evidence for his theological proposition certain affective states supposed to be our religious sense of the world as a whole. Sociologically, he claims that American society stands in spiritual need of a religious consensus about the value oriented creativity of the natural world as a whole. Scientifically, he purports to find support for the thesis of panpsychism from biology and physics. The first three of these contentions are more or less standard radical empiricist theology. The sociological and scientific contentions are more particularly Dean's.

These disagreements with pragmatic humanism appear in different versions in two of Dean's books. In the first of these, *American Religious Empiricism,* Dean assigns the name "God" to what he claims to be a general and so far unchanging orientation of change throughout the entire natural world in the direction of ever more beautiful complexity.[20] This tropism toward greater complexity in natural history gives a worth to human history that makes a vital difference. It elicits "God" language from at least some people. This trend engenders a response in the beholder that qualifies as religious experience because (a) a feature of change that seems to be everywhere in the natural world causes it and (b) it is the ultimate experiential evidence that life in this world is worth living.

In this first version, Dean treats the religious experience of God as an epistemological medium that operates between our beliefs and the rest of the world. He does so in terms of the Whiteheadian notion of causal efficacy. Causal efficacy is how we feel the power of the world with our bodies before we form beliefs about it. This initial impact of the world upon our bodies, thus, stands between the things of the world themselves and the beliefs that we form about those things. Causal efficacy is the ultimate experiential evidence to which our various beliefs, including theological ones, have to be adequate. Dean refers approvingly to Whitehead's claim for "the primitiveness of causal efficacy" and to his contention that "the primary aim of knowledge is to elucidate with as little abstraction as possible the immediacy of causal efficacy."[21]

The best way to accomplish this aim for theology, Dean suggests, is through a so-called empirical aesthetic which

> would seek to bring to some dim awareness that intimate concourse of the body with the aesthetic worth of the world . . . to attend directly to that physical reaction to the world which says with incorrigible indefiniteness . . . [among other things] "This is lovely."[22]

So, at bottom, the contention that value oriented creativity is a function of the natural world as a whole, and not primarily of human beings, derives from someone's sense that the entire natural world has a bias in favor of the production of beautiful things.

In his more recent *The Religious Critic in American Culture,* Dean articulates these contentions in terms of what he calls conventions.[23] He agrees with pragmatists that our cognitive dealings with the world are functions of our selective interests. Conventions are ways of knowing and doing that are products of such selective interestedness. They originate

Religious Naturalism

with individuals and then, sometimes, "take on a life of their own."[24] Newtonian mechanics, for instance, started as Isaac Newton's "brainstorm" and then went on to outlive him, becoming the way of understanding motion taught to subsequent generations of physicists. This is what Dean calls "epistemological conventionalism." So far there is nothing here for pragmatists to disagree with. Dean's conventions are the practices formed and reformed along the Darwinian lines that James first suggested.

Dean goes on to argue that our connection to the rest of the world, as knowers and as creatures who act in the hope of making things better, is insecure unless conventions characterize the entire natural world and not just its human portion. Dean calls this thesis of continuity, according to which the basic constituents of the natural world possess at least proto-mental properties, "ontological conventionalism." Ontological conventionalists, he says, "have described convention-making in nature and have suggested that nature, itself, is a history of conventions."[25]

We need to affirm ontological conventionalism, Dean says, because "without it, epistemological conventionalism is not fully intelligible." He asks,

> What sense does it make to affirm the openness of epistemological conventionalism if convention-making humans are bound and gagged in the machinery of nature? . . . If the environments in which people live are causally determined, what chance is there that free and indeterminate conventions can take bold in those environments? Conventional forms of knowing, it would seem, must occur in a world that is itself conventional; otherwise the imagination that would offer new conventions can have no effect in the world beyond imagination and, thus, no pragmatic meaning.[26]

Dean concludes from this that "any sensible, defensible epistemological conventionalism simply requires an ontological conventionalism."[27] Rather than defending ontological conventionalism on metaphysical grounds, he appeals to recent developments in the special sciences. John Wheeler's speculations about a participatory universe in which all entities are observers are supposed to be one such development. A neo-Lamarckian theory in biology according to which E. coli can choose to produce genetic mutations when placed in a hostile environment is another. Obviously ontological conventionalism, according to which decision making characterizes the natural world at its most fundamental levels, is panpsychism with a different name.

Dean's theological and epistemological disagreements with pragmatic humanism recur in this conventionalist context. First, he claims again that there is a bias running through the entire natural world in favor of aesthetic complexity. This, he explains, is a natural convention that supports and lures human creativity and the conventions that we produce. Referring again to Whitehead, Dean says that "God's power lies in persuading the world to enjoy richer forms of experience."[28] He proposes the following "practical argument" for the reality of a universal divine convention that favors aesthetic complexity. This divine creative power, as it is felt experientially by creatures, is what stimulates them to be creative in the first place. Were it not for this naturalistic God, Dean claims, "There are creatures who otherwise could have been as addicted to repetition as they have become addicted to aesthetic novelty."[29]

Second, he continues to claim that we know of this natural value oriented creative power through certain affective states. At this point Dean introduces one new and important qualification. He no longer claims that the nonpropositional affective states described in his earlier book are the ultimate evidence in terms of which we have to justify our beliefs. Beliefs, including those about the nature of the world as a whole, have to pay their way. We should assess an idea "for whether and how it works in society," not for its adequacy to the epistemologically primitive subject matter of causal efficacy.[30] That experiential medium, he now says, plays a much more limited epistemological role. It serves as a plausibility criterion with reference to which to distinguish beliefs that are worthy of being tested for their usefulness from those not worth taking seriously. Specifically, our affective sense of the world as a whole serves to narrow down an otherwise long and arbitrary list of possible theories about the nature of the whole world to a manageable short list of plausible candidates. He says,

> Apart from such an epistemological consideration, there is no clear way to distinguish in advance those few propitious estimates of the whole that might be advanced from those hundreds that are sheer accidents, mere projections of wishes, or simply self-interested objectives.[31]

Dean fears that without at least this residue of empiricist epistemology we will be left to say, as Rorty once said of Galileo's new ideas about bodily motion, that he just lucked out. Apart from experience,

Dean says, "proposals about the meaning of the whole are simply arbitrary or random."[32] He continues, "When experience is disregarded, Jesus or Martin Luther King becomes just statistical freaks; they have this incredibly lucky streak, stumbling from one lucky spiritual choice to another."[33] This reluctant concession as to the epistemological role of experience is Dean's halfway covenant with Rortian pragmatic humanism.

Pragmatic humanists break completely with empiricist epistemology, radical or otherwise. As Dean is well aware, this break with empiricism is crucial. It denies the epistemological authority of the very affective states on which radical empiricist theologians base their case for a naturalistic God whose power is beyond that of merely human creativity.

A principal reason that pragmatic humanists reject empiricist epistemology outright is that it buys into the problem of knowledge about the external world. Consider causal efficacy. As Dean describes it, causal efficacy is subjective in the following sense. These affective states, which are supposed to serve as a person's evidence for what they believe about the rest of the world, are specifiable without reference to anything else in the world apart from them, i.e., without reference to the things that they are evidence for. As Donald Davidson argues, it is logically possible that these experiential states and the beliefs based on them vary independently of what is going on in the outside world. It is logically possible, in short, that all of our beliefs about the outside world are false.[34] This is the possibility that philosophical solutions to the problem of knowledge about the external world are designed to rule out.

Pragmatic humanists follow Peirce by supposing that beliefs are rules of action. We follow James by using the Darwinian analogy to understand our connection as creatures with beliefs to the environment. The survival of creatures in a given environment all of whose rules of action are false is about as likely as their survival were all of their organs maladapted. This is one reason why pragmatists since Peirce say that Descartes was wrong to claim that inquiry should start by doubting everything we believe at once, by taking the possibility that all of our beliefs are false seriously and then trying to rule it out. Like it or not, radical empiricist theists have to take this possibility seriously because of their commitment to the subjectivity of experience and of the beliefs based on it. Their distinctive theological and metaphysical claims are designed, in part, to resolve this problem that their empiricist epistemology creates in the first place.

Dean's claim that rejecting empiricist epistemology makes religious leaders like Jesus and Martin Luther King out to be "statistical freaks" is the result of a misunderstanding of pragmatic humanism. Those of us who adopt the Jamesian account of the formation and evolution of beliefs do not suppose that every "brainstorm" anyone has is equally worthy of serious consideration. As James put it in the "Great Men" essay,

> Not every "man" fits every "hour." Some incompatibilities there are . . . . Now, the important thing to notice is that what makes a certain genius now incompatible with his surroundings is usually the fact that some previous genius of a different strain has warped the community away from the sphere of his possible effectiveness. After Voltaire, no Peter the Hermit; After Charles IX and Louis XIV, no general protestantization of France . . . and so on.[35]

For example, would-be bright ideas today about the motions of bodies are constrained, for better or for worse, by the previous ideas of the Newtons and Einsteins in our history. By the same token, not just any idea about the whole world and our connection with it is going to get serious consideration given our history with the ideas of Democritus, Plato, Jesus, Descartes, and Hegel in it. Pragmatic humanists agree with Dean that experience functions as a plausibility criterion. What we mean by experience, however, is not the empiricists' medium that stands between our beliefs and the rest of the world. It is the practices that develop and get passed on in human communities as these interact directly with their natural environment.

The moral of the pragmatic humanist intellectual self-image is that we do not need a theory of absolutely everything in order to go about our lives with the comfortable assurance that we are in a position to interact fruitfully with our environment. Specifically, we do not need a scientific or super-scientific theory that postulates ontological continuity between ourselves and everything else in the rest of the world.

James and Dewey explained the reasons for this when they talked about the influence of Darwin on philosophy. They saw that if we apply the same "logic" to the study of the human mind and culture that Darwin applied to the study of living things generally, we no more need a theory about the nature of the whole world in order to explain the connection of our ideas and linguistic practices to the environment than a biologist needs a theory about the nature of the whole world in order to explain the connection of organic structures to the environment.

Consider James's "Great Men" essay again, in more detail. That essay is an extended argument against the demoralizing effects of the scientific materialism of his day. Inspired by Darwinian biology, James argued specifically against the theses of the omnipotence of the environment and the passivity of the human mind in Herbert Spencer's evolutionary empiricism. Dean interprets this essay, with its Darwinian emphasis on the crucial role that "spontaneous" variations in our thoughts play in our intellectual adaptation to the environment, as a kind of "protoconventionalism."[36] In other words, as Dean reads it, James combats the deleterious effects of Spencerian metaphysics with a metaphysical thesis of his own, namely an early version of panpsychism.

I read this essay very differently. James proposed a methodological thesis, not a metaphysical one. He advocated bringing the selective attention that has made modern science successful in other areas to bear in the subject matter previously reserved for philosophy, i.e., the mind and its connection to the rest of the world. It may be the case that "a complete acquaintance with any one thing, however small, would require a knowledge of the entire universe."[37] As James goes on to note, the finiteness of the human mind "obliges it to see but two or three things at a time."[38] Our minds, he says, are partial and "can be efficient at all only *by picking out* what to attend to and ignoring everything else—by narrowing its point of view." James cites the differential calculus as a notable example of the success that such selective attention can bring.

Darwin's "triumphant originality," according to James, was to have recognized that there are two different sets of causes responsible for descent with modification. There are causes of production, which he treated as physiological and proceeded to ignore. And there are causes of preservation, which he paid attention to and studied "as functions of the cycle of the environment."[39] The point of this selective attention, according to James, is that

> since that environment is a perfectly known thing, and its relations to the organism in the way of destruction or preservation are tangible and distinct, it would utterly confuse our finite understandings and frustrate our hopes of science to mix in with it facts from such a disparate and incommensurable cycle as that in which the variations are produced.[40]

Similarly, James suggests that human mental and cultural adaptations to the environment result from the operations of two independent cycles of causes. One, which he proposes to disregard, operates inside of people. The other, to which he proposes to attend, operates from the outside. We can explain the adaptation of our thoughts and cultural practices to the environment by attending to the operations of the external environment on our individual mental and linguistic differences, while disregarding what produced these variations in the first place. Precisely what gets left out of this account is a theory about the nature of the whole in which these two cycles of causes are united. James recommends that we disregard the universal set of conditions which, taken together, might be supposed to be the sole source of our mental and cultural adaptation to the environment. That might be a fit subject for the omniscient mind of God. It is not for us. We should be content with describing the readily available environmental conditions that operate selectively on mental/linguistic variations, however the latter may have been produced in the first place.

James's message to the Spencerians of his day was not that the ultimate constituents of the entire natural world are proto-mental. It was that we do not need a theory about the nature of the whole world to understand our own more or less successful dealings with the environment. A theory couched in terms of proximate causes, in this case the selective operations of the environment on individual mental/linguistic variations, is sufficient. James's criticism of Spencer was not that he was guilty of bad metaphysics. It was that he had an obsolete view of science. The clincher for this methodological interpretation of James's essay is his comment that the fallacy of the Spencerians is a "practical one" which he will expose by assuming with them the "predestination of all human actions" although he believes in free will.[41]

James's methodological proposal for understanding our mental and cultural connection to the environment sets the stage for Dewey's later call to replace wholesale with retail philosophy. When Dewey talked about the influence of Darwinism on philosophy he reiterated James's contention that the selective attention which had made modern science successful can profitably be introduced into subjects heretofore reserved for philosophy. He recommended that people who call themselves philosophers attend to what passes for knowledge and other goods in our neck of the woods with an eye to improving on these values, while disregarding whether they are to be found in the original structure of the world. Dewey wanted philosophers to be creative artist/poets, engaged in local meliorative efforts, instead of theoreticians whose accounts of the nature of the whole world provide society with ultimate approval for its activities. Once we get it through our heads that we can account for the connection of our various cultural practices to the environment in the way that James suggested, there is no societal need for a theory about the nature of the world as a whole to rule out the enervating possibility that what we say and do has no purchase in the world.

Pragmatic humanism is a descendant with modification of James's and Dewey's introduction of the new "logic" of Darwinian science into philosophy. It is a retail philosophy that has no use for Dean's ontological conventionalism for exactly the reasons they first articulated. That is why pragmatic humanists see no need for the American religious consensus that Dean calls for in his most recent book. Dean fears that, apart from the version of Whiteheadian metaphysics that he would like to serve as the theoretical core of a new American public religion, we are left to doubt whether the creativity that we prize in ourselves is effective in the world. Without the thesis of ontological conventionalism, he claims, our epistemological conventions are at risk of spinning their wheels uselessly in a world that pays them no mind.

As pragmatic humanists see it, what we need to allay the fears that Dean describes is something less than general acceptance of the theory that the world as a whole is proto-mental and oriented toward the creation of beauty. A Jamesian account of cultural adaptation will do. Beyond this, what we imagine the nature of the whole world to be, how we envisage our connection with that, and how we express these things, are matters left quite properly to the preferences of individuals and voluntary associations thereof. Our feelings, longings, and imaginations with regard to the world as a whole are better left to song, dance, story, and drawing. These latter types of discourse have criteria of acceptability quite different from those typically found in the sciences that are designed to produce a consensus. There is no reason to expect this religious discourse to be the same as scientific discourse about the motions of bodies or about biological evolution. The former is bound to be more idiosyncratic than the latter. It is no worse for that. It is no less important in our lives.

Understood in this context, Rorty's call for the privatization of religion has nothing to do with the notion that it is a trivial matter. It is a function of the pragmatist dismissal of the philosophical mare's nest collected around the problem of knowledge of the external world, including the idea that nothing less than a theory about the nature of the world as a whole will finally resolve that problem. Once it is clear that the well-being of society does not hang on a theoretical consensus about the nature of the world as a whole, then the so-called naked public square, in which members of our society discuss matters of common concern without reference to any such religious consensus, doesn't look so denuded after all.

Pragmatic humanists take the natural world to be indifferent to things that we hold dear for at least two reasons. We are aware that the rain falls on the just and the unjust. We are impressed also with the silence of the natural sciences about entities in the inanimate realm that are value oriented in their nature or operations. As James once said of his own lack of belief in the Absolute, "the greatest enemy of any one of our truths may be the rest of our truths." What he said of the Absolute applies to Dean's naturalistic God. My belief in a universal tropism toward greater complexity, "based on the good it does me, must run the gauntlet of my other beliefs."[42] Pragmatic humanists can live with the mechanistic character of the modern scientific world picture. We have no vested interest in the revival and ultimate triumph of organicist theories. This is a special case of our contention that since the world has no preferred description for itself, descriptions should be judged by how well they serve our purposes.

Radical empiricist theists cannot rest so easily with mechanistic theories in the natural sciences. They have to trump them in some way. Dean attempts to do that in two different ways. In his earlier book, he appeals to the distinction between experiential knowledge that is concrete and scientific descriptions that are abstract. In his most recent book, he finds light at the end of the mechanistic tunnel in scientific theories that seem to support panpsychism.

In *American Religious Empiricism,* Dean explains the silence of the natural sciences about a natural power predisposed to create ever more beautiful things in terms of the abstractness of scientific descriptions. The concrete immediacy of causal efficacy and the divine tropism felt therein are beyond scientific descriptions because the latter are abstract.[43] This epistemological dualism between knowledge by acquaintance and knowledge by description calls the naturalistic credentials of radical empiricist theism into question for pragmatic humanists. There is no difference that makes a difference between a theological dimension of the natural world and the God of classical theism. Both are beyond the descriptive capabilities of the physical sciences. Given their common transcendence of scientific description, there is no more reason to locate Dean's divine tropism in the natural world of things that have scientific descriptions than in the supernatural world of things, like the God of classical theism, that do not.

In *The Religious Critic in American Culture,* Dean turns to the sciences themselves to make an opening for the proto-mental character of the natural world. To this end, he casts his lots with the prospects for a

Lamarckian revival in evolutionary biology.[44] He seems not to appreciate how radical that change would be were it to occur. Asa Gray once advised Darwin to adopt the notion of directed variations, as part of the "philosophy" of his theory, to make it more palatable theologically. Darwin declined on the grounds that were he to do so natural selection would be superfluous. Similarly, if the speculations about E. coli that Dean cites were to become biological orthodoxy, we would no longer have evolution by natural selection. We would have evolution by individual choice and dent of will.

I have no idea how Dean's Lamarckian hopes for the future of biology will pan out. Note that, to foster these hopes, he must waive the very plausibility criterion that he contends experience is supposed to supply. To suggest that, when it comes to theory assessment, speculations about organisms' inner choices are deserving of the same degree of initial plausibility as natural selection is to act as though three hundred years of scientific history never occurred. The postulate of an inner guidance system for biological variations has a high degree of initial implausibility to overcome precisely because of the track record of mechanistic theories, like Darwin's, in which such entities play no role as agents of change in the natural world.

Similar observations apply to Dean's use of Wheeler's work.[45] I waive the question whether it is proper to take Wheeler's thoughts on the subject of a participatory universe to be a matter of scientific theory rather than of metaphysical speculation about all possible universes. In any event, consider why Dean is interested in Wheeler's work in this context. Avowedly, it is a way to make the world safe for epistemological conventionalism. Epistemological conventionalism involves treating the world as if it has no preferred description of itself. Wouldn't it be nice if epistemological conventionalism were an accurate representation of the fact that the world is an indefinite something or other? That, of course, is just what Wheeler tells us. The physical universe, considered as a quantum entity, is in fact indefinite apart from acts of observation and/or description.

Contrast this with non-reductive physicalism. Rorty's contention that reduction is a relation between linguistic items rather than between ontological categories is another way of saying that the world has no preferred description of itself. In this instance there is no attempt to show, in terms of physical cosmology or anything else, that this depends on the ontological indefiniteness of the world itself apart from someone's descriptions of it. Pragmatic humanists treat this thesis about reduction as a product of someone's "brainstorm." This bright idea resulted in a different manner of talking, one in which we describe our own language use in terms of more or less useful tools rather than more or less accurate representations. This new way of talking about our own linguistic behavior has nothing more nor less than its fruits to recommend it. Its value does not stand or fall on whether it is an accurate representation of the ontological indefiniteness of the world itself apart from acts of description.

Pragmatic humanists view our relationship to the natural world as language users no differently than that of any other biological organism to the environment. Nature's lack of preference for any one of the various sorts of linguistic behavior that humans have exhibited over time is a special case of its lack of preference for any one of the various organic forms that have evolved over time. The natural world's indifference to how we describe it no more calls for ontological explanation than does its indifference to elephants or whales, birds' wings or fish's fins, the moles' burrowing behavior over the peacocks' mating behavior. Specifically, it does not require the speculative thesis that the world is physically indefinite until someone observes, and thereby describes, it.

The Darwinian view of the evolution of our mental/linguistic capacities spelled out by pragmatists from James to Dewey and, more recently, Rorty takes us a first step on the way toward a sense of belonging in the world. It makes the idea that our beliefs and desires are cut off from, and ineffective in, our environment utterly implausible. Consequently, there is no need to bridge any supposed gap between our mental/linguistic lives and the rest of the world with a universalistic gesture that postulates ontological continuity, panpsychism for example.

What further steps we take to consolidate that sense of belonging in and to the world are very much up to us. Pragmatic humanism has at least one obvious advantage over various sorts of naturalistic theism, including radically empiricist ones. When the sciences are silent about natural powers that care about any of the things that we care about, pragmatic humanists have no motive either (i) to claim that the relevant theological dimensions of the natural world are physically indescribable or (ii) to force the issue about the content of scientific theories in favor of those purported theological powers. As pragmatic humanists, our interest in the sciences is that they remain open to human creativity, not that their contents provide support for theistic beliefs.

NOTES

1. William James, "Great Men and Their Environment," *Selected Papers on Philosophy* (New York: E. P. Dutton & Co., 1961), pp. 165–197.

2. John Dewey, *A Common Faith* (New Haven: Yale University Press, 1968), pp. 50–52.

3. John Dewey, "The Influence of Darwinism on Philosophy," *The American Intellectual Tradition: A Sourcebook; Volume II*, second edition, edited by David A. Hollinger and Charles Capper, (New York: Oxford University Press, 1993), p. 172.

4. Richard Rorty, *Contingency, Language, and Solidarity*, (Cambridge: Cambridge University Press, 1989), pp. 16–17.

5. *Ibid.*, p. 61.

6. Richard Rorty, "Heidegger, Contingency, and Pragmatism," *Essays on Heidegger and Others: Philosophical Papers*, Volume 2 (Cambridge: Cambridge University Press 1991), p. 48.

7. *Ibid.*, p. 48.

8. Richard Rorty, "Pragmatism Without Method," *Objectivity, Relativism, and Truth: Philosophical Papers*, Volume 1 (Cambridge: Cambridge University Press, 1991), pp. 63–77.

9. *Ibid.*, p. 69.

10. *Ibid.*, p. 70.

11. *Ibid.*, p. 74.

12. *Ibid.*, p. 74.

13. *Ibid.*, p. 76.

14. Richard Rorty, "Non-reductive Physicalism," *Objectivity, Relativism, and Truth: Philosophical Papers*, Volume II (Cambridge: Cambridge University Press, 1991), pp. 113–125.

15. *Ibid.*, p. 114.

16. *Ibid.*, p. 115.

17. *Ibid.*, p. 116.

18. *Ibid.*, p. 115.

19. *Ibid.*

20. William Dean, *American Religious Empiricism* (Albany: State University of New York Press, 1986), p. 59.

21. *Ibid.*, p. 97.

22. *Ibid.*, pp. 94–95.

23. William Dean, *The Religious Critic in American Culture* (Albany: State University of New York Press, 1994).

24. *Ibid.*, p. 107.

25. *Ibid.*, p. 114.

26. *Ibid.*

27. *Ibid.*

28. *Ibid.*, p. 149.

29. *Ibid.*

30. *Ibid.*, p. 92.

31. *Ibid.*

32. *Ibid.*, p. 94.

33. *Ibid.*, p. 95.

34. Donald Davidson, "The Myth of the Subjective," *Relativism: Interpretation and Confrontation,* edited by Michael Krausz (Notre Dame, Indiana: University of Notre Dame Press, 1989), pp. 162–163.

35. William James, "Great Men," pp. 176–177.

36. Dean, *Religious Critic,* p. 123.

37. James, "Great Men," p. 165.

38. *Ibid.*, p. 168.

39. *Ibid.*, p. 170.

40. *Ibid.*, p. 171.

41. *Ibid.*, p. 167.

42. William James, *Pragmatism and The Meaning of Truth* (Cambridge: Harvard University Press, 1978), p. 43.

43. Dean, *American Religious Empiricism,* pp. 93–94 and 97–98.

44. Dean, *Religious Critic,* pp. 123–125.

45. *Ibid.*, pp. 115–122.

III. Rorty, Pragmatism, and Historicism

THE PRAGMATIC SECULARIZATION
OF THEOLOGY

Victor Anderson

At the turn of the twentieth century, American theologians such as Charles Augustus Briggs of Union Theological Seminary (1897, p. 39) and Augustus H. Strong of Rochester (1907, pp. vii–viii) vigorously contended that theology is a necessary faculty of the university because it centers the various faculties around an ultimate reality and value, namely, God. If a course of study excludes or brackets Christian theology, Strong said, it is intellectually impoverished. At the close of this century, American academic theologians struggle against critics who call into question the entire project of academic theology. Two such critics are Richard Rorty and Jeffrey L. Stout. They enthusiastically announce that as a major intellectual discourse, metaphysically ordering meaning in Western culture and determining the legitimacy of Western morals, theology has come to an end for the properly initiated secularist. This essay critically examines their arguments for this conclusion.

Secularization is a confused concept. It means different things to different people. I use the idea in three ways. First, secularization refers to an historical, intellectual process by which theological ideas are thought to be *displaced* by some competitive ideas and ideals. When applied to theology, the competitive ideas and ideals are then said to render theology, its justifications and substantive content, unreasonable or nonplausible. Second, secularization signals a process by which theological ideas are *expropriated* into the meaning of a rival system of ideas. When this happens the legitimacy of theology is undermined as if by a transfer of its content (that is, a certain transfer of ownership) to a conceptual competitor (Blumenberg, 1983, pp. 24 ff.). Third, secularization signals the pragmatic secularist's commitment to the idea that radical contingency circumscribes human intentions in knowledge, truth, and morals, and that pragmatism exonerates and makes regulative the humanistic values of Western liberal democracy without appealing to theological justifications or arguments. What unites Rorty and Stout is their consensus that pragmatism is incommensurable with theology because pragmatism is not translatable in terms of objectivist conceptions of metaphysics, grand teleologies, and traditional Western accounts of theism. Both Rorty and Stout define theology by these categories. On their accounts, pragmatism makes dubious theology.

I.

Rorty is profoundly silent about theology. It is a silence reminiscent of the absence of God in the writings of George Herbert Mead. In searching for God in the writings of Mead, one quickly comes to see Mead as a thoroughgoing and consistent naturalist whose pragmatism allowed no room for the God hypothesis. Rorty's writings are also comparatively silent and for similar reasons. He is determined to continue the critical project of pragmatism after post-analytic philosophy. Although Rorty is rather silent about theology, In *Contingency, Irony, and Solidarity* (1989), there are a few places where the topic is discussed. These instances are quite revealing of how he understands the pragmatic secularization of theology.

For Rorty, pragmatism does not only displace metaphysics and theology. More accurately, it usurps the legitimate domain left vacant by the displacement of theology. Rorty's critique of theology is coincident with his negative judgements about metaphysics. In telling the story of the rise, reign, and fall of Western metaphysics, Rorty also sees himself as simultaneously telling the tragic story of theology. Theology and metaphysics are the culprits which have fed the pretense toward perfectionism in Western moral and religious thought (1990, p. xii). They are discourses that "ask us to believe that what is most important to each of us is what we have in common with others—that the springs of private fulfillment and of human solidarity are the same," says Rorty (p. xiii). Rorty finds himself in solidarity with thinkers such as Nietzsche, Freud, and Davidson, among others, who regard "metaphysics and theology [as] transparent attempts to make altruism look more reasonable than it is" (p. xiii).

Rorty sees himself as carrying out the critical consequences of pragmatism in philosophy, displacing every attempt to account for human actions in ahistorical terms. According to Rorty, theology depends on justifying itself in terms of a priori foundations in philosophy, religion, and morals. Therefore, a theologian or metaphysician (terms used synonymously by Rorty) "believes in an order beyond time and chance which both determines the point of human existence and establishes a hierarchy of responsibilities" (p. xv). According to Rorty, what lies at the heart of theology and metaphysics are questions of ultimacy regarding the origins and destiny of human life which are answered in terms of God's existence (p. xv).

By contrast, pragmatism categorically rejects such theological self-justifications. It disarms theology of its pretense toward certainty in matters of truth, knowledge, and ultimate human fulfillment. Programmatically, pragmatism calls for a liberation of Western thought from both theology and metaphysics. It seeks the release of thought from the need for ahistorical foundations by making time and chance regulative. The secularization of Western intellectual history intends a substitution of "Freedom for Truth as the goal of thinking and of social progress," says Rorty (p. xiii). Rorty proposes that where metaphysics and theology are fundamentally justified in terms of *Truth*, and where *Truth* is unsettled by radical contingency, private irony, and linguistic solidarity, then both metaphysics and theology must suffer the fate of *Truth*. If metaphysics is no longer plausible, then theology is also no longer plausible.

In the position once occupied by metaphysical and theological ideas, a secular pragmatism (third humanistic use of secularization) ascends to fill the void. The ascendancy of pragmatism over metaphysics and theology makes possible the resurgence of an "utopian politics [that] sets aside questions about both the will of God and the nature of man and dreams of creating a hitherto unknown form of society" (p. 3). Pragmatism renders absurd proposals that human nature and culture cohere insofar as they are oriented toward the purposes of God and/or Nature. According to Rorty, theological fictions (kingdom of God, immortality of souls, afterlife, etc.) justify themselves on the premise that "the world is a divine creation, the work of someone who had something in mind, who Himself spoke some language in which He described His own project" (p. 21). Rorty thinks differently.

Rorty's pragmatism advances a non-metaphysical and non-theological version of intellectual history. It proposes that we view "[o]ur language and our culture as much a contingency, as much a result of thousands of small mutations finding niches (and millions of others finding no niches) as are the orchids and the anthropoids" (p. 16). Rorty calls for a thoroughgoing rejection of a priori metaphysics and theology. He proposes that "we try to get to the point where we no longer worship *anything*, where we treat *nothing* as a quasi divinity, where we treat *everything*—our language, our conscience, our community—as a product of time and chance" (p. 22). Rorty's pragmatism normatively commends "chance as worthy of determining our fate" (p. 22).

On Rorty's terms, neither metaphysics nor theology are plausible sources for constituting human meaning at the close of the century. They are displaced by a secular faith that rejects metaphysics and theological claims as just so many reifications of subjective states: fictions. And the functions that the metaphysical philosopher and theologian once served intellectually and morally are now usurped by iconoclastic social critics. Pragmatism spells the end of theology. These consequences of pragmatism are carried over into Stout's critique of theistic morals. The next section of this essay examines Stout's critique of theology in *Ethics After Babel* (1988).

II.

Like Rorty, Stout also sees our contemporary debates in moral philosophy as consequences of the demise of metaphysical ontology, foundationalist epistemology, and a loss of wide-spread agreement not only in ethics but also in theology. Central to the thought of Rorty and Stout is their common rejection of a unified system of ethics that has the capacity for overcoming moral disagreement by some universal or transhistorical principles or laws. Stout argues that faith in such a system is beset with the pretensions of Babel. However, he also thinks that the plurality of morals is a serious problem to be reckoned with. And his own position is that it is not a sign of "the confusion of tongues in a society that has fallen from the coherence and community of an earlier age" (p. 7). Neither are we warranted in undue skepticism, nihilism, and relativism. Rather, our contemporary moral situation is related to the plurality of social practices and institutions that we have reason to affirm (p. 7). He suggests that "[o]ur moral languages exhibit a division of conceptual labor, each doing its own kind of work. But they also sometimes get in each other's way" (p. 7). Stout finds himself uncomfortable with thinkers who regard the issue of moral pluralism frivolously; for he recognizes that the legitimacy of a great many values that we prize depend on whether our moral claims are true or false.

Stout is always careful to offer an account of pragmatism that resists its identification with moral relativism. However, his attempts to answer the charge leave an ambivalence between two concepts: justification/warranted assertability and truth. It is this ambivalence that leaves him a mitigated Rortian pragmatist. Stout rejects the charge that pragmatism necessarily suggests a commitment to moral relativism. He asserts that it is a matter of common sense that claims to moral disagreement make sense only if "there is some truth of the matter in ethics to disagree over and only if I am prepared to say of people who disagree with me over the truth of moral propositions that it is they who are wrong" (p. 24).

The difficulty occurs where Stout seems to identify truth with warranted assertability in his account of belief justification. At one point, he says that "truth is, for us, here and now, warranted assertability" (p. 26). However, later he also says that justifications are contextually relative, while truth is not (pp. 28-29). The problem occurs here. Stout insists that there are good reasons for holding truth claims in our contemporary moral debates, but that these reasons will be based on contextual wisdom. He also insists that truth claims are not relative in the same way that justification are. What is not clear in Stout's position is what one is to make of truth, since it is apparently connected with justified beliefs but not identified with them.

In a subsequent essay, "On Having a Morality in Common" (1993), Stout tries to clear up the ambivalence. He asserts that there is a conceptual difference between adjudicating moral disagreements, justifying beliefs, and moral truth (p. 228). While Stout is sure that both adjudication and justification are relative to specific contextual conditions, he nevertheless asserts that truth in ethics is not relative in the same ways as are either adjudication or justification (p. 228). After numerous attempts to clarify the concept of truth that will be acceptable to him without committing himself to something like absolute knowledge, Stout remains vague about this concept's pragmatic meaning. He insists only that truth behaves differently than adjudication and justified beliefs (p. 229). Truth behaves with a certain permanence, simplicity, certainty, and universality that is not characteristic of either adjudication or justified beliefs (pp. 228-29).

What is not clear is how these traditional philosophical marks of truth are compatible with the contextualist account of knowledge (p. 231). As I read Stout on this matter, the significant difference between justification and truth is one of simplicity and universality in contrast with relativity, fragmentarity, and fragility (p. 230). Because Stout defines truth in terms of traditional philosophy, simplicity, a high grade of certainty, and universality, his characterization of truth is hard to square with his Rortian rejections of both metaphysical ontology and metaphysical theology. That is, it is hard to talk about truth in the "traditional" senses that Stout commends without the benefit of the traditional metaphysics that supported traditional notions of truth. This is an ambiguity in Stout's pragmatism that renders him a mitigated pragmatist.

To be sure, Stout's talk about truth is directed to moral truths and not to religious ones. He insists that talk of moral truth is not incongruent with his secularist claims for pragmatism. He says, "countless moral truths—some known, others not known—have universal applicability. My kind of contextualist need not deny any of them" (p. 230). For Stout, there appears to be a pragmatic necessity for affirming moral truth claims, especially given human propensities toward radical evil and cruelty (p. 230). Moreover, he thinks that moral truth claims peculiar to Western liberalism can be defended in pragmatic terms without committing the moralist to either moral relativism or moral dogmatism.

Stout proposes that truth claims proffered in the languages of human rights and defining the moral and public commitments of Western liberal societies, however thinly conceived, achieve a remarkable level of rational consent and agreement among members of our societies. However, he is aware of the ways that radical moral disagreements obtain at local political levels (1988, p. 225). He argues that we must at least achieve some measure of "agreement with respect to justice and a partnership for the common good" (p. 241). His preferred metaphor for this sort of agreement is the moral garment made of many patches. In this case, we "take the many parts of a complicated social and conceptual inheritance and stitch them together into a pattern that meets the need of the moment. . . . The creative intellectual task of every generation, in other words, involves moral bricolage" (p. 292).

For all of his talk about moral bricolage, however, Stout can find little relevance for theology in the public debates on morals. When compared with Rorty, Stout's critique of theology is polemical and not simply non-theological. For Rorty, the plausibility of theology is simply a non-question because pragmatism usurps whatever relevant moral meaning theology once had in American intellectual culture. Therefore, the question of theology cannot be taken seriously as a mode of discourse on public morals. Stout also thinks that a secularist account of pragmatism excludes theology, but for him, theology nevertheless remains a serious contender to moral legitimacy. For him, the critique of theology is a consequence of pragmatism and remains a viable aspect of secular criticism (p. 109).

Stout is not concerned with the old anti-religious polemics that sought to deny the necessity of religious foundations for the legitimacy of morals. The view that religion is not a necessary basis for morality has long been accepted in the West. Therefore, the independence of morality from religious belief is no novelty of contemporary moral philosophy. Stout sees himself as maintaining the polemical posture of earlier secular moral philosophers who tended to regard religious ethics as the *other* against which secular moral philosophy defined itself (p. 109). However, he thinks that much of the prior secular polemics was merely reactionary, "never [developing] anything like a real dialogue, which might have allowed secular moral philosophy to work through its merely antithetical relation to the religious traditions" (p. 110). Stout's aim is to work through the merely antithetical relation of secular criticism to religious traditions.

For Stout, post-analytic philosophy creates a context where secular moral philosophers can rethink former critiques of religious ethics because the categories that once made it possible for analytic thinkers to separate the logic of morals from that of religion have collapsed in the wake of post-Wittgensteinian philosophy and the resurgence of pragmatism. Stout thinks that secular criticism can no longer simply dismiss theology by begging the question of its relevance on categorical grounds. Rather, he assumes that a real dialogue ought to be possible among pragmatists and traditions of religious ethics, and that theology ought to be a relevant mode of discourse on public morals even though it currently is not. Shortly, I shall argue that, contrary to his claims that dialogue with theology ought to be possible, in the end Stout makes categorical claims that undermine his overtures toward conversation. His position is that if the conversation between pragmatism and theology breaks down, it is because theologians often fail to contribute anything relevant to the conversation on public morals that other discourses do not already accept or say, or because others have no good warrants for accepting what theologians offer (p. 164).

Stout's argument is not that theology is irrelevant insofar as it signals the faith and practices of religious communities. This is the realm of discourse where he thinks it properly belongs. Therefore, theology as a function of ministerial education is not the point at issue. However, relegating the primary context of theological language to religiously specific cultic communities certainly limits the range of influence it is expected to have on a public morality that valorizes the privatization of religion (p. 164). Stout's critique is most accurately targeted at the academic theologies of the university—the public that he clearly has in mind when he constantly refers to theology's irrelevance among the educated secular public (pp. 163–64, 169, 187).

Stout insists that academic theologians cannot successfully communicate to an educated secular public the relevance that religious ethics holds for a common public morality without either alienating themselves from the distinctive religious traditions that they are supposed to represent or without alienating the public that they wish to influence, a public that no longer takes for granted or is persuaded by theological ideas (p. 164). If I read Stout's argument correctly, there are several reasons why he thinks that appeals to theological ideas are untenable among a secular public of moral bricoleurs. One, the success of moral bricolage depends on moral materials that can be patched together. However, this implies that some measure of agreement exists between the materials being patched. Two, moral bricolage has as its goal the upholding of a provisional outlook toward the patch work of moral languages that are suited for our common goods and values. Theology can meet neither criterion and remain theological; that is, if its moral claims are regarded as exclusive, distinct, and absolute. The absolutist and dogmatic disposition of theology, therefore, renders it incommensurable with pragmatism.

Stout's argument, which echoes MacIntyre's "The Fate of Theism" (1969), is that academic theologians are in a dilemma of irrelevance because they often intervene in public matters in ways that "merely repeat the bromide of secular intellectuals in transparently figurative speech," and because "theologians with something distinctively theological to say are apt to be talking to themselves—or, at best, to a few other theologians of similar breeding" (p. 163). Whether these theologies can speak faithfully for their religious traditions by articulating their ethical and political implications without also withdrawing to the margins of public discourse among educated secularists essentially unheard, signals the double bind of theology (p. 163).

Central to Stout's critique of theology is his insistence that a "conversable theology must have something distinctive, something recognizably theological, to say. It must at least make clear what difference theology makes and how an educated person could reasonably believe its distinctive claims" (p. 169). According to Stout, David Tracy and James M. Gustafson are academic theologians who try to clarify the distinctive contributions of theological claims to public discourse, only to find themselves alienated from the sources and legitimacy of the religious traditions with which they identify. They also fail to persuade the intellectual culture that they would like to influence about the viability of theology in moral bricolage. For this secular public is not likely to be persuaded by theological claims. The success of Stout's critique of

The Pragmatic Secularization of Theology 107

academic theology depends on whether it is sufficiently descriptive of the state and functions of theology in the academy. In order to raise doubts about Stout's critique of theology, I shall confine myself to what he takes to be the normative materials that define the function of theology in the academy.

In *The Flight From Authority* (1981), Stout tends to define theological discourse in relation to classical theism and the problem of lost authority. There he argues that in the theological tradition an appeal to authority was an appeal to the historical warrants for assuring the integrity of faith. And the supreme warrant for faith was located in theism and divine revelation. Stout tells the story of how these distinctive elements of theological reflection (theism and divine revelation) were progressively subverted and decentered by philosophical criticism among Christian humanists themselves. Consequently, theology became the handmaid of philosophy rather than philosophy's queen. The original function of theology, that was foremost concerned with the explanation of sacred doctrine, was progressively transferred to philosophical apologetics. And the languages of evidences (internal/external), proofs and demonstration, religious experience and nature, knowledge and reasonableness, supplanted theological authority. Stout's earlier book, therefore, restricts the normative materials of theology to theism and divine revelation, and it restricts the function of theology in the academy to its classical intention, namely, the explanation of sacred doctrine.

The critique of theology in *Ethics After Babel* presupposes the classical terms and functions of the discipline as constituting the normative voice of theology. If I am right, Stout's questions about whether appeals to theological ideas add anything viable for public morality today ought to be heard as a question about whether theism and divine revelation can add anything viable for a public morality. Stout thinks not—at least not for the educated secularist. Stout's criticisms are warranted in certain respects. He rightly supposes that theologians who insist on the viability of theistic morality for moral bricolage must be prepared to convince fellow secular bricolours why they also should be persuaded of the relevance of theistic morality for public debates on morals. Such theologians ought not to presume the viability of their discourse in debates on morals. Stout is also convincing when he insists that academic theologians who jettison claims for the distinctiveness of theistic morality in their attempts to speak relevantly to an educated secularist risk irrelevance. In agreement with Van A. Harvey (1981, 1989), Stout holds that academic theologians risk irrelevance simply because they have nothing distinctive to offer the secularist for critical musing. For the theologian, the problem is this: if theologians are to respond reasonably to Stout's criticisms, they would be warranted in turning to a fundamental theology or to theological arguments. However, Stout's anti-foundationalist critique of theology rules out from the outset any such turn on the part of the theologian. Therefore, his criticism effectively mitigates if not vitiates the possibility of theology answering its Stoutian dilemma.

To further the argument, I propose to take Stout's dilemma as a false one that is based on a categorical error. The error is Stout's identifying academic theology normatively with classical theism and functionally with the successful communication of sacred doctrine. Stout's normative definition of theology is couched in such a way as to beg the question of theology's multiple reoccupations in Western intellectual history. Sometimes theology normatively refers to the Doctrine of God. Sometimes it refers to the entire matrix of historical processes which are said to be directed teleologically toward some consummate end. And sometimes theology is equated with the cultural identity of a people, effectively taking the form of a political theology but signaling nothing of the classical terms. Therefore, defining the meaning of academic theology in terms of classical Western theism appears arbitrary in light of contemporary theology.

Stout stacks the rules of the game against the voice of theology. His exclusive insistence on the criterion of distinctiveness (distinctiveness meaning ownership of the traditional theological vocabularies of one's tradition), as the primary rule of the game, settles the game against academic theology from the outset. Again, the dilemma seems quite persuasive as long as we are talking only in terms of classical theism and atheistic secularism. Indeed, no theologian who intends to advance his/her theistic claims in order to convince atheistic secularists of theology's relevance for moral bricolage can do so without, at the same time, risking irrelevance. However, the burden and risk are peculiar to the exchange between theists and atheists. The impasse between such critics does not signal an authentic dilemma between theology and pragmatism, even if it does say a great deal about the incommensurability between theism and atheism.

On the terms provided by Stout, I suggest that there is no dilemma because there are no genuine lively alternatives in play, each of which are equally compelling or translatable the one into the other (at least not if the game is set up in terms of theism and atheism). If the issue is one of intellectual persuasion, theists (whether those overly preoccupied with the exclusive claims of their tradition or those who are eclectic) are not likely to succeed in persuading educated secular moral bricolouers (who may also happen to be atheists) of the legitimacy of theistic morality. Persuasion would mean blurring the categorical distinctions that identify atheists and theists.

If Stout's insistence on the criterion of categorical distinctiveness is given up, however, then perhaps the impasse to successful communication between theology and pragmatism can be overcome. Yet to be an atheistic secularist is precisely to resist the persuasion of religious perspectives and theological languages. The categorical differences between the theologian and the educated secular atheist are therefore a matter of definition and hence formal. Talk about the atheist's openness to persuasion by the academic theologian amounts to a rhetorical posturing that allows such critics to see themselves as oppositional to theology, confining the fate of academic theology to the impasse of intellectual and moral irrelevance, but without appearing merely arbitrary or without having to define themselves in terms of a categorical rejection of religious discourse (p. 187).

III.

In summary, Rortian pragmatism intends the further secularization of theology that renders pragmatism and theology incommensurable discourses. Rorty's position emphasizes a radical incommensurability between pragmatism and theology. In Rorty's discussion, pragmatism usurps the domain left vacant by the pragmatic explosion of theology's metaphysical criteria of legitimation. When compared to Rorty, Stout is a mitigated incommensurabalist. He remains intellectually invested in theology but accents pragmatism's displacement of theology. His distinction between "religious discourse" (as a linguistic activity proper to the faith and practices of religious communities) and "academic theology" holds for him the possibility of breaking from those critiques of theology and religion that are categorically oppositional toward religious ideas. Stout's is a mitigated pragmatism. His argument is that academic theologians cannot presume that their theistic moralities will have or ought to have influence on the debates concerning public morality. Theological ideas are not merely antithetical to the claims that Stout wants to proffer for public morality. They are also intellectually irrelevant when voiced by theologians as highly distinctive narrative utterances or when voiced by theologians who hold them as intellectual possibilities not only for themselves but also for everyone in dialogue with them.

Stout's restricting the relevance of academic theology to classical terms (theism and divine revelation) and functions (explanation and transmission of sacred doctrine) has an ironic result. While seeking to carry out a secularist critique of theology without defining his objections to theology in categorical terms, Stout's insistence on the criterion of distinctiveness (in this case, between theists and atheists) assures the cogency of his critique only by insisting on the categorical opposition of atheistic secularism to theistic morality.

Like Rorty and Stout, I also hold that the tensions that characterize our present debates about the marginalization of theology in American public life can be accounted for adequately in terms of the pragmatic secularization of theology. However, I also hold that pragmatism and theology need not be regarded as incommensurable discourses. Rather, I am led to think that while pragmatists and theologians may pose different answers to our cultural questions about meaning, value, human intentions and ends, communicative understanding and agreement are possible insofar as our various discourses are centered around shared realities and oriented toward the moral fulfillment of common goods. My position is optimistic. Yet, mine is an optimism that undergirded the pragmatists' reconstructive philosophy throughout the disciplines, including theology. And it is an optimism that classical pragmatists bequeathed to the future of American theology.

WORKS CITED

Blumenberg, Hans. *The Legitimacy of the Modern Age*. Cambridge, Mass: MIT Press, 1984.

Briggs, Charles Augustus. "The Scope of Theology and its place in the University," *American Journal of Theology*, 1897, 1: pp. 38–70.

Harvey, Van A. "The Dilemma of the Unbelieving Theologian," *American Journal of Theology and Philosophy*, 2/2 May: 1981, pp. 46–54.

———. "On the Intellectual Marginality of American Theology," in *Religion and Twentieth-Century American Intellectual Life*, ed.

Michael J. Lacey. Cambridge: Cambridge University Press, 1989, pp. 172–92.

MacIntyre, Alasdair, and Ricouer, Paul. "The Fate of Theism," in *The Religious Significance of Atheism*. New York: Columbia University Press, 1969, pp. 3–29.

Rorty, Richard. *Contingency, Irony and Solidarity*. Cambridge: Cambridge University Press, 1989.

Stout, Jeffrey L. *The Flight From Authority*. Notre Dame: University of Notre Dame Press, 1981.

———. *Ethics After Babel*. Boston: Beacon Press, 1988.

———. "On Having a Morality in Common," in *Prospects for a Common Morality*, Gene Outka and John P. Reed, Jr. Editors. Princeton: Princeton University Press, 1993, pp. 215–32.

Strong, Augustus H. *Systematic Theology*. Valley Forge: Judson Press, 1907.

HABET DEWEY ANIMAM?

J. Harley Chapman

It is certainly conceivable and in fact often hauntingly troubling that for all the undeniable virtues a philosophy may possess, it may be deficient in a central or significant way such that the contemporary issues facing men and women can hardly be addressed. Can pragmatism, a philosophy fundamentally oriented to the issues of people's lives, adequately deal with what is most intimate and fascinating, with what may be the most readily available (albeit most neglected) and potentially the most fruitful way into the divine—namely, soul?[1] Specifically, can the philosophy of John Dewey provide adequate resources for dealing with questions of soul— *Habet Dewey animam*? Puckishly, if not malevolently, I have alluded to the scholastic debate of the Middle Ages: Does a woman have [a] soul (*habet mulier animam*)? Both the obvious and the non-obvious commingle here. Indeed, by our lights, the debate is seen to be misguided, silly, and unjust. Yet, theological context and cultural assumptions aside, the question throws into relief the perennial issues of centrality and importance. Also with Dewey, Is something fundamental lacking? Does Dewey have [a] soul? Playful and profound, let the question—with its offense—stand.

I.

Let us begin in a Deweyan fashion by acknowledging a dubious or problematic situation, one with both theoretical and practical complexities. First, we have created in modern Western culture a theoretical impasse with regard to human selfhood and its full delineation. Unfortunately, neither the inherited religious teachings about human selfhood nor the current social-scientific depictions of human beings seem adequate to current experience. Secondly, the conditions of modern life make it practically impossible to express—or possess—a rich interiority, to enjoy a nuanced and textured experience of events, to integrate meaningfully death into life, and to sense and to respond wholeheartedly to the sacred, i.e., to live full, rich, and abundant lives. If the first produces confusion for the mind, the second produces stultification of life. Along with others, I shall call this situation, culture-wide, the "loss of soul." Reasons will emerge as I elicit responses from three different representatives.

The American philosopher William Barrett has written *Death of the Soul*, in which he traces the fate of mind or consciousness in the modern epoch, roughly the period of development from Descartes to artificial intelligence. Despite the unprecedented and brilliant advances in science and technology, "our understanding of human consciousness," he writes," has become more fragmentary and bizarre, until at present we seem in danger of losing any intelligent grasp of the human mind altogether."[2] In the modern period the language about human selfhood has constantly fluctuated; "spirit," "self," "soul," "ego," "the I," "mind," "reason," "consciousness," "psyche," "subject," "person," to name several, have all had currency. For Barrett, soul is more than reason, the ego, or the conscious mind. He is concerned to speak for the "concrete density of the self,"[3] that is, for the soul with its sensitivities and sufferings, its longings for meaning, beauty, and the divine, and its unique ability to ripen into wisdom.[4] Unfortunately, this reality has been painted out of the dominant cultural picture. Come to think of it, why is it so hard to imagine scientifically- or epistemologically-oriented philosophers—bright, informed, even brilliant—as ripening into wisdom? Are their own philosophies sufficiently self-reflexive to account for their own commitments to their programs, their careers, the values they espouse (or ought to), and their destinies? Generally not. This is no doubt one dimension of Dewey's concern to overcome the split between science and human values, neither of which we can forfeit.

Also using the same language of "the death of the soul" in a new work entitled *New Maladies of the Soul*, Julia Kristeva arrests us with the question: "These days, who still has a soul?"[5] The implications are stunning: something fundamental to humanity can weaken, atrophy, get lost, and die. A contemporary French psychoanalyst in the Freudian-Lacanian tradition, she is concerned with the "spectacular reduction of private life."[6] There is a desperate attempt by many in the culture to substitute television serials for genuine emotional life. As a linguist also, she worries that the structure of meaning, that bond of language between one speak-being *(parlêtre)* and another, can die. The death of the soul would rob the body of any ability to act. As a therapist, she faces the challenges that contemporary neurobiology and pharmacology, now standard adjuncts to psychiatry, bring to mental and emotional healing. Though pharmacological assistance is of some acknowledged value at some stages of human distress, it still cannot be maintained, for example, that Prozac creates soul. Neither soap operas nor a renewed interest in religion suffice as psychic prostheses to replace an amputated subjectivity. What is needed is "the time and space . . . to create a soul for ourselves."[7] Despite the fact that many will take such a suggestion as frivolous, what is desperately needed is an "inner zone, a secret garden, an intimate quarter . . . a psychic life."[8]

A third area of witness to the problematic situation of our culture is archetypal psychology, which, though having ancient roots and varying cultural instantiations, finds its twentieth-century expression in the later Jung, in James Hillman, Robert Sardello, Thomas Moore, David Miller, Daniel Noel, Lynda Sexson, Edward Casey, and Robert Avens, to name only a few. For them, loss of soul is a serious dissociation of soul from conscious life. Nearly thirty years ago James Hillman provided what is a classic expression of this situation, quoted here *in extenso:*

> Anthropologists describe a condition among "primitive" peoples called "loss of soul." In this condition a man is out of himself, unable to find either the outer connection between humans or the inner connection to himself. He is unable to take part in his society, its rituals, and traditions. They are dead to him, he to them. His connection to family, totem, nature, is gone. Until he regains his soul he is not a true human. He is "not there." It is as if he had never been initiated, been given a name, come into real being. His soul may not only be lost; it may also be possessed, bewitched, ill, transposed into an object, animal, place, or another person. Without this soul, he has lost the sense of belonging and the sense of being in communion with the powers and the gods. They no longer reach him; he cannot pray, nor sacrifice, nor dance. His personal myth and his connection to the larger myth of his people, as *raison d'etre,* is lost. Yet he is not sick with disease, nor is he out of his mind. He has simply lost his soul. He may even die. We become lonely. Other relevant parallels with ourselves today need not be spelled out.
>
> One day in Burgholzli, the famous institute in Zurich where the words *schizophrenia* and *complex* were born, I watched a woman being interviewed. She sat in a wheelchair because she was elderly and feeble. She said that she was dead for she had lost her heart. The psychiatrist asked her to place her hand over her breast to feel her heart beating: it must still be there if she could feel its beat. "That," she said, "is not my real heart." She and the psychiatrist looked at each other. There was nothing more to say. Like the primitive who has lost his soul, she had

lost the loving courageous connection to life—and that is the real heart, not the ticker which can as well pulsate isolated in a glass bottle.

This is a different view of reality from the usual one. It is so radically different that it forms part of the syndrome of insanity. But one can have as much understanding for the woman in her psychotic depersonalization as for the view of reality of the man attempting to convince her that her heart was indeed still here. Despite the elaborate and moneyed systems of medical research and the advertisements of the health and recreation industries to prove that the real is the physical and that loss of heart and loss of soul are only in the mind, I believe the "primitive" and the woman in the hospital: we can and do lose our souls. I believe with Jung that each of us is "modern man in search of a soul."[9]

In light of the above it would seem that modern culture has placed us in mortal danger. We are more or less cut off from the deep psychic springs of life; and we do not know how shallow our emotional lives are, whether our religious quests are true journeys of the soul, whether we are capable of genuine responses to love, beauty, and death. Apparently, we are capable of genuine psychic dissociation (with the resulting alienation) and of not knowing it at all.

II.

Can Dewey, as a representative of the pragmatists, contribute to "the Deweyan project" of applying a method of intelligence between a problematic situation ("loss of soul," as described above) and its solution (a more-or-less pervasive cultural situation in which a living transaction obtains between consciousness and the depths of experience). I propose that we reconstruct a notion of soul, with the help of both Dewey and others, capable of accessing the depth dimension of human experience and of opening up concomitantly the possibility of experience of the sacred.

It must be admitted at the onset that not all interpreters of the pragmatic movement are sanguine about the prospects of Dewey's providing much help in this project. John E. Smith claims that the pragmatists, and especially Dewey, were "masters of analysis of the outer life, the public sphere," never developing a satisfactory account of human interiority.[10] He further claims that "the possibility that the ego has depths not to be apprehended by the experimental method or mastered by the instrumental intelligence was quietly passed by."[11] I tend to agree with this judgment; however, since our goal is a reconstructed notion of soul, we may with profit avail ourselves of whatever Dewey can offer.

In an early essay "Soul and Body" Dewey argues that psyche or soul is immanent in the body, directing the body toward an end.[12] Furthermore, in order to attain that end the soul selects some activities and inhibits others; it responds to some and controls others; it adjusts and coordinates the complex whole in a most economical fashion to attain its end. This activity cannot be the work of matter, which cannot of its own act for an end, i.e., teleologically. Soul also transcends body/matter in that the body as the organ of the soul becomes such by being *made* to be the organ. The body stimulates but does not cause the soul to make its own creative response, transforming the body's activities to be the soul's end. Though echoes of Hegel, Aristotle, and St. Paul can be heard, one can also hear themes that will later have a Deweyan ring: creativity; acting for an end; organizing the various sub-activities to achieve the desired end; immanence; unifying of polarities or opposing forces; and the complex whole.

Not long after this early effort Dewey abandoned any systematic use of the word "soul" despite the fact that psychology tended to be of continuing interest to him. Individual psychology, however, more or less gave place in Dewey's thinking to social psychology, as his 1922 *Human Nature and Conduct* clearly shows. Darwin intervened, as did William James; physiological psychology became important to him. Later he was to say what had become central in his thinking: "Biology has revolutionized conceptions of soul and mind."[13] Dewey's most systematic reflection on the issue of soul appeared in his 1929 *Experience and Nature*. Because of the aptness and suggestiveness of his observations, I wish to quote at length:

> ... "soul" when freed from all traces of traditional materialistic animism denotes the qualities of psycho-physical activities as far as these are organized into unity. Some bodies have souls preeminently as some conspicuously have fragrance, color, and solidity. To make this statement is to call attention to properties that characterize these bodies, not to import a mysterious non-natural entity or force. Were there not in actual existence properties of sensitivity and of marvelously comprehensive and delicate participative response characterizing living bodes, mythical notions about the nature of the soul would never have risen. The myths have lost whatever poetic quality they once had; when offered as science they are superstitious encumbrances. But the idiomatic non-doctrinal use of the word soul retains a sense of the realities concerned. To say emphatically of a particular person that he has soul or

a great soul is not to utter a platitude, applicable equally to all human beings. It expresses the conviction that the man or woman in question has in marked degree qualities of sensitive, rich and coordinated participation in all the situations of life. Thus works of art, music, poetry, painting, architecture, have soul, while others are dead, mechanical.[14]

First to be noted is that soul need not be a trans-natural activity or process. For Dewey, it cannot be; moreover, the traditional mythology suggesting animism and mysterious non-natural entities and forces is to be rejected as a "superstitious encumbrance." Soul plays in and around the events of the natural world and everyday experience; there is no necessary reason why soul should be seen as coming from afar. On the other hand, there are dimensions of soul, it may be argued, that are more remote, that entwine themselves with mystery and the depths of nature; soul cannot be restricted to the foreground. The issue of soul is tied up with how rich and deep nature (and naturalism) can be allowed to be.

Second, soul has to do with qualities, immediately felt, of sensitivity and participative responsiveness. Dewey is right to start with the idiomatic and non-doctrinal uses of the word as a way into what is directly experienced. He is further on target in linking soul to aesthetic qualities, even to works of art. Soul is yoked with richness as well as sensitivity. Though Dewey at this point has little to say about the aesthetic properties, his intuition here is accurate. It is beyond the scope of this paper, but his aesthetic thinking, which flowered in *Art as Experience*, would be the appropriate focus of attention for an extended treatment of Dewey's notion of soul.[15] A second, and revealing area of investigation, would be Dewey's own poetry, which reveals qualities not otherwise obvious.[16]

Third, soul can be more and less. He is right to acknowledge that we speak of soul when the qualities in question are present to a "marked degree." Thus we speak of the "great-souled" as those who possess the qualities of richness, sensitivity, and coordinated responsiveness in ways which transcend the expected and ordinary. Presumably, those qualities were not always present or manifest with such insistence even among those gifted soul-wise; they were nurtured, developed, and refined. Since it lives, soul can grow.

Fourth, soul has to do with the organization into unity of psychophysical qualities. The emphasis has to be on the active and never-ending process of the unifying of various and disparate sub-activities. The question is, How tight must the "organization into unity" be to be soul?

Habet Dewey Animam?   119

Some soul activities evince an amazing intentionality, intelligence, and wisdom; some do not. Some activities have at best only a loose association with the central process of consciousness and will. The kinds and degrees of organization, co-ordination, and unity are matters for empirical investigation; the issue should not be settled aprioristically.

The above statements indicate how Dewey might be a genuine resource for a reconstructed notion of soul. Dewey himself was not at all sure that traditional words like "soul" and "spirit" could be salvaged, so fraught were they with traditional baggage; for the needs of science and philosophy he was willing to jettison them. "But," we may be pleased to hear him say, "the realities are there, by whatever names they might be called."[17] It is now for us to press on with our program of reconstruction, using, in addition, other and contemporary resources.

The contemporary cultural movement most alert to the possibilities of soul, and presumably most able to help in the reconstruction of the notion of soul, is archetypal psychology, to which I alluded earlier. Rooted in the later Jung, it nonetheless has its own integrity as a discernible psycho-cultural approach to reality. James Hillman, the thinker-psychologist most identified with this movement, began using the term about 1970. He has been joined by a host of others in Europe and in both South and North America.[18]

The central image is soul, indefinable but glimpsable through its manifestations—ambiguous, insistent, shy, boisterous, fey, bold, pulsing—and its configurations—twisted and warped as well as regular and symmetrical. We must listen for soul in the rhythms and figures of speech, in silences; watch for it in gesture, manner, and display; stick to it in image, metaphor, and dream; circle it in play, fantasy, and joke; and acknowledge it in the maze of confusion and multivalenced complexity of life.

We know that souls can be troubled, in a mess, possessed, lost, innocent, inspired. Souls can be searched, go on journeys, be on trial, be on fire, be on ice. Soul is seen in eyes; experienced in gospel and blues; savored in poetry, enjoyed in cornbread and black-eyed peas; endured in wailings, dirges, and wakes; and honored at battlefields and cemeteries. In all this we are speaking of living experiences—concrete, colorful, tactile, poignant, profound, zestful.

Soul is there, real, but not a thing or a substance—a living process, a dimension, a perspective perhaps. Not body, though sticking to each cell. Not mind, with its cogitations, sharp distinctions, and bright reasonings; rather, soul is reflective, cool, allusive, and connecting. Not fiery spirit, with its hot-spurred ambitions, dry abstractions, its upward and outward thrusts, its peaks, its sun-lit moralism and defensive fundamentalism. Rather, soul, however it is best thematized, is to be followed in its inward and downward movement, its vales, its moisture, its entanglements, its desires, its descent into darkness and into the underworld of dream, perversity, madness, and death.[19]

Soul is that component that makes meaning possible (Edward Casey speaks of "possibilizing"); it expresses itself through image and is experienced through the imagination.[20] Soul deepens events into experiences through its capacity for reflection, for memory, and through its affinity with death. An eros towards persons, plants and animals, and things, it communicates itself in love. Sensitive to the sacred in all its myriad manifestations, the soul loves the mystery, the imagination, the arts of religion—its stories, pageants, and rituals; its simplicity and stillness; its peculiar affirmations and directives. Further, soul responds appreciatively to art, to beauty in all forms, natural as well as cultural.[21]

Soul winks and peeps through language, challenging all attempts to speak only literally, directly, and propositionally. Even our most determined efforts to speak solely objectively and abstractly in the sciences and in philosophy, to "tell it like it is," are doomed to failure. Sooner or later, we are all poets, who can only, in a Dickensonian way, "tell the truth slant." Theories house the most amazing metaphors; categories often emerge from imaginative encounters with the natural world and the transactions of everyday life; observations and low-level hypotheses are often inexpungeably image-riddled. It could not be otherwise since, as Hillman puts it, "soul is the poetic basis of mind."[22] Human discourse is rhetorical as well as logical, mythical as well as dialectical, as Plato so amply demonstrated. To speak honestly is to speak soulfully. Every reasonably accurate "picture" of the world must have an important place, fundamental to both its structure and functioning, where the language only points, suggests, teases, reveals, idles, plays, breaks down, doubles back on itself, and generates alternate outcomes and paradoxical effects. This is the role of soul. It expresses imaginal reality *(mundus imaginalis).*[23] In such role it serves to deliteralize practical assumptions and theories about the world. This imaginal world is the between-world, the metaxic realm, mediating between matter and spirit, body and mind, consciousness and world.

III.

Let us move to closure "the Deweyan project" of reconstructing the notion of soul to meet the crisis of the "loss of soul" by considering the ends-in-view, the purposes, the outcomes, the effects. The goal of the reconstruction is to make possible both for contemporary individuals and for the culture generally theoretical and practical means by which a living connection, an on-going, ever-enriching transaction can obtain between the depth of experience (soul) and conscious thinking, doing, undergoing, and enjoying. Culture as currently configured makes such difficult, if not impossible.

If we take seriously a reformulated notion of soul, what follows? At least four consequences, the first three of which serves a negative-critical function and the fourth a positive-creative one. First of all, taking seriously the potentialities of soul would lead to the de-rationalizing of experience. This first consequence is difficult to state without distortion, if not caricature, because, on the one hand, experience without rational interpretation, direction, and decision hardly deserves to be called human; yet, on the other, experience over-interpreted, over-guided, or overborne by reason becomes thin, predictable, stultified, even demonic. Historical examples of both tendencies abound in the modern period. Dewey himself preferred the concept of intelligence to that of reason, which preference has decided merit; intelligence, unlike reason, does not tend to suggest a bias toward the *vita contemplativa* over the *vita activa*, nor for theory over praxis. It is easier to speak, as some educational researchers do, of seven types of intelligence than of seven types of reason. Dewey wanted to fold in both the practical and the purposive into his view of intelligence. This is important; yet Dewey's notion is too instrumental, too purpose-oriented to meet fully the needs of soul with its desire to experience the depth of things, to make contact with what fascinates, with what holds the promise for enrichment, with what oddly completes and peculiarly satisfies—whether or not bread is baked, sense made, or problems solved. Apparently, soul is not overly impressed with the story of the progressive development of human intelligence, either at the level of the species or of the individual. Soul opens up the imaginative underbelly—even the dark shadow side—of reason, displaying its complexity, its opacity, its vulnerability, its dysfunctionality, and its perversity. Underneath every abstract argument and chain of such, soul is working/playing with images; weaving memories onto perceptions; making connections among feelings, anticipations, fears, fantasies, bodily sensations, and intuitions; punning, caricaturing, and riddling; in short, making a somatico-rhetorical nest for all the mind's hatchings. No doubt, all this under-world activity is usually not conscious at all. When it is glimpsed, it is seen through the silences, the lacunae, the anacoloutha, the logical breaks; it is manifest in imagery, in peculiar locutions; and it presents itself, insistently or shyly, in moods, dreams, homophones, and jokes. Loving the concrete, the odd, the peculiar, the exception, the vivid, the intense, soul finds little of interest in the Categorical Imperative, the Identify of Indiscernibles, or the Principle of Sufficient Reason. What this means practically as well as theoretically for rational activity and discourse is that such approaches never tell the whole story and are often forced to share the stage with an unpredictable and sometimes outrageous partner. Reason rests in and draws its strength from an inescapable rhetorical matrix; it can never scrub itself totally clean of its bloody birth. This means that starting points are never totally obvious or self-certifying; that assumptions can at best be only partially clarified through indirection and circumambulation; that arguments depend in unexpected yet important ways on aesthetic factors; and that endings which do not connect with the affections can hardly convince. The purpose of these reflections is not to exalt soul nor to condemn reason; rather, it is to place reason, powerful but limited, into a larger framework of understanding and significance.

Secondly, taking soul seriously would de-literalize claims and assertions about experience and the world, about the sacred and our destinies. Literalists have enormous trouble in taking claims with a certain lightness, so serious are they about the Truth they wish to uphold and about their own (laughless) persons and their responsibilities as *defensores fidei* (whatever the faith). All literalizing moves aim at smoothing out variations of light and dark, high and low; discounting differences in weight and importance; dampening nuance; organizing dynamic tendencies into mechanical patterns and grids; removing anomalies; in short, literalizing aims at managing the anxiety which inheres in any living process. Literalizing ("making letters," like handles, to put on the world) always aims at getting a grip on things, at controlling experience.

For all its capacity for intensity and urgency of expression, soul has no stake in controlling, partly because of its protean nature and internal complexity, partly because of its function as a reflecting medium, and partly because of its eros toward all things. Soul needs and wants something other than itself—in fact, many others to which it can relate. Soul relaxes all need for control. It drops all the modernist pretensions of certainty and self-containedness; it dissolves all rigid dualisms and fixed polar oppositions (honoring, however, dualities and polarities); and it quells the fear that fuels all fanaticisms and fundamentalisms. This last point is particularly important since, as David Miller, religion scholar and archetypal psychologist, once put it in a public discussion, "we are all fundamentalists somewhere." There is for most human beings a non-negotiable point, an ideological *axis mundi,* an Archimedean *pou sto.* For its part, however, soul knows that a good story is just that—a good story. An engrossing narrative can be so thrilling, enriching, and suggestive of possibilities that, for the time being, anything else is hardly imaginable. But, soul knows: another time, another story. And so on, world without end.

Thirdly, and organically related to the previous point, soul is a demonizer. It deconstructs the dominant and privileged perspective through its sheer display of multiplicity, its internal juxtapositions and paradoxes, its protean self-expression, its un-summability. Soul's perspective is happily pluralistic; it sees no reason to opt for one story, one principle, one deity, one angle of vision. Rather, the variety of perspectives playing off each other, naturally filling in missing details, mirroring each other like the jewels in Indra's net, effects an unimaginable increase in riches and dazzling beauty. From soul's perspective pluralism is a decided strength, not the failure of a unitary vision sufficiently to account for all (important) data. Soul sees such totalizing attempt as fatuous and thoroughly misguided.

Soul has a preference for eaches over alls. It savors the unique value-contribution of each thing. It views all attempts to establish a monism either as an abstraction by a thinning out of the idiosyncratic values of each thing in the interest of some grand unity (for what purpose?) or as an act of political suppression and domination such that one interest is to be served by all others. Soul is fascinated by the diversity of individual things in all their dappled glories, their uniquenesses, their irreducible natures, styles, and signatures.

Soul honors many principles and worships many gods and goddesses. Reality reveals a number of centers of value, and the sacred expresses itself through many media. Strict monotheists are always alarmed by soul's penchant for worshipping at many altars, either concurrently or serially. But soul wishes to honor the value experienced in each deity at each shrine. Concrete richness always has more interest for soul than abstract unity or ethical consistency. Thus, soul is little attracted to creeds and universalizing codes of ethics: "Oh, all this is well and good in its place (but, of course, there are lots of places!)."

A penultimate summary: Not with animus or in competitiveness but by its ownmost nature and functioning, soul is a relativizer of all human efforts to make reason lord and master, to literalize all metaphorical and symbolic expression, and to sum up all experience under one rubric. Soul simply goes its own way imagining this and imagining that, unashamedly fascinated by the endless variety of things—loving, honoring, and enjoying each thing in its sacred thisness.

Fourth and positively, taking soul seriously, i.e., experientially, opens up the sluice gates of creativity by encouraging play, reverie, receptive thinking, and intuition, all of which are strengthened simply by being given time and loving attention. A certain freshness and vitality obtain, and a sense of adventure develops when experience is stimulated at its fundamental levels. Culture is then rooted in the deep springs of life; and the problems of contemporary persons become more nearly solvable since new energies, new perspectives, and new resolves are brought into play.

The above-mentioned developments resulting from taking soul seriously conspire together to effect "the enlargement of sensibilities," which may, after all, be the most pragmatically important, the most pervasive and enduring outcome which humans can intend. In any case, it aids in the overcoming of the "loss of soul," with which problematic we began. Dewey wanted to solve the real problems of men and women, not simply to test his ingenuity on inherited philosophical puzzles. Though it was not his language or explicit concern, rooted as he was in a different era, it is conceivable that he would have acknowledged "the Deweyan project," sensitive to the problem of the "loss of soul" delineated above and hopeful for a solution which a reconstructed notion of soul could assist in providing. At least, as he put it, "the realities are there."[24]

NOTES

1. I have chosen to address the general theme of the conference, pragmatism and religion, by raising the question of soul, and this for at least two reasons. First, as a movement pragmatism is ambivalent toward both religion and soul, particularly the latter. Pragmatism has cast its lot with the public, the secular, the humanistic, and the immanent; and good work has been done. In light of what has been ignored—the interior, the private, the mysterious, the sacred, and the transcendent—perhaps should

be revisited. If, as has been charged, pragmatism is a philosophy of the foreground, the introduction of soul, with its implications of background, interiority, and depth, will either extend and complement the categories already in use or create trouble. Either way, valuable work will be done.

Second, "soul" may not be a Buberian *Urwort*, but it denotes a range of experiences—mysterious, subtle, elusive, profound—which can never be well-captured in more rationalized patterns or discourse. "Soul" may indeed be an embarrassment for some, but whether or not the term can be dropped without loss is a serious and open question. It is interesting to note some recent social-scientific thinking about the inexpungeability of soul, even for scientific discourse. See, for instance, *On Losing the Soul: Essays in the Social Psychology of Religion*, eds. Richard K. Fenn and Donald Capps (Albany: State University of New York Press, 1995). Psychoanalytically-oriented readers will be interested to consult Bruno Bettleheim's *Freud and Man's Soul* (New York: Alfred A. Knopf, 1982), where he claims that Freud's German *Seele* has been corrupted in the standard [English] edition of Freud's work, fundamentally skewing Freud's intent. If this is true, then profound rethinking of Freud's program is in order. This along with other suggestive treatments of soul by a wide range of artists, philosophers, poets, mystics, cultural critics, theologians, psychotherapists, and scientists can be found in *Soul: An Anthology* ed. Phil Cousineau (New York: Harper Collins Publishers, 1994).

A word about strategy. In the latter part of the paper I resort to displaying as much as is possible within the limits of an essay what soul is. It seems to me that, granted the current cultural context, to provoke, to suggest, to require settled agreement over premises, is hardly open to us. Sometimes we simply have to say, "Come over here and look at this."

2. William Barrett, *Death of the Soul* (New York: Doubleday, 1986), p. xvi.

3. *Ibid.*, p. 14.

4. *Ibid.*, p. 160. Barrett's discussion of the ripening into wisdom is illustrated from the work of a poet over time. It should be true *a fortiori* of a philosopher, a lover of wisdom.

5. Julia Kristeva, *New Maladies of the Soul*, tr. Ross Guberman (New York: Columbia University Press, 1995),

6. *Ibid.*

7. *Ibid.*, p. 27.

8. James Hillman, *Insearch: Psychology and Religion* (New York: Charles Schribner's Sons, 1967), pp. 43–4.

9. John E. Smith, *The Spirit of American Philosophy* (New York: Oxford University Press, 1966), p. 129.

10. *Ibid.*, p. 196.

11. John Dewey, "Soul and Body" in *The Early Works*, 1882–1898, Volume 1 (Carbondale and Edwardsville: Southern Illinois University Press, 1969), pp. 93–115.

12. John Dewey, *A Common Faith* (New Haven: Yale University Press, 1934), p. 31.

13. John Dewey, *Experience and Nature* (New York: Dover Publications, Inc., 1958), pp. 293–294.

14. John Dewey, *Art as Experience* (New York: G. P. Putnam's Sons, 1934). See also the insightful study of Dewey's aesthetics by Thomas M. Alexander in his *John Dewey's Theory of Art, Experience, and Nature: The Horizons of Feeling* (Albany: State University of New York Press, 1987).

15. Jo Ann Boydston, ed., *The Poems of John Dewey* (Carbondale: Southern Illinois University Press, 1977). For the significance of his poetry I am indebted to Steven C. Rockefeller's masterful study *John Dewey: Religious Faith and Democratic Humanism* (New York: Columbia University Press, 1991), ch. 7.

16. John Dewey, *Experience and Nature*, p. 294.

17. The best brief account of the movement is James Hillman, *Archetypal Psychology* (Dallas: Spring Publications, Inc., 1983). C.G. Jung and Henry Corbin are the immediate forefathers of the movement. Behind them are the German Romantic tradition; Renaissance theologians, particularly Ficino; the Neoplatonic thinkers, Plato, and Heracleitus. Both Freud and Nietzsche also play important roles, the latter the subject of a fine study by Graham Parkes, *Composing the Soul: Reaches of Nietzsche's Psychology* (Chicago: The University of Chicago Press, 1994). James Hillman's numerous writings are of course foundational. They are best presented in *A Blue Fire: Selected Writings by James Hillman*, introduced and edited by Thomas Moore (New York: Harper and Row, Publishers, 1989). Thomas Moore has also written two works which have further given archetypal psychology a large public exposure with his best-selling *Care of the Soul* (New York: Harper Collins Publishers, Inc., 1992) and *Soul*

Mates (New York: Harper Collins Publishers, Inc., 1994). To this must be added two suggestive works by Robert Sardello, *Facing the World with Soul* and *Love and the Soul*, both published by Harper Collins, in 1992 and 1995, respectively.

18. These reflections owe much to James Hillman, *A Blue Fire*, chs. 1 and 6.

19. See Edward Casey, *Spirit and Soul: Essays in Philosophical Psychology* (Dallas: Spring Publications, Inc., 1991) for an outstanding reflection on imagining, remembering, and the soul in time and space. His statement that "imagining *is* possiblizing" is found on page 277.

20. James Hillman, *A Blue Fire*, chs. 1 and 12. Thomas Moore, *Care of the Soul*, is also suggestive with regards to the soul and beauty.

21. James Hillman, *A Blue Fire*, "The Poetic Basis of Mind," ch. 1.

22. The phrase *mundus imaginalis* is acknowledged to be Henry Corbin's. See Hillman, *Archetypal Psychology*.

23. John Dewey, *Experience and Nature*, p. 294.

JUDGING THEOLOGIES:
Truth In An Historicist Perspective

Sheila Greeve Davaney

Many current depictions of the contemporary theological scene reflect widespread cultural and intellectual changes resulting from the deepening sense of the historical character of human existence. The theological movements designated postliberalism and revisionist theology are often described as two prominent expressions of what is being labeled the historicist turn in contemporary thought, two expressions that are taken by many to be the epicenter of present day theological shifts. When these two theological perspectives focus the theological debate certain questions and concerns become pivotal and controlling. In particular, questions concerning the relation of the present situation to the founding narratives or classics of the Christian tradition come to the fore, shaping subsequent issues of theological method and norms.

I would like to contend that these mainline cartographies or depictions of the theological landscape do not exhaust the possible ways of construing historicist understandings of theology today. In particular, I want to suggest there is emerging another option that I term pragmatic historicism or, as Delwin Brown calls it, constructive historicism.[1] When we focus on this historicist trajectory, new possibilities for theology take shape and a fundamental reconsideration of theology's task, including revisionist and postliberal versions of it, is called for.

One important area in which both historicism in general and the particular claims of the perspective I am advocating require such significant reconsideration concerns the question of norms, the question of how we assess our various efforts to interpret reality and our human place within it. Now these questions of adequacy or truth are not easy issues for any historicist perspective today. They are formulated in light of the relentless erosion of traditional bases for claims to truth and in the context of a culture that seems to fluctuate between the concession that all views are equal and the passionate declaration of the superiority of one's local vision. This essay will examine the question of norms, first exploring revisionist and postliberal interpretations as serious attempts to set forth historicist responses to these issues. But it will also suggest that from the perspective of a fuller historicism these efforts are not successful and that pragmatic historicism offers a more compelling alternative.

In relation to questions of truth, adequacy and the adjudication of theological claims, George Lindbeck's work has centered the discussion of postliberalism.[2] Lindbeck has developed an interpretation of religious traditions as historically derived and highly specific streams of interpretation within which humans live their lives and gain orientation and meaning. All such meaning, according to Lindbeck, is thereby contextual, emergent within and dependent upon particular historical traditions for content and significance. Moreover, it is these very traditions that provide the norms and criteria for assessing all their own claims and adjudicating among competing assertions. The norms for evaluation and judgment are not provided by a universal reason, shared by rational humans everywhere, nor are they disclosed in some form of pre- or supra-rational dimension of experience that characterizes human life as such. The arena for arguing for the validity of theological claims is not a public realm structured by common reason or shared experience. Instead all theological claims and the norms for assessing them are historical and context dependent.[3]

Lindbeck further construes the nature and location of historical norms in a very particular way that follows from his understanding of the nature of historical traditions. Lindbeck has specified his interpretation of historical religious traditions by likening religions to languages which gain their distinctive character and maintain their ongoing unity through the persistence of an inner logic or depth grammar. Thus historical traditions, including those encompassing ones called religions, are given their identity through the articulation of basic grammars that then come to structure all subsequent variations and expressions of these traditions. This construal of religious traditions as akin to languages with stable grammars and attendant rules for articulation has led Lindbeck and his followers to a very specific interpretation of truth as primarily intrasystematic.

Lindbeck's intrasystematic view of truth can be seen to have a number of components. First, judgment takes place within a tradition, according to norms specific to that tradition. There is no appeal to broader criteria; indeed such appeal is, for Lindbeck, an impossibility. Apologetics has little or no place in postliberalism. Second, the internal norms by which theological assertions are to be evaluated and adjudicated stem from the regulative principles or directives of a tradition. Third, these directives or basic grammars are located in the past, assumed to be emergent from and authoritatively expressed in the founding narratives of the tradition. The grammar of a tradition is, fourth, assumed to be identifiable and stable and possessing a unified character. Out of these assumptions, then, theological adequacy or truth comes to mean the faithful representation of and conformity to this normative grammar or to the regulative principles of the Christian tradition. Theological validity is determined by faithful adherence to the internal rules of the Christian tradition.[4]

Such adherence does not entail, for Lindbeck, an uncreative and rote repetition of these normative claims. Later developments do and should evidence novelty and creativity as they give expression to the authoritative depth grammar of the faith; changing times demand new interpretations. And just as a language such as English can say all sorts of different things while still remaining "good" English, so Christian doctrines and theological claims can make varied, even tension-filled, assertions and still be valid Christian positions as long as they adhere to the original normative articulations of the Christian narrative, to "the self-identical story" found in the Bible.[5]

But who is in the position to render judgment about what conforms and what diverges, what is novel faithfulness and what is unfaithful deviance? Lindbeck's answer to this question also flows from his views of the nature of historical traditions. Traditions, in his view, make reference back to themselves; they give imaginative portrayals of reality but offer no way to get out of themselves in order to ascertain whether or not they correspond to some external reality. Indeed, that is not their primary purpose; religious traditions and their doctrines are thoroughly practical rather than propositional. They provide the interpretive means for getting around in life, for negotiating historical existence. And they succeed in doing so to the extent that their vision of reality is inculcated in their adherents. Thus for Lindbeck, it is finally the adept, the skillful practitioner of a tradition, the one who has most thoroughly internalized and lives most fully out of the tradition who is in the best position to determine the adequacy of theological claims and developments.[6]

While Lindbeck places most of his emphasis upon this intrasystematic definition of truth, he also nods minimally in the direction of the notion of truth as correspondence to reality, but with his own particular twist. First, he claims that while individual doctrines, as doctrines, are not propositional claims to truth but rules or guidelines for living within a tradition, nonetheless, a tradition or religion as a whole might be interpreted as one large proposition that "may as a whole correspond or not correspond to what a theist calls God's being and will."[7] But how is that gigantic proposition to be tested? Once more Lindbeck refers us back to the practice of religion; a religion interpreted as a single proposition about reality can claim validity as true to the extent that its vision is interiorized by its adherents in such a manner that their lives can be said to correspond "to the will of God." Thus Lindbeck, far from jettisoning the notion of truth as correspondence, locates that correspondence in lives rather than in free floating ideas. He does not, however, provide us with any means to ascertain such correspondence outside the terms offered within and by the historical tradition.

Lindbeck's views of truth raise many questions concerning historicist interpretations of theology, especially postliberal versions of historicism. As Timothy Jackson notes in an insightful analysis of Lindbeck's position entitled "Against Grammar," a strong intrasystematic view of truth coupled with an anemic correspondence theory of truth remains unacceptable to realists who demand firmer grounding for their claims. What Jackson calls Lindbeck's "relative insouciance about ontological truth" seems to many, especially more conservative commentators, to be an acquiescence to relativism, emptying Christianity of its historic claim to ontological truth, leaving it as just one story among many, with little or no reason to adhere to this story instead of another.[8]

For our purposes, however, I am interested in the problems that emerge from the perspective of pragmatic historicism as developed in this paper. This approach shares Lindbeck's hesitancy in advocating a correspondence theory of truth, concurring with his sense, contra traditional realists, that humans are not in the position to ascertain with absolute certainty the adequacy of our visions to the way things really are. It rejects, like him, extra-historical appeals whether to universal reason, to privileged experience, or to special revelation as the means for justifying theological claims. But while sharing this historicist reluctance with Lindbeck, pragmatic historicism finds many other elements of Lindbeck's view problematic.

Much of Lindbeck's view of truth rests upon his underlying assumptions about the nature of historical traditions. Utilizing the analogy to language, he asserts a stability at the core of traditions, a grammar that does not change despite the variety of its instantiations. Lindbeck's use of the language analogy is sometimes illuminating, especially as it focuses attention on language as a form of social practice. His portrayal of grammar as static and stable, however, appears to be an abstraction made at the service of theological ends. It is simply not the case that vocabularies and lexicons change over time but grammars and their rules do not. First, languages, including their grammars emerge over time; they do not appear, complete in all essentials, in some instantaneous moment of birth. Second, while relative stability may eventually develop, it is never total, and its form can not be established ahead of time but can only be discerned in hindsight.

Moreover, once we move from languages to living traditions themselves Lindbeck's claims become even more suspect. Delwin Brown has captured well the interlinking assumptions that ground Lindbeck's positing of authority in the past when he states, "Lindbeck . . . assume(s) that a canon is unitary in its fundamentals, that this unity is reasonably demonstrable, that it can be conformed to, and that such conformation is necessary to preserve the authentic identity of the tradition."[9] The view being contended for in this paper suggests that each of these presumptions is problematic; there is not and never has been one self-same story found in the originating narratives of the Christian tradition; there have been various stories, of God, Jesus, what it means to be human, and these cannot be reduced to one another or to an abstract set of rules. Even at the beginning, there was not one Christian story, agreed upon by all. Christianity's origins, like the rest of its history, are unstable and contested.

Furthermore, the historical traditions of Christianity are also internally plural, appropriating and transforming earlier Christian stories, intermingling them with other traditions, and creating novel understandings of reality in the process. While historical developments certainly evidence continuities with what has gone before, they are not continuities of the sort Lindbeck envisions wherein a Platonic-like unchanging form—the singular self-identical Christian story—is, to use Lindbeck's words, fused with a changing historical reality without the abiding Christian story being affected in any way by such a fusion. If we are to understand those developments at all we must understand them as concrete and specific, not as the ephiphenomenal expression of static principles which in the end provide them with their only claim to validity.

This is to say that Lindbeck's location of authority in the narratives of the past is predicated upon the prior assumption that these narratives are stable and unified and, further, that his assertion that truth or adequacy is measured by conformity to these static cores depends upon his interpretation of later theological claims as historical containers, if you will, of this self-same, never changing story. But once the stability at the origins of Christianity is questioned and once the historical variability of

Christian theological claims is recognized, then Lindbeck's version of truth as conformity begins to appear as an arbitrary assertion of authority that protects theologians and religious practitioners alike from the hard task of justifying their beliefs and practices in an historicist age. In the name of unity and purity, Lindbeck forgoes the messiness of history, reinscribing an authoritarianism that can easily dismiss all hetreodoxy as illegitimate deviation from the pristine, self-identical core of Christian faith presumed the same from age to age, supposedly adequate for all.

Lindbeck's reinscription of an authoritarian view that allows theology to be, as Linell Cady puts it, reduced to the citation or designated authorities rather than open inquiry or argumentation is also evident in his view of the incommensurability of traditions.[10] Because religious traditions are all-encompassing and fully historical, for Lindbeck, they are assumed to be incommensurable, non-reducible to one another and finally, seemingly non-translatable into one another. This self-enclosed character of traditions reinforces, for Lindbeck, the notion of truth as intra-systematic. If there are no ahistorical vantage points for ascertaining absolute truth, neither are there cross-traditioned perspectives that can confirm or challenge the claims of a tradition. Each tradition goes its own way, turning, with all legitimacy, a deaf ear, if it chooses, to those outside its borders. But pragmatic historicism also challenges this view, arguing that humans do not reside so neatly within traditions and hence are forced, in a manner unaccounted for in Lindbeck's version of truth and tradition, to make their varied assumptions cohere with one another and not just with an ancient past. Moreover, pragmatic historicism also contends that there is another way traditions are not self-enclosed, that is, in their effects. Wherever we reside today, our actions and beliefs impact others, and it is imperative that we be open to the challenge and critical evaluation of those whose lives are, for good or ill, affected by them.

Turning now to revisionist theology, David Tracy's work can be seen to provide the access to distinctively revisionist assertions concerning truth and adequacy. Tracy has developed a notion of theology as a hermeneutical enterprise with a method of correlation as its centerpiece.[11] Such an approach has grown out of Tracy's convictions that human life is thoroughly historical and his construal of that historicity as essentially an ongoing interpretive process whereby human identity comes into being through encounter with the other, be that other a text, person or event. But Tracy's rendering of theology has been based on particular specifications of this interpretative mode of being. For while all of our interactions bear this hermeneutical character, Tracy has most forcefully focused upon the relation of past and present, specifically upon the relation of the contemporary situation and a tradition's "classics."

Tracy's early articulation of hermeneutical theology and the method of correlation were predicated upon certain assumptions that characterized a good deal of hermeneutical theory. In particular, he espoused the notion that all human beings have existential questions to which the classics of their specific traditions offer answers. These classics were almost always located in the past, having gained their designation over time as "expressions of the human spirit" that contain both a permanence and excess of meaning that give rise to their longevity and capacity for creative appropriation. These classics, for Tracy, disclosed truths about reality especially as they displayed what Tracy poetically termed an "instinct for the essential."[12]

Tracy also defended the notion of *religious* classics. For humans do not just have existential questions; they also have questions about fundamental meaning and value, about the limits of life and about the character of ultimate reality. It is to these most basic questions that religious classics respond. As such they have a unique character. They not only disclose truth about reality; they disclose something concerning the whole of reality and thereby make a particular claim for truth upon those who encounter them.[13]

Concerning each of these kinds of classics, non-religious and religious, notions of truth are relevant in the form of disclosure, manifestation, and realized experience of the essential. Out of the encounter of the present with the classics of a tradition some essential aspect of reality, previously concealed, is made known, at least in part. And in relation to religious classics it is not only some part of reality that is now partially unveiled but the whole of reality, ultimate reality itself. In all of Tracy's terminology there is the clear indication that some antecedent truth is there to be discovered, revealed, made known through the hermeneutical encounter. Moreover, there is the strong presumption of the authority or adequacy of those texts, persons, doctrines, events designated classics, that make them, and not other historical artifacts, appropriate locales for the disclosure of such truth.

In recent years Tracy has modified his position a good deal as he has moved in a self-designated postmodern direction.[14] Such movement has several important implications for Tracy's position. First, Tracy is far more careful about the universalizing tendencies of his perspective, suggesting now that while all humans have questions of meaning and value neither they nor their classical answers can be reduced to a common set of existential concerns and responses. Insisting that while there is enough similarity-in-difference to make conversation possible, Tracy has nonetheless focused his attention on otherness in a new way.[15] Moreover, and most importantly for our purposes, Tracy seems to have altered his notion of classic. He has opened the category of classic; at times now it seems that almost anything can be a classic. He has also pointed to the instability of the classic; whereby once it seemed that something was a classic by virtue of its permanence and excess of meaning, now things gain and lose that status for far more complex historical reasons, including reasons of power and interest. And finally, the tendency to grant a presumptive positive value to tradition has been modified by Tracy's intensified acknowledgment of the ambiguous and mixed character of all aspects of historical reality, including those designated religious classics.[16] The result of these movements has been demonstrated in Tracy's insistence on the critical character of theology whereby theology is not just the appropriation of the authoritative givens of a tradition but the mutually critical correlation of the present and the classics of that tradition.

However, despite the relativizing of the classics and the emphasis upon the critical dimensions of theology, Tracy continues to articulate much the same view of theology as he did earlier. The classics of the past, while chastened, still remain center stage. And the central task is still to interpret them, thus implicitly continuing presumptions of their adequacy; theology is still primarily a hermeneutical enterprise, not a constructive one, whose primary conversation partners are the powerful interpretations of a bygone era.

Linked to the continuation of a primarily hermeneutical approach to theology is Tracy's ongoing emphasis on truth as a primordial manifestation.[17] The motifs of concealment/ disclosure and recognition on the part of interpreters still permeate Tracy's account of classics. But what truth as manifestation means has never been and is not now very clear in Tracy's work. It appears, at the least, to refer to the fact that whenever encounters of any type take place some interpretation of such interaction emerges. But Tracy seems to want to make more far-reaching claims than that. For he asserts that in genuine encounters or conversation the other is revealed in such a manner to make a claim to truth upon us. But what does this mean? Are all claims upon us to be assumed to be valid? Are all disclosures "true"? True to or about what? How does Tracy's growing recognition of the ambiguity of history play into his notions of manifestation? Philosopher Richard Bernstein has critically focused on this lack of clarity in Tracy's thought. As he states, "we must also always ask whether what is manifested is a true or false manifestation. The hard question that Tracy does not fully confront is what is the source of authority or legitimacy of truth as manifestation. Is the 'source' of this legitimacy to be found in the manifestation, in the disclosure/concealment, or in the communal critical practices of validating the claims to truth?"[18]

Accompanying this confusion about truth as manifestation is lack of clarity concerning Tracy's connected notion of the relative adequacy of interpretation. Tracy suggests that while classics manifest the truth in the dialogical moment, interpreters, for their part, seek to give the best possible expression to that truth through their interpretations. Such interpretations cannot be seen as absolute or timeless, Tracy avers, for as with all things historical they are always limited, temporary, and fragile.[19] Hence all interpretation can ever aspire to is a relative adequacy that is always open to revision and challenge. On the one hand, Tracy's modesty here is commendable and certainly consistent with historicist insights. On the other hand, it doesn't help matters much. This is the case for several reasons. First, it is seemingly impossible to distinguish between the classic that is interpreted and our interpretation of it. As Tracy notes, we only have interpreted classics, not classics that are then subject to interpretation. Thus adequacy cannot be judged by comparing the "manifestation" and the interpretation of it. Moreover, as was noted above, when we are pushed back to the manifestation it is totally unclear what is to count as a true or false manifestation or on what bases such judgments should be rendered. Tracy's tendency to assume that we'll know one when we see one simply won't do.

All this becomes even more problematic when the topic is religious classics. For these classics do not present some finite claim to validity but manifest the "whole of reality" through a particular finite reality. Not only does this seem to negate the particular significance of a finite historical reality by making it an occasion for ultimate reality to reveal itself, but it clouds the notions of truth as manifestation and relative adequacy even more. How does one assess as true or false a manifestation of the whole of reality through a finite moment? On what basis does one decide that this interpretation rather than another is relatively more adequate?

Now Tracy acknowledges that these are difficult questions, and in part he tries to answer them by arguing that our various claims to adequacy of interpretation must be tested in the communal and public realms. That is, we must offer reasons. And Tracy has lately suggested, appealing to William James, that those reasons have to do with how our claims cohere with what "we otherwise know, practice and believe"[20] and with the consequences of such claims for life. These two norms, coherence and consequences, he links to William James's pragmatism. And as we will see, they do indeed resonate with the neo-pragmatism this paper is espousing. But how these norms connect with the idea of manifestation and what content the pragmatic norm might have remains undeveloped. And while Tracy has recently referred to the need to develop interpretations of reality that foster resistance and hope, the reasons for moving in this direction rather than another also remain unarticulated.

In sum, this analysis suggests that Tracy has embraced a number of assumptions that are compatible with the position I am taking. But there are other dimensions of his thought that lend confusion to his own position and clash strongly with the approach being developed here. His notion that "truth, in its primordial sense, is manifestation" smacks of an ongoing romanticism that presupposes that the really real, especially the ultimately real, resides behind finite reality waiting to be discovered and disclosed.[21] Such romantic presuppositions seem, moreover, to continue to tie Tracy to the classics of a tradition even though he has widened the category and now treats these artifacts of the past with a much more critical edge. And although Tracy now refers to pragmatic norms and criteria of coherence, the question of how they connect with assumptions about disclosure and manifestation remains much of a mystery. Thus, while Tracy has insisted, over against the postliberals' interpretation of revisionists, that hermeneutical theologians have been engaged in an internal critique fostered by growing historicist insights for several decades, key elements of that earlier tradition can be seen to remain in Tracy's own thought and to sit uneasily with the historicist directions his work seems now to be pursuing.

The analysis offered in this paper suggests that while postliberalism and revisionist theology both reflect significant historicist insights, their interpretations of theological norms revert to positions that call into question the depth of their historicist commitments. It is now the moment to explore what the emerging trajectory of pragmatic historicism asserts concerning these issues of theological norms and adjudication.

Pragmatic historicism presupposes a dynamic, non-essentialist interpretation of human cultures and religious traditions and human life within them. It rejects what Wilfred Cantwell Smith once termed the Big Bang Theory of religions that considers what is most important about religious traditions to have been present in their origins and endorses the idea that traditions are essentially complete, revolving around a static and unchanging core. Instead, pragmatic historicism stresses both the ongoing funding of the present by the past *and* the changing and open nature of traditions wherein the plural inheritances from the past are continually transmuted; that is, it insists on the radical historicity of human subjectivity and its creations. For pragmatic historicism, the acknowledgment of such historicity leads not to an obsession with origins but to engagement with the broad reaches and depths of traditions now recognized to be comprised of diverse and plural strands of historical existence which do not have stable cores and unchanging identities.

If the historicist temper of contemporary thought is turning our attention to the thick histories of particular traditions it is also leading us to recognize that humans, especially in the contemporary world, are multi-traditioned, the products of intersecting, sometimes overlapping but often contending influences. This perspective suggests that out of all sorts of bits and pieces of traditions, beliefs, and influences, late twentieth century persons and communities are constructing their personal and group identities, living, in the phrase of cultural theorist James Clifford, an "existence among fragments."[22] The creation of any identity is not found in the recapitulation of a settled and assumed to be adequate-for-the-present-past, even in its creative appropriation, but in the ongoing inventive construction out of the materials of diverse pasts and plural presents. As Clifford testifies, "twentieth century identities no longer presuppose continuous cultures or traditions. Everywhere individuals and groups improvise local performances from (re)collected pasts, drawing on foreign media, symbols and languages."[23] It is, not only with internally plural single traditions that theologians must traffic but with multiple traditions and histories as well.

This interpretation of historicity has led pragmatic historicists such as myself to argue that while indeed historical beings are shaped by their histories and by their present contexts, this is a creative process, always carried out through the ongoing reconstruction and extension of historical sources and issuing forth in novel forms of existence. The theologian's task, in light of these assumptions, is a critical and constructive one whose goal is to contribute to the development of personal and communal identities viable for today. Moreover, the norms for assessing the validity of these efforts are, in this view, primarily pragmatic ones focused upon the concrete consequences of living out of particular interpretations of life.

In order to understand better the meaning of a pragmatic interpretation of theological validity it is important to clarify what it is not. Pragmatic historicists concur with postliberals that correspondence theories of truth are difficult to enact from historicist perspectives. While our interpretations of reality certainly "intend the real," as Gordon Kaufman asserts, humans are not in the position to make definitive judgments about whose version of reality corresponds most closely to what is. And while we are called upon to give reasons for our positions, those reasons are now recognized to be contextual and thoroughly historical. However, both the postliberal and revisionist alternatives to a correspondence theory of truth are also, as this paper has argued, misdirected, assuming, either explicitly or obliquely, the adequacy of the past for the present and failing to develop notions of norms that are consonant with a fuller historicism.

In contrast, the pragmatic historicism I am articulating seeks to give a more complete voice to such historicist insights. This means, first, that while we are absolutely required to engage our varied inherited traditions both to understand where we have come from and what those histories might offer for today, those pasts are not the authoritative site for judging the adequacy of contemporary views. The past may indeed offer lessons that we do well to learn. And tracing the resonance between our current claims and past ones, tells us, like good psychoanalysis, something about where we have come from. But it does not tell us who we should be; it does not provide us with the criteria for determining the validity or adequacy of our contemporary claims.

These judgments, while influenced by the past, are finally the responsibility of each generation. We need to articulate norms for our time, recognizing their location in the present though granting their historical debt to what has gone before. This is to say, that for pragmatic historicists, we need to forego notions of sites of authority and replace them with sites of responsibility. And for pragmatists, it is the present which is finally the locus of accountability.

Locating our judgments and the norms that inform them in the present requires that we must also grant the contingent and ambiguous character of our visions and our assessments of them. For pragmatic historicists there can be no pleading for privileged epistemological or ontological status for our present claims any more than for those that have emerged from earlier times. Contemporary visions and norms are, like all others, thoroughly historical and hence partial, reflective of location, infused with interest and laden with power; they are transient, contingent, and eminently revisable, just as they are finally unavoidable.

But if the past does not yield privileged norms to judge our visions and if reason and experience are always thoroughly historical in nature, providing no secure means for assessing what is adequate and what is not, how should such inevitable judgments be made? What standards should we invoke, what criteria should we use to test our construals of reality and the ways we live our lives? The response being advocated here is that these norms should be pragmatic ones, relating to the consequences of adopting and living out of particular visions of reality.

Historicists of this ilk argue for pragmatic norms not only because other avenues to relative certitude seem impossible in our age but for the more positive reason that our traditions, our interpretations of reality are fundamentally practical in nature. They are, as postliberals also noted, for the purposes of negotiating our way through life; they are the means by which we traffic with reality. And the question is finally how well they make sense of life, how well they provide guidelines for living and criteria for decision making.

Now the group of people I have brought together under the rubric of pragmatic historicism have generally concurred that pragmatic criteria must be used to assess the final validity of our claims. However, sometimes such pragmatic norms have been invoked without substantive development of their content and at other times differing content has come to the fore. Nonetheless, I think certain pragmatist guidelines are emerging in theology that suggest both what the practice of pragmatic evaluation should look like and something of its substantive content.

First, because this form of pragmatism is deeply linked with an historicist interpretation of human subjectivity and human cultures and traditions, the norms for judging our visions must relate to specific examples of historical existence. That is to say, we must ask what practical and material repercussions for particular forms of life might result from living out of one set of values and visions rather than another. We can never ask these questions generally and for all times and places but only concretely and specifically. What are the consequences for these bodies, for these communities, for the planet at this time and place under these historical conditions?

But while we ask these questions about specific people, communities and places such specificity does not result in a narrow range of concern, a pragmatic narcissism or local utilitarianism. The view being contended for in this paper has asserted that while all historical existence is particular, it is not self-enclosed and isolated either in its constitution or in the range of its impact. To be historical, as an individual or a community, is to be particular but this particularity arises from the interaction of multiple influences; furthermore, how communities and individuals constitute themselves reverberates across the universe, affecting positively or adversely how others can live out *their* historical existence, and being affected by others. Hence, the pragmatic historicism asserted here is an expansive one, insisting that pragmatic testing demands the broadest field in relation to which we must assess our interpretations, values and commitments.

This assertion that the range for pragmatic testing should be broad and inclusive has several important implications for the understanding of theology. It suggests, to begin with, that such evaluation entails a commitment to radical democratic practices that include the voices of everyone impacted by our interpretations, visions and values. In direct contrast to the postliberals, pragmatic historicists assert that precisely because historical existence is social, interconnected and interdependent we cannot assess the adequacy of our visions by turning solely to the experts or the adept within a local tradition. We must inquire not only concerning the consequences of a worldview for those who benefit most from it but also for those who are its victims; we must ask our questions not only at the centers of traditions but at their margins and of those who are not practitioners of a tradition but who experience its impact daily. It will not do to ask only what a version of Christianity means to its Christian adherents unless we also interrogate its implications for Jews and Buddhists and Muslims. Nor will it suffice to assay the value of a religious vision according to the privileged elite within its ranks without also hearing from those who are ruled deviant, heretical, unclean and sinful.

Such inclusion of voices means, for pragmatic historicists, that theological analysis must attend to the dynamics of power that invest some perspectives with great legitimacy while dismissing others; not only must we be skilled cultural analysts but we must also be cognizant of the political dimensions of all of historical existence, including life lived out of religious interpretations of reality. And perhaps most importantly we must recognize that to commit ourselves to the inclusion of multiple voices as the field for pragmatic consideration entails a concomitant commitment to changing unjust power arrangements that render those lacking power silent.

This interpretation of pragmatism as entailing an inclusive field for testing our claims rather than a narrow, self-interested one can be concretely seen in relation to positions advocated by several of the theologians I would label pragmatic historicists. First, the pragmatism advocated by liberationists such as Simon Maimela, Kwok Pui-lan and Cornel West, as well as myself, has insisted that pragmatism is not the utilitarian tool of the powerful.[24] Rather, when historicism and pragmatism are wed, such a union requires further solidarity with those whose views have not been considered heretofore and a preferential testing of claims not against how well they further the well-being of the powerful but how well they support the historical existence of those without power.

William Dean, Sallie McFague, and Gordon Kaufman have taken this union of historicism and pragmatism in another, equally important, direction.[25] They have argued that the arena in which we must evaluate the validity of our claims must not only include all humans but must also extend to the natural sphere out of which we have emerged, upon which we depend, and which bears the marks of our human decisions and actions. William Dean has noted that most historicism and pragmatism have limited themselves to the human community, assessing the value of human claims in terms of how well they further human goals. But such versions of historicism and pragmatism are inadequate, failing to recognize both that human historical existence is material to its core and that natural existence is not static, waiting for us to act on it for our purposes, devoid of value or dynamism. Hence all three of these thinkers call for an understanding of human historical existence that does not cut it off from nature and for a form of pragmatism that includes nature in the arena of pragmatic evaluation. Thus, as Dean states, what is required is an historicized naturalism and a naturalized historicism.

Another way to state pragmatic historicism's commitment to an inclusive arena for the assessment of theological claims is to state that it seeks to be a form of critical public theology. This does not entail the assumption that all humans share a common set of principles, reasons or experiences that can readily be called upon to adjudicate among competing claims. Rather, to contend for our theological claims in the public forum and to insist that they be evaluated not only in relation to the internal values of a bounded community is to affirm once more that human particularity is not insular but porous and permeable, constituted by multi-influences and having effects beyond narrow boundaries. Linell Cady has proposed that one way of avoiding the intractable tension between particularity and publicness is to acknowledge we have no common notions of the good but we do, across all traditions, share a common life; we are part of an interconnected web of social and natural life that does not vitiate our historical particularity but makes it possible.[26] Thus for pragmatic historicists, to recognize this common life requires that we put forth our visions of reality not in an arena in which everything is already settled by virtue of a given commonality but in a public process wherein we, and others, consider the implications for our common historicized existence of our varied views.

Invoking pragmatic norms does not, however, end the debate about how these norms should be substantively construed. What should count as positive or negative consequences, life-affirming or destructive repercussions all remain difficult questions to answer. On the one hand, these can only be decided in local settings in relation to specific issues; what is life generating in one time and place may be the purveyor of death in another. And the only way to decide them is through painstaking and protracted debate about what, in this context, given these sets of circumstances and in light of these localized and far-reaching consequences is the best judgment to render now. But while acknowledging the particularized character of our judgment and their localized significance, all the persons I have gathered together as pragmatic historicists suggest that a general norm, always requiring specification in every context, should inform our judgments—namely, the substantive criterion of how well our visions, beliefs, or practices enhance or fail to enhance our historicized existence, an existence that is embedded in the thick web of natural and human history.

We can see a particular interpretation of theology and its normative criteria emerging from the foregoing analysis. The task of theology, for pragmatic historicists, is the identification, critical examination and constructive extension and transformation of encompassing worldviews that we heuristically call religious traditions. Theologians carry out this work not only within particular traditions but at the crossroads of intersecting traditions. Theology, in this mode, seeks to contribute to the articulation of visions of reality that protect and enhance historical existence, including its natural forms. It is indebted to the past, both recognizing its ongoing power and searching to learn from its triumphs and tragic losses. Its loyalty, however, is to the present and to future generations. Pragmatic historicism asserts, therefore, that it is the present that is finally the site of responsibility for judging our human efforts to make sense of life.

Judging Theologies

For pragmatic historicists, these fallible and contingent evaluations should be predicated primarily on the repercussions of our various visions for concrete lives. The call for the pragmatic assessment of our claims means that theologians will be less concerned with questions of undecidable ultimate truth than with the effort to offer the best reasons we can muster given our historical location. We will, moreover, welcome affinities with the past but not reckon such resonance an adequate ground for espousing a vision today. Out of our expansive understanding of historicism, we will seek to test our views and the views of our communities in relation to the broadest range of voices and in conversation and debate with all who are willing to participate.

I stated at the outset of this essay that questions of adequacy and truth are not easy in our age. Many of the traditional sources that seemed in other historical periods to provide certainty and sure means for assessing our human efforts now have been seriously, perhaps fatally, undermined. This essay has argued, however, that embracing the historicist turn does not lead us to a nihilism that forgoes all judgment or a confessional isolationism that employs ahistorical interpretations of tradition or a romantic interpretation of truth. Instead, pragmatic historicism, in its linking of an expansive historicism and a tentative pragmatism returns contemporary persons to the messiness of concrete history, to the fallible and ever difficult task of rendering judgments according to the best reasons we can articulate today and to unprotected conversations with the widest range of participants available. This is no easy task but it is, finally, the one to which we are called.

NOTES

1. Delwin Brown, *Boundaries of Our Habitations* (Albany, NY: State University of New York Press, 1994), esp. Ch. 5.

2. See George A. Lindbeck, *The Nature of Doctrine: Religion and Theology in a Postliberal Age* (Philadelphia: Westminster Press, 1984).

3. *Ibid.*, p. 32 f.

4. *Ibid.*, esp. Chaps. 3, 4.

5. *Ibid.*, p. 83.

6. *Ibid.*, p. 36.

7. *Ibid.*, p. 51.

8. Timothy P. Jackson, "Against Grammar," *Religious Studies Review*, Vol. II, No. 3 (July 1985), p. 241.

9. Brown, p. 125.

10. Linell E. Cady, *Religion, Theology, and American Public Life* (Albany, NY: State University of New York Press, 1993), p. 49, for a view of theology based upon authority.

11. See esp. David Tracy, *Blessed Rage for Order: The New Pluralism in Theology* (New York: Seabury Press, 1975); and Tracy, *The Analogical Imagination* (New York: Crossroad Publishing Co., 1986).

12. Tracy, *The Analogical Imagination*, p. 110.

13. *Ibid.*, esp. Ch. 4.

14. Tracy, *Plurality and Ambiguity: Hermeneutics, Religion, Hope* (San Francisco: Harper & Row Publishers, 1987).

15. *Ibid.*, pp. 20–21, 72.

16. *Ibid.*, pp. 69–71.

17. *Ibid.*, p. 29.

18. Richard J. Bernstein, "Radical Plurality, Fearful Ambiguity, and Engaged Hope," in *Journal of Religion* Vol. 69, January 1989, p. 82.

19. Tracy, *Plurality and Ambiguity*, pp. 27, 81.

20. David Tracy, "Lindbeck and New Program for Theology: A Reflection," in *The Thomist*, No. 49, p. 470.

Judging Theologies   147

21. Tracy, *Plurality and Ambiguity*, p. 29.

22. James Clifford, *The Predicament of Culture: Twentieth-Century Ethnography, Literature, and Art* (Cambridge, MA: Harvard University Press, 1988), p. 14.

23. *Ibid.*

24. See Simon Maimela, "Black Theology and the Quest for a God of Liberation," in *Theology at the End of Modernity*, ed. Sheila Greeve Davaney (Philadelphia: Trinity Press International, 1991); Kwok Pui-lan, "Mothers and Daughters, Writers and Fighters," in *Inheriting Our Mothers' Gardens: Feminist Theology in Third World Perspective*, ed. Letty M. Russel. *et al.* (Philadelphia: The Westminster Press, 1988); Cornel West, *The American Evasion of Theology: A Geneaology of Pragmatism* (Madison, WI: The University of Wisconson Press, 1989).

25. See William Dean, "Humanistic Historicism and Naturalistic Historicism," in *Theology at the End of Modernity*, ed. Sheila Greeve Davaney (Philadelphia: Trinity Press International, 1991); Sallie McFague, *The Body of God: An Ecological Theology* (Minneapolis, MI: Augsburg Fortress, 1993); Gordon D. Kaufman, *In Face of Mystery: A Constructive Theology* (Cambridge, MA: Harvard University Press, 1993).

26. Cady, pp. 73–74.

PRAGMATISM, POSTMODERNISM, AND POLITICS

Mary Doak

Since the 1970s, the inequality of income in the United States has been increasing so that there is now greater inequality than at any time since figures were first collected in 1947, and we stand dead last among major industrialized nations in economic equality.[1] The various alarming statistics on income and wealth distribution are so frequently cited that the observation that the rich are getting richer and the middle-class and poor are getting poorer has perhaps become trite but nevertheless remains an accurate description of our national economy. At the same time, severe reductions in social services are being proposed, and public education in inner-City areas has deteriorated to such an extent that many are calling for the abandonment of our public educational system. These aspects of our current situation have persuaded me of the wisdom in the many analyses that detect an atrophying of concern in our nation for the commonweal, the public good.

I mention these obviously selective and well-known facts because in this paper I would like to evaluate the socio-political consequences of two contemporary forms of pragmatism, the work of Richard Rorty and of Cornel West. Both of these thinkers claim the heritage of John Dewey, and both develop agendas for the future of philosophical thought which have important implications for our public lives. Further, because so much politically engaged work in the humanities has for perhaps the last 10 years looked to postmodern ideas to provide the basis for truly radical and liberating perspectives, the pragmatisms developed by Rorty and by West are particularly important as attempts to be nonfoundationalist while going beyond the political limitations of the French poststructuralists.[2]

For those of us dissatisfied with postmodern approaches that promise radical politics but tend toward impotent irony, unable to take any position seriously, it is worthwhile to explore other alternatives with an eye to the differences they might make. Since pragmatism advocates that we test the validity of theories in terms of their consequences, it is entirely fair to ask of Rorty and West what effects their ideas may have in our current situation. Do they offer resources for a country plagued by poverty and greed that poststructuralist thinkers cannot offer? Because Rorty and West provide very different political theories based on similar forms of pragmatism, engaging these two thinkers together will provide insight into the political as well as the philosophical strengths and weaknesses of the ideas they hold in common.

Rorty and West both offer forms of pragmatism that include the insights of poststructural thought but promise to overcome its limitations. Rorty, for example, agrees with poststructuralists that we have no direct access to reality but wants to move beyond postmodern irony and its continual unmaskings to recover a sense of liberal hope, along with the possibility of seriously considering specific plans of action.[3] West, on the other hand, argues that the recognition of contingency and historicity is not fully developed either by Rorty or by the poststructuralists insofar as they fail to provide socio-economic analyses of the specific historical circumstances of people's lives.

Let us first look more closely at Rorty's theory. Beginning primarily with his 1979 work *Philosophy and the Mirror of Nature*, Rorty has been arguing for a return to pragmatism on the grounds that we have no non-linguistic access to the world.[4] Since we cannot step outside of language and compare our statements about the world with the way the world really is, Rorty encourages us to give up any concern with truth as "correspondence to reality," and to ask instead about the usefulness of a vocabulary and its descriptions of the world. Vocabularies should be chosen and statements affirmed not because they are "true" in the sense of mirroring nature but because they serve our purposes better than other vocabularies do. This rejection of truth as correspondence could lead to the explicit self-contradiction involved in claiming that the truth of our human predicament is that we cannot know the truth of our human predicament, but Rorty avoids such a self-contradiction by acknowledging that his own view is not "the way things really are" but is only a new vocabulary or redescription that he believes to be more useful than our former talk of truth.[5]

Rorty's linguistic turn thus provides him with an entrée back into pragmatism: since thought is so informed by the historical and contingent effects of language that it cannot determine universal truths, philosophy should quit trying to discover the nature of things and investigate instead how we cope with our environment through language. Poststructuralists need not, then, focus solely on what thought *cannot* do (i.e., escape its own contingency and discover eternal truth) but ought more helpfully to attend to what thought *can* do, which is to provide more or less successful plans of action.

Given my concern with the practical implications of Rorty's ideas, it is important to note how Rorty moves from this rejection of truth to his argument in *Contingency, Irony, and Solidarity* for a radical separation of the public and private spheres of our lives, a separation which, I believe, erases much of the difference between Rorty's pragmatism and a purely textual postmodernism. Rorty argues that, because thought cannot determine the essential nature of things, there is no possibility of discerning what human nature is or what the true fulfillment of a human life would be. Apparently presuming that to give up certain and universal knowledge about human fulfillment is to give up public argumentation about such topics altogether, Rorty further insists that ideas about the meaning of life or about human fulfillment are best left to one's private life, which he understands to be the aesthetically rich arena wherein one creates one's self through experimentation with new vocabularies and with the beliefs, desires, and goals these vocabularies imply. The public sphere, on the other hand, has the obligation to prevent cruelty and to provide the freedom necessary for the creation of our private vocabularies.[6] Personal fulfillment and public obligation are thus severed; political proposals are to be evaluated solely according to the publicly shared criteria of protecting freedom and alleviating cruelty, and not according to "private" ideas about the meaning of life or the goals we ought to pursue.

This division between the spheres of the private and the public results in a limited idea of the role of the public and causes Rorty to focus (with the poststructuralists) on private play with creative vocabularies and personal possibilities rather than on concrete political plans of action, as Dewey did. In order to experience being truly self-creative, Rorty advocates that we take an ironic attitude toward the languages and beliefs in our private lives and experiment deeply. However, as Rorty sees it, experimentation clearly cannot go on to the same extent in the public sphere, where we depend on what we hold in common to provide the basis of our decision-making. Rorty finds sufficient common ground for the public realm in a liberal abhorrence of cruelty and a solidarity based on our perceived similarities, so that further philosophical ideas are neither necessary nor helpful. Even though the rejection of cruelty and the commitment to expanding our sense of solidarity initially achieved their position of acceptance in society based on metaphysical arguments and religious traditions, it is the sentiments themselves that we need (and have found useful) and not their metaphysical or religious grounding. "Freeloading" anti-metaphysicians and atheists can thus be grateful for the existence of these sentiments, acknowledging that they serve us well and that we have no reason to change them nor any need in our public lives to add to them.[7] With the notable exception of the contribution stories can make to expanding awareness of other's feelings, artistic as well as religious and philosophical construals of the purpose and value of life are thus relegated to the realm of private redescriptions and are considered irrelevant to processes of political decision-making.

I suggest that Rorty is led (though not forced) into this separation of the public and the private by the logic of his position as described thus far. By arguing that we should judge ideas according to how well they achieve our ends, pragmatism begs the question of how we determine what our ends will be. Dewey tried to resolve this problem with his argument that the proper end of all of our actions is growth, but it is doubtful that Dewey was able to provide a consistently pragmatic argument to support this goal.[8] In my reading, Rorty has recognized this problem of determining pragmatic ends and has concluded that when we give up a correspondence model of truth we give up also the possibility of providing either a universal goal for our actions or conclusive public arguments about what our goals should be. Linguistic redescriptions (the source of our goals and values) cannot be debated publicly since they are chosen according to personal taste and are therefore private. In public, Rorty argues, we base our political discussions not on such "private" beliefs about the meaning of life but rather on the minimal common ground (especially the abhorrence of cruelty) that we happen to share and that has served us well.

I have no dispute with Rorty's premise that there is no need to establish through argument what is already agreed upon, but there are two crucial tenets of his view I find seriously problematic. First, I am not persuaded that commitments to expanding our sense of solidarity and to the prevention of cruelty are widespread enough to be taken for granted in our society. Mistrust and even violence across racial, class, ethnic, and gender lines are flourishing, as is an unwillingness to share economic resources to alleviate the dire consequences of poverty. Second, I question the idea that the role of government can and should be limited to the securing of liberty and the prevention of cruelty, notwithstanding the importance of these goals. Questions about the value of an unpolluted environment or about the proper distribution of economic opportunities and resources, for example, do not fit easily into such a narrow definition of the role of government. It is important to note that if either of these two tenets (that government has such a limited role and that social solidarity can be taken for granted) are rejected, Rorty's attempt to avoid the need to provide public arguments for social goals fails. Have we any choice, then, but to find some way of allowing, indeed encouraging, public discussion of society's goals, a discussion that must be informed by religious, artistic, and philosophical views on the meaning of life?

Before turning to an exploration of Cornel West's answer to these questions, a brief political evaluation of Rorty's argument is in order. What possibilities for political thought has Rorty provided that postmodern arguments do not, and what are the political consequences of accepting his philosophy likely to be? As noted above, Rorty does move us somewhat beyond the limitations of textual strategies with his re-envisioning of philosophy as the pragmatic and conversational adjudication of ideas-considered-as-plans-of-action. However, in developing his strict separation between the concerns of the public and those of the private, he directs our attention to the creative self-fulfillment of private life, which he holds to be largely irrelevant to public concerns. Rorty's emphasis on private fulfillment through linguistic redescriptions presumes that we can live creative and fulfilled lives without addressing the material conditions of our lives and interactions with other people, thus encouraging us to abandon politics and to revert to the aesthetic and creative play of private linguistic strategies.[9] Further, and regardless of his own political intentions, Rorty's construal of the public as concerned only with protecting basic liberties (including, of course, the right to be free from cruelty) has very specific implications in the context of our current national debates: a Rortian government would safeguard the separation of Church and State and would prohibit prayer in public schools, but it would also be unable to justify those public programs and services designed to increase the opportunities of the disadvantaged or the quality of life for all of us. The idea that the proper role of government is to ensure that we are not unduly interfered with requires the cancellation of all social programs that cannot be defended strictly as necessary to prevent cruelty, even when they have very real effects in our public life and in many private lives. Surely sound politics requires a broader understanding of the public's interests than this.

Finally, I would like to consider the fact that Rorty himself has shown remarkably little interest in politics for a pragmatist. He admits he has little to offer our public sphere: we can imagine a better society, he says, but at this point in time we cannot envision how to get there.[10] This acknowledgment that there is no clear path forward no doubt strikes a chord with many of us, but his declaration that this lack of political clarity is due not to any weakness of will or failure of thought but is simply inevitable in our situation is not only a questionable counsel of despair but also one that undermines any philosophical position proposed as a useful redescription for our times. Cornel West is a pragmatist who does not accept this counsel of despair and who not only believes that pragmatism is capable of providing specific plans for political action but also attempts to develop such plans.

West accepts Rorty's linguistic approach to pragmatism and agrees with him that rejection of an understanding of the mind as a mirror of nature enables philosophy to renounce the search for eternal truths and to become thoroughly historicized. West argues that philosophers should not, however, focus on debating theories about the meaning of truth, but should concentrate instead on explaining their socio-historical contexts. By drawing on economic, historical, and sociological analyses, philosophy can shed important light on specific cultural and social practices and guide the development of effective political strategies. This philosophical project can best be realized in the form of a cultural criticism that provides genealogical accounts of our ideas and practices as arising within particular situations and as playing a role in the dynamics of those situations.[11]

In addition to his commitment to a more specifically political cultural criticism, West further differs from Rorty in his understanding of the nature of public life and of the relation between the public and the private realms. In West's view, a fully realized life is not achieved solely through the creativity of one's personal linguistic redescriptions, but rather through participating in the struggle to re-create the material and cultural conditions of our lives, a struggle aided by disciplined philosophical thought. West's point is not to deny *any* distinction between the private and the public, nor to sacrifice individual happiness for the sake of the community, but rather to argue that personal fulfillment cannot be achieved apart from certain conditions of communal life. The flourishing of individuals, West repeatedly insists, requires communities with just institutions. Democratic participation in economic and political decision-making is thus championed as indispensable for individual fulfillment.

While this concern for economic democracy is evidence of the Marxist influence on his thought, West is nevertheless a pragmatist in his emphasis on ideas as plans of action to be evaluated according to their consequences. He too cannot avoid the pragmatist problem of the selection and defense of goals, especially given his broad and controversial understanding of the purposes to be achieved in public life. Unable to accept either Rorty's confidence that agreement has already been achieved or Dewey's belief that rational defense is possible, West instead acknowledges the nonrational character of his goals and attempts to persuade through public witness rather than through philosophical debate. The fact that his goals come from a particular religious tradition (Christianity) and cannot be supported by rational argument does not preclude the possibility of others being attracted by his vision and adopting his goals. Purposes and values should be publicly proclaimed so that social goals can be chosen through a process not unlike the nonrational selection of personal vocabularies that Rorty advocates. The role of rational argumentation is not to defend the goal of radical democracy but rather to determine through socio-economic analyses the best plans of action to lead to this democratic state.[12]

West has, then, three significant (and related) disagreements with Rorty's concept of public life. In addition to rejecting Rorty's sharp distinction between public concerns and personal fulfillment, West opposes the exclusion of discussion of values from the public realm and the resulting minimalist view of the role of government in protecting public interests. Whether one considers West to have successfully reconceived the public realm and resolved the problem of selecting society's goals depends, at least in part, on whether one is willing to give up reasoned public debate over these goals as well as whatever safeguard reason provides against the whims and demagoguery that have the greatest number of voters currently supporting them.

In any case, it should be noted that West's appeal to religious traditions as the source of public goals is a further indication of the importance of history in his pragmatism. The source of our goals is to be found not only in religions but in all of the potentially subversive historical traditions that include memories of more just ways of living and forming communities. "To keep alive a sense of alternative ways of life and of struggle requires memory of those who prefigured such life and struggle in the past," West argues.[13] A concern for history is, then, a crucial aspect of West's pragmatism, both because of the importance of historical analyses of socio-economic structures and because of the need for historical traditions of subversive memories.

West sharply criticizes other forms of postmodern thought (including Rorty's pragmatism) for being so preoccupied with playful verbal redescriptions that they fail to undertake the study of historical causes and the recovery of memories. Redescription through the development of new vocabularies, which Rorty emphasizes, is certainly important for us individually and politically, but it is insufficient without the re-creation of the material as well as the cultural conditions of our lives.[14] West further argues that a thorough historicization of philosophy must contribute to political restructuring through the development of holistic or "totalizing" narratives able to account for multiple facets of an historical situation. West believes that such totalizing accounts, though distrusted by many postmodern thinkers, are indispensable for political engagement.[15] One of West's major contributions to contemporary political debate may well be his own historical narrative linking economic structures with cultural and moral problems, and explaining the problems of inner-city communities as due both to the contraction of economic resources and to the simultaneous undermining of morality by the market values of capitalist consumerism.[16]

Given his emphasis on concrete, historicized philosophy, the political consequences of West's pragmatism are developed in much greater detail than are Rorty's. Specifically, West addresses the socio-economic conditions that I mentioned at the beginning of this paper by pointing out the serious threat to individual lives and to our collective experiment in democracy posed by poverty and by a devalued public realm. Since a democracy depends for its success on the quality of its public conversations, a citizenry with the opportunities to be well-educated, well-informed, and virtuous is crucial if a democratic form of government is to succeed. (While Dewey was certainly aware of this need, Rorty seems either to presume that we already have such an educated and virtuous citizenry or to underestimate its importance.) West also explores the economic processes and governmental policies that have contributed to the increasingly unequal distribution of wealth and income that threatens our democracy, and he encourages formation of grassroots organizations and alliances working for such specific goals as better school funding and a more just system of taxation.[17]

My concern is less with the actual politics or the levels of political specificity in these thinkers' works, however, than with the political implications of the basic tenets of their forms of pragmatism. Because he rejects Rorty's separation of public interests and personal fulfillment, West develops a more profound grasp of the role of the public sphere and of historical traditions in the enrichment of individual lives. He is then able to avoid the denigration of the public realm that Rorty's work implies

Pragmatism, Postmodernism, and Politics 157

and that I believe is one of the most dangerous political attitudes in the United States today. Presuming that one is persuaded by West's project, at least in its fundamentals, the question yet needs to be asked why this move to a thoroughly historicizing cultural criticism is not more frequently followed by those who accept Rorty's and West's presuppositions about the linguistic and contingent nature of thought. The answer may be the severe tension, if not outright contradiction, that I find between the rejection of a correspondence view of truth and the development of thick historical analyses. This tension, though it more clearly emerges in Rorty's argument, finally undercuts West's position as well.

Let us return to Rorty's central claim that, given the linguistic character of thought, we ought to stop concerning ourselves with a putative reality beyond our statements and concern ourselves solely with the usefulness of these statements and vocabularies for achieving our goals. I find a serious problem here not only for Rorty's thought (given the prominence avoiding cruelty and alleviating suffering have in his argument) but also for any attempt to take history or politics seriously. Surely Rorty presumes that there is cruelty and that people are suffering apart from our linguistic descriptions of such things. Why would we want to develop vocabularies about suffering people if there are not in fact people out there whose suffering more or less corresponds with the description? Without real people suffering, what valid purpose would such a vocabulary serve?

If a concern for correspondence is indispensable for linguistic descriptions of others' sufferings, such a concern is equally crucial for those linguistic descriptions we call "historical." Is not history distinguished from fiction precisely by the intention of history to provide an account adequate to the traces of the past, that is, an account faithful to the documents and evidence we have from the past and that we therefore hope is a relatively adequate rendition of what actually happened?[18] To evaluate narratives solely in terms of their usefulness obliterates any real distinction between historical and fictional narratives. Those who accept Rorty's argument that we should focus on the usefulness of our vocabularies, rather than on what they refer to, ought to speak of "fiction" (or of mythology) rather than "history," since calling one's narrative "historical" only invites people to raise the supposedly useless question of the accuracy of its account of what happened.

There is another option, a path not taken by Rorty and West, but one that I believe would serve them better. I have no quarrel with the argument that we have no unmediated access to the world, that we cannot escape the confines of our language and compare our statements to the world itself. It does not necessarily follow, however, that our beliefs and ideas do not or cannot correspond to reality; such a position would be self-contradictory if it claimed to be true, as Rorty knows. What does follow is that our ways of knowing the world are always influenced by our circumstances and interests, and are fallible. Nevertheless, these conditioned and fallible accounts are not simply any stories we find useful but rather ones that give the best account of available evidence; some sense of correspondence, at least as an aim we strive for, is thus presupposed. To paraphrase Charles Hartshorne, the two extremes: we know exactly what happened, and we know nothing of what happened, are both unjustified.[19] Granting the impossibility of an "objective" history that perfectly corresponds to the past as it actually happened, historical narratives must nonetheless be judged not solely in terms of usefulness but also in terms of their relative adequacy in providing accounts faithful to the traces of the past. Otherwise, we give up history altogether and simply tell useful stories.

For West's position to be consistent philosophically, I believe he must take this middle path and acknowledge a distinction between history and fiction, since his argument, which works as an historicizing of philosophy, would not work as a fictionalizing of philosophy. Too much of his argument depends on the presuppositions that history refers more or less adequately to the past and that socio-economic analyses do correspond more or less well to the actual conditions of people's lives. This may be why West does not belabor the rejection of a correspondence theory of truth; to give up this part of Rorty's pragmatism would not hurt West much. It would only mean that his argument for a prophetic pragmatism (a philosophy become cultural criticism) would be based on arguments defending the need for such a pragmatic philosophy, and not on the untenability of any other type of philosophical argument.

What, then, is the outcome of Rorty's and West's attempts to surpass the political limitations of postmodern thought? I believe that the argument against a correspondence theory of truth which Rorty and West both use as the basis of their return to pragmatism undercuts the political viability of their ideas. Because ideas-as-plans-of-action are ideas evaluated according to their usefulness in achieving our goals, accounting for the selection of these goals is a problem for pragmatists. Rorty responds to this difficulty by privatizing all discussion of worthwhile goals and values, and suggesting a very limited realm of public concern that mitigates against public responsibility and encourages us to seek a fulfilled life primarily through verbal creativity. West, on the other hand, recognizes the public nature of goals and values and develops what I believe is a more adequate and helpful understanding of the dynamic interplay between public and private. However, he is forced by his rejection of truth as correspondence to make the choice of these very important goals fairly arbitrary, while he nevertheless depends on the possibility of knowledge that corresponds at least to some extent to our historical past and to real social and economic circumstances. It is my contention that, at least if we agree with West on the importance of historical thinking for political resistance, belief in the inescapably self-referential character of language (i.e., that we cannot know about the world out there) is a serious political liability.

NOTES

1. See William H. Shaw and Vincent Barry, *Moral Issues in Business,* 6th ed. (Belmont, CA: Wadsworth, 1995), pp. 101–102, for statistical trends on income and wealth distribution. For an insightful interpretation of social policies and attitudes toward economic stratification in the United States, see Michael Lind, "To Have and to Have Not," in *Harper's Magazine,* vol. 290, no. 1741 (June 1995), pp. 35–47.

2. Throughout this paper I will use the term "postmodern" to refer to those who accept the general ideas, especially the rejection of metanarratives, developed by poststructuralists and deconstructionists. I reserve the term "poststructuralist" more specifically for the major thinkers identified with poststructuralism (especially, in this paper, Michel Foucault and Jacques Derrida) and for those who adhere strictly to their ideas.

3. For his criticism of the tendency of much politically engaged thought to produce "articles that offer unmaskings of the presuppositions of earlier unmaskings of still earlier unmaskings," see Richard Rorty's "Thugs and Theorists," in *Political Theory,* vol. 15, no. 4 (Nov. 87), pp. 564–580.

4. Richard Rorty, *Philosophy and the Mirror of Nature* (Princeton: Princeton University Press, 1979).

5. For a concise presentation of this argument, see Rorty's "Pragmatism, Relativism, and Irrationalism," in his *Consequences of Pragmatism* (Minneapolis: University of Minnesota Press, 1982), pp. 160–175.

6. This argument is most clearly worked out in Rorty's *Contingency, Irony, and Solidarity* (Cambridge: Cambridge University Press, 1989), esp. pp. 23–72. While he develops the political implications somewhat differently in other works, I believe the basic distinction between public and private and the concomitant problems remain. See especially his "The Priority of Democracy to Philosophy," in *The Virginia Statute for Religious Freedom*, ed. M. D. Peterson and R. C. Vaughan (Cambridge: Cambridge University Press, 1988), and his "Thugs and Theorists."

7. See Rorty, *Contingency*, pp. 73–95.

8. See John Dewey, *Reconstruction in Philosophy* (Boston: Beacon Press, 1948) and also his *The Public and Its Problems* (Denver: Swallow, 1927). For an excellent discussion of Dewey's political philosophy, see Robert Horwitz's "John Dewey" in *History of Political Philosophy*, 3rd ed., ed. Leo Strauss and Joseph Cropsey (Chicago: University of Chicago Press, 1987), pp. 851–869.

9. It is interesting to contrast Rorty's linguistic view of creativity with the lives of the great saints, whose creativity often lay not primarily in their development of original vocabularies but rather in practicing deeply, in their particular circumstances, an ancient vocabulary of the Christian Church.

10. "This inability to imagine how to get from here to there (a future of dignity, freedom, and peace) is a matter neither of loss of moral resolve nor of theoretical superficiality, self-deception, or self-betrayal. . . . It is just the way things happen to have fallen out," Rorty argues in *Contingency*, p. 182.

11. For the development of his understanding of pragmatism, see West's *The American Evasion of Philosophy* (Madison: University of Wisconsin Press, 1989), esp. pp. 182–243. For a more complete understanding of West's own project, see his *Prophetic Thought in Postmodern Times*, vol. 1, and *Prophetic Reflections*, vol. 2, *Beyond Eurocentrism and Multiculturalism*, (Monroe, Maine: Common Courage Press, 1993).

12. For clarification of the role of religion as the source of his goals, see West, *Prophetic Reflections*, pp. 183–198 and pp. 223–234.

13. West, *Prophetic Reflections*, pp. 229–230.

14. West develops this criticism of postmodern preoccupation with verbal play especially in the concluding chapter in West, *Evasion*, pp. 211–239.

15. For a discussion of the importance of totalities in relation to Lukács and Deleuze, see West, *Prophetic Reflections*, pp. 69–70.

16. This argument is made particularly well in West's *Race Matters* (New York: Random House, 1993), especially pp. 15–32.

17. See especially West, *Prophetic Reflections*, pp. 203–221 and his *Race* pp. 17–31.

18. For similar criticisms of Rorty's argument, see Charles Hartshorne, *Creativity in American Philosophy* (Albany: State University of New York Press, 1984), pp. 248–261, and Richard Bernstein, "One Step Forward, Two Steps Back," in *Political Theory* vol. 15, no. 4 (Nov. 1987), pp. 538–563. For a well-developed argument that history *intends* to refer to the past as it actually was, see Paul Ricoeur, *Time and Narrative*, vol. 1 (Chicago: University of Chicago Press, 1984), pp. 175–225.

19. "The two extremes: We know exactly what things are, We know nothing of what they are, are both unjustified," is Hartshorne's actual statement. He adds, "If Rorty's view is not the second extreme, it is not easy to see the distinction." Hartshorne, p. 261.

MINDS, BODIES, EXPERIENCE, NATURE:
Is Panpsychism Really Dead?[1]

Warren G. Frisina

I.

Richard Rorty's paper titled "Dewey between Hegel and Darwin"[2] argues that, while it is appropriate to describe John Dewey as a radical empiricist and panpsychist, it would be better if we allowed those aspects of his thought to atrophy and eventually disappear. He claims: "If one looks at the end of the twentieth century rather than at its beginning one finds pragmatism enjoying something of a renascence but no similar renascence of panpsychism. The philosophers of today . . . tend to speak about *sentences* a lot but to say very little about ideas or experiences, as opposed to such sentential attitudes as beliefs and desires."[3] Rorty goes on to argue that the atrophying of panpsychism enables us to better see what was truly innovative and important in Dewey's thought and in the thought of the other classical pragmatists.

Rorty is surely correct in noting that the percentage of active philosophers who take panpsychism seriously is smaller than it was during the earlier parts of this century.[4] Nevertheless, and despite Rorty's ethnocentric views on philosophical argumentation, we ought not to assess a theory's value simply by virtue of how many people happen to be using it at a given time. Rather, it remains our responsibility to ask whether a theory might help us (as Rorty sometimes says) *cope* with the contemporary philosophical situation as we see it. In this instance I believe a case can be made that panpsychism has an important role to play and ought to be promoted rather than excised from our vocabulary. Were we to interpret ourselves and our world using biological metaphors derived from a panpsychist position, we might be better able to accept, understand and interpret recent research by physiologists and neuroscientists who continue to blur the lines between minds, brains and bodies. We would also have disposed of much that has been troublesome in traditional epistemology and have a more fruitful, that is to say, more pragmatic understanding of the relationship between knowledge, value and action, which in itself would be helpful when it came to thinking about matters of science, ethics, and even religion.

II.

Before beginning my defense of the usefulness of the panpsychist metaphor, I should outline Rorty's argument against it. He begins by conceding that panpsychism was important to Dewey, William James, and Charles Sanders Peirce.

> A survey of the most interesting and original philosophers of the year 1900 would indeed show . . . that most of them wanted to close the epistemological gap between subject and object by some form of the panpsychist claim that the two were somehow continuous. For panpsychism seemed an obvious way to perform what Kloppenberg calls "the marriage of Hegel and Darwin."[5]

The image of Dewey as the thinker best prepared to "marry Darwin and Hegel" becomes a vehicle for Rorty to explain what he finds fruitful in Dewey's work and what has shown itself to be less than helpful. Though panpsychism was important to pragmatism's founders, Rorty argues it has not turned out to be particularly relevant to thinking in the late twentieth century.

Pointing to the work of Donald Davidson, whose "distal theory of meaning . . . [and] . . . philosophy of language has no use for Locke's and Hume's specifically psychic terrain, intermediate between physiology and linguistically formulated beliefs," Rorty says he would like to construct "a *hypothetical* Dewey who was a pragmatist without being a radical empiricist, and a naturalist without being a panpsychist. The point of constructing such a Dewey is to separate out what I think is living and what I think is dead in Dewey's thought and thereby to clarify the difference between the state of philosophical play around 1900 and at the present time"[6] (italics added).

In developing this hypothetical reconstruction of Dewey, Rorty emphasizes Dewey's relationship with the historicist side of Georg Wilhelm Friedrich Hegel. Here he follows Manfred Frank who describes Hegel as having removed the Archimedean point in historical consciousness, leaving us no "transhistorical frame of orientation beyond linguistic differentiality."[7] The roots of the linguistic turn are thus traced back to Hegel (and ultimately to Johann Herder and Wilhelm von Humboldt) who "made it possible for us . . . to think of 'transnational and transhistorical reason' as an 'image of the world' inscribed in a linguistic order."[8]

In tracing the linguistic turn back to the historicist implications of Hegel's thinking, Rorty defines historicism as "the doctrine that there is no relation of 'closeness of fit' between language and the world: no image of the world projected by language is more or less representative of the way the world really is than any other." This definition of historicism is designed to contrast with scientism, by which he means "the doctrine that natural science is privileged above other areas of culture, that something about natural science puts it in closer touch with reality than any other human activity."[9]

Viewed in this context, Dewey becomes for Rorty a "philosopher of the *via media*" between historicism and scientism. While many followers of the pragmatic tradition see Dewey as someone who brings together Hegel and Charles Darwin "by finding a holistic, panpsychist way of describing the relations between experience and nature," Rorty argues that Dewey's real accomplishment was in finding a "historicist, relativist, way of describing Darwin's claim upon our attention. By a historicist and relativist way, I mean a way of seeing natural science in general, and Darwin in particular as simply one more description of the world to be placed alongside others, rather than as offering the *one* image that corresponds to reality."[10]

Rorty goes on to point out that a true historicist is never in the position to complain that her opponent's views are out of joint with reality. She cannot resort to "notions of misleading abstraction" or "misplaced concreteness" since all descriptions must be viewed pragmatically as "more useful for the following purposes."[11] By substituting such expediency for representational accuracy, Rorty believes that the true historicist is forced to opt for only *one* of the two famous formulations of the pragmatic theory of truth.

Citing William James, Rorty praises the formula that sees truth as "only the expedient in the way of our thinking, just as 'the right' is only the expedient in our way of behaving."[12] Rorty contrasts this with what he describes as James' unfortunate alternative formulation of the pragmatic theory of truth, namely that "ideas (which themselves are but parts of our experience) become true just in so far as they help us get into satisfactory relation with other parts of our experience."[13] The former definition is compatible with Rorty's "historicist sense of truth as a property of linguistic entities," while the latter is not. He believes the latter necessarily points to a nonlinguistic realm of human activity which is ultimately the "germ of panpsychism:"

> "getting into satisfactory relation with other parts of our experience" will be acceptable as an account of true beliefs only if both the distinction between the propositional and the nonpropositional, and the distinction between properties of the agent and properties of her environment, are blurred in the way in which Dewey blurred them in *Experience and Nature*.[14]

For those who have taken the linguistic turn, there is no fruitful philosophical work to be found in discussions of nonpropositional experience. Moreover, if one believes that philosophical reflection should be confined to discussions of what takes place within language, it is particularly important that we not confuse the language user with that to which she refers or to whom she speaks.

Put another way, Rorty simply has no use for the distinction Dewey draws between primary and secondary modes of experience and the principle of continuity that governs so much of Dewey's thinking. Rorty makes this clear by discussing the relationship between Darwinism and pragmatism.

> Darwinism requires that we think of what we do and are as continuous with what the amoebae, the spiders, and the squirrels do and are. One way to expound this continuity is suggested by the second formula: we may think of these members of other species as sharing with us something called experience—something not the same as consciousness or thought, but something of which consciousness and thought are more complex and developed forms. This way of obtaining continuity is illustrated by Locke's attempt to tell a story about how we get from the baby's mind to the adult's—by adding in more simple ideas and then joining them up to produce complex ideas. This way of procuring continuity blurs the distinction that Peirce draws between cognitive and noncognitive mental states—between, for example, sensations and beliefs. As I have argued in my *Philosophy and the Mirror of Nature*, it also blurs the distinction between the question "what causes our beliefs?" and the question "what justifies our beliefs"—a blurring that is essential for any representationalist theory of knowledge.[15]

I quoted this statement at length because it captures much of what Rorty finds objectionable in radical empiricism and panpsychism. Rorty cannot conceive of a reason to explore a link between cognitive and noncognitive mental states. Whether the latter exist simply cannot be established. And even if they did exist, we would have no means of describing or knowing anything about them, except propositionally. They are, therefore, irrelevant to philosophical reflection of the kind Rorty prefers.

Rorty's objections are rooted in his conviction that despite historicist leanings, Dewey remained under the influence of a "representationalist theory of knowledge." For Rorty, *any* talk of experience raises the specter of representationalism and all of the negative consequences that it entails. Ultimately, Rorty believes that panpsychism simply doesn't accomplish what it advertises. Instead of resolving long held epistemological problems it masks them by redefining the terms. He says that "when we invoke panpsychism in order to bridge the gap between experience and nature, we begin to feel that something has gone wrong. For notions such as 'experience,' 'consciousness,' and 'thought' were originally invoked to *contrast* something that varied independently of nature with nature itself."[16]

According to Rorty, the problems motivating over 2500 years of epistemological reflection in the West have always been rooted in the distinction between appearance and reality. Though Dewey's objective was to dissolve such epistemological problems by redescribing truth in terms of warranted assertability, Rorty complains that by relying on the term *experience* Dewey placed himself within the orbit of traditional epistemological problems. Dewey's attempt

> to get rid of . . . [the] appearance versus true reality distinction, and to replace it with a distinction of degree between less organized and directed and more organized and directed *empeiria* . . . was futile because his fellow philosophers insisted on language in which they could discuss the possibility of our being "out of touch with reality" or "lost in a realm of mere appearance." Dewey often rejoined by insisting that we replace the appearance-reality distinction by a distinction between beliefs useful for some purposes and beliefs useful for others. If he had stayed with that rejoinder, he would have been on firm ground. But unfortunately he also rejoined that his opponents had "misdescribed experience." This rejoinder was utterly ineffectual.[17]

Dewey's second response was ineffectual, according to Rorty, because by retaining the term experience he could not avoid giving implied consent to the possibility that experience might, in some contexts, be out of joint with reality. Thus, Dewey's theory of experience was viewed by his critics as dodging "hard epistemological questions by redefining the terms in which they had been raised,"[18] rather than by resolving them.

Rorty essentially agrees with Dewey's early critics. Unlike those critics, however, Rorty wants to press the historicist side of Dewey's thinking to its ultimate end, dropping forever the notion that mind mirrors world. Thus, he would have preferred it if Dewey had let go of epistemology completely and dropped the term *experience*. "He should have agreed with Peirce that a great gulf divides sensation and cognition, decided that cognition was possible only for language users, and then said that the only relevant break in continuity was between non-language users (amoebae, squirrels, babies) and language users."[19] This seems to be the heart of Rorty's understanding of the implications of the linguistic turn for his reading of Dewey. Rorty sums up his arguments with the following statement:

> Dewey's and James' attempt to give a "more concrete," more holistic, and less dualism-ridden account of experience would have been unnecessary if they had not tried to make "true" a predicate of experience and had instead let it be a predicate of sentences. For then they would not have thought of "ideas" (which are themselves but parts of experience) becoming true or being made true. They would not have set themselves the bad question, Granted that truth is in some sense the agreement or correspondence of experiences with reality, what must experience and reality be such that they can stand in such relations[20]

As Rorty reads them, James and Dewey both tried to redefine *agreement* and *correspondence* so as to overcome the assumption that these terms entailed copying reality in thought. Insofar as their redefinitions were merely other ways of saying "truth is what works," Rorty finds them helpful for twentieth-century thinkers. Rorty observes, however, that "James and Dewey thought of them as more than that, and that is why they were led down the garden path of radical empiricism."[21]

Rorty is objecting to what he takes to be a common assumption shared by James, Dewey, and a number of other late nineteenth and early twentieth century thinkers that "an appropriate philosophical response to Darwin required a kind of vitalism—an attempt to coalesce the vocabulary of epistemology with that of evolutionary biology."[22]

Instead of relying on panpsychism to legitimate a marriage of Hegel and Darwin, Rorty believes that *historicism* should be used to temper the excesses in each. Thus, Darwin's description of evolution as both *random* and mechanistic can be used to overcome Hegelian teleological tendencies that place humankind and Spirit at the center of a single unfolding drama whose end is ultimately predetermined. Those same evolutionary mechanisms are also quite sufficient for explaining both oral and written language, and the meaning systems they imply. From a Darwinian perspective language is an adaptation, pure and simple. It occurs for the same reason birds build nests and sing songs. These were spontaneous adaptations which, over the centuries, proved themselves to be useful. According to Rorty, there is no need to posit a substratum called "experience" which all beings share and which gradually grows more complicated as we move up the evolutionary chain.

At the same time, a historicist understanding of science undoes the scientistic pretensions to ultimacy or finality which sometimes accompany the Darwinian scientific mentality. Randomness and mechanism are part of Darwin's elaborate metaphor, "survival of the fittest," which has shown itself to be a helpful tool for understanding ourselves and our relationships with nature. It is not, however, a final description of what is real about either ourselves or nature.

Rorty's hypothetical Dewey would, therefore, show us a way between the "reductionist use of Darwin and the rationalist use of Hegel." Dewey's contribution, as Rorty sees it, is to lead us to recognize the fruitfulness of replacing traditional questions about ultimate reality and human nature with Deweyan questions such as "which community's purposes shall I share, What sort of person would I prefer to be." Coupled with the increasing prominence of language as a topic for philosophic reflection, Rorty's Dewey helps us to "spend less and less time talking about the nature of ultimate reality"[23] and more time exploring how our communities shape themselves.

In sum, Rorty begins by positing a hypothetical Dewey, one for whom a commitment to historicism outweighs a commitment to empiricism and panpsychism. According to Rorty, a historicist does not expect mental entities to map onto or represent the world. Concepts or ideas are components of a continually changing linguistic system whose properties can best be explored within the context of reflections on propositional attitudes.[24]

Insofar as the real Dewey was interested in experience, especially in experience of a non-cognitive sort, he showed himself to be still under the thrall of a representationalist theory of knowledge, one that requires some explanation for why it is that appearance so often varies from reality.

Struggling with questions such as these led Dewey down the "garden path" toward radical empiricism and panpsychism.

But radical empiricism and panpsychism have proven to be unproductive. The linguistic turn outstripped earlier efforts to plumb the depths of nature and rendered talk of experience (in any but a linguistic context) obsolete. Rorty prefers to imagine a marriage between the historicist side of Hegel and the evolutionary vision of Darwin. Rorty's hypothetical Dewey, one who was a historicist rather than a panpsychist, would perform the honors by charting a *via media* that rejects Hegelian teleology and Darwinian scientism and in their place provides us with a vision of philosophic reflection that focuses our attention on resolving human problems.

So, where does this leave those of us who harbor panpsychist thoughts? Ought we to follow Rorty's therapeutic suggestions and just get over them? Should we put aside any hope of a thoroughgoing naturalism? In what follows I would like to suggest some reasons for retaining Dewey's panpsychist and empiricist tendencies.

III.

In addition to Rorty's portrayal of panpsychism as a response to crises engendered by Darwin's evolutionary biology, the panpsychist option may also be viewed as potential remedy to a number of more "old fashioned" philosophical puzzles such as the problem of the one and the many, mind/body dualism, and, most importantly, the Enlightenment separation of facts from values and objectivity from subjectivity.

Whitehead, for example, was surely influenced by Darwin. Nonetheless, Whitehead's panpsychism, which is far more radical than most of the figures Rorty cites (including Dewey), is better described as an alternative account of causality, one that replaces the billiard ball metaphor derived from Newtonian physics with an organic metaphor more suited to the twentieth century's revolutionary notion that matter is a form of energy and that all movement (both within bits of matter and among them) is the transfer of energy.

Although Darwin's evolutionary theory played an important role in the development of Whitehead's process ontology, I suspect Darwin's most significant impact involved providing Whitehead with a rationale for speculating on how things might look were we to make *biology* the "queen of the sciences," and use biological metaphors rather than metaphors derived from Newtonian physics to frame our understanding of ourselves and the natural world.

Whitehead's panpsychism is thoroughgoing in the way that Rorty, and most critics of panpsychism disparage. He argues that existence is inherently relational, that to be anything at all is to be a perspective on that which already is, that "being" is actually the process of coming to develop such a perspective, and most importantly, that the process of developing such a perspective is ultimately value-laden.[25]

Whitehead uses many metaphors for describing this process, but the one he shares with Dewey is *experience*. All of the "actual entities" constituting the universe are, according to Whitehead, "drops of experience." Each is a "perspective" on the whole of things, and there is nothing outside the plurality of perspectives that have been actualized or the potential perspectives still to be achieved.

There is one detail of Whitehead's cosmology that is important to note in the context of a discussion of Rorty's critique of panpsychism. For Rorty, any talk of experience, especially talk of what amounts to "precognitive" or "non-propositional experience," raises the problem of appearance vs. reality and puts one on the wrong side of a line drawn in the sand by those who have taken the linguistic turn. I would like to suggest, however, that there is a way to see Whitehead's use of experience as more anti-representationalist than would ever be possible for those who eschew metaphysical reflection.

Though Whitehead uses the metaphor of experience to describe the activity of actual entities, and says that each entity has both a "mental" and a "physical" pole, he is not attempting to smuggle in a representationalist theory of knowledge. Rather, his concern is to provide a metaphysical basis for *value*. Prehending entities do not "represent" mental images of previous entities, they incorporate previously actualized values directly into their own self constitution. That which is prehended enters *causally* into the constitution of the concrescing entity. Prehensions are not micro-mental pictures of the world. They are better understood as dynamic acts of energy transfer.

The term *experience* might lead one to assume a prehension is a "mental" representation, much like a photograph or a movie image. But this simply is not the case. At the microcosmological level mentality is valuative feelings of aversion and attraction. Since actual entities are best described as evaluative responses to the whole of things, and since these responses (actual entities) are the "final real things," a prehending entity is not *representing* other perspectives so much as prioritizing and incorporating them. Thus, on my reading, Whitehead's panpsychism is not representationalist in any of the ways Rorty is concerned about. On the microcosmological level there is no problem of "appearance versus reality." Instead, Whitehead has described a causal system which is non-reductive and physicalistic.

I choose the terms non-reductive and physicalistic to echo Rorty's call for a non-reductive physicalism that would erase long-held assumptions about an internal realm of the mind that is struggling to make contact with and come to know an external physical world.[26] My suggestion is that Whitehead's microcosmology is physicalist in the sense that it is essentially a description of a causal system. There is no "internal" mind that is separated from and trying to make contact with a world where physical causation holds sway. Moreover, Whitehead's panpsychism is non-representationalist, since an actual entity's mental pole is evaluative rather than representational.

Of course saying that Whitehead's microcosmology is not representationalist does not absolve him from representationalism on all fronts. To respond to the spirit of Rorty's concerns it would be necessary to examine the epistemology Whitehead builds upon this panpsychist hypothesis. But that is another paper.[27] My main concern is to point out how Rorty's assumptions about panpsychism do not apply to one of the most radically panpsychist positions available. Of course, to see that this is true one would have to take speculative metaphysical reflection seriously, something that Rorty, by his own admission, finds hard to continence.[28]

What I have said about Whitehead's panpsychism should make it clear that I view his position as more radical than Dewey's. While there is no doubt that experience is central to Dewey's thought, he was unwilling to assert that experience is an ontological category, a feature of all forms of existence. In fact, in *Experience and Nature*, Dewey indicates that there is a clear delineation between situations that engender experience and those which do not. In discussing the distinction between inorganic and organic activity he says: "the difference between animate and inanimate objects lies not in the fact that the latter has something in addition to physico-chemical properties, but rather in the way in which those energies are interconnected and operate, evoking different consequences."[29] Thus, for Dewey, there is a level of physico-chemical interaction which is not organic. If, therefore, Dewey is not a panpsychist in the same way Whitehead is, then what kind of a panpsychist is he?

Rorty reads the entire panpsychist movement through the lens of Darwin's impact on nineteenth century thought. As I see it, however, Dewey is like Whitehead in that his panpsychist leanings are of a piece with his metaphysical concerns. Though Dewey is not interested in either micro or macro cosmology, he is a process thinker (in a broad sense) who is eager to experiment with hypotheses that a process orientation makes possible. Like many of his late nineteenth and early twentieth century colleagues, Dewey flips the Newtonian metaphor and begins by presuming that individual existence is a cognitive construction and that ontological priority ought to be given to the systems that set the context for and thereby give rise to those things which we normally believe stand alone. Viewed from Dewey's perspective, there is no such thing as "individual" existence, if by that one means ontological status apart from the system out of which the "individual" emerges.

This aspect of Dewey's process vision extends to the inorganic realm, where he describes molecules and atoms as patterns of movement within a larger system of movement. Though he did not follow Whitehead in pressing the "organic metaphor" down to the microcosmological level, Dewey was clearly influenced by recent discoveries in physics and was responding to them in his own way.

The impact of Dewey's shift to a systemic-process paradigm ought to be considered in any discussion of his empiricism and panpsychism. Throughout his career Dewey worked tirelessly to undo our habit of viewing organisms as isolated, self-contained individuals that only happen to be placed within an environment. While Rorty points out how "Darwinism requires that we think of what we do and are as continuous with what the amoebae, the spiders, and the squirrels do and are,"[30] he does not acknowledge that part of what made Darwinism possible was a "paradigm" shift from thinking in terms of self-contained species (placed on earth by the divine hand) to thinking in terms of ecosystems and their impact on the development of species through evolutionary means. Whether this shift belongs solely to Darwin or is part of some larger nineteenth century movement need not concern us. My main point is that Dewey's use of the term *experience* must be seen as of a piece with the Darwinian turn toward ecosystems. Dewey recognizes that to understand organic activity we can no longer ask, What is the nature of the organism under discussion? Rather, we ought to be looking to the broader environmental *situation* which makes possible and supports this particular form of organic activity. All of these assumptions lay behind the priority Dewey gives to what he calls the "situation." In fact, as Dewey uses the term, "situation" has a kind of priority over experience. Thus, to understand Dewey's panpsychist tendencies is to see them as an outcome of his "situationalist" approach to organic activity.

For Dewey, organisms are systems of organized activity nested within larger systems. In fact, he defines an organism as a pattern of movements with the capability of either maintaining or restoring its equilibrium when there are changes in its broader environment. This hierarchy of systems within systems is both compatible and incompatible with the linguistic turn as Rorty describes it. On the one hand, the linguistic turn allows us to see that any aspect of language is dependent on a broader linguistic system. Thus, Davidson's holistic approach to meaning and language, for example, seems like a natural outcome of both the linguistic turn *and* the turn toward systemic thinking in the late nineteenth and early twentieth centuries. On the other hand, Rorty seems to see in the linguistic turn a rationale for bracketing one organic system, that having to do with human language, from all other organic systems. This assumption, if it is true to the spirit of the linguistic turn, runs contrary to the spirit of the times, and is, as far as I see it, completely out of line with Dewey's instincts.

Rorty is right to press the historicist implications of Dewey's thinking. I agree that Dewey is a far more radical thinker than he has been made out to be by either the scientistic types who see in him the ultimate justification for a hegemony of the scientific method, or the meliorists who read him as a lonely optimistic voice amidst the gloom that characterized the first half of the twentieth century. Nonetheless, Rorty is just wrong if he thinks he can create a recognizable image of Dewey (hypothetical though it may be!) who will allow human language to be the only organic system about which we cannot ask the question: What makes this kind of organic activity possible?

Dewey's understanding of experience is necessarily related to his urge to describe organic activity as a set of practices that emerge from and are in continuity with their larger surroundings. Such an approach does not entail the "representationalist" implications that Rorty is so concerned to avoid. For Dewey, *experience* is a term describing the capacity of an organism to adjust to, or cope with its environment. As Rorty himself points out, such adjustments (or coping) have little to do with mental mirroring of the world. Thus, I suspect Dewey would agree with Rorty's overarching effort to rid us of the specter of the ghost in the machine. Rorty's error, as I see it, is in assuming that *any* talk of experience necessarily entails such a ghost.

Perhaps some personal testimony will help drive home the point I am trying to make. When I first read Dewey's *Experience and Nature*, I was smitten by the overall process vision, and by the way in which Dewey provided a completely naturalistic understanding of value and the role it plays in the constitution of organic activities. Dewey did all of this without appealing to God or eternal objects, Whiteheadian concepts which I found especially problematic. Nonetheless, I was confused by his use of the term *experience*. Written in the margins at a number of key points is my own impatient scrawled question "whose experience?!!" What I came to understand upon successive readings is that in *Experience and Nature* Dewey was working to undo any lingering Cartesian assumptions about what we mean by the term experience. Experience is not an essential characteristic of an independently existing subject. It is, rather, a *trait* exhibited within organic situations and in that sense should not be seen as "owned" by any individual. Since it is not "owned" by an individual it is much harder to see in Dewey's use of the term the mental representationalism that Rorty fears. Organic systems are continually adjusting to changes within the broader environment. Experience is the term Dewey uses to describe those adjustments.[31]

IV.

Having described why I think neither Whitehead's nor Dewey's panpsychism can be viewed as representationalist, I would like to turn to a brief discussion of what Whitehead calls causal efficacy and Dewey calls primary experience. Any analysis of their panpsychism ought to at least try to highlight why both felt compelled to include in their descriptions of human experience a level of human activity which, though well below the "cognitive" or "propositional," must still be described as experiential.

Rorty, of course, would prefer to rule consideration of such feelings out of philosophy altogether. His desire is motivated by what he perceives as an unbridgeable "gulf" between perception and conception. As I see it, however, ruling them out of philosophy *assumes* rather than *justifies* a dichotomy between feeling and cognition; minds and bodies; experience and nature. The Whiteheadian and Deweyan suggestion that we attend to such feelings serves as a reminder that we ought not start from a position which pre-determines our conclusions.

Whitehead, for example, poses the Humean question: What justification do we have for claiming that who we are at this moment is continuous with who we were a moment ago? He answers that we *experience* a physical confirmation of that continuity over time. So long as we keep in mind that Whitehead understands experience as the continual adjustment of an organism to its environment, there is no reason to presume, as Rorty does, that talk of such "physical feelings" smuggles in a Cartesian ghost who "has" the feelings. Rather, because Whitehead's cosmology allows no division between the mental and the physical he can argue that experience of this physical compulsion appears to be a characteristic of all organic activity. Moreover, Whitehead's description of causal efficacy as a response to Humean skepticism has an advantage over say Immanuel Kant's *a priori* transcendental explanation by virtue of its not having to explain how a purely cognitive *a priori* compulsion (e.g., temporality, causality, etc.) relates to the body and an external physical world.

Most importantly, Whitehead's willingness to take seriously the notion of non-cognitive physical feelings provides him with a way to understand those vague but powerful emotional overtones that color cognitive experience but have no explicit connection to cognition as we normally describe it. Understanding "feelings" such as rage, love, repulsion or attraction, feelings which seem so clearly to blend both physical and cognitive responses to situations, is more difficult for those who take Rorty's version of the linguistic turn.

Dewey follows a route similar to Whitehead in urging that we attend to what he calls primary experience and the role it plays in relation to secondary experience. When he talks about primary experience he is generally referring to the immediate "havings" and "doings" that constitute the vast majority of an organism's interactions with its environment. As Dewey describes them, organisms exhibit a rhythmic movement from equilibrium to stress and back to equilibrium. When stressed, perhaps in need of food, the situation calls forth from the organism a response which is rooted in its physicality. As is true of Whitehead, Dewey feels justified in calling such responses experience because they are the micro-adjustments the organism is making to its environment. Moreover, Dewey agrees with Whitehead in attributing to this level of experience the vague yet powerful emotional responses that are the background for our more sharply defined cognitive or secondary experience.

Since Rorty views the appearance of language as akin to genetic mutations, he feels justified in leaving it to the neurologist to describe the connections between our organic responses (e.g., brain states) and the higher order cognitive activity which language makes possible. No "explanation" is needed since language, like opposable thumbs, appeared spontaneously and has proven itself *de facto* to be a useful mutation. The problem with such a response, however, is that it ignores the ways in which this particular "mutation" is both dependent on and integrated with that which preceded it. Language *can* be viewed as a spontaneous mutation of human behavior. And Rorty is correct to describe language as a coping tool rather than a mapping device. Nonetheless, there is no reason for imagining that the differences between perception and cognition are so great that we cannot learn something from the way one (i.e., cognition) is dependent on the other (causal efficacy or primary experience). Moreover, there is no reason to allow an awareness of language's limitations to prevent us from recognizing that our organic responses are also efforts to cope with the world and in that way continuous with language as Rorty understands it.

Sometimes, the way Rorty describes language gives readers the impression that he imagines us trapped within a fluid linguistic system with metaphor as our only escape and the world as an unknowable *ding an sich*. Actually his position is more subtle. He wants to undo the distinction we draw between world and language and replace it with an image of selves that are constituted only as a web of beliefs which are continually weaving and unweaving so as to realize specific goals.[32] Whitehead and Dewey would probably find much to agree with in Rorty's metaphor of the self as a web of beliefs. According to both, cognitive experience gains its precision by virtue of selecting particular perspectives from which to respond to things. An epistemology rooted in perspectivalism is less inclined to worry about getting things "right" and more inclined to worry about getting things done.[33]

Ultimately, Dewey and Whitehead are both naturalists in a way that Rorty could never be. They see a continuity among all of the ways we struggle to cope with the world. In doing so, they do not reduce them all to the same thing, a fear implied throughout Rorty's critique of panpsychism. Perceptions are different from conceptions, and neither Dewey nor Whitehead would deny the distinction. Nonetheless, they do not insert unnatural dichotomies where they are not needed.

V.

At the beginning of his article Rorty says he intends his paper to "clarify the difference between the state of philosophical play around 1900 and at the present time."[34] Rorty's ethnocentric approach to questions of truth and knowledge bars him from saying more than that panpsychism is out of fashion at the present time. Beyond that, the most he can do is retell philosophy's story over the last century in a way that highlights why he believes panpsychism is out of fashion and why it should remain so. By telling the story in the way he does, Rorty hopes to convince us that panpsychism is not responsive to problems in the current philosophical situation.

I will not fault Rorty for failing to tell Dewey's story in the way that I would. After all, Rorty signals his intentions right from the beginning by announcing that he is going to describe a "hypothetical" Dewey, one who better fits Rorty's own vision of the current philosophical situation. Though it is probably useless to protest that Rorty misreads Dewey, it is appropriate to complain that Rorty seems out of touch with the cultural and philosophical world beyond a fairly narrow group of colleagues. Much of his critique of panpsychism hinges on what he takes to be the general acceptance of the linguistic turn and the gulf it creates between perception and conception. As a result Rorty unintentionally leaves open the possibility that panpsychism might be relevant at a time when such a gulf is not perceived to be as wide as he thinks it is. In the following pages I would like to point to some general evidence and one particular study that indicates we are living in a time when we should be re-reading Whitehead and Dewey, along with many of the other panpsychist thinkers from the late nineteenth and early twentieth centuries. Having thought long and hard about radical empiricism and panpsychism, they have much to teach those of us who are seeking for a way to understand the relationship between minds, bodies and nature.

In light of recent philosophic movements in the late twentieth century, it seems clear to me that philosophers are now better positioned to take seriously the Deweyan and Whiteheadian call to attend to vague emotion-laden causal feelings than they were in the period between the mid 60s through the mid 80s. In recent years phenomenologists have published a broad range of material exploring the "bodily" background to higher level cognitive knowledge. Though it would be wrong to assume that phenomenologists are necessarily panpsychists, it does seem fair to say that whereas Rorty (operating from within the assumptions of the linguistic turn) wants to draw a sharp line of demarcation between perception and conception, most phenomenologists are engaged in exploring the continuities that link them.

Feminist theorists represent another group of contemporary philosophers who have refused to allow the linguistic turn to circumscribe philosophic reflection. While most feminists readily acknowledge that we should attend to the way language structures experience, many also regularly appeal to modes of awareness which are not propositionally structured and which have not been taken seriously in the recent philosophic past. Again, I am not arguing that feminists are, or ought to be, panpsychists. Rather, I am claiming that panpsychism's emphasis on modes of experience which extend beyond the cognitive should make it a fruitful resource for feminist thinkers.

Sparked in part by both phenomenology and feminist theory, there has been a recent explosion of interest in the body. This interest cuts across many fields including philosophy, anthropology, history, religion, Asian studies, etc. Rorty, of course, is aware of this work. What I find surprising is that he does not see in it a favorable context for naturalist philosophy and especially the panpsychist specification of naturalism. He might want to argue that all such work is unlikely to be productive if it does not take seriously the fact that thoughts are always embedded in linguistic systems. But that seems a tenuous stance for an ironist who refuses to allow that there is any value to philosophy other than its therapeutic resolution of philosophic problems. Phenomenologists, feminist theorists, and philosophers of the body all seem hard at work providing therapeutic responses to the excesses of positivism and an overly dogmatic understanding of the linguistic turn. I find it hard to believe that Rorty would want to rule these modes of philosophic reflection useless, yet his argument against panpsychism seems to turn on precisely such logic.

Having suggested why I believe the general philosophic climate is more hospitable toward panpsychism than Rorty suggests, I would like to look briefly at Mark Johnson's remarkable book *The Body in the Mind: The Bodily Basis of Meaning, Imagination, and Reason*,[35] which will serve as a concrete example of the kind of philosophic work I see going on in a variety of contexts.

It is important to note at the outset that though Johnson is self-conscious about the fact that his position is unorthodox, he locates his work squarely in the center of contemporary philosophy, psychology and cognitive science. He makes no appeals to the American pragmatic or process traditions, and therefore cannot be seen as related in any but an indirect way to them. I am citing Johnson's work not only because I think he makes an interesting and powerful case for the embodied mind, but also because I take his work to exemplify the new climate at the end of the twentieth century that is more hospitable to, and would be well served by, a fuller discussion of panpsychism and radical empiricism.

As the title indicates, Johnson's aim is to develop a theory of meaning which takes proper account of the way our body sets the stage for and contributes to human understanding. The book opens with an exposition of what he calls "objectivism," which asserts that:

> The world consists of objects that have properties and stand in various relationships independent of human understanding. The world is as it is, no matter what any person happens to believe about it, and there is one correct "God's-Eye-View" about what the world is really like. In other words, there is a rational structure to reality, independent of beliefs of any particular people, and correct reason mirrors this rational structure.[36]

The most problematic feature of the objectivist position, according to Johnson, is the way it assumes that rationality transcends the "structures of bodily experience."

Citing philosophical arguments from both Rorty and Hilary Putnam, as well as empirical studies that examine the way we deal with categorization, metaphor and polysemy, Johnson argues that the objectivist position has been theoretically discredited, though it continues to define the "context in which our most popular theories of meaning and rationality are articulated."[37] Johnson views his book, and parallel efforts in linguistics and cognitive science, as the beginning of a new description of thought and understanding designed to avoid objectivism's limitations.

It is ironic that Johnson cites Rorty's *Philosophy and the Mirror of Nature* as the text which best sums up the story of the development and decline of objectivism.[38] On the one hand, Rorty sees the problem as Johnson does. Both agree that philosophy has suffered under the tyranny of an inadequate metaphor for knowledge (vision), one that mistakenly describes thought as outside of time and truth as the equivalent of a cognitive mirror of objective reality. On the other hand, Rorty's insistence on the centrality of the linguistic turn runs directly counter to Johnson's proposed remedy to the crisis engendered by objectivism's collapse. Where Rorty praises Donald Davidson for arguing that there is no "psychic terrain, intermediate between physiology and linguistically formulated beliefs,"[39] Johnson argues that "bodily experience and problem-solving," produce a vast network of "image-schematas which contribute directly to human imagination and understanding."[40] In this way Johnson turns to an analysis of "the nonpropositional, experiential, and figurative dimensions of meaning and rationality" in order to lay out the extent to which these patterns of bodily movement set a context for our higher order cognitive structures.[41]

Johnson's argument for the existence of bodily generated image-schematas rests on his ability to make some sense of the notion of *nonpropositional* experience. He approaches this task from two directions. First he asks us to attend to what he calls the nonpropositional aspects of our experience. "My present sense of being balanced upright in space at this moment is surely a nonpropositional awareness that I have, even though all my efforts to communicate its reality to you will involve propositional structure."[42] Johnson's point is that this vague awareness of being balanced precedes any cognitive awareness we may have, and more importantly, is rooted in the physical feeling of being balanced.[43] Having made the first point, Johnson goes on to describe how this nonpropositional sense of balancing shapes our imagination and the way we use language, especially metaphor, to describe ourselves and the world we inhabit.

For example, Johnson argues that our sense of what it means to be physically balanced serves as the metaphorical basis for what we mean when we talk about balanced systems, a balanced argument, an imbalanced personality, a balanced judicial decision, balanced morals, and mathematical equality.[44] In all of these ways our imagination and our higher order cognitive processes are shaped by image-schematas that are derived directly from patterned responses of our body to its environment.

It is at this point that Johnson's position both resonates with and goes a step beyond what I described above in my discussion of Whitehead's causal efficacy and Dewey's primary experience. For all three, experience can be understood as patterns of adjustments by an organism to its environment. Moreover, all three see those adjustments as the background against which humans cultivate higher order cognitive activity. Johnson, however, goes beyond Whitehead and Dewey by developing extended analyses of the image-schematas themselves.

> In order for us to have meaningful connected experiences that we can comprehend and reason about there must be pattern and order to our actions, perceptions, and conceptions. *A schema is a recurrent pattern, shape, and regularity in, or of, these ongoing ordering activities.* These patterns emerge as meaningful structures for us chiefly at the level of our bodily movements through space, our manipulation of objects, and our perceptual interactions.[45]

In this book Johnson touches on some twenty-seven different image-schematas, though he acknowledges that there is ultimately no end to the many ways our bodies develop patterns of interaction with the world. He says, "there is clearly nothing sacred about 253 patterns versus 53 or any other number of patterns, but it is certain that we experience our world by means of various image-schematic structures whose relations make up the fabric of our experience, that is, of our understanding."[46] The task of creating an inventory of image-schematas and analyzing each is a clear step beyond the kind of work that Dewey and Whitehead did in their discussions of primary experience and causal efficacy.

While Johnson's position is largely neutral with respect to naturalism, panpsychism and radical empiricism, my hope is that juxtaposing his work with that of Whitehead's and Dewey's will make it clear how pragmatic and process philosophers have a right to assume that the panpsychist dimensions of their work can contribute directly to contemporary philosophical discussions. Contrary to the impression Rorty tries to convey in his article, it is possible to argue that Johnson's work would benefit directly from a willingness to engage in the hypothetical metaphysical speculation that has been at the center of both the process and pragmatist movements from their beginnings.

VI.

Throughout his career Richard Rorty has remained keenly attuned to the role that metaphor plays in both philosophical and everyday discourse. For Rorty there is a sense in which all language is metaphorical. Words, phrases and ideas are originally metaphors that lose their metaphoric glow when they become commonplace truths. Nevertheless, though the glow may be gone, it would be wrong to assume that a metaphor is ever anything but metaphorical. And in that spirit, it is important to note that some metaphors can regain their "metaphorical glow" if they are cast again into a new context.

In his attack on panpsychism Rorty is largely concerned about the presence of the term *experience*. He sees in it all of the bad old things he has fought so hard to overcome: essentialism and a world that knowledge mirrors; subjectivism and objectivity; appearance and hard core reality. In this paper I have tried to suggest some of the reasons Rorty's fears are misplaced. In sum, my argument is that Rorty has failed to appreciate the way panpsychists like Whitehead and Dewey took an old term and put it to new metaphorical uses.

For a long time I wondered what it was that rendered Rorty tone-deaf to Deweyan naturalism. If "Dewey Between Hegel and Darwin" is a true indicator of his position, it turns out, unsurprisingly, to be his early commitment to the linguistic turn and the gulf it creates between conception and perception. I say unsurprising, because his early work in that area was a signal moment in American philosophy, and I guess one cannot begrudge him attachment to what was accomplished.

On the other hand, my own attachments are to ideas which, once unfashionable, have gained new currency in a world newly fascinated by the way bodies, minds, experience and nature are all interwoven into a complex organic network. We live in a time when advances in brain research and artificial intelligence are calling for us to rethink what we mean by bodies, minds, experience and nature. Rorty's response is to emphasize the gulf between perception and conception and argue that there is no interesting philosophic work to be done in discussing the way our bodies play a role in shaping our understanding. The other response, marked long ago by panpsychists like Whitehead and Dewey, and now taken up by contemporary philosophers like Mark Johnson, is to retrieve the metaphor "experience" and use it to describe the way all organisms struggle to cope with their environment. Viewed this way, panpsychism is likely to remain relevant in both the near and long terms.

NOTES

1. I am grateful for the fruitful questions and comments at the 1995 Highlands Institute for American Religious Thought conference that enabled me to improve upon the original presentation there. In particular I would like to thank Richard Rorty, J. Wesley Robbins, David L. Hall, and an anonymous reader, all of whom made very helpful suggestions.

2. Richard Rorty, "Dewey between Hegel and Darwin," *Modernist Impulses in the Human Sciences 1870–1930*, Dorothy Ross, ed. (Baltimore: The Johns Hopkins University Press, 1994), pp. 54–68. This paper can also be found in *Rorty and Pragmatism: The Philosopher Responds to His Critics*, Herman J. Saatkam, Jr., ed. (Nashville: Vanderbilt University Press, 1995). Page references in this article will be to Ross' volume.

3. *Ibid.*, p. 55.

4. Rorty himself notes the neo-Whiteheadian school, which he describes as centered around Charles Hartshorne. He also identifies Thomas Nagel as a panpsychist. *Ibid.*

5. *Ibid*.

6. *Ibid*., pp. 55–56. In the past Rorty has been chided by contemporary pragmatists for presenting a distorted picture of their philosophical heroes. It remains to be seen whether this "hypothetical" approach, which has the virtue of greater honesty, will help ameliorate the anger Rorty evokes among those who prefer to remain faithful to Dewey's original intentions. To his further credit, Rorty goes out of his way at the end of the article to point out that his reading makes Dewey sound "more Nietzschean than most of his commentators take him to be" (p. 67). In the end, of course, Dewey himself would likely concede that the issue ought not to be who remains most loyal, but rather whose vision of philosophy best contributes to resolving the problems that we face.

7. *Ibid*., p. 56. Rorty is citing from Manfred Frank, *What is Neo-Structuralism?* trans. by Sabine Wilke and Richard Gray (Minneapolis, University of Minnesota Press, 1989), p. 87.

8. *Ibid*., p. 56 citing Frank, p. 11.

9. *Ibid*., p. 56.

10. *Ibid*., p. 57

11. *Ibid*.

12. *Ibid*., p. 57. Rorty is citing William James, *Pragmatism* (Cambridge: Harvard University Press, 1978), p. 106.

13. *Ibid*., p. 57, James, *Pragmatism*, p. 4

14. *Ibid*., p. 58.

15. *Ibid*.

16. *Ibid*., p. 59.

17. *Ibid*.

18. *Ibid*., p. 60.

19. *Ibid*.

20. *Ibid.*, pp. 60–61.

21. *Ibid.*, p. 61.

22. *Ibid.*, p. 62

23. *Ibid.*, p. 66.

24. The book-length argument for this conclusion is found in Rorty's *Philosophy and the Mirror of Nature* (Princeton: Princeton University Press, 1979).

25. In an important early article that in many ways anticipates concerns articulated in his critique of Dewey, Rorty argues that by including within his philosophy things that are beyond the realm of experience (e.g., actual entities) Whitehead effectively surrenders the most important aspect of Descartes' legacy and returns to a premodern dependence upon vacuous explanatory categories. While he acknowledges the value in Whitehead's emphasis upon the fact that all knowledge is a perspectival construction, Rorty agrees with Sellars and other early ordinary language philosophers that we can avoid the felt need to appeal to undescribable entities through "a more careful deployment of our ordinary resources for describing mental acts." "The Subjectivist Principle and the Linguistic Turn," *Alfred North Whitehead: Essays on His Philosophy*, George L. Kline, ed. (Englewood Cliffs: Prentice-Hall, Inc., 1963), pp. 134–157.

26. Richard Rorty, *Objectivity, Relativism, and Truth: Philosophical Papers, Volume I* (Cambridge: Cambridge University Press, 1991), pp. 113–25.

27. See my "Knowledge as Active, Aesthetic and Hypothetical: An Examination of Whitehead's Theory of Knowledge," *The Journal of Speculative Philosophy*, Vol. V, No. 1, 1991, pp. 42–64.

28. Richard Rorty, "The Subjectivist Principle and the Linguistic Turn," p. 147.

29. John Dewey, *Experience and Nature* (New York: Dover, 1958), p. 254.

30. *Ibid.*, p. 58.

31. Viewed this way, Dewey's use of the term remains compatible with Whitehead's, though Dewey does not have a parallel microcosmology to fill in the details.

33. In "The Subjectivist Principle and the Linguistic Turn" Rorty points out appreciatively the importance of Whitehead's recognition that knowledge is perspectival. See p. 153.

34. Richard Rorty, "Dewey between Hegel and Darwin," p. 56.

35. Mark Johnson, *The Body in the Mind: The Bodily Basis of Meaning, Imagination, and Reason* (Chicago, University of Chicago Press, 1987).

36. *Ibid.*, p. x.

37. *Ibid.*, p. xxix.

38. *Ibid.*, p. 215.

39. Richard Rorty, "Dewey between Hegel and Darwin," p. 55.

40. Mark Johnson, p. xx.

41. *Ibid.*, p. xxxvii.

42. *Ibid.*, p. 5.

43. Johnson's phenomenological approach is structurally similar to Whitehead's appeal to attend to our feeling of continuity with who we were a moment ago.

44. *Ibid.*, pp. 80–96.

45. *Ibid.*, p. 29.

46. *Ibid.*, p. 127.

FROM LONELINESS TO SOLITUDE:
The Pragmatist's Path To Salvation

David L. Hall

I.

The treatment of the religious sensibility within the context of American pragmatism can hardly be a straightforward enterprise since many of our principal pragmatists themselves felt a certain uneasiness about it. Both William James and John Dewey were notoriously uncertain as to the manner of approaching the subject of religion. Throughout his career James was saddled with the apologetic need to provide at least qualified support of theism by recourse to a philosophical vision that, though religious to the core, was rather unfriendly to theistic ideas per se—and downright hostile to the transcendent monism that often accompanies traditional theistic beliefs.

Dewey struggled throughout his life to overcome the rather narrow moralistic religion of his childhood. All that groaning and travailing finally led in his later years to *A Common Faith,* a thin, timid, wind-egg of a book which he surely must have regretted ever having written. Though one can certainly find far profounder religious ideas secluded in his poetry, and in works such as *Human Nature and Conduct* and *Art as Experience,* this only reenforces the view that Dewey was reticent to provide any comprehensive presentation of his views on religion.[1]

Moreover, pragmatic resources for understanding the religious interest have been obscured through both misconstrual and neglect. As Emerson complained of his generation, American philosophers in the mid-twentieth century have too often looked to the "courtly muses of Europe" for their insights. Continental philosophies, particularly those associated with Germany, were directly imported through the migration of European philosophers and theologians in the wake of the second world war. The influence of European ideas, and those British modes of thought which supported both positivism and its subsequent transformation into analytic philosophy, were strong enough to eclipse for a while any sustained interest in home grown philosophies.

A consequence of this neglect is that even some participants in the recent renewal of pragmatism arrive at the texts of Ralph Waldo Emerson,

Charles Sanders Peirce, James, Dewey, and George Herbert Mead with distinctly nonpragmatic backgrounds, motives, and agendas.

Often this means that those interested in considering the religious side of pragmatism are predisposed to interpretations of religious experience and expression motivated by systematic and metaphysical, or analytic and reductive, aspirations which do not accord well with the pluralistic and nonreductive aspects of pragmatism.

To complicate matters even further, the thinker most associated with the renewal of a general interest in pragmatism proclaims himself an atheist. And though Richard Rorty's protests against religion often possess the tone of one who comes to scoff but, even yet, might stay to pray, the cumulative effect of his considerable influence is to reenforce neglect of the subject of religion, at least on the part of those who would lay down their crosses and follow him.

An effective engagement of the religious sensibility by contemporary pragmatists, one having both constructive and apologetic force, would address at least the following issues: first, the tensions within pragmatic philosophy that urge its proponents continually to shift back and forth between moral and aesthetic interests, a shiftiness that qualifies in a most important manner the treatment of the religious interest, particularly as regards the preference for theistic or mystical interpretations. A second, allied, issue is the general collapse of theological notions of transcendence along with the theistic interpretations of these notions, an event which has transformed the apologetic context within which the religious interest may be assessed.

The first of these issues allows for the possible extrication of the religious sensibility from bondage to strictly moral concerns by allying it more closely with the aesthetic interest. This in turn facilitates effective recourse to mystical and experiential interpretations of religion. The second issue, which advertises the general ineffectiveness of theistic metaphors, frees the pragmatist from having to speculate about the cultural importance of ideas associated with a transcendent law-giver, again reenforcing the possibility of an experiential rather than a dogmatic approach to religion.

A third issue, a distinctly pragmatic one, is simply whether the mystical, nontheistic interpretation of the religious sensibility suggested by a reevaluation of the pragmatic sources such as I shall propose is really worth the effort.

II.

The sibling values of "truth" and "rightness" have dominated the cultures of modernity. Other values, such as aesthetic beauty, or religious holiness, or philosophical importance have been clearly less significant. So much is this so that we are more likely to wonder whether it is *true* that x is beautiful than to consider the beauty of x in itself. And many of us will allow our interest in the *rightness* of something beautiful, its moral effects, to overrule any nascent aesthetic interest.

The Kantian division of cultural interests into the spheres of science, art, and morality is both effect and cause of our generally truncated and reductive approach to cultural self-consciousness. Immanuel Kant's three critiques were constructed and sustained by the philosophical superscience, the arbiter of cultural importances. Of course, religion was denied its own critique, and thereby its autonomy.

This organization, *mutatis mutandis,* was effectively ratified by Georg Wilhelm Friedrich Hegel who, however, gave religion the status of "pictorial representations" *(Vorstellungen),* aligning it more closely with art. Kant and Hegel designed the two masks behind which religion has subsequently been forced to hide. Of the two disguises, the moral and the aesthetic, it is the Kantian mask which has been most employed. Thus we more often than not find the true face of religion obscured by a moral shroud.

One of the important achievements of pragmatism is an effective reconstitution of the evidential matrix to which appeal must be made in discussing prominent philosophical issues. And though most of us will likely remain corrupted by the Kantian organization of cultural interests for some time to come, and will continue to affirm the irreducibility of at least some of the cultural interests promoted by that organization, the final escape from the strictures of Kantian philosophy, and from the unswerving belief that we have divided the experiential pie in the only viable manner, will be achieved through buying into something like the novel problematic of pragmatism.

III.

It was Peirce who most self-consciously bypassed the Kantian organization of the value spheres.[2] He did this by holding aesthetics to be the fundamental science, adjudicating logic and ethics.

Underlying Peirce's organization of the ways of knowing are his principles of Firstness, Secondness, and Thirdness. Appeal to these categories allows Peirce to provide a radical revisioning of the Kantian faculties of Feeling, Willing, and Knowing and the value spheres associated with them—namely, the aesthetic, moral, and scientific.

> The true categories of consciousness are: first, feeling, the consciousness which can be included with an instant of time, passive consciousness . . .; second, consciousness of an interruption in the field of consciousness, sense of resistance . . .; third, synthetic consciousness, binding time together, sense of learning, thought.[3]

By replacing Kant's category of Willing with the sense of action and reaction, the "polar sense,"[4] Peirce was able to relativize the Hebraic-Christian concept of "volition" (inherited from Augustine) which had narrowed the Platonic notion of "spirit" and contributed, at least as much as René Descartes' *cogito*, to the increased subjective bias of modern thinking. Also, Peirce's replacement of the "cognitive faculty" by the notion of "learning" or "acquisition" brings process notions to bear upon the enterprise of thinking and co-opts Platonic "Eros" for process philosophers in a manner supplementary to that by which A.N. Whitehead achieved the same result. Peirce's revision of the Kantian taxonomy provided a means whereby consideration of the religious sensibility could be allied with predominantly aesthetic, rather than moral concerns.

Peirce's recognition of the preeminence of the aesthetic is but one illustration of the commitment of American philosophy to the distinctly aesthetic interest. Beginning, in fact, with Jonathan Edwards, the strain of what may be called "aesthetic pluralism" which, perhaps better than any other term names the genius of American philosophy, is in evidence.[5]

Edwards' entire theology presumed the primacy of beauty. Reading Edwards, one is constantly confronted by the word "beauty" in places one would expect to see "goodness" or "truth."[6] Further, when Edwards claims that "God is the fountain and foundation of all being and beauty,"[7] he is reversing the relations of being and unity, making the former prior to the latter as a metaphysical principle. Beauty is defined as "consent to being." And since beauty is the principle of unity, it must conform to the conditions of consent set by the character of specific beings. Paradoxically, the principal condition is that of plurality. Manyness precedes oneness. Thus, God's beauty entails diversity.[8]

Emerson's conception of beauty and the aesthetic sensibility was put forward as a response to the democratic pluralism of his society in a manner not unlike Edwards' response to the presumed ontological pluralism associated with a being's consent to Being. For Emerson, knowledge is not of essences, universals, or natural kinds. What we seek to know the meaning of is "the meal in the firkin; the milk in the pan; the ballad in the street; the news of the boat; the glance of the eye. . . ."[9] Knowledge is of the congeries of particularities encountered in immediate experience.

For William James, the universe is a context within which "things are 'with' one another in many ways, but nothing includes everything, or dominates over everything. The word 'and' trails long after every sentence."[10] Both monism and pluralism are grounded in aesthetic intuitions. Beliefs such as "nature is simple and invariable; makes no leaps or makes nothing but leaps . . . express our sense of how pleasantly our intellect would feel if it had a nature of that sort to deal with."[11]

I could continue to rehearse the aesthetic pluralism of American thought by appeal to influential pragmatists such as Dewey, Mead, Rorty, and others. Such a rehearsal, however, would be somewhat strained, for there is a definite moral impulse in pragmatism existing alongside of and in tension with that of the aesthetic. What I take to be the real genius of American thought, its commitment to aesthetic pluralism, has yet to free itself from what Dewey would term the "crust of conventionalized and routine consciousness."

IV.

Whether conceived as the Divine Mind[12] of Plato (or Johannes Kepler, or Albert Einstein) or the Great Mechanic of Isaac Newton (or Benjamin Franklin) or as the Arbitrary Will of Augustine (or John Calvin), or the Telos of Nature of Aristotle (or Pierre Teilhard de Chardin, and sometimes Dewey), God has been held to transcend the world of physical nature and human experience.[13]

Beliefs associated with the various construals of theism served to undergird the sort of objectivism guaranteeing meaningfulness on the broadest scale. The world conceived as a rational pattern, paradigmatically expressible in formal mathematical terms, receives its warrant from the metaphor of God as Divine Mind. This metaphor in due course became secularized into the notion of the Principle of Sufficient Reason, or Absolute Spirit, or simply as the Laws of Nature construed in mathematical formulas. In fact "Reason" with a capital "R" is little more than a translation of this theistic metaphor.

Alternatively, the world understood as a set of causal interactions ultimately reducible to matter and motion does not have to "blindly run," but can receive the benefit of a perfectly mechanical explanation. The metaphor of God as "Great Mechanic" served that function.

The metaphor of "Arbitrary Will" is one which best articulates the sense of radical contingency to which many perforce must appeal in order to make some sense of their circumstances. There is of course a certain wildness admixed with the conditions of human experience that must be explained and controlled. Some individuals function best when they are able to organize their lives in terms of "authority" and "obedience."

The Telos of Nature was one of the most familiar and influential tropes in our culture. Its primary function was to articulate the notion of God as, in Alfred Tennyson's words, "that far off divine event towards which all creation moves."

It would be vain were one to seek a means of rendering rational, mechanistic, volitional, and teleological understandings coherent; it is sufficient to note that each has played a role in underwriting the various objectivist values and beliefs of important segments of our culture. And it is a significant comment upon our recent past to note that these objectivist interpretations have been served up, explicitly or tacitly, in a theological guise.

The naturalized religion urged by American pragmatism cannot but abandon these notions of strict transcendence upon which Western theism has been grounded from the beginning. And though metaphors of transcendence were still powerful enough throughout the classical period of pragmatism that pragmatists had to contend with them, our cultural situation today is considerably less friendly to such notions. This makes the naturalizing efforts of the pragmatist far less complicated.

Beginning with Feodor Dostoevski and Friedrich Nietzsche, and moving well past the middle of the twentieth century, Anglo-European intellectual culture experienced the "Death of God" movement in which theological interpretations of God were assaulted in such a manner as to lay to rest among large segments of the intellectual community the notion of God as source or ground of objectivist appeals. No more dramatic evidence of the intransigent copresence of these four models of Deity considered above may be found than that the Death of God movement occasioned *four* announcements of God's demise. Each of the characterizations of the death of God is an expression of some aspect of the generalized assault upon the notion of transcendence that has come to characterize our late modern period.

Some champions of the Death of God movement took as their theme the essentially Weberian notion of the disenchantment of the world through processes of secularization. Harvey Cox's *Secular City* addressed a "world come of age" in which many of the forms and functions associated with religious belief and ritual had been reconstituted in the nurturing and mediating activities of the modern city. Technology has the potential to fulfill promises associated with spiritual hope. The Great Mechanic who disposed the apparatus of our world in a beneficent manner has passed away. He has been replaced by those technical processes that reshape our world in humane terms. Yes, God is dead. But we may receive some comfort from the knowledge that He did, after all, have a long, full life—and finally died of natural causes.

God as Telos of Nature has passed on as well. As our kenotic theologians have testified, the transcendent God has poured himself into the world, and we are now served by immanent modes of spirituality. New Age religions, eclectic combinations of Christian, Buddhist, Hindu, and Sufi beliefs and practices, filtered through quasi-scientific world views, have become an expression of the spiritual activity of a large number of so-called religious individuals. God so loved the world that He gave up the life transcendent and is, indeed, defunct. We are asked to face the embarrassment of His suicide as honestly as we can.

Nietzsche's death sentence is perhaps the most familiar. The existential strain of theology associated with Nietzsche's Dionysian aspect defined human existence as a project of individual will, rendering the notion of Divine Will inimical to human autonomy. God as Arbitrary Will had to die that human beings might achieve authenticity. Thus God is dead yet again. This time a victim of patricide.

Finally, the notion of Divine Mind which had served those who defined their lives in terms of a search for truth has collapsed under the strain of both internal and external events. The union of the God of the Jews and of the Platonic Greeks presented from the very beginning an unresolvable problem of uniting passion and perfection. This problem, along with the many futile attempts to overcome it, has had consequences far beyond theological circles. The more refined the theological defense of transcendence and aseity, the more distant and effete this God was felt to be. Recently, process theologians have attempted surgical intervention to repair the internal rupture, but to no avail.

The last best member of the Quaternity expired on the operating table.

V.

The principal effects of the deaths of God have been either to underwrite a general disinterest in religion on the part of some, or to turn others away from theistic religion toward the a/theism of deconstructive, or so-called "postmodern," philosophies of religion,[14] or to lead yet others to move away from doctrinal and toward mystical interpretations of the religious sensibility.

Of the two responses which continue to take religion with some seriousness, the "postmodern" alternative proposes an aestheticized religion which in a sense merely offers the aesthetic interest as a replacement for the moral. The mystical turn promises autonomy for the religious interest and best exploits its practical relevance. Since it is essentially irrelevant to pragmatic concerns, I will leave aside the postmodern movement and deal with the reinterpretation of religious interest in what, for *serious* want of a better label, we have come to call "mystical" terms.

The first thing to stress is that the mystical turn is only partly in evidence in the most influential pragmatists. Largely this is so because the theistic metaphors did not come under full-scale attack until the mid-twentieth century. If we look at the writings of Dewey, for example, we can see that the mystical leanings are qualified by moral (and, tentatively, theistic) interpretations of religion.

The tension between moral and mystical strains in Dewey's thought can be illustrated by taking *A Common Faith* as largely representative of the former and the scattered references to mystical religion in *Experience and Nature, Human Nature and Conduct,* and *Art as Experience* as representing the latter. Note this rather typical citation from *A Common Faith*:

> I should describe this [religious] faith as the unification of self through allegiance to inclusive ideal ends, which imagination presents to us and to which the human will responds as worthy of controlling our desires and choices.[15]

Here we have Dewey trying to invoke the since-defunct "telos of nature" metaphor. Compare that statement with others from the less restrained Dewey:

> When a sense of the infinite reach of an act physically occurring in a small point of space and occupying a petty instant of time comes home to

From Loneliness to Solitude 195

us, the *meaning* of a present act is seen to be vast, immeasurable, unthinkable.[16]

The religious experience is a reality in so far as in the midst of effort to foresee and to regulate future objects we are sustained and expanded in feebleness and failure by the sense of an enveloping whole. Peace in action, not after it, is the contribution of the ideal to conduct.[17]

Any experience becomes mystical in the degree in which the feeling of the unlimited envelope becomes intense—as it may do in the experience of an object of art.[18]

First, we should note that mystical experiences per se are not theistic. Theistic concepts may be employed to interpret any given mystical experience, but the direct accounts of mystical encounters are much more diffuse than is suggested by the categories by which they are framed in theistic religions.

Further, mystical experiences do not essentially involve absoluteness or overarching unity. The "infinite reach," "enveloping whole," and "unlimited envelope" of which Dewey speaks, if the meanings of these phrases are to cohere with the rest of Dewey's philosophy, apply to an indefinite totality of things. Further, the sense of "oneness" is as much referenced to the singular detail which is to be contrasted with the totality, as to the totality itself. In a description similar to those of Dewey cited above, Whitehead makes this point rather directly:

When we survey nature and think however flitting has been the animal enjoyment of its wonders, and when we realize how incapable are the separate cells and pulsations of each flower of enjoying the total effect—then *our sense of the value of the details for the totality* dawns upon our consciousness. This is the intuition of holiness, the intuition of the sacred which is the foundation of all religion.[19]

A mystical experience can have as its primary focus the singularity and insistent particularity of the detail in its contribution to the totality. Whether, in any given phenomenological account, one stresses the "totality" or the "detail" is a matter of experiential urging. In Dewey's words:

Religion as a sense of the whole is the most individualized of all things, the most spontaneous, undefinable and varied. For individuality signifies unique connections in the whole.[20]

The most comprehensive forms of mystical experience are likely to be envisioned as pluralistic, if we translate "totality" and "whole," not as "unity," but as "all of the many things," and if we affirm the independent significance of each finite detail for this totality. It is a prior belief in monotheism, or in some form of metaphysical monism, that disposes toward monistic interpretations of mystical experience.[21]

As pragmatists, we really have no choice but to take mystical experiences with some degree of seriousness. The difficulty with rejecting them out of hand was pointed out long ago by William James:

> The existence of mystical states absolutely overthrows the pretension of non-mystical states to be the sole and ultimate dictators of what we believe.... For there can never be a state of facts to which new meaning may not truthfully be added, provided the mind ascend to a more enveloping point of view. It must always remain an open question whether mystical states may not possibly be such superior points of view, windows through which the mind looks out upon a more extensive and inclusive world.[22]

It is a question-begging enterprise, to say the least, if we exclude *ex hypothesi* the experiences of the few by appeal to the standards of the many. There are many other areas, notably in the arts, in which we permit those of greater sensitivity in this or that particular to add to the depth of our own perceptions.

The pragmatic reinterpretation of the religious sensibility would involve an essential abandonment of traditional forms of theism and the acquisition of an open attitude toward mystical reports. Such a move would allow religion to be a productive topic of reflection since it would reenforce the essentials of pragmatism construed as a form of aesthetic pluralism—that is, as a naturalistic, nominalist, radically empiricist manner of dealing with the world.

The abandonment of theism involves the jettisoning of two fundamental ideas that have had profound effects upon our social and cultural self-understanding throughout the modern period. The first is the notion of transcendence which guarantees the objective grounding, and thereby the truth and rightness, of our beliefs and practices. The second is the connection of the religious sensibility with distinctly moral and ethical concerns.

All forms of theism have provided a transcendent source undergirding, at its best, a faith and a set of beliefs which promoted a search for Truth and, at its worst, a sense of the finality of the beliefs and practices of a specific social grouping. The most significant of the beliefs and practices grounded by theisms have been moral in nature. Religious experience interpreted in terms of its moral content involves conformity with objective mind, will, purpose, or causal conditions modeled by God's nature and creative activity. Construed in mystical terms, experience is less cognitive and, moreover, carries no adjudicating moral content.

The reference of morality is to some finite selection of others over some finite temporal span—to friends, family, nation, the human species, in the short or long run. Religion refers to the relations of particulars to the unlimited totality of things, over the interminably long run. Thus morality lies somewhere between the immediacy of aesthetic experience—the experience of this, here and now—and the experience of the relation of a particular to the indefinite totality of things. It is the mystical rather than the doctrinal and theistic character of religion that best allows us to understand its distinctness and autonomy.

VI.

While a seminarian at the Chicago Theological Seminary, I heard a sermon by Paul Tillich entitled "Loneliness and Solitude," the theme of which was the contrast between "existential loneliness" and "essential solitude." In the condition of human existence, we are born, suffer, and die alone since the depth of communion or communication with others of our kind can never overcome the outsidedness of all existential relations. In reference to the Ground of Being, however, we experience the uniqueness and particular preciousness of our individual being.

I was reading Whitehead at the time of hearing Tillich's sermon and so was tempted to conflate Tillich's words with Whitehead's well-known definition of religion: "Religion is what the individual does with his own solitariness."[23] Ever after I have tended to think of the religious problematic as constituted by the tension between loneliness and solitude. Even after discarding Tillich's "Ground of Being" and yielding the theistic superstructure informing Whitehead's "Consequent Nature," the loneliness/solitude dynamic retained its evocative and interpretive significance for me. This poetic contrast, therefore, seems as effective a means as any of focusing the final issue with which I am presently concerned: Is anything truly worthwhile to be gained by the sort of speculations regarding the religious interest suggested by my remarks this far?

In the "Conclusions" to his *Varieties of Religious Experience,* William James notes that

> The warring gods and formulas of the various religions do indeed cancel each other, but there is a certain uniform deliverance in which all religions appear to meet. It consists of two parts:
> 1. An uneasiness; and
> 2. Its solution.[24]

I would say that underlying the many socio-psychological problems besetting contemporary societies is a kind of pathological loneliness. This is an appropriate name for the uneasiness which religion would be found to advertise if ever one looked beyond the canceled gods and formulas of what are oxymoronically called "spiritual institutions." The solution comes with the transmogrification of loneliness into solitude.

Among contemporary philosophers, Rorty has offered as telling a characterization as any of the uneasing effects of loneliness. Strained through his disjunctive categories of the private and public self, Rorty's analysis of loneliness reads as follows: We are alone, and loneliness is painful. This fact applies finally and with intransigence to our private selves. Of course, the public sphere is finally derived from the creative efforts of a fortunate few individuals whose metaphors catch on and serve to provide the interpretive matrix within which all of us wander. There is, therefore, a sense in which the private parts of some of us are infused into the set of public meanings, and thus some of us might feel less alone than others. Finally, however, this is of little consequence since there is no permanent set of metaphors. Accompanying all fame is the ironic recognition of its transitoriness. There is some hope for the mitigation of loneliness at the level of public existence, however. Solidarity with others provides us the only palliative we might reasonably expect to acquire.

Rorty stops well short of any appeal to mystical experiences which might give us a sense of the "vast, immeasurable, unthinkable meaning" of any given act, a sense of meaningfulness which finally offers us "peace in action." He does this in large measure, I believe because he is skeptical of the idea that one can have anything like religion without appeal to "Something or Somebody Bigger Than Ourselves,"[25] which in turn would reenforce our tendencies to have God, or the Absolute, or Objective Reason, do most of our work for us.

Rorty is finally left with efforts to overcome loneliness through solidarity with other human beings. Such solidarity is instanced throughout his works as various forms of "we-consciousness": "we Wittgensteinian therapists," "we Deweyan historicists," "we bourgeois liberals," "we citizens of North Atlantic democracies," "we liberal ironists," "we freeloading atheists," "we mortal millions."

At least for myself such appeals to solidarity are noble, but also somewhat desperate and futile. Rorty claims that solidarity groupings have "no foundation except shared hope and the trust created by such sharing."[26] But it seems to me that solidarities of the sort most in evidence in our contemporary period exist pretty much without any shared hope, are not at all characterized by trust, and have lost thereby any moral impulse. With truly few exceptions, our solidarity groupings express a kind of "morality bereft of emotion," leading them to exemplify passionless activities motivated by calculated self-interest, fainthearted political correctness, or both. Further, the vast number and variety of "we"s, and their seemingly *ad hoc* character, surely mocks the notion of solidarity.

Granted that there need be no "divine event" grounding general consensus, at least some of our ends ought be sufficiently "far off" to guarantee a degree of impartiality. But too often our loyalties are immediate, finite, and transitory. Further, the motives for our coming together shift like the desert winds, finally canceling one another as surely as do the competing gods and formulas of the various religions. Institutional religion, which in our country alone accommodates the Church Universal, the Moral Majority, and the Branch Davidians, is one more set of warring solidarities, populated by the fearful and the lonely. We need to face the reality that, in that Great Gittin' Up Mornin' we are all likely to be gittin' up at different times, and with altogether different projects in mind.

Along comes the pragmatists' mystical religion to save us by asking that we accept solitude in trade for our loneliness. This we can do only by broadening in an indefinite manner our sense of solidarity, by seeking first that kingdom in which we may share what is truly unique about us—the insistent particularities which guarantee our preciousness. Doing this we may gain a sense of vast, immeasurable meaning, a sense of the value of the details for the totality, a sustaining sense of peace in action. These feelings underlie the only unassailable form of solidarity.

Now what's wrong with this? The Church of the Insistently Particular will remain, as all churches should, Invisible. No one will be enjoined to recite creeds, pound beads, or torch the unfaithful. The members of the invisible fellowship of those who prize peace in action will make themselves known (as they always have) here and there, in this manner and that, without aspiring to a place in the *Lives of the Saints*.

But even if such a religious sensibility is not harmful, the pragmatic question remains: Is there anything finally to be gained by promoting religious interest in this form? What are the consequences of a sense of *vast, immeasurable, unthinkable meaning, of the value of the details for the totality*—of *peace in action?* I will simply assert, without argument here, that the principal consequence of recognizing that we belong to a community of precious particulars, irreplaceable details, is the maintenance of that sensitivity and strength required of any individual who would, at least occasionally, avoid falling into total self-absorption, or (what is worse) absorption into the sleazier modes of solidarity.

If such is in fact a possible consequence of trading in our loneliness for solitude, it seems the pragmatist really has no choice but to clear a broader path for the religious interest.

NOTES

1. In his *John Dewey—Religious Faith and Democratic Humanism,* Steven C. Rockefeller manages an exhaustive treatment of Dewey's approach to the religious sensibility from the beginning to the end of his career. This work demonstrates that Dewey was a remarkably "spiritual" individual in private.

2. Richard Rorty has called Peirce "the most Kantian of thinkers." See "Pragmatism, Relativism, and Irrationalism" in *The Consequences of Pragmatism* (Minneapolis: The University of Minnesota Press, 1982), p. 161. I'm not sure what he means by this other than that Peirce, like Kant, was given to taxonomies and architectonics. I would argue that the effect of Peirce's speculations, including his (always tentative) metaphysical and taxonomic activities, was to offer a creative and constructive alternative to Kant.

3. Charles Sanders Peirce, *Collected Papers* (Cambridge, MA: Harvard University Press, 1965), Vol. 1., par. 377.

4. *Ibid.,* par. 380.

5. I have discussed the aesthetic pluralism of American thought in greater detail in my *Richard Rorty—Prophet and Poet of the New Pragmatism* (Albany: State University of New York Press, 1994). See pp. 66–80.

6. Here are some citations from Edwards:

> God is God, and distinguished from all other beings, and exalted above 'em (sic!) chiefly by his divine beauty, which is infinitely diverse from all other beauty.

> It was more especially the Holy Spirit's work to bring the world to its beauty and perfection out of chaos; for the beauty of the world is the communication of God's beauty.

> [Miscellanies, #293 Yale Library Collection of Edwards Manuscripts. Quoted in Roland Delattre, *Beauty and Sensibility in the Thought of Jonathan Edwards* (New Haven: Yale University Press, 1968), p.183.]

7. Jonathan Edwards, *The Nature of True Virtue* (Ann Arbor: The University of Michigan Press, 1960), p. 15.

8. "One alone cannot be excellent, inasmuch as, in such case, there can be no consent" ["Miscellanies" p. 117, *Yale Collection of Edwards Manuscripts* (Sterling Library, Yale University).]

9. Ralph Waldo Emerson, "The American Scholar" from *The Complete Essays and Other Writings of Ralph Waldo Emerson* (New York: Modern Library, 1950), p. 61.

10. William James, *A Pluralistic Universe* (Cambridge: Harvard University Press, 1977), p. 145.

11. William James, *Principles of Psychology*. (New York: Dover, 1950), Vol. II., p. 673.

12. Somewhere, I believe it is in a note at the bottom of one of the pages *of Art as Experience*, Dewey comments that the effect of Capitalization on German thought has not received proper attention. Surely, we need wonder about its effect on all forms of theological thinking, as well.

13. I have discussed the principal models of Deity and their distinctive demises in some detail in *The Uncertain Phoenix—Adventures Toward a Post-Cultural Sensibility* (New York: Fordham University Press, 1982). See Chapter 3, "What Hath 'God' Wrought?"

14. See, for example, Mark Taylor's *Erring—A Postmodern A/Theology* (Chicago: The University of Chicago Press, 1984).

15. John Dewey, *A Common Faith*, in Jo Ann Boydston, ed., *The Later Works of John Dewey, 1925–1953* (Carbondale, Illinois: Southern Illinois University Press) Vol. 9, p. 23.

16. John Dewey, *Human Nature and Conduct* (New York: The Modern Library, 1950), p. 263.

17. *Ibid.*, p. 264.

18. *Art as Experience* in Jo Ann Boydston, ed., *The Later Works of John Dewey, 1925–1953*, Vol. 10, p. 197.

19. A.N. Whitehead, *Modes of Thought* (New York: Capricorn Books, 1958), p. 164. My italics. Whitehead continues:

> In every advancing civilization this sense of sacredness has found vigorous expression.
>
> It tends to retire into a recessive factor in experience, as each phase of civilization enters upon its decay.

It is not altogether clear whether Whitehead wants to claim that the sense of sacredness is itself a civilizing factor, or merely an accouterment of civilization. I assume that he, and Dewey, would support the former view.

20. John Dewey, *Human Nature and Conduct*, p. 331.

21. See William James' offbeat essay, "A Pluralistic Mystic," in *William James—Writings 1902–1910*, Bruce Kuklick, ed. (New York: The Library of America, 1988), pp. 1294–1313.

22. William James, *Varieties of Religious Experience*, in *William James—Writings 1902–1910*, Bruce Kuklick, ed., p. 385.

23. A. N. Whitehead, *Religion in the Making* (New York: Meridian Books, 1960). p. 16.

24. In *William James—Writings, 1902–1910*, Bruce Kuklick, ed., p. 454.

25. See Rorty's "Comments on Taylor's Paralectics." I have seen only an unpublished draft of this piece.

26. Richard Rorty, "Objectivity, Relativism, and Truth," *Philosophical Papers*, Volume I (Cambridge: Cambridge University Press, 1991), p. 33.

CORRESPONDENCE, COHERENCE, SATISFACTION, POWER:
The Four Elements Of James's Pragmatic Theory Of Truth

Fred W. Hallberg

I.

Introduction. William James was a master literary stylist. His lectures on *The Varieties of Religious Experience* (1902), *A Pluralistic Universe* (1909), and *Pragmatism* (1907) constitute a stunning philosophical and literary achievement. Yet he has had a terrible time persuading fellow academics of the merits of his views. Half the essays in his *The Meaning of Truth, A Sequel to 'Pragmatism'* (1909) consist of complaints about having been misunderstood by his critics. We find further complaints about having been mistreated by his critics in *Pragmatism* itself. He says concerning his earlier (1896) essay *The Will to Believe*:

> I wrote an essay on our right to believe, which I unluckily called the *will to believe*. All the critics, neglecting the essay, pounced on the title. Psychologically, it was impossible, morally, it was iniquitous. "The will to deceive," "the will to make-believe," were wittily proposed as substitutes for it. (*Pragmatism*, p. 168.)[1]

Given my own high estimate of James's achievement, I want to be fair to him in ways in which he claims his critics were not. Yet I too have found that he often gave his critics the rhetorical tools with which they dismantled his views. Honesty requires that I acknowledge *both* the tools he gave his critics *and* his positive achievements. I shall attempt to do this by proposing some modest re-formulations of James's theses which acknowledge his occasional slips and inconsistencies while preserving what I believe is most important about his pragmatic theory of truth.

II.

Pragmatic Truth as Warranted Belief. Had I been the editor of the published version of *Pragmatism*, I would have proposed that the sixth lecture, entitled "The Pragmatic Conception of Truth," be re-titled "The Pragmatic Conception of *Warranted Belief.*" I would have further proposed that the phrase "pragmatic truth" be replaced by "pragmatically warranted belief" wherever it occurs throughout the lectures. Had James been persuaded to make such a modification, the bulk of his rhetorical inconsistencies would have disappeared, and his critics' main objections would have been avoided.

James would never have accepted such a suggestion. He would have resisted because he wished to defend an ontology of genuine novelty and becoming (pp. 167–168). He wished to defend these ideas because novelty and becoming were for James essential features of *life,* and he was committed to defending a view of nature as having a *life,* the way a human being has a life which embodies growth and change. He also wished to ground the value of our personal efforts and achievements by reference to the way they contributed to the evolution of the cosmos itself (pp. 166–167). The correspondence theory of truth, which James usually called the "intellectual" or the "agreement" theory, entailed for James the *negation* of this prized thesis concerning cosmic growth and change. He reasoned that if "truth" is simply what corresponds to the book of nature, and if that book is already written, then novelty and becoming must be illusions (pp. 167–168).

I believe this worry was entirely unjustified. The inference from "truth" as correspondence to the unreality of novelty and change depended on a too simple and inadequate version of the truth. *If* there is genuine novelty and change, *then* a true account of nature must adequately reflect, or "agree with" that fact.

The history of science since James died in 1910 has been very favorable toward his views concerning the reality of cosmic novelty and change. The only two examples of novelty he could offer were Darwinian evolution (p. 79) and human cultural inventiveness (pp. 53, 164–166). Consensual science has since added at least three items to this list. First, the discontinuities and indeterminacies postulated by quantum mechanics have been massively confirmed.[2] Second, the phenomenon of cosmic expansion entails the continuous creation of negative entropy which can be understood as a source of novelty in nature.[3] And finally, Ilya Prigogine's work with "dissipative structures" functioning in regimes far from thermodynamic equilibrium shows how such systems can spontaneously generate and sustain new structures which cannot be predicted by causal means.[4] If we add these three to James's two examples, we get five kinds of genuine novelty in the world which any *true* account of nature must incorporate or express.[5]

III.
Pragmatism Applied to Objective Knowledge of Matters of Fact. If we read James as I have suggested, as defending an epistemological account of warranted belief, what he proposes is very sophisticated and captures much of what would be required of any adequate epistemology. James is proposing what I might call an "ecological" or a "contextualized" theory of warranted belief, in which genuine answers to legitimate questions are understood to be as diverse as the list of human interests or concerns. Ian Hacking has (in private conversation) contrasted Leibniz's idea of the "book of knowledge" with the idea of the "magazine of knowledge." Pick up any general interest magazine such as *Scientific American*. You will find it is composed of the most amazing variety of articles. What on earth do these topics have in common? Nothing, beyond *being of interest to* a certain group of readers.

Our system of received knowledge exhibits a similar absence of substantive uniformity. It is organized into disciplines, but it is as difficult to say what holds a discipline together as it is to say what articles in a general interest magazine have in common. They are unified mainly by having contents that are of interest to a fairly stable community of inquirers. That is why James denies we have any *general* obligation to speak the truth if that obligation is understood to exist in abstraction from the speakers' interests (pp. 150–151). I would argue it is this background of relevance to human interests which ties *warranted* beliefs to *those beliefs it is good for us to hold*. (Actually, James links knowledge and value by identifying *truth* with humanly warranted beliefs [p. 145]. But this move is unnecessary so long as warranted belief is always linked to the relevant interests, as it is when the warrant arises in a community defined by a common research project.)

Given this background assumption, that the answers sought in an inquiry are those which are relevant to the interests of the members of the community of inquirers, what can we say about the *kinds* of knowledge which inquirers are typically able to secure concerning the world as objective, scientific, fact? James gives two very similar lists of four such kinds of knowledge of objective fact, the first in Lecture VI and the second in Lecture VII (pp. 132–133, 138–139, and 160). The first list runs as follows: 1) statements about the manifest traits of small numbers of dry-goods-sized objects which are accessible to immediate observation, 2) statements about logical or mathematical truths, 3) statements about the dispositional traits of material objects, and 4) statements about the past.

I have a problem with his second category because he applies the "agreement" or "correspondence" theory to mathematical truths just as he does to truths about material objects. This would imply a very strong version of Platonism concerning the nature of mathematical truth, a view which is not supported by any sort of strong consensus among contemporary philosophers.[6] I notice James omits any mention in this list of statistical generalizations about classes of elements based on an allegedly "representative" sample. Yet he *refers to* this form of judgment when he speaks of generalities which are *funded by* observable data the way a credit system is funded by a small cash reserve (p. 137). Since statistical generalization constitutes an important type of objective knowledge about matters of fact, and since the peculiarities of mathematical knowledge are so peripheral to his main philosophical concerns, I propose that we simply replace his second category with that of statistical generalization. The resulting list of four categories does seem to me to constitute a reasonably adequate and accurate description of the most frequently employed types of objective knowledge about matters of fact.

Concerning these four types of knowledge, James accepts what I would call a "realistic" definition of truth as "correspondence with reality." (He actually uses the phrases "the intellectual definition" or "agreement with reality" to designate this idea [p. 132].) But he then asks the further question: What does agreement with reality *mean* in this context? "Agreement" is a metaphor. How can it be unpacked?

James argues quite persuasively that the notion of "agreement" can only be given a literal interpretation in the case of the first sort of judgment about the traits of small numbers of dry-good-sized objects accessible to immediate observation. His example is a statement about a clock on the wall of the lecture hall where he is speaking. One can, in this case, provide a literal specification of the three components of the "agreement" formula. There is first the linguistic proposition which James asserted and which his hearers understood about the time which the clock indicated. Second, there are the criteria which would have to be manifested by the clock to make his statement about it true. And third, there is the actual dusty, metal-encased and glass-faced object to which the criteria may be applied to ascertain whether what he said was in fact true.

In this domain and this domain alone James is happy to endorse the "intellectualist" analysis of truth as agreement with, or as correspondence to, fact. But this only covers a small proportion of the sorts of truth-claims we are concerned to validate in ordinary life, and in none of the other cases can we unpack the relevant metaphors to yield an unambiguous and literal sense. Consider my second category of statements about classes with numerous inaccessible members. Suppose James said in addition to the fact that the clock on the wall registered 8:10, that the wall clocks at Harvard were generally more accurate than were those at Columbia where he was speaking. This sort of claim about large numbers of objects distributed across only partly accessible regions of space and time could never be verified by direct inspection the way one could verify the statement about the present individual clock. We would be driven in the case of the comparative generalization to use *sampling* methods to test the directly accessible members of the class and then to *project* the results of these tests onto the larger target population. The "agreement" formula still seems to be applicable, but unavoidable uncertainty about the accuracy of the sample makes this a very different sort of epistemological beast. The vernacular complaint about "lies, damned lies, and statistics" highlights the risky nature of all such claims. They may rest on a system of epistemological "credit" as James proposed, but all too often no one has the time or resources to determine whether the credit is actually sound (p. 137).

The third type of knowledge claim concerns dispositional properties determined by deliberate manipulations. His example is the *elasticity* of the spring which presumably drives the mechanical clock on the wall. Elasticity is not an individual substance or event which could be directly observed. It is a *potentiality* which is expressed by subjunctive, counter-to-fact conditional sentences such as: "*Were* the spiral spring to be wound more tightly than it was originally and released, then it *would* exert a force on the clock mechanism which would operate the clock until the spring returned to its original, unwound state." This potential can be counted on to manifest itself in a regular law-like way in the future *even if* it is not currently being manifested. It shows itself not in any *one* instance, but in its *repeatability across* instances. Since this power cannot be directly observed in any one replication, the criteria cannot be applied directly to their object here as they can in the case of an individual thing.

The fourth and final kind of objective knowledge of matters of fact which James discusses is our knowledge about the past (pp. 139, 141). There can be no direct application of criteria to things in this context, because experience is bound to the present (p. 141). Recent past events may be known by memory and testimony, but these witnesses to the past can only be relied on in the context of corroborating evidence. The operative criterion of correctness here is *coherence among* these elements, not "agreement" or "correspondence" as in the case of the clock (pp. 141–142, 146, 152). Our knowledge of the *remote* past, such as the acts of Julius Caesar or "the antediluvian monsters," can only be known by inference from circumstantial evidence (p. 141). To speak of "agreement" or "correspondence" in this context is to engage in hand-waving by means of metaphors which *cannot* be unpacked into *any* literal content, even in principle.

IV.

Shift from Fact to Value: The Satisfaction and Power Criteria of Pragmatic Truth. To summarize James's argument so far, there are at least four distinct types of warranted belief-affirmations about objective matters of fact. The correspondence theory of truth can only be applied in the literal sense to statements of the first type, which are far from the most important or most frequently employed type of statement which we seek to warrant by means of inquiry. At the very least, James's pragmatic theory of truth is a brief in favor of active experimentation as opposed to passive observation as a means to significant knowledge, together with the claim that *coherence* among items of evidence is far more important for warranting significant truth-claims than is correspondence to fact. So far the argument seems to be perfectly correct and even uncontroversial. But this description of the spectrum of types of objective knowledge obscures the main thrust of James's argument. His central thesis is not merely that the correspondence theory of truth does precious little work in the over-all economy of our system of knowledge. It is rather that this entire spectrum of objective knowledge of matters of fact merely provides the stage setting and backdrop for the really important issues of our lives. The important questions are not about matters of fact, but about our justification as persons and whether our lives are worth living.

The status of personal justification has become a problem in modern culture because the explosion of knowledge of fact since the seventeenth Century. The rapid growth of this type of knowledge has at least suggested to some observers that *knowledge of objective matters of fact may be the only real knowledge there is.* (James lists Spencer, Darwin, Ostwald, and Mach as informed contemporaries who had come to precisely this conclusion.) The Epicureans had shown us how knowledge of value could be added to knowledge of objective fact by treating the value of pleasure and the dis-value of pain as observable traits of sentient beings. The problem with this view is that the over-all balance of pleasures versus pains imposed by the necessities of nature is pretty certainly negative in the normal course of events. Young persons might be able to sustain a preponderance of pleasures over pains, but by middle age this will have become exceedingly difficult, and all hedonistic aspirations will finally be undone by the ravages of time.

The grim prospects of a purely hedonistic life may be transcended for a while by shifting one's concern from the passive consumption of pleasure to the active realization of freely elected projects. Are you bored or unhappy? *Get a hobby!* The great personal advantage of what James calls "the strenuous life" is that it circumvents the problem of the "sick soul" which James sees as the cost of a disengaged and contemplative life style (pp. 179–180, 186).[7] But even the strenuous life devoted to the realization of one's self-selected projects is going to be undone by senescence and death. So why not why not opt for a comparatively quick and painless suicide as a means of escaping the frustration which constitutes a life lived within the horizon of objective fact?

James was like his philosophical soul-mate John Stuart Mill, in that he had a history of difficulty with depression.[8] We might attribute this propensity to a physiological vulnerability, or to unresolved feelings of competitiveness and hostility toward powerful male figures in their lives. Whatever the cause, James found the world when viewed from what Husserl called "the objective standpoint" to be depressing because it allowed no conceptual resources for even addressing the question of whether life was worth enduring at all.

James was enormously impressed by an argument articulated by the British statesman A.J. Balfour in his (1879) *A Defense of Philosophic Doubt* and his (1895) *Foundations of Belief*. Balfour argued that both naturalism and theism rested on principles which could not be proved by reference to data (such as the "principle of the uniformity of nature" for naturalism and the "providence of creation" for theism). Since neither set of fundamental principles could be decided by reference to data, Balfour argued, we are intellectually free to consider *other* reasons when making our choice. The life-affirming optimism of theism made it more worthy of our affirmation than did the nihilism implied by a rigorous naturalism.[9]

This is essentially the argument defended by James in his (1895) essay "Is Life Worth Living?" and in his (1896) essay "The Will to Believe."[10] James is concerned in *Pragmatism* to limit the authoritarian pretensions of the "intellectual" definition of truth and to defend the reality of novelty in nature. But he is concerned above all to clear a cognitive space within which questions of merit and justification may be addressed and settled in an affirmative manner. That is why the status of religious beliefs looms so large in James's philosophy. The rhetorical structure of *Pragmatism* is built on the polar opposition between "tender minded" and "tough minded" personalities and styles of philosophy. (This structure of polar opposition corresponds exactly to that in Balfour's *Foundations of Belief*.) The great advantage of pragmatism, according to James, is that it is catholic enough to permit both poles of this opposition to be explored without prejudgment. Pragmatism enjoins us to affirm whatever symbol-system addresses our deepest need for a relation to a source of authentic value (p. 33) and which enables us to sustain this relation in the long term and on the whole (p. 145).

James does not advocate simply shutting our eyes to unpleasant realities. The vision of the good which we instantiate in our account of the real must be compatible with both current sense experience (such as that of the clock on the wall), and with the entire body of propositions which have been confirmed in the past. He quotes Emerson in reply to those who complain that his pragmatism can be used to justify too much. "If anyone imagines this law to be lax, let him keep its commandments for one day" (p. 152).

The whole point of James's pragmatic theory of truth is to ensure that the system of objective truth about matters of fact does not close the lists of the real. The total set of truths about nature understood as objective fact leaves, according to James, the issue of whether life is worth living entirely open and undecided. But *how* are such issues to be addressed within the pragmatic theory of truth? At this point James unveils *two further* criteria of truth (beyond correspondence to fact and coherence with existing fact). These are the criteria of satisfaction and power.

Concerning the first criterion of satisfaction, James says precious little that is specific. He does say that truth is one species of good (p. 59), and he attempts a quasi-Kantian "transcendental deduction" of that claim. He argues that if this essential connection between value and truth did not obtain, the idea that truth is important would never have become a widely-held dogma (p. 59). He claims that *"The 'true' . . . is only the expedient in our way of thinking, just as the 'right' is only the expedient in the way of our behaving. Expedient . . . in the long run and on the whole of course. . . ."* (p. 145). What James means by "expedient" here cannot mean what it does in ordinary life. Yet what he *does* mean is never made explicit with further analysis or examples.

I believe there are several good reasons why James leaves the criterion of "satisfaction" undeveloped. The most important is the bewildering variety of legitimate interests which persons may pursue in the course of their everyday lives. That is why he denies we have a *general* obligation to acknowledge truths. He says:

> Truth with a big T, and in the singular claims abstractly to be recognized, of course, but concrete truths in the plural need be recognized only when their recognition is expedient. A truth must always be preferred to a falsehood when both relate to the situation; but when neither do truth is as little of a duty as falsehood. If you ask me what o'clock it is and I tell you I live at 95 Irving Street, my answer may indeed be true, but I don't see why it is my duty to give it (pp. 150–151).

The variety of interests engaged by inquiry may make it difficult to say very much that is systematic about the important forms of human satisfaction. But it does not make the task impossible. John Stuart Mill, to whose memory James dedicated his lectures on pragmatism, accomplished some useful work along this line. The theory of intrinsic good defended by J.S. Mill's father and by Jeremy Bentham was simple and intelligible, but patently false. Bentham held that pleasure was good and the only good, and that all pleasures were qualitatively identical. They differed in quantity not merit or status. Against this view Mill argued there are at least five distinct categories of intrinsic good.[11] He listed:

1) Pleasure is good but some pleasures are better than others. "Better Socrates dissatisfied than a pig satisfied" (*Utilitarianism*, Ch. 2, p. 197).
2) The development of intellectual mastery is good, even if it hurts. "The truth of a proposition is part of its utility" (*Essay on Liberty*, Ch. 2, p. 274).
3) The development and exercise of *any* talent, whether athletic, artistic, or social, is good, even if it hurts (*Essay on Liberty*, Ch. 3, p. 306).

4) The exercise of personal autonomy is good (*Essay on Liberty*, Ch. 3, p. 324; this is a direct repudiation of Bentham's ideas for prison reform and for the role of "experts" in the task of improving the "vulgar' in the thought of both Bentham and his father).

5) Sympathy is good (*Utilitarianism*, Ch. 2, p. 201, also see *Autobiography*, Ch. V, pp. 83–87 and Ch. VI, p. 111; the sort of relation of mutuality and reciprocity which he had with Harriet Taylor is an indispensable component of the good life).

James did in fact describe and analyze most of these sources of intrinsic good in his occasional essays. He defended what Mill meant by "sympathy" in his (1899) essay "On a Certain blindness in Human Beings."[12] He defended the prudential imperative of developing and exercising our abilities in his (1899) "What Makes Life Significant?," in his (1907) "The Energies of Men," and in his (1910) "The Moral Equivalent of War."[13] Of course the whole of *Pragmatism* breathes with the value of intellectual and personal autonomy, where acceptance of heteronomy is treated as the vice of a "sick soul" (pp. 86, 188, 193). There is enough material here to enable us to confidently project how James might have developed a more systematic account of the authentic forms of "satisfaction" had he chosen to do so within his lectures on pragmatism. It would have been very similar to Mill's account of the sources of intrinsic good.

What about the other half, the *power* component, of the criteria of non-factual pragmatic truth? When discussing pragmatism and religion in his concluding eighth lecture, James asks why must *all* be saved? There is after all real loss in life, so why not contemplate losers as well as winners in the domain of religious justification (p. 190)? This comment should be read together with his comment in the sixth lecture that pragmatic truth is what is expedient in the long run and on the whole. This reference to the "long run" is an allusion to Peirce's "convergence theory of truth" as "that which all inquirers will eventually agree upon" (p. 145).[14] This conjoint affirmation of expediency, winners and losers, and the convergence theory moved Bertrand Russell to comment as follows:

> This philosophy, therefore, although it begins with liberty and toleration, develops, by inherent necessity, into the appeal to force and the arbitrament of big battalions. By this development it becomes equally adapted to democracy at home and imperialism abroad.[15]

Russell's crack about pragmatism justifying imperialism abroad is plainly unfair to James, who happily identifies his own tolerant pluralism with the "irresponsibility" of those who advocate Home-Rule for the Irish and who suppose Filipinos are fit for self-government (p. 169).[16] The appeal to "power" by James and Peirce is *not* the power of "big battalions" as Russell supposes. It is rather the *persuasive* power of an idea in the context of inquiry protected by the moral requirements of due process and free expression.

I must confess I did not always appreciate the importance of this "power" component in the legitimation of belief. Modern philosophy began with Descartes as a reaction against the religiously and politically motivated repression of dissent, such as the Church's condemnation of Galileo. To protect himself from such threats, Descartes invented and defended the myth of the lonesome, heroic, knowledge-seeker, who could critique his entire culture and ratify a new system of belief entirely out of his own resources. This myth of the individual critic and creator of new cultural forms endured through the entire tradition of empiricism up to the late versions of Logical Positivism defended by A.J. Ayer after World War II.

The current critique of "foundationalism" in epistemology consists in large part of the repudiation of this Cartesian myth of the individual knower. I first encountered the force of this anti-foundational critique when, as a youthful Cartesian empiricist, I read Nowell-Smith's (1957) *Ethics*. Nowell-Smith's book was an attempt to defend a version of rule-utilitarianism on neo-Wittgensteinian grounds. The argument in the book which stopped me in my tracks arose from the question of the alleged similarity of the ratification procedures concerning judgments in ethics and judgments about matters of fact.[17] Nowell-Smith asked: What are the background conditions which are necessary to make out the distinction between appearance and reality in either domain? The starting point in either case would be an initial conflict among reported judgments by the parties involved. Consider the case of judging the weight of an object, such as a heavy reference book. If I attempt to carry such an object on a long hike, it will *seem* to grow heavier as my walk proceeds. Whereas if I ask members of a group of persons to heft it and judge its weight, I will receive a *wide range* of differing judgments. We do not suppose in such contexts, Nowell-Smith argued, that the book actually becomes heavier as my walk proceeds, or that it weighs a different amount in each person's hands. We instead distinguish between the *real* weight of the book and what it *seems to* weigh at different times to different observers. What must we suppose, Nowell-Smith asked, about both the world and about human practice for such a distinction to be successfully employed?

Nowell-Smith arrived at two necessary background conditions (to which I have, upon reflection, added a third). First, there must be an available decision procedure which is accepted as relevant by the overwhelming majority of the participants in the inquiry. In this case the relevant procedure would be to *weigh* the book on a calibrated scales. Second, the procedure would have to be such that when applied, the *initial range* of conflicting intuitions would become *markedly smaller* than they were originally. (The practice off weighing or measuring the traits of objects will generally yield such a convergence of results. Those who have actually attempted precision measurement in the context of laboratory experiments or of tool and die making will be painfully aware that *no* such measurement yields *exactly one replicable result*. The best one can hope for is to reduce the *range* of variability within specified limits.) Finally, the third condition (which I have decided was missing from Nowell-Smith's original list) is that the procedures must be such that they do not of themselves bring about any one outcome, as would be the case if one held one's thumb on the scales.

If these three conditions are met, we will be able to successfully employ the distinction between the way something *appears* to a particular observer, and the way it *really is* from an objective point of view. This analysis works for determining such primary physical traits as an object's mass, size, or duration. But what about the non-physical objects of belief which James discusses in his third and eighth lectures, such as whether we should believe in God or whether we should view our selves as justified or our lives as worth living? Can we define objectivity in this sort of context *without* the use of physical measuring instruments?

Of course we can. We can never be separated from the "instrument" for detecting meaning and value. This "instrument" is the perceptions and judgments of intact, functioning persons who have mastered the relevant language and who participate in some communal arena of inquiry. The "procedures" for applying this "instrument of measurement" are none other than the moral requirements of freedom of expression and fairness of treatment of differing perspectives in the decision making process. *Robert's Rules of Order* is one version of these moral requirements. Those elements of the U.S. constitution and in the history of federal case law which protect expression and which require that everyone be treated equally before the law are another. Kant's "three formulations of the Categorical Imperative" is perhaps the most adequate succinct statement of these requirements. What all these sets of requirements share in common is protected expression and a procedure of decision-making (by a plebiscite, for example), which ensures that all points of view are heard and are allowed to influence the outcome. When such moral requirements are widely recognized as relevant for legitimate decision-making, and when they are applied to the actual decision making process, there is almost always a marked *movement toward* consensus. Whenever such conditions and procedures generate such an uncoerced movement toward consensus, then we are able to apply the distinction between appearance and reality to the difference between the early confusion and the late agreement. These procedural considerations apply to decisions about warrant across the board, whether the subject matter is about matters of fact on the one hand, or about faith and morals on the other. Since the very same requirements and procedures apply equally to both domains, the philosopher must either be a skeptic in both domains or in neither. Selective skepticism would be pragmatically inconsistent.

I have so far followed James's order of exposition in his sixth lecture on pragmatic truth. I have begun with our encounter with physical facts (such as the clock on the wall), and have moved down through judgments which are ever more remote from such "data" (such as judgments about the elasticity of the spring or about events in the remote past). I finally arrived at the satisfaction and power criteria of pragmatic truth which are necessary to yield warranted judgments concerning matters of faith and morals. But this rhetorical "progression" is philosophically misleading. Our allegedly "direct" perception of the physical facts about the clock on the wall is itself informed by a set of interpretive categories which *also* exist for evaluative reasons. The very concept of "clock," and of the "hours" and "minutes" indicated by hands of differing length, as well as the division of the 24 hour day into a 12 hours of "a.m." and "p.m.," are all human constructs which have been created and ratified by the very same procedures of uncoerced consensus-formation which we employ to make decisions concerning human concepts of justice and value. "The trail of the human serpent is over everything," says James, even over the "data" of immediate sense apprehension (p. 53; see also pp. 163–166.) What is fundamental to inquiry is neither data nor interpretative frameworks, but those *legitimate procedures of uncoerced consensus formation* which enable us to distinguish objectively warranted judgments from merely subjective opinions.

V.

The Social Dimension of Pragmatic Truth. The philosophical revolution on which James has embarked is not yet complete. We have moved from data to theories to the procedures by means of which judgments may be objectively warranted. But such procedures exist, if at all, as the *institutionalized* practices of *historically extant communities of persons.* Objectively warranted judgments are possible, therefore, only in the context of *institutions* of a certain sort. James neglects to say anything specific about this institutional background of legitimate knowledge.

What sort of institutions are required in order to make knowledge possible? The fully functioning and participatory members of communities of inquiry must have mastered a native language which enables them to formulate the relevant questions and apply the categories necessary to participate in the discussion. But the acquisition of a language requires at least the functional equivalent of a nursery within which children could be cared for and in which the complex structures of the language could be mastered. There must be, in other words, something like the institution of the *family* in which mothers would have the safety, resources, and leisure necessary to bring their pre-linguistic infants to the status of functioning participants in the linguistic community. Beyond the rudimentary linguistic skills acquired in the nursery, there must be some sort of extended educational enterprise by means of which the more specialized and demanding knowledge and skills of the culture may be transmitted from the older masters to their more youthful apprentices. A minimum precondition of the existence of ratified pragmatic "truth," in James's sense of the term, must be the *power* of such institutions to *perpetuate themselves across generations.* This is the cultural correlative to species "viability" in neo-Darwinian evolution. An idea is *true* (or more precisely, *objectively warranted*) by the pragmatic criterion only if it demonstrates the *power*, in actual history, *to generate institutions which endure.* In the context of religious belief, an idea is pragmatically "true" (i.e., objectively warranted) only if it leads to the creation of an ecclesiastical organization which endures for generations. Otherwise the religious idea is pragmatically "false."

This is a consequence of Peirce's social consensus (or "power") definition of truth which James missed entirely. James remained to the end so focused on the issue of the status and autonomy of the individual that he never perceived the necessity of dealing with the role of institutions in the procedures for warranting truth-claims. His (1902) *Varieties of Religious Experience* was devoted entirely to the religious experiences of individuals, and simply omitted any mention of the structures of shared experience within an ecclesiastic community. But apart from such institutionalized communities of belief, with their (at least sometimes!) legitimate procedures for distinguishing orthodoxy from heresy, the question of objective warrant cannot be coherently addressed. (That was the point of Nowell-Smith's argument concerning objective judgments in ethics.) James thus led those, who like himself were fascinated by the facts of religious experience, down a dead end epistemological path. The individualism of James's approach to religious experience is what enabled contemporary critics like Wayne Proudfoot to reject the facts which James so painstakingly catalogued as irrelevant to the objective warrant of religious beliefs.[18] Of course Proudfoot's critique *only* applies to the experiences of isolated individuals, and not to the legitimacy of warrant arrived at by means of due process within institutionalized religious communities.

Alasdair MacIntyre has argued, in two concluding chapters of his (1988) *Whose Justice?, Which Rationality?*, that the procedures by means of which a non-native-born person is initiated into the language and practices of an (initially) alien institution, is so similar to that by means of which the native-born member is apprenticed into that same institution, that such "conversions" of adult outsiders cannot be forbidden without rendering the entire institution illegitimate.[19] This implies that each warranting institution is in a state of implicit competition with all others for membership, and that those institutions which embody (or are at least close to) pragmatic truth reveal that about themselves not merely by *enduring* across generations, but by *growing* relative to the competition.

The relation of perseverance and growth to the power criterion of pragmatic "truth" shows why it is unhelpful and confusing to try to change the meaning of truth as ordinarily understood (that is, to change it from what James calls the "intellectual" or "agreement" theory of truth). What James is really talking about in the context of "pragmatic truth" is the procedures by means of which our beliefs are *warranted*. But as James of all people knew, what is warranted by evidence and arguments today may not be warranted tomorrow. *That is why the category of "truth" must be used sparingly and cautiously, and almost exclusively for judgments about the past.* The quest for naked truth is much like a Kantian's quest for things in themselves. As James says, access to things themselves is not (literally) available to us (p. 162–163). I conclude that it is best to *surrender* the claim of truth in most everyday contexts, and to speak of *warranted belief* instead. If we disconnect from the conflicts and party factions of the present day, however, we *can* get a purchase on what has come *close to the truth* through long stretches of historical time. One would not need statistics or complicated sociological analyses to discern that Paul's version of Christianity has proven itself to be closer to the truth than, say, Mithraism. One might hazard the plausible guess that Luther's and Calvin's version of Protestantism has been closer to the truth than the Anabaptist teachings of Menno Simons, given the enduring size and influence of the resulting denominations. But would anyone dare say whether contemporary Lutheranism or contemporary Presbyterianism is closer to the truth? Only God could tell.

Notice that the procedures of legitimation encompassed under the power criterion of pragmatic truth do *not* imply a total victory on the part the winners, and an unconditional surrender on the part of the losers. It is rather that the relation of the winners to the losers is symbiotic, like that of predators to prey in a dynamic eco-system. The very legitimacy of the winners' status depends on the existence of the dissenting losers in order to ratify the legitimacy of the winner's victory. Small dissenting denominations like the Mennonites function in the total economy of religious legitimation the way the Satan's rebellion functioned to ratify God's majesty and glory in the theological economy of Milton's *Paradise Lost*. The failure of their dissent to yield any significant positive social effects is necessary in order to make evident the legitimacy of those institutionalized systems of belief which are able to fill churches or temples with enthusiastic participants for decades and centuries on end.

NOTES

1. William James, *Pragmatism*, edited by R. B. Perry (New York, NY: Meridian Books, 1955 [1907]). All page references will be to this edition of his lectures on pragmatism.

2. Nick Herbert, *Quantum Reality* (Garden City, NY: Anchor Press, 1985), Ch. 7.

3. David Layzer, *Cosmogenesis* (New York, NY: Oxford University Press, 1990), Ch. 9.

4. Gregoire Nicolis and Ilya Prigogine, *Exploring Complexity* (New York, NY: W. H. Freeman and Co., 1989), Ch. 3.

5. Of course these facts about real becoming do have significant metaphysical implications. If becoming is real there must be an irreducible asymmetry between past and future times. Only the present and past would be fully determinate or individuated, and there would have to be a framework of absolute time in which to locate this metaphysically real transition from past to future. Fortunately for James, absolute time is no longer a problem, since general relativity allows a version of "absolute" time determined by reference to cosmic expansion. Since not all future states of an expanding cosmos can be predicted from the past, James need not have worried about his spiritual freedom being suffocated by a causally closed natural order (pp. 82–86).

6. Penelope Maddy, *Realism in Mathematics* (New York, NY: Oxford University Press, 1992), Ch. 1.

7. William James, "The Absolute and the Strenuous Life," in *The Meaning of Truth* (Cambridge, MA: Harvard University Press, 1975 [1909]), Ch. X, p. 124.

8. William Dean, *The Religious Critic in American Culture* (Albany, NY: State University New York Press, 1994), pp. 42–45.

9. John Passmore, "Pragmatism and Its European Analogues," in *A Hundred Years of Philosophy* (London: G. Duckworth and Co., 1962), Ch. 5, p. 100.

10. William James "Is Life Worth Living?" in *Essays on Faith and Morals*, edited by R. B. Perry, (New York, NY: Meridian Books, 1972), pp. 1–31; and "The Will to Believe," pp. 32–62.

11. John Stuart Mill, *Essential Works of John Stuart Mill: Utilitarianism, Autobiography, On Liberty, The Utility of Religion,* edited by Max Lerner (New York, NY: Bantam Books, 1971). All page references are to this edition.

12. William James, "On a Certain Blindness in Human Beings," in *Essays in Faith and Morals* (Op. Cit., 1972) Ch. IX, pp. 259–284.

13. *Ibid.*, "What Makes Life Significant?" Ch. X, pp. 285–310; and "The Energies of Men," Ch. VII., pp. 216–237; and "The Moral Equivalent of War," Ch XI, pp. 311–328.

14. C. S. Peirce, "Critical Review of Berkeley's Idealism," in *Values in a Universe of Chance*, edited by Philip P. Wiener (New York, NY: Doubleday Anchor, 1958 [1871]), pp. 81–82.

15. Bertrand Russell, "Pragmatism," in *Philosophical Essays* (New York, NY: Simon and Schuster, 1966 [1909]), Ch. IV, p. 110.

17. P. H. Nowell-Smith, *Ethics*, (New York, NY: Philosophical Library, 1957), Ch. 4, Sec. 2, pp. 46–50.

18. Wayne Proudfoot, *Religious Experience* (Berkeley, CA: University of California Press, 1985), Ch. VI and Conclusion, pp. 190–236, esp. pp. 230–236.

19. Alasdair MacIntyre, *Whose Justice?, Which Rationality?* (Notre Dame, IN: University of Notre Dame Press, 1988), pp. 363–365, 374–375, 388.

PRAGMATISM, PHILOSOPHICAL RESPECTABILITY AND THE MEANING OF LIFE

Yeager Hudson

I shall argue that paleo-pragmatism, despite some appearances to the contrary, concerned itself in a very substantial way with the problem of finding life worth living, which is after all the most pressing of *human* concerns, whether *philosophers* are willing to admit it or not. Indeed, during most of the twentieth century that concern disqualified anyone for the title of philosopher, or "real" philosopher, or professional philosopher. What is remarkable about the paleo-pragmatists is that they managed to maintain a measure of philosophical respectability because of their successful pursuit of *sanctioned* interests while at the same time keeping in touch to an admirable degree with living, breathing human beings and their concerns.

We think of existentialism as the movement that was sensitive to the pervasive and creeping sense of meaninglessness or absurdity characteristic of so much of the twentieth century. They were the ones who sacrificed all claims to being real philosophers by their dabbling with evil, suffering, anxiety, futility, nothinglessness—questions of *meaning*, in the sense of the *purpose*, if any, of human existence. Paleo-pragmatism, in apparently sharp contrast with the existentialists, and especially in the person of Charles Sanders Peirce and John Dewey, gave every appearance of being concerned with what some in that era called the *science* of philosophy, with philosophy worthy of the purified sense of the term *science*. The pragmatists were concerned with *cognitive* meaning and scientific method, and thus sustained a modicum of philosophical respectability because they could be thought of as treating existential issues as subordinate or peripheral. Of course, William James lectured and wrote quite shamelessly about *human* issues and about religion, but Peirce's predominate concerns were quite abstract and technical, having to do with such things as making our ideas clear, with operational definitions of scientific terms such as "hard," "force," and "weight," and with the refining of scientific method—topics far enough removed from any of the mushy claims of hidebound philosophy to leave even a logical positivist feeling relatively safe and unthreatened. Even Dewey talked enough about "scientific method," "experimentation," and "verification" to throw the superficial observer off guard, although a closer look revealed a disconcerting vagueness which might suggest a lack of mastery of genuine philosophical [i.e., analytic] techniques. At least he realized the importance of science and attempted to make use of its methodology rather than to pontificate from a philosophical bully pulpit when he turned his attentions to such practical matters as how to educate our children, improve our social institutions, unionize our professors and our blue collar workers, and, generally speaking, how to promote democracy. "Real" philosophy, philosophy which was to be regarded as worthy of the name, was on its way to avoiding any involvement with practical matters, and the conventional wisdom emerging at the time was that philosophy had to become "professional," which ruled out anything as cracker-barreled as values, purpose or religion. We can say in defense of Dewey's philosophical respectability that he mostly avoided any involvement with religious ideas. Indeed, he turned his attention explicitly to religion only in one little book, *A Common Faith,* and then only because the lecture series he was invited to give at Yale, from which the book came, required that the lecturers address the subject of religion in an age of science.

It was the absolutists like Josiah Royce who were the chief source of embarrassment to those who wanted to make philosophy scientifically respectable. And despite James' preoccupation with religious and existential issues, at least he brought to his study of them the skills of a medically trained mind, and a measure of scientific detachment. To his credit in the eyes of the "real" philosophers, he explicitly embraced empiricism, but on the negative side from their point of view he also firmly insisted that empiricism *must* be radical: that is, it must take account of *all* kinds of human experience, including moral, aesthetic and religious experience, and not just sense experience. Despite this, his recognition of the importance of cognitive meaning and his discussion of meaning in terms of empirical verification succeeded in attracting the very *enfant terrible* of positivism, A. J. Ayer, to write an introduction to the Harvard reprint of James' *Pragmatism and The Meaning of Truth.* Whether Ayer's interpretation of James' philosophy is correct or fair is a matter open to debate.

And yet, despite the surface appearance of philosophical respectability, a closer examination will show that all three of the "classical" pragmatists were actually very much concerned about the "meaning-of-life" issues which the existentialists would later popularize through their novels, plays, and essays. In fact, I will argue that the classical pragmatists succeeded, to a greater extent than any other twentieth century philosophers, in being just what philosophers in my [never sufficiently humble] opinion should be. That is, they disciplined themselves in an effort to achieve what is really valid and valuable about "professionalism" in philosophy while at the same time stretching in the opposite direction to sustain a significant line of communication with the real-life issues with which the infamous "person on the street" is primarily concerned.

I propose here to lift up ever so briefly certain themes of the three paleo-pragmatists which anchor their claim to a measure of philosophical respectability even in a time like the philosophical dark ages of the twentieth century, *and* a few themes which illustrate my claim that they were very strongly devoted to "human," "existential," or "meaning-of-life" issues. I will conclude with a plea to the effect that such a two-pronged enterprise is just what philosophy that is *really* worthy of the name should always attempt.

I.

Peirce. As everyone knows, Peirce was head and shoulders above Dewey and James when it came to technical, science-oriented, and rigorous logic-grounded philosophy. Dewey and Peirce both wrote a fair amount about logic, but Dewey's logic was really a rather general interpretation of scientific reasoning in terms of what he called his "five-step analysis of a completed act of reflective thought." He insisted that all reflective thought, from the simplest puzzlement about some momentary issue up to and including the most technical research problem in any one of the sciences is really just an application in straightforward or in complexified ways, of the five steps. He was distressingly vague, however, concerning just how these steps might be elaborated into rigorous methodology.

Peirce had a hand in the creation of the new logic which transformed what had been thought of as a static and largely finished discipline into a very dynamic and rapidly developing one. Murray G. Murphey says of Peirce that he "was one of that group of men, including George Boole, Augustus De Morgan, Gottlob Frege, and others, who revolutionized logic and prepared the way for Whitehead and Russell's

Principia Mathematica."¹ He contributed importantly to the logic of relations, and he discovered quantification—a discovery which Frege had also made some six years earlier. As a logician, Peirce holds a position of first rank among the most creative philosophers of the twentieth century, an accomplishment which earns him the status of "real" or professional philosopher in the minds of even the most hard-line of the positivists and analysts.

In the field of epistemology he took a no non-sense position designed to expose mistakes he believed to be almost universal among philosophers. In so doing he partly anticipated Dewey's exposure of the foolishness of philosophy's perennial quest for certainty. A key point involved the distinction of logical from psychological certainty. He points out that validity in reasoning is often assumed to be present when our process of thought is such that we feel very strongly inclined to accept— or even find ourselves unable to doubt—the conclusion. This error, as Peirce sees it, comes to us from Descartes' teachings about clarity and distinctness and has characterized much subsequent philosophy. Descartes had asserted that whatever we perceive clearly and distinctly must necessarily be true. And many of those philosophers who would not agree with Descartes' notion that God would not allow us to be mistaken about what we perceive clearly and distinctly still believe in self-evident knowledge, which they insist is incorrigible. Clarity and distinctness, to the extent that it attainable, is, of course, very important, but it is not synonymous with a strong impulse to believe. There may indeed be things which we simply cannot bring ourselves to doubt, but this does not prove them to be indubitably true. We admit, of course, that truth is sometimes, as we say "counter-intuitive," but we assume that this is rare and that we will quickly recognize those rare cases. Peirce warns us that we are in fact quite prone to arrive at beliefs by paths that cannot be expected to transcend this distinction between psychological conviction and logical truth. He insists that truth is stubbornly just what it is regardless of our inclination or disinclination to believe it. Only the method of science, which involves repeated observation and confirmation by the whole community of qualified thinkers, can be trusted to result in that convergence toward agreement in which truth consists. This method will ferret out and hold up to the cold light of objective scrutiny any beliefs whose plausibility is merely psychological or intuitive.

Peirce carefully considers phenomenalism but finally embraces epistemological realism. He remarks that "all our knowledge may be said to rest on *observed facts.*"² And he insisted upon empirical verification long before Ayer and the other positivists made such an issue (and such a mess) of it. And yet his doctrine of fallibilism insured his rejection of the foolhardy quest for certainty whose disastrous prevalence in modern philosophy Dewey so well documented. It also saved him from the positivist dogmatism of scientific certainty which the verifiability criterion naively presupposed. In other words, he insisted on logical rigor and on careful scientific verification in a spirit of humility engendered by a recognition that certified knowledge or warranted truth is something we approach asymptotically but are not entitled to claim to have attained merely by virtue of a bit of positivistic verifying observations we may have carried out.

If his work in logic and the philosophy of science—sometimes as eccentric as it was rigorous—was enough to earn Peirce a title to respectability among the positivists, his recognition of the crucial importance of syntactics, grammar, and semantics should certainly earn him a place in twentieth century philosophy of language. His work here was, if anything, even more abstruse, filled with distinctions and subdistinctions, and shackled to an idiosyncratic vocabulary of his own making. He declared that logic in a general sense is another name for semiotic, the doctrine of signs. And he designated pragmatism itself as a theory of meaning (and not a theory of truth). It is here that he emphasizes operational definitions and denies distinctions of meaning where observable, practical differences are not to be found.

Even if not all of Peirce's efforts were altogether successful—whose ever are?—he must be recognized as deserving a place among real, professional philosophers even as understood in the twentieth century. He dealt with the right issues, and did so in ways that the philosophical orthodoxy of the era recognized. What remains for me to show is that while doing so, he also manifested a concern for the kind of meaning-of-life issues that constitute, in my judgment, the neglected but essential other side of philosophy.

Peirce writes unabashedly about metaphysics. The word had not yet become a term of ridicule. He argues that metaphysical beliefs are simply hypotheses of a much higher level of generality than ordinary scientific hypotheses but verifiable by techniques which are not different in principle from those appropriate in the sciences. His cosmology depicts a universe evolving from a paleo-condition of chaos toward increasing order, so that the determinism which some believe science implies is only the ultimate limit of the process lying in the very remote future. His concept of tychism involves the notion that the uniformity of nature is not yet rigid, so that instances of disorder may still occasionally appear and so that human free will has a place. Although he calls Hegel's doctrines a "cardboard model of philosophy," there is an unmistakable echo of the Hegelian dialectic in Peirce's own triadic metaphysics. The three concepts of firstness, secondness, and thirdness and those of tychism (or discreteness), synechism (or continuity), and agapasm (evolutionary love) involve a progression that certainly appears dialectic. He contrasts the tychastic philosophy of greed prevalent in nineteenth century America with the synechastic gospel of love taught by Christ, and finds their synthesis in agapasm, a concept that he explains by comparison to Empedicles' notion of love and hate as the driving forces in the universe. But Peirce insists that hate is subordinate to love.

Peirce's concept of agapasm as a cosmic principle suggests an interest in grounding human morality and religious devotion in a form of life which is beyond "mere" human brotherhood. He spoke out with considerable force against the socials evils most prevalent in his day, against "man's inhumanity to man," especially as represented by social Darwinism's gospel of greed. There is in his own mind a sharp contrast between the rigorous logical reasoning that applies to science and the function of sentiment in the realm of ethics and religion. Orthodox twentieth century emotivism in ethics would find his disclaimers about moral knowledge and his affirmation of sentiment deserving of a doctrinal imprimatur, but it seems to me quite unnecessarily differential. It seems to me that his epistemology and metaphysics might have served as a cognitively respectable grounding of morality. He might have argued quite forcefully, for example, that Social Darwinism's use of the image of "nature red in tooth and claw" to justify ruthless exploitation of the poor working class by a handful of robber barons represented a transitional stage of tychism which morality dictates must give way to the principle of synechism as represented by Christian charity and as grounded in the cosmic principle of agapasm or evolutionary love.

His own interest in religion, especially toward the end of his life, suggests a desire to show that human existence does after all have a meaning and a value—even in a cosmic and not merely a humanistic sense. In it we seem to glimpse something not altogether unlike James' sayings about the "reality of the unseen." He denies that logic or science can prove the existence of a supreme being—an expression he rejects as linguistically ill-formed—but at the same time he insists on the "reality of God," something which, he asserts, would be obvious to anyone who would "open [his/her] eyes—and [his/her] heart, which is also a perceptive organ . . .".[3] He rejects all of the arguments for the existence of God, but he offers what amounts to a vague, almost mystically phrased, version of the argument from design. He claims that what the pragmaticist means by the word "God," is to be found in the obvious answer to the question

> whether all physical science is merely figment—the arbitrary figment—of students of nature, and whether the *one* lesson of Gautama Boodha, Confucius, Socrates, and all who . . . have had their ways of conduct determined by meditation on the physico-psychical universe be only their arbitrary notion or be the Truth behind the appearances . . . and whether the superhuman courage which such contemplation has conferred upon priests who go to pass their lives with lepers and refuse all offers of rescue is mere silly fanaticism . . . or whether it is strength derived from the power of the truth.[4]

Peirce seems deliberately to keep his arguments about religion vague, presumably because he believed that it is sentiment rather than logic which predominates in such matters. It is perhaps an admirable epistemological modesty but in my judgment an excessive one. In his forceful denunciation of social evil and his almost poetic presentation of our religious sentiments, he illuminates the human-centered value-dimension of philosophy which has been so lamentably neglected during much of twentieth century philosophy.

II.

Dewey. We have already had occasion to note in passing Dewey's conviction, essentially in agreement with Peirce's, that scientific method is the clear path to knowledge and that it can be used in every arena of human endeavor, including philosophy. Dewey claimed, again in agreement with Peirce, that the function of human thought is to serve practical concerns. Ordinarily our behavior proceeds according to habit. It is only when genuine puzzlement occurs, when an attempt to achieve some desired goal is blocked, that the mind awakens to a process of reflective thought. When it does so, it follows a routine which is essentially the same, however simple or complex the problem. Dewey presents again and again in many of his writings the basic structure of human thought which he conceives as a five-step process, and he emphasizes the importance of careful observation, both at the initial stage of figuring out what the problem is and formulating hypotheses and that of testing and verification.

He also points out how logic is used in the process of verification when we infer from the hypotheses the conditions we can expect to observe if we perform the testing operations. He grounds his epistemology in evolutionary theory by pointing out that organisms whose cognitive strategies put them in touch with the world as it really is are the ones which would survive and prosper through natural selection. Thus the application of Dewey's five-step process of reflective thought, while it does not produce the kind of absolute certainty philosophy has long demanded, does produce practical results which are entirely worthy of being called knowledge.

One of Dewey's most important philosophical contributions was in his thorough discrediting of philosophy's impassioned and obsessive quest for certainty. In his book by that name[5] he showed that philosophy has been blighted since Greek antiquity, but especially since the time of Descartes, by a virtually unquestioned dogma to the effect that nothing is knowledge unless it carries a certification equivalent to the conclusion of a deductive logical syllogism or a proof in geometry. Furthermore, it has been almost unquestionably assumed that it is the business of philosophy to generate knowledge of just this kind, and indeed that nothing should be allowed to count as philosophy which does not bear the crest and insignia of absolute indubitability. It was this obsessive misunderstanding which drove the logical positivists to denounce several branches of philosophy which they believed were not susceptible of such indubitability, and thus to reduce the field of philosophy to that shrunken and atrophied handful of activities they believed could achieve it. The result was a philosophical fundamentalism fully as dogmatic as religious fundamentalism. With commendable clarity, Dewey showed that the dogma about indubitable knowledge and the assumption that only such knowledge constitutes philosophy are quite without warrant. The standard appropriate for knowledge-claims varies depending on the subject-matter—i.e., depending on what is possible in each area of human inquiry. It would, of course, be the height of folly to call a conclusion in geometry knowledge if it did not conform to rigorous standards of proof. To settle for an approximation of the sum of a column of figures would be unjustified, precisely because an exact figure is within the reach of human capacity. Even in astronomy, many predictions, such as the exact instant at which an eclipse will begin or exactly what effect a comet of measured mass would have on the orbit of an asteroid of a certain proportion of mass if it passed within a certain range of distance can be ascertained with remarkable precision. But the exact effect on economic growth of raising the interest rate by half a percent, or the precise extent to which reinstituting public hangings would affect the crime rate defies the same kind of precision. If considerable exactness is reasonably demanded with regard to certain questions in chemistry, the same degree of exactness cannot be expected in sociology. Indeed, even in that remarkably exact science of astronomy, we saw clearly in the summer of 1994 that the precise effect of the collision of large fragments of a comet with the planet Jupiter could not be predicted in detail. Dewey argued that our expectations with regard to the various areas of human endeavor must be adjusted to what we discover to be possible in dealing with the issues in those areas.

To refuse to call the conclusions of biology knowledge when they have been reached by the most careful application of the most appropriate methods of research in that field simply because they do not equal the precision of geometry is unreasonable—indeed irrational. And yet this is just what, by implication, philosophy's misguided dogma of indubitability explicitly proposed to do. It was also what the verifiability criterion of logical positivism implicitly assumed. Even in their effort to escape the perceived traps into which Descartes' work had led modern philosophy, the positivists along with nearly everyone else assumed a foundationalist epistemology grounded in indubitable atomic sense perceptions from which, with presumedly infallible logical procedures, we could generate absolutely certain knowledge. Dewey showed us quite clearly that such assumptions and such efforts are completely misguided. The quest for certainty is an effort to force the physical, the social, and the psychological world to conform to the standards of mathematics. Such an effort is a seriously mistaken.

This work of Dewey in epistemology and the philosophy of science certainly entitles him to the status of "real" or "serious" philosopher— even though some of its implications were diametrically opposed to, and by implication, highly critical of the epistemic orthodoxy being developed by those who were bent on making philosophy respectable. His concern with morality and with meaning-of-life issues took a direction different from that of Peirce or James, but he gave such concerns an important place nonetheless. It is ironic that his essay titled "Theory of Valuation" was invited for inclusion in the *International Encyclopedia of Unified Science*, the envisioned standard reference work of positivism, because the essay turned out to be explicitly critical of the whole project of the sponsors of the *Encyclopedia*. In contrast, on the one hand, to those who would reduce moral discourse to emotive, expressive, or imperative speech, and on the other hand to those who championed one or another of the supposedly objective moral theories, Dewey insisted that moral discourse must be grounded in careful observation and analysis of the problematic situation and must make use of informed intelligence to project and to select desirable courses of action which could realistically be expected to lead to a resolution of the problem. It is intelligence, the unique human faculty which evolution has produced and refined, that can assess information, evaluate situations, compare imagined possible outcomes, and select a path toward a better state of affairs. It is precisely this process of intelligence, making use of the five-steps of a completed act of reflective thought, in which moral reflection consists.

Unlike Peirce, who became increasingly religious, increasingly Christian—indeed increasingly Episcopalian—as he grew older, and unlike James, who affirmed a less sectarian variety of theism, Dewey manifests a growing dissatisfaction with the Congregationalism of his childhood, with institutional religion in general, and, in fact, with theism itself. Yet this "outgrowing" of religion and of supernaturalism yielded, not hostility toward things spiritual nor an agnostic indifferentism, but rather a robust naturalistic humanism which depicts humans as children of the physical universe, at home in the natural world, and stewards of their environment and their destiny.

In *Experience and Nature* Dewey insists that our perceptions and thoughts, and even our aspirations and feelings have "ontic reach." They do not merely put us in touch with our own thoughts and ideas, as subjective idealism taught. Rather, they reveal to us the way nature itself really is. He speaks of how we long, amidst a troubled world, for safety, stability, permanence, assurance—forgetting that what gives significance to our experiences is the very conditions of nature which give rise to longing.[6] He even goes so far as to say that "as such nature itself is wistful and pathetic, turbulent and passionate."[7] Intelligence, our unique human faculty, is the faculty that nature has produced to enable us to survive, make a living, understand the universe, and flourish in the natural world. He sweeps aside three hundred years of tortured epistemological drudgery with its passionate but hopeless attempts at achieving certainty and shows us how the nature in which we are immersed and of which we are a part has equipped us to get into touch with those objects of our experiences with which we need to deal. Our knowledge is of a practical sort, neither infallible nor illusory, but altogether adequate to our purposes in designing for ourselves happy and creative lives. In a world without a supernatural dimension and shaped by evolutionary processes this is just what is to be expected of an organism with a history and pedigree like ours. Organisms unable to grasp the real nature of objects in their environment would soon be eliminated through natural selection. As we come increasingly to recognize that our destiny is in our own hands and not in the hands of some deity, we can learn how to imagine a society that enables and promotes the realization of the highest of human values, and to work toward its realization.

Meanwhile, of course, with much muffled weeping and wailing and carefully disguised gnashing of teeth, most philosophy in the English-speaking world, especially positivism, analytic philosophy, and linguistic philosophy, continued its desperate and ill-begotten quest for Shanghai-la, showing its frustration and dimly recognized sense of futility through its petulant dismissive attitudes toward everyone and everything but the strictly orthodox, as defined by itself. It is perhaps ironic how epistemology, especially since 1963, when Edmund L. Gettier introduced the gimmick, has distilled itself into a process of story-telling, each story designed to illustrate how some epistemic formula fails to capture the precise meaning of whatever word was selected for the game. It matters not at all how contrived, concocted, *ad hoc*, improbable, trumped up the story might be, since after all no longer is there any sense of connection with anything practical. It is ironic, because this process of making up wildly far-fetched stories is conceived by the epistemologists as a rigorous philosophical method radically to be distinguished, they would insist, from philosophy as story-telling in Rorty's sense. The suggestion that their stories had anything to do with the existential concerns of live human beings would offend these philosophers deeply—not that anyone would ever any longer imagine that they did.

III.

James. With James the story is somewhat different. He is clearly committed most enthusiastically to the practical, meaning-of-life issues, with virtually no hang-ups about respectability, orthodoxy, or professionalism in philosophy. Such confidence evidences a competence that the nervous, status seeking philosophers could only envy. James produced important work that deservedly earned him a place among those philosophers who did have serious hang-ups about professionalism.

James' credentials are solidly scientific, including an MD and some years of teaching human anatomy in the Harvard Medical School. He also founded America's first experimental psychology laboratory at Harvard, and contributed importantly to the process in which psychology was engaged in separating from philosophy and becoming an independent discipline. It is, perhaps, his prodigious work, *The Principles of Psychology*, that most substantially grounds his place among "serious," professional philosophers. A spectacular synthesis of empirical and rational or speculative psychology, and epistemology, based to a certain extent on his own work in the experimental psychology laboratory, but involving extensive library scholarship as well, it deserves to be ranked alongside John Locke's *Essay* and David Hume's *Treatise*. James contributed fundamentally toward moving the field of psychology from the arm-chair, where its primary method had been introspection, to the laboratory where it came increasingly to be recognized as a legitimate science.

James brought to the study of religious experience and mysticism the sharp, analytic mind of the scientist who scrutinized and classified types of experiences and then raised probing questions about them, questions such as what credence we should place on them, how they were similar to and different from the experiences characteristic of psychopathology, whether the noetic claims they make are to be credited, and generally speaking what significance they have for understanding humans and their world. His *Varieties of Religious Experience* still stands today, more than ninety years after its publication, as the most substantial and credible study of the phenomenology of religious experience. It brings nononsense scientific methodology to bear upon these experiences, while at the same time taking them seriously and conceding that they do indeed tell us something important about human beings and their world.

It is in his popular philosophical essays such as "The Will to Believe," and "Is Life Worth Living?" that he seems to depart farthest from tough-minded rigor, and it is these that have been most severely criticized. His eagerness to communicate with non-specialists resulted in some looseness of expression that left him open to criticism, but much of the criticism is the result of the carelessness with which his critics read his works. The parodies that called his essay "The Will to Deceive" or "The Will to Make-Believe" reflect a very superficial understanding of what James actually said, and the charge that James authorizes us to believe anything that makes us feel good is really a rather absurd misunderstanding. James makes it entirely clear that we must always base our beliefs on the best evidence and the strongest reasons we have, that when the evidence is even slightly stronger on one side than the other, we must believe the claim that these best reasons support. It is only when the evidence is so evenly balanced that we cannot detect a preponderance either way, and only when the issue is urgent and cannot await the accumulation of more evidence, that we are justified in exercising our "passional nature" and willing to believe the doctrine that we believe will contribute most to our well-being.

The book titled *Pragmatism,* one of his most popular, is explicitly devoted to elaborating a philosophical position that takes a middle path between two extremes of philosophical professionalism in order to satisfy the needs of people he calls "philosophical amateurs," namely, intelligent plain people who want their philosophy to be empirical, scientific, and rigorous but also want it to be in touch with human religious and moral concerns. The extremes he calls tough-minded and tender-minded, the one thoroughly empirical and scientific, the other rationalistic and mystical. Both contain elements that the intelligent public cherish, but both also involve aspects that informed amateur thinkers find unacceptable. Pragmatism, James asserts, brings together the tough-minded empiricism and concern for facts and science with the tender-minded recognition that there is a value dimension and a spiritual significance to reality and human life. It is just this sort of philosophy that intelligent non-philosophers in any era need and desire. It is easy to see that twentieth century English-speaking philosophy went on its head-strong way, paying very little heed to the sage warnings of either James or Dewey. And much professional philosophy today, in the 1990s, continues to spin out its elaborate webs of esoterica, still largely unconnected to anything that is significant to living human beings.

I suppose that an attempt to do for today what James attempted to do for his day would involve not a contrast between the tough-minded and the tender-minded, but between the analytic philosophy of the English-speaking world and the post-modern, post-structural philosophy of the European continent. Perhaps some might be willing to characterize the former as tough-minded and the latter as tender-minded [or fuzzy-minded?]. Despite the fact that there has been much disillusionment with positivistic, analytic, and linguistic philosophy in the last few decades, and not very much confidence in whatever it is that the Europeans are writing about, not many philosophers have taken up the challenge to make philosophy relevant again to important human concerns. The outlines of a melioristic philosophy in the spirit of James's pragmatism, designed to capture what is legitimate and intelligible in the two philosophical extremes of our century, have not yet appeared. The need for it is patent and is being grudgingly recognized by a few.[8] Rorty's path of essentially abandoning philosophy or declaring it dead and defunct is not, in my judgment, what we need. Philosophy as social commentary or as literary theory is valuable, but it stops short of providing the moral vision and leadership which should be a role of philosophy. Even anthropologists, those stalwarts of cultural relativism during most of the twentieth century, are beginning to recognize the urgent need for intelligent evaluation of social practices and the condemnation on *moral* grounds of some that inflict needless suffering, that victimize the weak, and that perpetuate oppression. It is essentially the almost hysterical dedication to certainty and the "physics envy" which longs to gain for philosophy the prestige of science that continues to block the process of intelligent and relevant philosophizing. Dewey urged us to turn aside from our preoccupation with indubitability for its own sake and instead to engage our thought with the urgent problems that confront the human race, so that we may assess the resources which might be brought to bear upon them as we attempt the very practical process of making the social world for which we are responsible more habitable and more conducive to human well-being. Philosophy's old-fashioned way was to attempt to create an all-comprehensive system of ideas alleged to be infallibly true of the entirety of reality and to delay any attempts at practical reform until the time that such a system yields designs to transform the world into paradise. Philosophy's new-fangled, twentieth century way has been to claim that the role of philosophy is to solve, again with absolute infallibility, that limited range of technical problems which remain once the vague, value-centered, meaning-of-life issues have been thoroughly renounced and rooted out. Dewey's claim makes much more sense, that philosophy makes progress as we tackle particular problems piece-meal and envision courses of action that can actually be taken which will serve, not so much to create heaven on earth, as to diminish the severity of a particular problem and to open up possible future paths to alleviating other related problems. This process is precisely the function of intelligence, the faculty that nature, through the evolutionary process, has given us as our means of survival and prosperity. We need philosophers with the vision to recognize what such pragmatic philosophy could do and with the courage to risk being called "unprofessional" or not "real" philosophers, so that they might actually be about the business of the calling and vocation of philosophers who are *really* worthy of the name.

By reaffirming the place of rational, philosophical critique and evaluation in the religious, aesthetic, political, and moral dimensions of human life, a renewed pragmatism might contribute toward rescuing religion from the fundamentalists, aesthetics from the "theorists," politics from the demagogues, and morality from the relativists. If this has to be

Pragmatism and the Meaning of Life 237

achieved at the cost of sacrificing a bit of the carefully cultivated illusion of philosophy's being "scientific," or by descending a step or two from the studied indifference of our "professionalism," so be it. Indeed, that process would not only benefit those causes I have named; it would also contribute toward making philosophy itself a little less stuffy, pompous, and irrelevant.

NOTES

1. "Charles Sanders Peirce," by Murray G. Murphey, in *Encyclopedia of Philosophy* (New York: Macmillan Publishing Company, 1967). Vol. 6, p. 71.

2. C. S. Peirce, "Abduction and Induction," in Justus Buchler, *Philosophical Writings of Peirce*. New York: Dover, 1955), p. 150 [Peirce's italics].

3. *Ibid.*, p. 377 f.

4. *Ibid.*, p. 376 f.

5. John Dewey, *The Quest for Certainty* (New York: Minton, Balch & Company, 1929).

6. John Dewey, *Experience and Nature* (La Salle, Illinois: Open Court, 1923), p. 55.

7. *Ibid.*, p. 56.

8. Cornel West is one example; his recognition of the point is not grudging.

RADICAL EMPIRICISM AND THE HOLOGRAPHIC MODEL OF REALITY

Jennifer G. Jesse

When we hear the word "hologram," most of us probably think of those little pictures on our credit cards. Or if we've been to a holography exhibit, we think of it as a new and spectacular form of art. In fact, holography is one of the furthest advances of physics that promises to take us beyond the two-dimensional images of computers and electronic information into something whose implications we are only beginning to sense. It represents a whole new dimension of scientific inquiry through which we are making startling discoveries about the deep structures of reality and, as such, it has particular relevance for radical empiricism.

For a long time now, we radical empiricists have carried on a lover's quarrel with science. We realize that the continued vitality of our philosophy relies on a commitment to interdisciplinary study with all branches of culture. Alongside the arts, the sciences have served as the greatest impetus to focus and redirect our energies. At the same time, we are ever vigilant against uncritically incorporating any materialistic methods, principles, or conclusions into our own thought. For those of us who strive to broaden the boundaries of experience and meaning, the traditional empirical method of science represents closure of meaning because it attempts to measure experience in purely quantifiable, objective terms. This method "impoverishes the world of experience. It destroys the capacity to appreciate the 'surplusage' of experience."[1]

But science has embarked on a new age. Quantum physics has altered the objective boundaries of traditional science and is pushing the human mind into dimensions which it has never before conceived —dimensions for which quantifiable measurements of time and space have no relevance. Holography is an integral part of this quantum revolution, which aims to expand the boundaries of meaning. Consonant with the elemental principles of radical empiricism, holographic science is a method of inquiry that attempts to focus on the "More" of human experience, and to restructure the scientific method to take account of new data that do not fit into the old epistemological categories.

This raises the question whether holography may not be a valuable stimulus for developing the language and ideas we use in radical empiricism. I suggest that the image of reality it proposes is a powerful one that can help us sharpen our articulations about the structure of the universe we experience and understand more intimately how it works. I will argue that the holographic model directs us to a deeper awareness of what is ultimate in reality by focusing our attention on the broadened understanding of perception and experience that is so central to radical empiricism. Another aspect of holography is the degree to which it satisfies the pragmatic test, always a necessary part of this tradition. Holography is a fact, if you will; it is the result of the actions of existing physical laws. This pragmatic factor confirms the belief that holography reveals something essential about reality, and lends persuasive force to long-held beliefs of radical empiricism.

In the following section of this paper, I introduce briefly some of the basics of holography and their relevance to the radical empirical vision. In the next section, I suggest some ways in which holographic principles would affect radical empiricism. In the last section, I comment on implications of that model for the empirical task.

I.

The first hologram was created more or less by accident in 1948, but it was in the 1960s, with the creation of laser light, that the history of holography really began. Laser light is a coherent form of light that produces more uniform waves than normal light. A hologram is an image formed by the interference pattern of two waves of light. A laser light is split into two separate beams. One beam hits the photographic plate after being reflected off the object being photographed; the second, called the reference beam, is reflected directly onto the photographic plate. The plate, or film, records the light wave interference pattern created by these two beams. If you look at this plate under normal circumstances, you see either nothing at all or faint, incoherent rings. But when a bright light or another laser is passed through the film, the interference pattern recorded there causes the light to diffract in a pattern that recreates the photographic moment, producing a full three-dimensional image of the original object.

There are two particularly fascinating things about the hologram. The first is that if this film is cut in half and illuminated, each half still contains the whole image. In fact, no matter how many pieces the film is cut into, each piece will still show the image of the whole object, though that image will become less distinct the smaller the piece becomes. Second, an incredible amount of information can be contained in a holographic plate. The finer the grain of the film, the more detailed depth the image reveals.[2] Further, many different images can be recorded on the same surface, simply by changing the angle of light at which the image is recorded and viewed.

Two basic principles scientists believe are revealed by holography are, first, that the wave properties of matter are at least as fundamental, if not more fundamental, than its particle properties. A particle conception of matter—the traditional conception of modern science—gives rise to atomistic and objectified views of the universe. "Particle thinking" grounds our conceptions of distinct identities but offers no basis from which to posit any essential relatedness between them. A wave conception of matter leads naturally to an organic image of the universe. While two particles cannot occupy the same space at the same time, a great many waves can do so, without losing their distinct forms. The second principle is that the whole is a more elemental reality than its parts. (This is based on subquantum theory, described below.)

These principles arose primarily through the work of two scientists who, independently of one another, developed theories about the holographic nature of the universe. Karl Pribram, a neurophysicist at Stanford University, used the principles of holography to explain how memory and perception are distributed throughout the brain, each bit of information being simultaneously present in every part. David Bohm, a quantum physicist at the University of London, proposed that holographic principles explain many anomalies in standard quantum theories.[3]

The results of their work have led these scientists to suggest that the universe may be one vast hologram, with the world as we know it being a projection from another level of reality whose logic is holographic.

In his work on vision, Pribram proposes the idea of the brain as a frequency analyzer that functions as a holographic projector. For example, when we see something, its image exists on the surface of our retinas, and yet we experience the object as being "out there," not on our retinas. The same is true of every other kind of perception or experience. Every experience, which is actually internal, is projected by the brain as being external. The implication for Pribram is that reality is a vast domain of wave frequencies, akin to the seemingly incoherent rings we see on an unilluminated holographic plate, and that out of this, our brains project the world we recognize. Likewise, quantum physicists like Bohm have recognized that subatomic particles, called quanta, manifest themselves as particles only when they are being observed, and otherwise act as waves. Bohm is betting that our perception creates matter as we know it. As Michael Talbot explains:

> Our brains mathematically construct objective reality by interpreting frequencies that are ultimately projections from another dimension, a deeper order of existence that is beyond both space and time: The brain is a hologram enfolded in a holographic universe.[4]

This does not mean there is no "there" out there. But it does mean that the objective nature of things is not all there is; what we see is only one possible manifestation of underlying wave patterns.

Bohm develops his conception of the relation between our projections and the reality underlying those projections by referring to the Explicate and Implicate Orders of the universe. To account for the anomalies in quantum physics, he theorizes the existence of a subquantum level of reality, which he calls the Implicate Order. This elemental level of existence gives rise to the world projected through our perception, which he calls the Explicate Order. The Implicate Order is one fundamental whole operating at the subquantum level to organize the behavior of all the parts that arise out of it. This subquantum theory exemplifies the second principle mentioned above, that the whole is more elemental than the parts. At the subquantum level, everything is interconnected. There can be no phenomenon that occurs in one "part" that does not occur in all other "parts." For Bohm, what we think of as separate entities are merely reflections from different angles, as it were, of one and the same whole. Bohm takes this logic even further to say that there is no meaningful separation between subjectivity and objectivity. These terms signify abstractions that exist only at the level of the Explicate Order and do not reflect any separate reality on the Implicate level. In Bohm's theory, we are not only creating the "objective" world by perceiving it, but are ourselves part of the cosmic hologram being projected.

The relevance of these theories and principles to the philosophies and theologies of radical empiricism is obvious. I will mention here only a few of the basic themes constant throughout the radical empirical tradition.

(1) The American empiricists rejected the Cartesian dualism between subject and object, conceiving of experience as a field or matrix

of interdependent subjective and objective aspects in which each is co-constitutive of the other, what Henry Nelson Wieman called "creative interchange." Like the overlapping waves of the holographic model, this view overcomes any strict epistemological dualism, whether between the self and the other, or God and the world.

(2) William James and John Dewey expanded the traditional concept of experience beyond the five physical senses to include affective and qualitative feelings. They believed that experience is constituted by an elemental and organic relatedness between the experiencing subject and the experienced environment. Bernard E. Meland's notion of "lived experience" includes these "felt qualities" through which we are able to apprehend, in part, something of the "structures of experience," the "surplusage" or depth dimension of existence, which gives a fringe or penumbral quality to all human knowledge. The defining phrase for Meland is that "we live more deeply than we can think."[5]

(3) The "givenness" of relations (à la James) and the claim that relations are felt and experienced as immediately as anything else is another key theory of radical empiricism. This concept of the organic interrelatedness of events as being constitutive of reality at its most elemental level was one of Alfred North Whitehead's central themes. And Bernard Loomer used the term "size" to express the capacity for relational depth, intensity, and complexity.

(4) The organicism of the radical empiricists encompasses and is grounded in all these other ideas. The whole, which is the ultimate source of meaning, was conceived by these thinkers as a radically living event, animate all the way down, and as a network of interrelatedness in which there is no separation between self and other or between spirit and nature. In *Art and Experience,* Dewey spoke of the quality of the whole as a "consummatory" experience, most directly encountered in aesthetic feelings.

There are other themes just as important in the radical empirical tradition, such as its process orientation, its dynamic interpretation of the human mind, and its cautions against closure based on the tentativeness of all conceptualizations in the context of the More beyond rational intelligibility. Each of these themes is relevant to the holographic model of reality. Both areas of inquiry direct us to expand the concept of experience to be more attentive to, and to recognize the reality of, the deep structures of experience that operate according to a holographic kind of logic where there is no separation of subject and object, and the organic interrelatedness of events is constitutive of reality at its most elemental level. Once one grants the possibility of a holographic reality, statements such as James's hypothesis that "the conscious person is continuous with a wider self through which saving experiences come"[6] do not sound quite so theoretical as they once did.

II.

The scientists' development and explication of the principles of holography offer some intriguing ideas to radical empiricism. Before assimilating those ideas, however, we need to consider critically the way they have been articulated. Following Bohm, the language we have used so far to characterize the worldview extrapolated from the holographic evidence is basically the same as we used to describe the hologram. We have portrayed our reality as a "projection" or "reflection" of another, more "original" level of reality, just as a hologram is generated by a projection of light waves from an original source. Further, we have attempted to represent this worldview using such terms as subjective, objective, internal, and external—a highly problematic tack when applied to a dimension in which these concepts no longer apply in any distinctive way. This language—particularly Bohm's articulation of the Implicate and Explicate Orders—translates the logic of the hologram itself literally into a metaphysical theory. But it does not necessarily follow from the holographic evidence that the world we experience is literally a giant hologram, a projection from another, more original, realm. Such a view would be merely another version of natural-supernatural dualism. We can say, however, that the hologram analogically discloses in the realm of physics something inherent in the nature of the reality we experience.

This linguistic issue is well-known to radical empiricists. The problem is that the actuality intimated by our experience outruns any attempt to express it adequately, which is why empiricists such as James and Meland resorted to such elusive terms as "pure experience" and "lived experience." The problem here is the same: holographic and subquantum theories lead to a worldview for which we have no language adequate even to the idea of it, let alone the experience itself. Until such a time as our linguistic skills improve, we must use our words metaphorically, always conscious that we apply them to reality not literally but heuristically.

Given that caveat, I believe the holographic model of reality has valuable images and ideas to lend to the development of radical empiricism. For example, George F. Dole, a Swedenborgian theologian who has been working with the holographic model for some time, uses holography to image human consciousness as constituted by the intersection of two wave patterns, the "subjective" constructed from "within" the self, and the "objective" flowing in from "outside" the self, through experience. Consciousness is the interference pattern itself, which cannot be understood without reference to both wave patterns.[7] This could be another way to support the process and radical empirical view that individuals are neither wholly autonomous nor completely determined from without. We construct our own perceptions, but by using the materials made available to us. This is also a fundamentally social view of the self, which begins to blur the boundaries between what is "within" and "without."

There are many such ideas that holography can lend to radical empiricism. The most important, I think, is the attention it focuses on the deepening of our perceptual senses. In his Vision of the Last Judgment, William Blake poses the issue this way:

> What it will be Questioned When the Sun rises do you not see a round Disk of fire somewhat like a Guinea O no no I see an Innumerable company of the Heavenly host crying Holy Holy Holy is the Lord God Almighty I question not my Corporeal or Vegetative Eye any more than I would Question a Window concerning a Sight I look thro it & not with it.[8]

The first option, in which the corporeal eye sizes up the rising sun to be somewhat like a guinea, communicates the absurdly reductive conclusions reached by a materialistic understanding of human perception. The other is more to the point for Blake. He and the radical empiricists are concerned to broaden our perceptual capacities, which means that the reality realized by those expanded perceptions will not be the same as that envisioned by the five senses of our corporeal nature. For Blake, "the Suns Light when he unfolds it / Depends on the Organ that beholds it."[9] Expanded perception reveals a reality that is radically animate and "Organized," which is to say, indivisible.

This is the direction in which we find ourselves headed when we enter the holographic universe. That worldview places a special emphasis on the expansion of our perceptual power as the key to realizing reality. We see this focus on perception in the fundamentally perspectival nature of holography. Our vision of any given image depends on the angle from which we view it. While this is also a characteristic of normal vision, it is sharpened by the holographic image to a point of elemental importance.

With the hologram, the ability to vary the angle of vision makes the difference not merely between seeing different aspects of an image, but between seeing radically different appearances of an image, or between seeing an image clearly and not being able to see it at all. What is invisible to the corporeal eye may be ineluctably evident to the holographic eye.

This perceptual emphasis gives rise to two hypotheses which, though implicit in radical empiricism, take on primary importance in a holographic empiricism. First, every vision in the holographic universe "reflects" or in some way enacts the organic whole of which we are all creative participants. Holographic logic heightens the radical empirical emphasis on relationality to a radical organicism. Everything reflects the whole not merely in the sense of being a participant in it, as the radical empiricists already have said, but in the sense that every participant contains the entirety of the whole within itself. This is not by any means a monochromatic interpretation of reality, where everything is reduced to being somehow the same. It is just the opposite because it is a whole of great "size," to use Loomer's term. Reality is conceived as a continual flow from a deep and expansive source that is felt through a direct path (the laser's "reference beam") and an indirect path (the beam reflected from the object). It is the meeting of these paths in an interference pattern that carries meaning, and that pattern manifests a perpetually new and unique disclosure of this indivisible organism, which changes and expands with every new explication.

Second, this dynamic quality of the whole leads to a very strong inkling about perception in the holographic universe. If in the depths of this organism "subjectivity" and "objectivity," imagination and reality, are not separate things, then reality may be, finally, a construct of the mind—time, space, matter, our own bodies, all being imagined explications of the thoughts, hopes, and fears of the organism which we all embody. Might it literally be possible, then, to create reality as we perceive it? Those who have worked with the holographic paradigm have described matter as a habit of mind, constantly born anew out of the Implicate Order because our brains keep generating it that way. The mind is conceived as organizing itself according to layers of templates that continually explicate energy along the same repetitive patterns. Those patterns, like bad habits, are hard to break. Understanding conceptually that we perceive things into being does not mean we can simply think them away in the wink of an eye. These elemental perceptual patterns may be recalcitrant to change by the higher levels of consciousness because those levels may not partake of sufficient depth to unseat them. Nevertheless, if reality is a construct of the mind, it might be possible for us to perceive our way into a new and better world.

It is not only the content of ideas such as these that the holographic model lends to radical empiricism. We may wonder whether holography may not be considered a pragmatic test of the tenets of radical empiricism. No system of philosophy or theology has a very high degree of sticking power without solid pragmatic underpinning. And the fact is, holograms work. They form three-dimensional images from the interference patterns of light, and every part of the holographic plate contains the whole image. Holographic science is already being used as a technique of surgery, medical and chemical research, industrial manufacturing, sound transmission, and virtual reality exploration. The strength of radical empiricism depends in part on its ability to develop pragmatic tests that enable us to judge the truth of our beliefs about the nature of reality, about how God works in history, about how the interrelatedness and organic quality of reality is more than just a "poetic" idea. What does it mean for radical empiricism that holograms work? Might the holographic arts and sciences serve in some way as pragmatic tests of the claims of radical empiricism?

III.

I have suggested that the holographic model of reality would add significant nuances to radical empiricism in the direction of a radical organicism and the creative nature of perception, and that it may strengthen and promote the further development of empiricism's pragmatic side. In conclusion, I briefly discuss some implications of incorporating the holographic paradigm into radical empiricism.

One of the most challenging aspects of holographic thinking, as is evident from this essay, is conceptualizing the holographic worldview without allowing our language to confine the reality or experience we are attempting to relate. Empiricists like Meland remind us that, no matter how self-conscious we try to be about the limits of our language, our experience is nonetheless deeply affected by whatever language we use to describe it. Perhaps the primary danger in using the holographic model is that of re-importing into our theology a traditional-style image of divine transcendence, which radical empiricism already has discarded. Because the bipolar logic of our language preserves the fundamental idea that holographic reality involves the reflection of the whole, a dichotomy may arise in our thinking—along a traditional type of subject-object boundary—between that which reflects and that which is reflected. Any such dichotomy lends itself to positing a higher reality separate from this one which this reality reflects. And because we come to know that more holistic reality through its reflection, a certain mystification of the divine Other may creep back into our theology. After all, these are patterns of logic that have been honed to a lightning efficiency over millennia of theologizing.

Nevertheless, the radical empirical tradition is uniquely qualified to monitor the terms and ideas used in holographic theories because of the sensitivity it has encouraged toward the problem of language. That sensitivity may enable radical empiricists to improve and further develop the words and concepts used in holographic theories. For instance, we may find in James's concept of pure experience a way to stave off the dualistic tendencies in holographic discourse. James holds in creative tension the idea that there exists "one primal stuff" of which everything is made with the assertion that there is "no general stuff," no primal quality of being that can be differentiated from the thoughts and things that manifest it.[10] This may help us articulate beliefs about the holographic universe while avoiding a misleading elementalism. Another example of the development of holographic theory that would be provoked by the empirical framework is based on the critical stance empiricists would bring to assumptions about the holographic universe. The proponents of the holographic paradigm consistently refer to the depth level of reality, or Bohm's Implicate Order, as a monistic whole. Many empiricists have argued, however, that the experience of organicism does not translate neatly into a concept of ultimate Oneness or coherent unity because, for them, such a notion is not sufficiently sanctioned by the facts of experience. Is it beyond the limits of holographic logic to suppose that the Implicate Order we experience may be only one of many such orders? Would it not be in the very nature of holographic logic—based as it is on the principle of infinitely overlapping wave patterns—to assume that the Implicate Order may itself be radically plural in dimensions, not one whole but multiple wholes?

The implications of a holographic empiricism also go well beyond matters of language and conceptualization. Radical organicism and the claim that perception is an inherently creative force constitute a powerful combination which would mean that not only our actions but all of our thoughts, feelings, and perceptions would have an efficacy reaching much further than what we have conceived of in the past as "ourselves." If everything we do, think, feel, and perceive affects the whole cosmic organism, which each of us explicates, then all these activities would be matters for ethical consideration. While it is an accepted philosophical and theological practice to treat actions, and even thoughts and feelings, as ethical concerns, perception itself is not usually thought of as a moral issue. But given its fundamentally creative character in the holographic paradigm, even perception—indeed, perception above all—would be a matter of grave ethical import because whatever we perceive in the holographic universe affects our fundamental reality. If we perceive the world according to materialistic and utilitarian principles, those will form the pragmatic rules by which this reality functions. And as experience shows, that which we create is very real. Reality at the explicate level is a product of innumerable layers of perceptual patterns whose formation goes back literally to the beginning of time. Patterns so elemental are not changed easily. But holographic logic tells us that, with effort, change is possible and, in a holographic empiricism, re-perceiving reality becomes the primary ethical concern.

The thoroughgoing organicism of holographic logic also would call for a theology that extends beyond human concerns. Humanity, understood as something that stands above, or in any way apart from, its natural environment, could not be the principal interest of a holographic theology. Though it may be inevitable that our theology centers in human experience, I question whether a holographic empiricism could remain primarily concerned with the condition of humanity. If reality is radically organismic, then humanity is only one explicate form among others, all of which contain the whole. Are there principles in the holographic paradigm that could justify valuing the human explication of the whole as superior to any other explication? Would Loomer's concept of "size" or Whitehead's "complexity" serve as adequate criteria here? Or would the radical nature of a holographic organicism level all such attempts to assign degrees of value among the many wondrous forms of this living organism? And what would that mean for the difficult choices facing us today in regard to the survival of our global community?

Finally, what image of God would a holographic empiricism generate? The logic of the holographic image gravitates persistently in Loomer's direction: if we identify God as the concrete, organic whole itself, which is present in its totality in every part, and if our fundamental perceptions and experience of this whole are valuationally ambiguous, how are we to distinguish God from the evil and the energy of sheer destruction we experience as present within that whole? It would seem that we could only arrive at a belief in an exclusively benevolent God by abstracting from our actual perception and experience. But is there a sound holographic principle by which to perform this abstraction? And if not, what is the implication for the faith communities which this theology would support? Is it possible that one may believe in an ambiguous God whom one still finds worthy of worship?

Observations and issues such as these are only a small indication of the challenges presented by a holographic empiricism. It will take a far more in-depth study and development of the premises and principles of the holographic paradigm to discern the effect those theories may have on radical empirical thought.

NOTES

1. Henry Nelson Wieman, *Seeking a Faith for a New Age: Essays on the Interdependence of Religion, Science and Philosophy*, Cedric L. Hepler, ed. (Metuchen, NJ: The Scarecrow Press, Inc., 1975), p. 51.

2 There is a hologram of a microscope at the Museum of Holography in Chicago, and if you walk up to that microscope and put your eye to the image of the eyepiece, you see the microscopic material on the plate below magnified with complete accuracy.

3. The holographic theories of Pribram and Bohm can be found in Pribram's *Languages of the Brain* (Monterey, CA: Wadsworth Publishing, 1977) and Bohm's *Wholeness and the Implicate Order* (London: Routledge & Kegan Paul, 1980). The theories of both scientists are described by Michael Talbot in *The Holographic Universe* (New York: Harper Collins Publishers, 1991).

4. Talbot, p. 54.

5. Meland, *Fallible Forms and Symbols: Discourses on Method in a Theology of Culture* (Philadelphia: Fortress Press, 1976), p. 24.

6. James, *The Varieties of Religious Experience* (Cambridge, MA: Harvard University Press, 1985), p. 405.

7. Dole, *Sorting Things Out* (San Francisco: J. Appleseed & Company, 1994), pp. 84-85.

8. William Blake, *The Complete Poetry and Prose of William Blake*, David V. Erdman, ed., newly revised edition (Garden City, NY: Anchor Press, 1982), pp. 565-66.

9. *Gates of Paradise* 1 (Erdman, p. 260).

10. James, *Essays in Radical Empiricism* (Cambridge, MA: Harvard University Press, 1976), pp. 4–19 (emphasis in original).

RORTY'S NEOPRAGMATISM AND THE RELIGIOUS HUMANIST OPTION

Mason Olds

In Book X of Plato's *Republic*, there is the rather well known discussion about beds. At one level the issue deals with the validation of censorship in the just state. The argument is that works of art are attractive, and that such works seduce citizens away from the truth; therefore works of art are potentially dangerous and should be censored. To support this claim, reference is made to three different understandings of the word *bed*. First is the idea or the "form" of the bed, a mental or metasensory entity containing the essence of what a bed is. It is a universal, unchanging form which "exists" in "the intelligible world" and was created by the gods. This kind of bed is grasped or intuited or apprehended by those well-trained, rational minds. Second is the physical bed in which we sleep. Created by craftsmen out of perishable materials it is a rough copy of the form of the bed. It exists in the "world of appearance" and is perceived with the senses, most particularly that of sight. Third is the artist's painting of the bed, a poor, further removed copy of the physical bed. The argument runs, if truth and reality appropriately apply to the form of the bed, if the physical bed is a once removed copy of the real bed, and if the painting is a copy of the physical bed, then it is even further removed from reality. Thus, art, according to Plato, rather than leading us to the truth, leads us away from the it.

Rorty's Neopragmatism. In exploring Richard Rorty's neopragmatism Plato's metaphor can be useful. Rorty would take Plato to task in his discussion about the beds. In fact, he would claim that it is the artist's perspective that should claim our attention. Each of the understandings of the bed presupposes a final vocabulary: if the form of the bed is real, the vocabulary of Platonic idealism is true; if the physical bed is real, the final vocabulary of Lockean empiricism must be true; if the work of the artist is to be convincing, Rorty's final vocabulary of neopragmatism must be persuasive. Deciding which final vocabulary is the "truth" is as impossible as determining which of three paintings of a bed is "true" when the style of one is realism, another impressionism, and the third expressionism. There simply is no metastylistic perch or God's-eye perspective from which one can "see" what a real bed is, and then determine which style best captures "reality."

What is neopragmatism? Rorty offers some insights in his discussions of the "edifying philosopher" and the "liberal ironists." In some contexts Rorty contrasts "edifying" with "systematic" philosophers. Since the modern period, systematic philosophers have focused on epistemology. Edifying philosophers have been suspicious of epistemological theories, seeking instead "new, better, more interesting, more fruitful ways of speaking."[1] However, Rorty acknowledges that it is possible to be both a systematic philosopher and revolutionary. Revolutionaries establish new schools of philosophy or new paradigms within which normal, professionalized philosophy can be practiced; often they are constructive and provide well thought out arguments for justifying their claims. René Descartes, Immanuel Kant, and Bertrand Russell represent systematic philosophers who were revolutionary. In contrast, such edifying philosophers as Søren Kierkegaard and Friedrich Nietzsche dreaded the thought that their vocabularies should ever be institutionalized. Nietzsche, for instance, said that he sought fellow creators, not disciples. The great edifying philosophers react to the well-established systematic philosophy of their time, and they attempt to debunk it with satires, parodies, and aphorisms, not with well conceived rational arguments. Of course, their work loses its force when the period they are reacting against has passed. Their place is intentionally on the periphery of the philosophical establishment. As Rorty says, "For edifying discourse is *supposed* to be abnormal, to take us out of our old selves by the power of strangeness, to aid us in becoming new beings."[2]

We turn now to Rorty's understanding of the "liberal ironist." Following a definition of Judith Shklar, Rorty says that liberals believe "that cruelty is the worst thing people do,"[3] suggesting that the liberal ironist is concerned with the causes of pain in the world and reducing suffering. What identifies the ironist is the realization that one has no final vocabulary to justify giving priority to pain. Ironists have radical and continuous doubts about final vocabularies, because they realizes that others, with different final vocabularies, confidently appeal to them as if they had a firm epistemological foundation. Ironists also realize that arguments phrased in a present vocabulary can never remove these doubts about final vocabularies, nor do they think that their own final vocabulary is closer to truth and reality than any of the others. When pressed, Rorty acknowledges that there is no answer to the question, Why not be cruel?

The only response possible is that it holds conviction as part of his current vocabulary. The liberal ironist, then, acknowledges only the relative validity of one's convictions, yet stands by them unflinchingly.[4]

For the Platonist, on the other hand, such forms as justice and goodness are eternal, universal, and unchanging. They "exist" outside "the world of appearance" and are beyond history. A single permanent "form" or reality is located behind the many temporal appearances. Once it has apprehended this reality the rational mind cannot doubt the solid foundation upon which decisions about pain and cruelty are built. Such smug assurance about the foundation of truth is just what the liberal ironist doubts. The major difference between the two perspectives relates back to their final vocabularies: the Platonist does not seem to question his final vocabulary as the liberal ironist does.

In the end, the liberal ironist does not find Platonic dualism with its eternal forms useful, but neither does he find the theory of the correspondence between the physical bed in which one sleeps and the mental concept of the bed helpful. Again, there is no neutral perspective from which to compare one concept of a bed with another or to compare these concepts with the actual bed. So, for the liberal ironist the epistemological theory of empiricism has no more legitimacy than the theory of idealism. The artist creates in the painting his notion of a bed, and in so doing, creates rather than discovers the reality, like the idealist and the empiricist. Contrary to claims about foundations, Rorty maintains that both the empiricist and the Platonist are also creating their realities. They create the "Truth" and the "Reality," and then seek to justify them from the context of their final vocabularies.

Although Rorty eschews "systems," as mentioned earlier, his philosophy comes closer to the artist's than to the epistemological Platonist or the Lockean empiricist. He believes the edifying philosophers and the liberal ironists are more on target than the systematic philosophers or those who believe that truth mirrors nature. Rorty sometimes refers to his approach as postmodern, using the term in the narrow sense of having a "distrust of metanarratives."[5] He also calls his position "pragmatism," for he believes the important issue today to be "how to be useful rather than how to be right," or how to arrive at what is true.[6] Rorty says, for example:

> [Platonism is] the claim that the point of inquiry is to get in touch with something like Being, or the Good, or Truth, or Reality—something large and powerful which we have a duty to apprehend correctly. By

contrast, pragmatism must be defined as the claim that the function of inquiry is . . . to "relieve and benefit the condition of man"—to make us happier by enabling us to cope more successfully with the physical environment and with each other.[7]

With his neopragmatism, Rorty seeks to steer a philosophical path between the extremes of absolutism and relativism.

Closely associated with Rorty's neopragmatism is the concept, "the linguistic turn." Significant turns have occurred throughout the history of philosophy. The earliest Greek philosophers, for instance, were interested in identifying the fundamental substances. Eventually they came up with four: earth, water, air, and fire. Once they thought they had exhausted this problem with the tools at hand they shifted to morality. Socrates explored the moral problem of how ought one to live. In the modern period, philosophers have turned to epistemology, and Descartes and a host of others addressed the problems associated with knowing. Rorty, seeing a need for yet another change, proposes: "the linguistic turn":

> Once the philosophy of language was freed from ". . . the dogmas of empiricism," sentences were no longer thought of as expressions of experience nor as representations of extra-experiential reality. Rather, they were thought of as strings of marks and noises used by human beings in the development and pursuit of social practices—practices which enabled people to achieve their ends, ends which do not include "representing reality as it is in itself."[8]

By employing the linguistic turn, Rorty both includes and excludes concepts in his final vocabulary. He thinks that "intuitively" people believe there is a world out there, but descriptions of the world are created by human beings. The world is indifferent to the varied descriptions created by people. To say, therefore, there is a world out there is quite different from claiming there is truth out there. Humans describe the world in language, for there is no other way to do so. These descriptions of the world are true or false: humans decide; the world itself cannot. Likewise, there is no vocabulary "out there" awaiting discovery. The world does not speak, only humans do; so humans create rather than discover their languages. What we call truth is a property of linguistic entities—of sentences, not of experience. The major thrust of Rorty's concept of the linguistic turn is that only sentences can be true, and they are dependent upon vocabularies and grammar, both made by humans. Humans, therefore, create rather than discover the truth.

Once Rorty adopts the linguistic turn, he is led to "a nonepistemological sort of philosophy."[9] As he has maintained in other contexts, there is no standpoint outside our particular, historically conditioned, and temporal vocabulary from which to judge anything. Rorty therefore advises us to relinquish the notion that there can be reasons for using languages as well as reasons within languages for believing statements.[10] It is simply impossible to step outside our various vocabularies to find a metavocabulary that encompasses all possible vocabularies and all possible ways of feeling and judging. What is more, Rorty does not limit this claim about language to philosophical discourse. He includes the language used by scientists, poets, political thinkers—in other words *all* language. They all invent descriptions for their own purposes, but "there is no sense in which *any* of these descriptions, is an accurate representation of the way the world is in itself."[11] Even scientific revolutions bring about only a shift in paradigms, or "a metaphoric redescription" of nature, not new insights into the intrinsic nature of nature.[12]

Rorty acknowledges that he is "a historcist and a nominalist" who seeks to cure us of our great metaphysical need. During the Age of Enlightenment, distinctions were made between rational and irrational, relative and absolute, morality and prudence. Rorty contends these distinctions are outdated. Now they are impediments to the preservation and progress of democratic societies. Languages are means of communication, tools for social interaction, ways of tying oneself to other human beings.[13] New vocabularies are created by trial and error, not as a means for more correct expression or representation of the truth. The question is whether some of our words get in the way of other words.[14] A new language is a tool that works better for certain purposes than did a previous tool. As we have seen, the world does not provide us with any criterion for choice between alternative languages, so "we can only compare languages or metaphors with one another, not with something beyond language called 'fact.'"[15]

Contending that societies are held together by common vocabularies and common hopes, Rorty believes we should settle for narratives that connect the present not only with the past, but with "the utopian future." In order to persuade others, one employs resdescription rather than correspondence and inference. One defines one's views by their relationship to previous views rather than by their relationship to the truth.

One employs persuasion rather than force, so that whatever is true and good is whatever is the outcome of free discussion. According to Rorty, there is no teleology running through history, nor is there a common human nature; moral progress is the history of increasingly useful metaphors, rather than increasing understanding of how things really are. It is no longer useful to desire something that stands beyond history and institutions; in fact, Rorty believes such a notion has become unintelligible. Although beliefs may no longer be thought to be grounded in God, forms, empirical reality, or human nature, and although we now realize beliefs are created by human beings, beliefs continue to be important because they can and do regulate human action. Beliefs can still be thought worth dying for, even if they are based on nothing deeper than contingent historical circumstance.[16]

Perhaps these words best capture Rorty's understanding of the situation of the neopragmatist living within the Grand Narrative of the postmodernist de-divinized world. We are no longer

> . . . able to see any use for the notion that finite, mortal, contingently existing human beings might derive the meanings of their lives from anything except other finite, mortal, contingently existing human beings.[17]

According to Rorty, every reflective person has a final vocabulary. This suggests that a person is born into a culture and eventually learns its language. To learn how language is used, according to Ludwig Wittgenstein (who was a major influence on Rorty), is to learn a language-game. Through the language-game we are socialized in a specific way. If we had been born and nurtured in a different culture, we would view things differently, even be different selves. Thus, "to be a person is to speak a *particular* language, one which enables us to discuss particular beliefs and desires with particular sorts of people."[18] The final vocabulary consists of a set of words we carry around to justify beliefs and actions, to make judgments, and to tell the stories of our lives. If doubt is cast upon our judgment, we cannot make further appeals. The final vocabulary employs "thin, flexible, ubiquitous terms" such as true, good, right, and beautiful. But lying behind these terms are "thicker" more rigid terms such as "the Bible says," "the church teaches," "professional standards require," and "they say." The thicker terms are used to back up the thin terms. One whose final vocabulary is repudiated might respond with helpless passivity or resort to force. A final vocabulary, then, is a kind of final court of appeal where we account for our values, claims, and actions.[19] Rorty's explication of final vocabularies is based on a conviction that "language goes all the way down"—there is no way to reach outside the language-game to an account of the relations between the language-game as a construct and the world as content.

Rorty also employs the term *narrative*, in the sense of a Grand Narrative.[20] We are born into a culture where words, sentences, language-games, and final vocabularies are already in place. The child who is being educated receives the impression that solid foundations lie beneath these terms. Rorty believes this aids the child's psychological well-being. But the neopragmatist or liberal ironist, who believes that no certain foundations exist, relies upon the language-game of the culture to provide a context for response. Realizing the variety of language-games leads neopragmatists to be suspicious about all language-games, including their own. Rorty contends, "What is essential is telling a new story, suggesting a new language-game, in the hope of a new form of intellectual life."[21] It is "this telling of a new story" that leads to the concept of the Grand Narrative.

Underlying Rorty's Grand Narrative is a conviction that there are no truths, factual or moral, independent of language, nor a neutral ground from which to judge language-games. So he is left with a situation where he plays off scenarios against contrasting scenarios, projects against alternative projects, and descriptions against redescriptions. He says, "To be a person is to speak a *particular* language-game, one which enables us to discuss particular beliefs and desires with particular sorts of people."[22] He places his beliefs within the context of a Grand Narrative, and by playing his beliefs off against the views of other thinkers, he hopes to persuade others.

According to Rorty, then, people learn language-games, of which final vocabularies are a part; and final vocabularies are provided within a framework provided by a Grand Narrative. "Narrative means telling a story about something, like the world spirit, or Europe, man, the West, culture, freedom, class struggle. It is the story of some big thing like that, in which you place your own story."[23] The purpose of these narratives is to give some sense of meaning to our existence, and they provide a way for contemporary thinkers to relate to the great thinkers of the past.

Rorty's Grand Narrative tells the story about the modern movement whose primary focus has changed from religion to science to philosophy to literature. He finds the early writings of Hegel especially illuminating, for he discovers philosophical writing in narrative form, telling about the history of human nature.[24] Writing such narratives, Rorty believes, is the most fruitful path for post-epistemological philosophy today, for Hegel's Romantic view of history opened the way to a literary culture. Hegel also showed how reason might be temporalized, as the world spirit sought to become conscious of itself in the progressive development of various world cultures. This in turn led to the desire to perfect the self by appeal to literary sources. Hegel's effect was to create competition between science and philosophy, science and literature, and finally literature and philosophy as each sought to dominate the culture. Hegel, then, provided the basic dynamism for the transition from science and philosophy to literature as the constituting element of culture. In Rorty's reading of the situation, this literary culture is best articulated in terms of the neopragmatist concern for the utility of vocabularies. Much of Rorty's interest in the thought of Søren Kierkegaard, Friedrich Nietzsche, and Martin Heidegger "was to understand what happened after Hegel." The main components of his Grand Narrative are chapters in this story.

Religious Humanism at Its Formative Stage. We have attempted to understand what constitutes Rortyian neopragmatism. The second question we must answer is, What is religious humanism? My response to this question must be even briefer than it was to the first. I can offer here only the sketchiest outline of the most salient features of this distinctive approach to religion, which originated in the United States among Unitarians at about the time of the First World War. The movement eventually embraced two groups: one consisted of some Unitarians, Universalists, and Ethical Culturalists; the other was a group of academics. Notably among them were Roy Wood Sellars, a member of the philosophy department at the University of Michigan, A. Eustace Haydon, professor of comparative religions at the University of Chicago, and John Dewey, a member of the philosophy department at Columbia University. All three signed a very controversial document in 1933, entitled "A Humanist Manifesto," (the first draft was penned by Sellars), and all three wrote books contributing to the literary canon of religious humanism.

Using Rorty's vocabulary one could say they created a Grand Narrative in which they described the developmental stages of religion. Often they referred to "a primitive age of ignorance" characterized by dynamism and animism, and followed by polytheism, henotheism, dualism, monotheism, deism, pantheism, and finally naturalistic humanism. The development, of course, was far more complex and less progressive than I have suggested, but the early religious humanists were historicists and nominalists in Rorty's sense of the terms. Sellars, for instance, said, "Once we have cut the supposed bonds with the supernatural world, we see that religion is, and always has been a social product."[25] They also thought that the metaphors of past religions were dead, and that the new metaphors created by the religious humanists provided an appropriate direction for religion in their time.

The religious humanists were convinced that religion was created by humans, not gods who always speak the words of humans. These humanists provided a functional interpretation of religion: it was created by humans to serve certain purposes. Haydon spoke of religion as "the mother of dreams."[26] "The task is to impose human purpose upon the cosmic process, to shape the course of the flowing stream of life with its millions of conflicting drives, so that it will converge toward the practical expression of creative idealism."[27] Sellars maintained the function of religion was to preserve and further human values.[28] Generally, humanists thought of religion as "intelligent participation in the human quest for the good life in a shared world . . ."[29]

Theirs was "a religion without God." True, Dewey employed the word *God* to designate the process whereby the actual is transformed into the ideal, but his friend and colleague Corliss Lamont maintained that Dewey used the term to avoid offending the sensitivities of friends who were theists. However, the word caused such controversy that he repented of having used it. Several statements in *A Common Faith* about religion require no concept of God—for instance, "Any activity pursued in behalf of an ideal end against obstacles and in spite of threats of personal loss because of conviction of its general and enduring value is religious in quality."[30]

Haydon used the pragmatic test to judge claims about the helpfulness of the gods: "What the gods have been expected to do, and have failed to do through the ages, man must find the courage and intelligence to do for himself. More needful than faith in God is faith that man can give love, justice, peace and all his beloved moral values embodiment in human relations. Denial of this faith is the only real atheism."[31]

According to the religious humanists, people can be moral without belief in God. Sellars said, "[M]orality is primarily a group affair. It is a term for the customs which have grown up through the generations and which are absorbed by each new-born individual in his turn, much as he takes in the air he breathes."[32] Conscience, rather than being the voice of God in the soul of the believer, was viewed by the religious humanists as "a reproduction of tribal morality." To be moral, people do not need the supernatural sanction of a "heavenly policeman." Morality "must justify itself by its actual working in human life."[33] It is primarily a social product, a historical achievement.

By repudiating the notion of a brain/mind dualism, the religious humanists also repudiated belief in personal immortality. According to Sellars, the new naturalism "has realized that personality is in large measure a social product rooted in the social history of the group."[34] The humanists were convinced that consciousness was totally dependent upon the brain; if the brain is dead, so are the mind, and consciousness. Sellars maintained, "True religion and the spiritual are within you. They are the only Kingdom of Heaven."[35] But beyond these considerations, the concept of personal immortality had become a dead metaphor. The goal of religion is to promote the spiritual in humans, understanding that the spiritual has relevance only between birth and death. In this broad and general sense, "The spiritual emerges when there is intelligence of a fairly high order, a sense of right and wrong, an ability to set standards, a drive for creation in art and in social relations, a wealth of imagination."[36]

In summary, religious humanists viewed religion as a human creation to contribute to both personal and social well-being. Unlike the traditional understandings of religion, even the more liberal ones, it repudiated belief in God, the belief that humans could not be moral without the concept of God to support morality, and the belief that humans were immortal in any personal sense.

Rorty's Neopragmatism as an Option for Religious Humanists. This brings us to our third question, What might a religious narrative look like constructed within the general perspective of Rortyian neopragmatism? Religious humanism and Rorty's neopragmatism certainly seem compatible. Both promote naturalism and repudiate various forms of supernaturalism, and both interpret truth in terms of its pragmatic usefulness. Two areas, however, require some comment. The first is the differences between an earlier pragmatism and neopragmatism. Earlier pragmatism had a greater respect for an empirical epistemology; specifically, it employed the empirical method because it worked better in certain areas than other theories of truth. Using the empirical method because it works better in certain cases differs from using it because its concepts mirror nature; in fact, such religious humanists as Roy Wood Sellars often employed an empiricist epistemology to refute theistic beliefs. By adopting the linguistic turn, Rorty finds the grounds used by religious humanists to refute theistic claims equally as suspect as the theists' claims of divine revelation. Rorty, it would seem, would agree with the humanists' conclusions but not with their method for reaching them. The language of theism he finds simply not useful; its dead metaphors might best be discarded.

The second area requiring comment is religion itself. In his writings Rorty expresses the desire to live in both a post-metaphysical and a post-theological culture. He certainly considers language that encourages people to think of themselves as responsible to nonhuman powers contributes to an undesirable, even harmful understanding of the self, because it is contrary to the promotion of a liberal democratic society. According to Rorty, if we dropped these metaphors, a new kind of human being would arise. Rorty therefore wishes to discard both religious and philosophical accounts of a superhistorical ground for belief in favor of a completely secular culture with no trace of divinity.[37]

Do Rorty's beliefs entail a fully secular culture and a repudiation of all expressions of religion—including religious humanism, with its interpretation of religion without God—or may a neoreligious humanism be compatible with Rorty's neopragmatism? It certainly is tempting to associate him with either Paul Tillich's broad concept of religion as a state of being ultimately concerned, or Fred Streng's concept of religion as a means of human transformation. I especially found Rorty's *Contingency, Irony, and Solidarity,* not only intellectually provocative, but even inspiring, and I think one could make a case for Rorty's being a religious thinker in Tillich's and Streng's broad definitions of the term.[38] But I shall not succumb to the temptation of claiming that Rorty is religious without knowing it. However, since Rorty has published his ideas, they are no longer his alone; they now belong to anyone who wishes to use them. So I will explore how Rorty's neopragmatism might provide some useful metaphors for creating a neoreligious humanism.

Neoreligious humanists, in accord with Rorty, will maintain that religious belief consists of a language-game created by humans. Beliefs were neither revealed to humans by the gods, nor based on truths that mirror nature. They are solely the products of human imagination. Since many metaphors of traditional religion—God, soul, heaven and hell, and "doing the will of God"—are all now dead, they will be deleted from the religious humanist vocabulary. Language will be viewed as just a tool for trying to make sense of one's life. Since religious humanists will embrace a narrative in which there is no teleology or divine purpose in the world or in nature, the human enterprise will be construed as just one more among nature's experiments, not the culmination of nature's design.[39] The only purposes or goals are those created by individuals or institutions for themselves. Success or failure in reaching these goals depends solely upon human intelligence and effort. The world, apart from humans, is indifferent to human projects and purposes.

Rorty's neopragmatism has two broad goals, one private and the other social, that religious humanists might well endorse. The private goal is self-creation, and the social goal is reducing pain and cruelty. Rorty believes that it is better to be kind to others than to torture them. Neither of his goals can be validated outside the language-game. Others must be convinced of the desirability of these goals by persuasion, not force.

Personal autonomy is required for self-creation, a goal that Rorty believes not all humans are capable of understanding and obtaining. Of all those who hope to become autonomous human beings through the process of self-creation, only a few actually succeed.[40] Self-overcoming and self-invention are concepts associated with autonomy, which suggests that one of the goals of a liberal democratic society is to enable people to achieve their widely different private ends without hurting each other.[41]

Rorty offers two specific models for those engaged in seeking self-invention: the "ironist theorist" and the "strong poet," a term borrowed from Harold Bloom. The ironist theorists attempt to become autonomous by getting out from under an old final vocabulary and fashioning one of their own.[42] In so doing, they create the "tastes" by which they will be judged, and become in turn their own judges, not unlike Clamence, the judge-penitent in Albert Camus' *The Fall*. In other words, the ironists themselves judge their lives in their own terms, caring not about how they look to the universe, but how they look to themselves. Some ironist theorists will be primarily devoted to self-creation, and have little or no concern for social policy. Since such ironists are interested not in power but in personal perfection, one of their challenges is how to overcome authority without claiming authority.[43]

Like the ironist theorists, the strong poets also seek to become autonomous. They do so by refusing to accept someone else's description of themselves, or by refusing to play a role in a previously prepared script. They are quite capable of telling their story in words never before used.[44] They divide the old from the new, accepting what is relevant from the past and discarding the irrelevant. They are not concerned about separating the temporal from the eternal. To use a metaphor from Bloom, the strong poet "gives birth to oneself" and maintains that human nature is not intrinsic, but a "set of powers" to be developed or left undeveloped.

Life itself is a poem to be written by how one lives. In the liberal utopia, the strong poet—certainly not the warrior, the priest, the sage, the objective scientist, or the athlete—will be a cultural hero.

Rorty's neopragmatism also has concerns in the public or social sphere, apparent in his endorsing a liberal democratic society and in hoping for a liberal utopia. He believes that we need not only a new private vocabulary, but also a new public vocabulary. We need, therefore artists—poets, novelists, and playwrights—who will create narratives enabling us to see the effects of social practices and institutions, to realize the pain caused by racial discrimination, poverty, sexism, homophobia, and various prejudices. We also need artists who will help us to see the effects of our private behavior on others, to see how certain people are cruel to others. Often the works of psychologists and fiction writers will expose our blindness to the pain one kind of person is causing another; we may even realize how our attempts at personal autonomy, our seeking a certain kind of perfection, may blind us to the pain and humiliation we are causing those around us. Literary works may dramatize the conflict between duties to ourselves and to others. Rorty says, "Novelists can do something which is socially useful—help us to attend to the springs of cruelty in ourselves, as well as the fact of its occurrence in areas where we had not noticed it."[45]

The liberal democratic society will contain diversity and plurality. Conflicts will arise between those committed to an old final vocabulary, both public and private, and those committed to a new one. Yet they will seek to speak a common language in the public sphere, expressing the liberals' concern to lessen pain and increase justice; they will act according to John Rawls's theory of justice, which addresses inequalities by arranging them to benefit the least advantaged. Since freedom for it's citizens is a major concern of a liberal democratic society, citizens must abide by the outcome of such encounters and conversations.

Rorty's ultimate hope, a liberal utopia, will provide a culture in which strong poets and ironic theorists become heroes and irony is universal. This culture will achieve solidarity through an increasing sensitivity to the pain and humiliation experienced by others. We will learn to see unfamiliar sorts of people as "one of us" rather than "one of them." With a sense of solidarity, citizens will have reached a consensus that the point of social organization is to provide everyone a chance at self-creation to the best of their abilities, and that that goal requires, besides peace and wealth, the standard "bourgeois freedoms."[46] The literary artists and politicians will be the leaders in charting the new directions for the culture, which will not be a religious, or scientific, or philosophical, but "a poeticized culture." The novel, the movie, the play, the opera, and even television will replace the sermon and the metaphysical treatise as vehicles for moral change and progress.

Rorty offers two words of caution about utopian thinking. First, utopias are conceived by poets with creative imaginations. As a culture moves toward the hoped-for dreams, poets imagine still further utopias; therefore, utopia is not a fixed and static concept like a Christian heaven somewhere beyond history or a static Marxist concept at the end of history, but is a never-ending process *in* history. It focuses on an endless increase in the realization of freedom, not on some already existing "Truth." Second, Rorty is also well aware that there are language-games which speak of causal factors creating novel situations, and there is his language-game that expresses hope for a liberal utopia. It therefore is difficult to have a clear vision as to exactly how one might bring about the desired goal: "We cannot tell ourselves a story about how to get from the actual present to such a future. We can picture various socioeconomic setups which would be preferable to the present one. But we have no clear sense how to get from the actual world to those theoretically possible worlds, and thus no clear idea what to work for."[47] Yet Rorty is confident that our language-games influence our perceptions of ourselves and the world even though we cannot know how the process works. We shall have to feel our way by trial and error, especially when we deal with new goals for which we have not developed habits.

In summary, a dichotomy runs through Rorty's neopragmatism. The private sphere deals with such issues as the meaning of life, and Rorty embraces a private vocabulary expressing concern for such things as autonomy and self-creation, which are necessarily private, unshared, and unsuited for debate. In the social sphere, concerns are for human solidarity, for people in a culture must be bonded together if their institutions and public practices are to become more just and less cruel. The vocabulary of justice is necessarily public and shared, an appropriate medium for argument and debate. Issues about social virtues are the language of the tribe. Both languages, of the private and public spheres, are equally valid; yet Rorty views them as incommensurable. For any particular individual, there is no answer to the question, When should I struggle against injustice, and when should I devote myself to private projects of self-creation? Ultimately one must decide for oneself; the universe is silent about such dilemmas.[48]

Religious humanists can generally embrace the foregoing components of Rorty's vocabulary, but there is one metaphor they would like to add: an institution for those who desire some mediation between the public and private spheres. My construal of this institution will be informed by Rorty's vocabulary. For lack of a better metaphor, I shall refer to this institution as a liberal democratic church. It will provide a bridge in certain areas for those individuals who do not wish to go it alone, to move them from the private sphere to the public/private sphere of the church, and thence out into the completely public sphere of the secular world with the hope of improving it—not by making it more religious, but by making it a better place in which to live.

The liberal democratic church will be a voluntary association where people gather for serious conversation and human community. Such a church will be noncreedal and inclusive. A person's private beliefs—whether one be atheist, theist, or agnostic—will not be cause for exclusion from membership. Any who feel the need for human community will be welcomed. The political structure of the liberal church will be democratic, not hierarchical; "truth" will not be handed down from those at the top to those at the bottom. The members will select their leaders and, if need be, fire them. Likewise they will create their own religious agenda, and the church will be free and open to all varieties of opinion. Consensus will be derived from study, conversation, and debate among the members.

The purpose of the liberal church will be to provide a place and context for its members to struggle with issues dealing with the meaning of life, to provide members mutual support in facing the normal crises of life, and to provide a calendar celebrating the important stages of the life cycle—for instance, marriage, the birth of a child, the coming of age of an adult, and death. There also might be services to celebrate the changing seasons.

The focus of the liberal church will be on living in the natural world that is our home. The world has given us life, sustains us, and will be our final and eternal resting place; the natural world should inspire a kind of piety involving respect and gratitude, though it will be indifferent to these expressions of human thankfulness.

The ideals of the liberal church will include concern for both private and social well-being. The members will be encouraged to become their own creators, to become their own versions of strong poets and ironist theorists; they will be encouraged to participate in other institutions that seek to address important local, national, and international problems so that pain and suffering will be diminished and justice and living well will be extended. By means of a value-centered program, children will be educated so that they might grow up to be citizens of sound character and take on responsibility for creating "a liberal utopia."

Conclusion. Let us return to the discussion of beds. We can now see that Rorty has turned Plato on his head. The heroes and models of the liberal utopia will not be philosopher-kings who have apprehended truth and justice from outside the realm of history and change; rather, the new models will be the creative artists whose imaginations will help us to see, and feel, and desire things we have heretofore not dreamed of. If religious humanists opt for neopragmatism as broadly outlined here, they too will have to become "neo." They must move onto the new soft terrain provided by the post-epistemological turn, looking to, perhaps even becoming, imaginative, creative artists. The task of a religious humanist society is to address the twin concerns of encouraging individuals to become self-creators and challenging society to become more free and just, to express concern for the well-being of both individuals and the culture. Their Bible will not be the divinely revealed scriptures of the past, but the imaginative writings of the novelists, dramatists, and poets of the present. Their focus will not be on saving souls for heaven and avoiding hell, but in making life a bit less painful and creating a world to be a fit place for our progeny to dwell in the future.

NOTES

1. Richard Rorty, *Philosophy and the Mirror of Nature* (Princeton: Princeton University Press, 1980) p. 360.

2. *Ibid.*, p. 360.

3. Richard Rorty, *Contingency, Irony, and Solidarity* (Cambridge: Cambridge University Press, 1989), p. xv.

4. *Ibid.*, p. 46.

5. Richard Rorty, *Essays on Heidegger and Others* (Cambridge: Cambridge University Press, 1991), p. 1.

6. *Ibid.*, p. 5.

7. *Ibid.*, p. 27.

8. Richard Rorty, ed., *The Linguistic Turn* (Chicago: University of Chicago Press, 1992), p. 373.

9. Rorty, *Philosophy and the Mirror of Nature*, p. 381.

10. Rorty, *Contingency, Irony, and Solidarity*, p. 48.

11. *Ibid.*, p. 4.

12. *Ibid.*, p. 16.

13. *Ibid.*, p. 41.

14. *Ibid.*, p. 12.

15. *Ibid.*, p. 20.

16. *Ibid.*, p. 189.

17. *Ibid.*, p. 45.

18. *Ibid.*, p. 177.

19. *Ibid.*, p. 73.

20. Hall appropriately employs the term "Grand" Narrative to elucidate this component of Rorty's thought. See David L. Hall, *Richard Rorty: Prophet and Poet of the New Pragmatism* (Albany: State University of New York Press, 1994), pp. 21–23.

21. Richard Rorty, *Consequences of Pragmatism* (Minneapolis: University of Minnesota Press, 1989), p. 220.

22. *Ibid.*, p. 177.

23. Rorty made this comment in an interview with Borradori. See Giovanna Borradori, *The American Philosopher* (Chicago: University of Chicago Press, 1994), p. 114.

24. In the same interview Rorty said, ". . . in Hegel's early Writings, there is a kind of philosophical writing that is narrative in form; it is a story about the history of human nature. I believe that's become the dominant mode of philosophical thought . . ." p. 113.

25. Roy Wood Sellars, *Religion Coming of Age* (New York: Macmillan, 1928), p. 252.

26. A. Eustace Haydon, *The Quest of the Ages* (New York: Harper & Brothers, 1929), p. 205.

27. *Ibid.*, p. 207.

28. Sellars, *Religion Coming of Age*, p. 249.

29. Haydon, *The Quest of the Ages*, p. 230.

30. John Dewey, *A Common Faith* (New Haven: Yale University Press, 1934), p. 27.

31. A. Eustace Haydon, *Biography of the Gods* (New York: Frederick Ungar, 1941), p. 329.

32. Sellars, *Religion Coming of Age*, p. 256.

33. *Ibid.*, p. 259.

34. *Ibid.*, p. 239.

35. *Ibid.*, p. 247.

36. *Ibid.*, p. 244.

37. Rorty, *Contingency, Irony, and Solidarity*, p. 45.

38. Of Course, Rorty is aware of this issue, for he says, "When these terms are broadly enough defined, everybody, even atheists, will be said to have a religious faith (in the Tillichian sense of a 'symbol of ultimate concern')." See his *Objectivity, Relativism, and Truth* (Cambridge: Cambridge University Press, 1991), p. 182.

39. Rorty, *Contingency, Irony, and Solidarity*, p. 45.

40. *Ibid.*, p. 65.

41. Rorty, *Essays on Heidegger and Others*, p. 196.

42. Rorty, *Contingency, Irony, and Solidarity*, p. 97.

43. *Ibid.*, p. 105.

44. *Ibid.*, p. 28.

45. *Ibid.*, p. 95.

46. *Ibid.*, p. 84.

47. *Ibid.*, p. 182.

48. Rorty reveals that in one way or another he has been struggling with this problem since he entered the University of Chicago at age 15. He says, "Insofar as I had any project in mind, it was to reconcile Trotsky and the orchids." See his autobiographical essay in *Wild Orchids and Trotsky*, edited by Mark Edmundson, (New York: Penguin Books, 1993), p. 15.

RORTY AMONG THE THEOLOGIANS:
The Possibility Of Theology After The New Historicism

Hendrik R. Pieterse

In this paper I inquire into the radical challenge of the so-called "new historicism" for a postmodern understanding and justification of the reality of God in our culture. In a recent article (and a subsequent book), William Dean articulated this new historicist challenge with admirable clarity. According to Dean, the central claim that new historicists have espoused consistently is that there is

> not a deeper truth behind or beneath the events of social history, despite the long tradition that says that there is. Further, and more explicitly historicist, they have argued that actual truths are entirely historical creatures, conceived within history, directed at history, and grown in a historical chain, as interpretation refers to interpretation refers to interpretation throughout history (Dean 1986:261).

What makes the new historicism new is that it wants to replace an "older historicism." The older historicism is *theological* insofar as it claims that "there is more to history than the combined forces of freedom and destiny, that history is influenced also by an extrahistorical, universal, and eternal reality, usually called God, sometimes called the Absolute" (Dean 1988: p. 2). Even though theologians in this older "onto-theological" tradition did incorporate the ambiguous reality of history, finally, they all held out for something not "truly subject to the contingencies of history, and thereby still extrahistorical" (Dean 1988: p. 4).

New historicists, like Richard Rorty, deny that any claim for such universal, ahistorical, and eternal God or Absolute can be argued coherently. For them, ontological claims by older historicists typically appealed to three things: metaphysics, a theory of language as representational, and the transcendentalized subject. New historicists assert that such appeals are doomed to failure because postmodern historicist critique of these "modern" notions has thoroughly debunked them. From this Rorty concludes that the fate of theology is so entangled in the fate of the whole onto-theological tradition (Heidegger) of Western philosophy that the demise of metaphysics and Philosophy (Rorty's term for foundationalism generally), means that in a secular, "post-Philosophical" culture, it would no longer pay for us to use the vocabulary of theology. Like the Platonic tradition of which it is a part, theology has outlived its usefulness and is now best abandoned (Rorty 1982: p. xiv). A post-Philosophical culture is a "de-divinized" one, a culture from which the last vestiges of transcendence have been removed. It is a culture living without the "metaphysical comfort" of ahistorical, abiding realities (Dean 1988: pp. 4–5).

How does the postmodern theologian respond to Rorty's new historicist challenge? In a postmodern culture, is theology even possible in the precise sense of discourse about a God who is in some sense an ontological, transcendent Reality? Is it possible to develop a theology that bears the full imprint of the new historicism and yet manages to be *theology*? Would it be possible to justify such theological discourse in a publicly credible way?

In what follows, I place Rorty in critical conversation with University of Chicago theologian, David Tracy. Tracy, along with others, could be interpreted as arguing that Rorty's conclusions about the fate of religion in our postmodern culture are wrongheaded and positivistic. Rorty is too quick to dismiss religion and to "change the subject" (Tracy 1987: p. 85). Tracy argues that precisely a *postmodern* construal of reality and reason would restore the religious as an inescapable dimension of human existence, and would do so in a rationally credible way. I will show that Tracy's proposal ultimately fails because its phenomenological-transcendental argument for *homo religiosus* reckons insufficiently with the full impact of the new historicist deconstruction of metaphysics and foundationalism. The failure of Tracy's attempt may seem to provide a *prima facie* justification for Rorty's rather curt dismissal of theology. In the concluding section of the paper, I return to the question about the possibility of theology after the new historicism, specifically as interpreted by Rorty. I will ask about possibilities for theology, not by trying to "prove" Rorty wrong, but by pointing to *aporias* and tensions in Rorty's own model which may provide important toeholds for theology in a historicist culture.

David Tracy would agree with Rorty that we live in a culture in which theological discourse is increasingly being marginalized. The eclipse of theological discourse from the public realm and the consequent marginalization of the "classics" of religion (and art), is a direct consequence of the triumph of calculatory, instrumental, and formal rationality in the modern world, expressed most powerfully in 20th century scientism (Tracy 1981: pp. 7-8). With art and religion effectively marginalized to "reservations of the spirit," scientism and positivism attempt to ground the liberating possibilities of technology. However, technology's "obvious liberating possibilities occur hand in hand with the negative actualities all around us: privatization, population explosion, false economic hopes of continual growth and, looming over all as our technological solution, the threat of nuclear holocaust" (Tracy 1981: p. 342). For Tracy, what is required is a genuinely postmodern understanding of rationality. Such a postmodern rationality will be a more *comprehensive* view of reason, one which establishes the logical and ontological *limits* of instrumental reason precisely by retrieving the power of our present conceptual and symbolic languages (art, philosophy, religion) to negate intellectual, linguistic and societal oppression, while affirming the possibilities of personal and societal liberation (Tracy 1975: p. 13). Art and religion provide both the ethos and world view of society's life (Tracy 1981: p. 7) by asking "the fundamental questions" of human existence.

For Tracy, then, the retrieval of a more comprehensive postmodern rationality equates to a "multi-dimensional" view of reason in which religious classics are appropriate symbolic expressions of the "signals of transcendence" (Berger) within the life world of culture. In this way, the rational status of concrete Christian theological discourse is incorporated into a comprehensive *theory of rationality* for postmodern thought. Tracy advances this theory of rationality on the basis of an ontology of human being construed as intrinsically *homo religiosus*,[1] and thematized with the help of an explicit metaphysical argument. In other words, Tracy puts forward the strong claim that a phenomenological-transcendental excavation of human being as such will reveal an ineluctable "religious dimension" as the ultimate and grounding horizon to all of the self's experience and knowledge. Rendering that religious dimension conceptually coherent would put the one-dimensional, secular self on a journey to *authentic* being by exposing, negatively, his "forgetfulness" of Being, and, positively, his ontological "rootedness" in Reality itself. Moreover, for Tracy, the ontological structure of the self's experience is isomorphic with the structure of the world as a whole, so that the discourses of culture (science, art, morality) can be viewed as linguistic and symbolic objectifications of the self's experience. An argument justifying the religious dimension to the self's experience would *ipso facto* make plausible the reality of a religious dimension to culture. Once the reality and coherence of the religious dimension has been justified by philosophical argument, the justification of concrete theological discourse is not far behind. Some of the perennial questions about human existence asked by any reflective human being (Tracy 1984: pp. 231–232), are properly *religious* questions insofar as they are questions about "the Whole" implicit in the religious dimension to common human experience. Theological texts, *as* religious classics, "are classic human responses to . . . [these] perennial human questions" (p. 232). The tradition-specific discourse of the Christian classics receives its justification as *public* discourse when its epistemic relation to the religious dimension has been thematized. In a crucial way, then, the feasibility of Tracy's entire argument rests on whether or not he is successful in arguing for an universal religious dimension.

Tracy articulates the conceptual contours of the construct *homo religiosus* by way of several closely interlocked notions. It is important to note that these notions mutually imply each other: The *neo-Kantian* features of Tracy's anthropology allows him to assume that human knowledge must have ontological and epistemic limits. Tracy uses a phenomenology of *limit* (limits-to, limits-of) to thematize experience of the religious dimension. The various limits-to experiences of science, morality, and the everyday, may prompt the disclosure of a Reality "however named and in whatever manner experienced, which functions as a final, now gracious, now frightening, now trustworthy, now absurd, always uncontrollable limit-of the very meaning of existence itself" (Tracy 1975: p. 108). The ultimate limit (implied by the religious dimension) functions as ontological *foundation* in that it constitutes "the condition of the possibility" of all knowledge claims whatsoever. In the depths of its own experience, the postmodern self discovers the fundamental "ground," the ontological *foundation,* of all its activity, experience, and cognition in Reality itself, a reality Christians will name "God." The reality of God emerges as the necessary "objective referent" of the inescapable religious dimension of the postmodern self's experience.

The supposition of foundations commits Tracy's model to the logic of *epistemological foundationalism*. For the foundationalist, in order to prevent an infinite regress of justification, a class of beliefs (or sensations, intuitions, or experiences) must be identified which are foundational in the precise sense that they do not themselves require justification (*immediate justification*) but with reference to which all of one's other beliefs are justified (*mediate* justification) (Alston 1976: pp. 165-166). In Tracy's model, the prethematic religious dimension functions as ultimate foundation to *all* of the self's other experiences and discourse and bestows on them their justification as rational claims, while *as* foundation, experience of the religious dimension cannot be justified with reference to scientific, moral, and everyday experience. This requirement inherent in epistemological foundationalism that the ultimate foundation(s) be *self-justifying*, forces Tracy to argue for religious experience of the religious dimension as *sui generis*. Tracy accomplishes this by asserting that religious experience is *prelinguistic*, thus making it logically distinct from ordinary *linguistically* mediated experience. The claim for ontological and epistemic foundations to knowledge requires a centered self capable of complete *self-transparency*. The self accomplishes this through a relentless quest for self-transcending authenticity where authenticity equates to *full self-presence* (see Ray 1987: p. 128). On its part, the need for full self-presence allows Tracy to take a *transcendental* turn since only an explicit metaphysics is capable of rendering conceptually coherent the *a priori* "conditions of the possibility" of all knowledge as such. In this scheme, transcendental method gains a neutrality, an epistemic *objectivity*, vis-a-vis the methods of other discourses. It is precisely this objectivity which allows metaphysics to establish and maintain the "rational space" (Tracy 1992: p. 19) needed for fully public discourse. Taken together, these closely interconnected notions constitute Tracy's "theory of rationality" for a more comprehensive, postmodern construal of reason.

I am now in a position to advance a new historicist, Rortian critique of Tracy's model. The notion of an universal religious dimension to human existence is the key to the success of Tracy's argument, for it is precisely in religious experience that the transcendent reality of God is encountered. Therefore, *failure to make a coherent case for the religious dimension will* ipso facto *mean a failure to argue for the notion of God as an ontologically distinct Other*. I argue that Tracy's defense of a prelinguistic religious dimension (and thus his defense of God's transcendent reality) is unsuccessful for two interrelated reasons: (1) The idea of prelinguistic experience is conceptually incoherent, and cannot withstand the intrusion of language and history. (2) Tracy's appeal to transcendental method to guarantee the full presence and self-transparency required for the religious dimension, is rendered dubious by the new historicist deconstruction of metaphysics. In Tracy's model this is the result in part because of major shifts in his own thinking toward a more historicist position.

(1) Tracy's argument for a prelinguistic religious dimension is incoherent in three interrelated ways: (i) It is unable to establish the *epistemic status* of prelinguistic experience. Many theologians and philosophers (including Rorty) have called into question the very possibility of prelinguistic experience. S. Alan Ray cites Gordon Kaufman as one who, on Kantian epistemological principles, would object that "experience cannot be prelinguistic, but must always be experience of something distinct from the subject. . . . The idea that experience is separable from reflection and communication (language) and can serve as a valid source for theology, that is, that it has some content apart from language, has been consistently and systematically rejected by Kaufman as incoherent" (Ray 1987: p. 104). Tracy certainly wants to argue that the religious dimension disclosed in limit-experiences and mediated through religious-as-limit language has a definite content. As such, it is an identifiable *experience*. However, Tracy's program runs into trouble when he tries to specify the epistemic relation between a prelinguistic experience and its "phenomenal" expression in the linguistic forms of a particular symbol-system. As long as Tracy operates on the assumption that there is an experience of the self or a meaning always "deeper" than its manifestation in language, it means that once the religious experience becomes explicit in a language, it loses its *immediacy* and *self-evidence* (see Ray 1987: p. 108). When this happens, though, the religious experience loses its *foundational* status. This is the problem typical of any Kantian construal of experience and knowledge. Knowledge of the *Ding-an-Sich* is impossible, since all *knowledge* is always the product of the synthesizing activity of the mind. Knowledge is always knowledge of phenomena, never of noumena. However, as Rorty points out, this scheme means that "a Kantian unsynthesized intuition can exert no influence on how it is to be synthesized. . . . Insofar as a Kantian intuition is effable [knowable], it is just a perceptual judgment, and thus not *merely* 'intuitive.' Insofar as it is ineffable [unknowable], it is incapable of having an explanatory function" (Rorty 1982: p. 4). Tracy seems to have an analogous problem: To the extent that a prelinguistic limit-experience is mediated in the symbols and propositions of a particular language, it is just a belief dependent for its justification on other beliefs within that linguistic scheme. To the extent that it remains prelinguistic and extralinguistic, it is ineffable and thus incapable of exercising control over

how it is to be mediated in a particular language structure. If that limit-experience is incapable of exercising epistemic control (incapable of having an explanatory function) over how it is to be re-presented in language, it has the unfortunate result that it becomes impossible to specify what it would be for that prelinguistic experience to serve as justifying foundation for its re-presentation in a particular linguistic scheme. Here we are at one of the central problems for epistemological foundationalism, namely, specifying the relation between theory (here language) and foundation (here prelinguistic experience).

The problem here is, of course, one that every foundationalist epistemology faces: How to determine the epistemic status of the foundational belief(s). The appeal is usually to some form of *intuition*. Tracy indeed claims knowledge of the prelinguistic religious dimension by appeal to intuition. Religious-as-limit experiences are finally immediate because intuitive experiences (Tracy 1975: p. 106). However, Tracy's appeal to intuition saddles him with the same difficulties and incoherences experienced by other foundationalist uses of intuition. It is required of foundational beliefs that they be immediately justified; i.e., that they are self-evident and noninferential. This requirement is needed to prevent an infinite regress of justification. Bonjour shows the difficulty when one invokes intuition to determine the epistemic status of foundational beliefs. The difficulty has to do with the epistemic status of intuitions *themselves:* Are they cognitive states? If an intuition is a cognitive state, it is difficult to see why it should not itself stand in need of justification. If it is not a cognitive state, an intuition does not require justification, but seems apparently incapable of granting it (Bonjour 1978: pp. 10, 11). Moreover, Thiemann has shown convincingly that an appeal to intuition ordinarily conflicts with arguments for ordinary knowledge in that it trades on an *equivocal* use of the phrase "to know" (Thiemann 1985: p. 45). The problem surrounding intuition has lead Rorty to answer 'No' to this "bedrock philosophical issue: can one ever appeal to nonlinguistic knowledge in philosophical argument?" (Rorty 1982: p. xxxvi).

(ii) Even if one should grant Tracy an appeal to prelinguistic religious experience, he faces a further crucial conceptual *aporia* (see Thiemann 1985: p. 15): He is unable to show how God can function as the "objective referent" of a prelinguistic experience. As we saw earlier, Tracy holds that a particular religious experience, such as ecstatic love, discloses *in the same ec-statis* (Tracy 1981: p. 106) a Reality "however named and in whatever manner experienced" (p. 108) which Christians will name "God." The problem is this: "What warrants the move from a self-referential claim [ecstatic love] to a referential claim concerning a distinct other?" (Thiemann 1985: p. 31). How can a *subjective* prelinguistic experience *at the same time* be an experience of an *objective* Other (God)? Religious experiences are per definition *prelinguistic* and thus *beyond* the subject-object distinctions of ordinary linguistically mediated knowledge. Tracy's model does not solve this "conceptual incoherence" inherent in foundationalist arguments (Thiemann 1985: p. 15).

(iii) My critique thus far could be summarized by saying that Tracy gets the relationship between experience and language backward. Critics like George Lindbeck argue persuasively that language is always *logically* prior to any experience, including religious experience. Religious experience is the *product* and not the *cause* of a particular religious linguistic formation (Lindbeck 1984: p. 44). There are no uninterpreted, unthematized experiences. In fact, "we cannot identify, describe, or recognize experience qua experience without the use of signs and symbols" (Lindbeck 1984: p. 36). If this line of criticism is sound, it seems that Tracy's argument for the public rational status of theological discourse is seriously flawed. If religious language is *constitutive* of religious experience, if a network of beliefs and concepts logically (though not psychologically) antecedes all possible experience, then Tracy's attempt to ground the claims of a particular religious community in some universal religious dimension, must be adjudged a failure. He would be unable to render coherent any notion of immediate (in the precise sense of independent of other beliefs for its justification) justification, since if the above considerations are valid, all religious experience is justified in terms of a network of prior beliefs and practices. And in such a network, beliefs and practices presuppose one another, so that a particular belief is always justified with reference to other beliefs. There seems to be no way to argue coherently for a prelinguistic experience that could "ground" these other beliefs and practices. Moreover, to speak of an *universal* religious experience now appears implausible: There can be no universal common experience which different religious communities thematize and conceptualize differently. Rather, they have fundamentally different "depth experiences of what it is to be human" (Lindbeck 1984: p. 41). Of course, a Rortian view of things would find this kind of critique congenial, because it amounts to a radical *historicizing* and *temporalizing* of all knowledge claims as the product of potentially incommensurable language games.

(2) At this stage Tracy may concede to Rorty that human being is "interpretation all the way down." Or he, while conceding that the authentic self can never become transparent to phenomenology, can set out to devise an explicitly transcendental method to articulate the conditions of the possibility for the appearance of the postmodern self's deep meaning (Ray 1987: p. 108). Tracy pursues the latter option. An explicit metaphysics indicates the adequacy of any experience to human existence by "explicating how a particular concept (e.g. time, space, self, or God) functions as a fundamental 'belief' or 'condition of possibility' of all experience" (Tracy 1975: p. 71). Metaphysical analysis renders conceptually coherent the central cognitive claim of the Christian faith, namely, that God is the sole and single objective ground to all reality (p. 147). Since only metaphysical mediation can raise to "full consciousness" the "basic beliefs" which function as conditions of possibility of our existing and understanding at all, this discipline alone is able to articulate how the religious limit-experience can function as "the most basic belief" or condition of possibility of *all* the self's experience (pp. 154–155). Tracy's understanding of metaphysics expresses an assumption that somehow Philosophy (Rorty) constitutes an ahistorical or foundational vocabulary (Magnus 1985: p. 2). Rorty has shown that there simply is no meta-philosophical method which is *tradition-neutral* and *objective*, and thus able to adjudicate the often incommensurable claims of communities of inquiry. There is no discipline called Philosophy which defines the nature of "reason" and "rationality" by virtue of its privileged attachment to reality (Magnus 1985: p. 6). Transcendental effort like Tracy's, says Rorty, "is the impossible attempt to step outside our skins—the traditions, linguistic and other, within which we do our thinking and self-criticism—and compare ourselves with something absolute" (Rorty 1982: p. xix). This is simply the Platonic urge to escape from the finitude of one's own time and place all over again (p. xix).

I could cite many of Rorty's claims against this transcendental turn, but in an important way Tracy has done Rorty's work for him. For in Tracy's later work, especially in *Plurality and Ambiguity*, Tracy goes a long way toward incorporating in a radical manner the dimensions of history and language into *all* thinking and doing. This represents important shifts in Tracy's thinking which, on their part, create difficult *aporias* and tensions in Tracy's overall project. In particular, Tracy's historicist turn problematizes two of his key claims: (1) The possibility of full self-presence or self-transparency, and (2) the *privileged* status (objectivity) of metaphysical discourse. The radical intrusion of history and language in postmodern thought (as in Derrida and Foucault, for example) has displaced the centered ego from its false pretensions to mastery and certainty: "We are all de-centered egos now" (Tracy 1987: p. 50). Historical ambiguity presents us with *systemic* distortion and evil. There is a split within consciousness *itself*: "The split self of postmodernity is caught between conscious activity and a growing realization of the radical otherness not only around us but within us" (Tracy 1987: p. 77). This leads Tracy to conclude:

> The fact is that we have left modernity behind. We have left any belief in the transparency of consciousness to itself. Reality and knowledge are now linked to language. And with a heightened sense of language, the interruptive realities of history and society entered consciousness anew (1987: p. 78).

Notice the difficulty Tracy now has: We said earlier that Tracy's argument for prelinguistic religious experience *presupposes* a self capable of self-transparency insofar as he is able to *know*, to *experience*, the ontological limits of his cognitional activity. But it is precisely *this* attempt at self-presence that Tracy now dismisses as a futile hangover from modernity. A crucial question now becomes: Given the loss of self-presence, how will the postmodern self account for *religious* experience? How will the self recognize an experience precisely *as* limit-experience when the self-transparency necessary for that experience cannot be had? If complete self-presence is impossible, the ability to *experience* and *identify* a religious limit-experience becomes impossible. But if the plausibility of an universal religious dimension cannot be stated coherently, how will Tracy continue to justify his argument for *homo religiosus*?

Notice that to appeal to transcendental method now is not going to get Tracy very far. Hermeneutical acknowledgment of the "linguistic turn" and radical historicity means that *no* discourse—not even metaphysics—escapes the all-encompassing nature of language and history. *All* understanding is hermeneutical. Transcendental method is as ideologically situated and systemically distorted as any other discourse. As Tracy himself acknowledged, every discourse, including metaphysics, bears within itself the anonymous and repressed actuality of highly particular arrangements of power and knowledge (Tracy 1987: p. 79). This means that metaphysics and transcendental method, precisely as *historical* discourses, lose their privileged position, their epistemic objectivity, and become just one more historical language game.

Given the historicist critique so far with its emphasis on the pervasiveness of language and history (as well as a historicizing trend in Tracy's later work), the basic components of Tracy's model seem in jeopardy: The notion of an extralinguistic, ahistorical religious dimension cannot withstand the constant invasion of language and history. Moreover, the demise of metaphysics leaves us without an "objective" discipline capable of creating the "rational space" for *public* discourse, where any claim to truth and reason can be adjudicated. Lastly, the incoherence of the religious dimension, but especially the demise of metaphysics as metadiscourse, undermines the theologian's attempt to justify the truth-claims of theological assertions. Once it is admitted that there is no discourse capable of securing complete self-transparency, it becomes impossible to illuminate the epistemic relation between the tradition-specific claims of the Christian faith and the supposed universal religious dimension. Theology's truth depends vitally on its ability to "re-present" this religious dimension. How will the claim to truth of Christian statements be justified if the very method necessary to secure that re-presentation is itself the victim of a particular history's ideologies and evils?

Despite the historicizing turn, the foundationalist moorings of Tracy's model remain. Much of the tension remaining in Tracy's later thought has to do with his unwillingness to accept the full implications of the utter historicity of all thought and *praxis*. Although radical linguistic plurality and historical ambiguity leads to a decentered self, Tracy retains his *neo-Kantian ontology of human being*. For Tracy, the *a priori* nature of the "structures of consciousness" that define human being as such, confers on them an universality which transcends the strictures of language and history (see Tracy 1975: pp. 68–69, 154–155). It is the ontology of human being as *homo religiosus* that Tracy finally protects from the vagaries of temporality and historicity. I just do not see how he can make a coherent case for this claim any longer. Tracy has not as yet provided us with a plausible reconstruction of these issues, and until he does, one may certainly remain unpersuaded of his claim to have advanced a comprehensive "theory of rationality" for postmodern language and practice.

Let us return for a moment to Dean's distinction between the new and the older historicism. It seems clear from our analysis that Tracy could be classified as an "older historicist." In the final analysis, he *does* try to argue for an "extrahistorical, universal, and eternal reality . . . called God" (Dean 1988: p. 2) as the "objective referent" of an extrahistorical, prelinguistic and universal religious dimension. And, perhaps Rorty would say (rather impatiently): for Tracy's model to be less than successful should come as no surprise, since it is just a version of the failed history of Western philosophy to find ahistorical Archimedean "natural starting points" that transcend cultural practice. *That* foundationalist Platonic tradition has outlived its usefulness and should be abandoned (Rorty 1982: p. xiv). But, one may wonder, why should one accept *that* conclusion about philosophy? Here Rorty simply concedes that there is no noncircular, non-question begging way of arguing for or against the Platonic tradition. One makes a decision simply "by reading the history of philosophy and drawing a moral" (Rorty 1982: p. 174). I will treat briefly the "moral" that Rorty draws from this disappointing history, and then, in the light of Rorty's musings, ask the questions with which we started out: In a post-Philosophical, postfoundationalist culture, is it even possible to speak coherently about God as a transcendent Reality? Depending on one's answer, what implications would that have for theology as public discourse?

From Rorty's response it seems that the claims of theology are completely incompatible with the new historicism. This is so because theology's implicature in the "Plato-Kant canon" causes it to go the way of all foundationalist epistemologies. Rorty thinks that the demise of Western philosophy's onto-theological tradition provides an opening for treating everything—our language, our conscience, our community—as products of time and chance (Rorty 1989: p. 22). Historicists proclaim the radical thesis that

> there is nothing deep down inside us except what we have put there ourselves, no criterion that we have not created in the course of creating a practice, no standard of rationality that is not an appeal to such a criterion, no rigorous argumentation that is not obedience to our own conventions (Rorty 1982: p. xlii).

Rorty denies that there is, as Tracy would hold, some such thing as "human nature" or "the deepest level of the self." Instead, the radical historicist holds that

> socialization, and thus historical circumstance, goes all the way down–there is nothing "beneath" socialization or prior to history which is definatory of the human. Such [historicist] writers tell us that the question "What is it to be a human being?" should be replaced by questions like "What is it to inhabit a rich twentieth-century democratic

society?" and "How can an inhabitant of such a society be more than the enactor of a role in a previously written script?" (Rorty 1989: p. xiii).

In fact, for Rorty, talk about the human being or the world as somehow possessing an intrinsic nature which may be "discovered" by the poet or the scientist, is simply an unfortunate remnant of an outdated *theological* view which understood the world as a divine creation, as "the work of someone who has something in mind, who Himself spoke in some language in which He described His own project" (Rorty 1989: p. 21). *Pace* theologians like Tracy, Rorty counsels that we drop this "quasi-divine" notion and realize that "we have no prelinguistic consciousness to which language needs to be adequate, no deep sense of how things are which it is the duty of philosophers to spell out in language. What is described as such a consciousness [by foundationalists like Tracy] is simply the disposition to use the language of our ancestors, to worship the corpses of their metaphors" (p. 21). For the radical historicist, to be human is a project of *self-creation,* with the human self akin to a centerless "web of beliefs and desires" constantly reweaving itself to accommodate new sentential attitudes (Rorty 1991: p. 93). Historicist thinkers realize that truth (including the truth about the "nature" of the self) is *made* not *found* (Rorty 1989: p. 3). This means that notions like "reason," "rationality," and "justification" are *temporalized* and *historicized.* Therefore, for the pragmatist, justification of claims to knowledge and truth is a matter of *social practice*: Nothing counts as justification unless with regard to what we already accept. That means that there is no way to *transcend* social practice—*our* beliefs and *our* language—to find some test other than coherence (Rorty 1979: p. 178). There simply is no ahistorical *metadiscourse,* such as metaphysics, in terms of which to adjudicate conflicting claims and even vocabularies. "Final vocabularies" are ultimately "floating, ungrounded conversations" (Rorty 1982: p. 174). For a belief to be "rational" means no more than the presence of, or hope for, agreement among inquirers (p. 355). Criteria of justification are no more than "temporary resting places constructed for specific utilitarian ends" (Rorty 1982: p. xli). "Truth" becomes a function of the coherence of a particular social practice, a function of the historical standards of the inquirers involved in a particular language game (Rorty 1979: p. 178). The philosopher in the post-Philosophical culture becomes a cultural critic, with his only specialty being his ability to see similarities and differences between historical paradigms or sets of descriptions and to show "how all the ways of making things hang together hang together" (Rorty 1982: p. xl).

In Rorty's post-Philosophical historicist culture there is simply no place for theological claims, especially the claim that God is a transcendent Reality. It is not that Rorty argues that God does not exist. He just does not know how to make sense of the idea of a transcendent Reality; consequently, his historicist culture is a radically *detranscendentalized* one.

How does the theologian respond? Clearly, she will agree with Rorty that to argue for the transcendent reality of God in the way that Tracy has, does not appear to get us very far. Should she simply abandon the theological enterprise altogether? A case for that can certainly be made. However, I believe there is another option. This third option begins by finding fault with some of Rorty's distinctions.

I agree with Richard Bernstein that one of Rorty's more dubious strategies "is the way in which he reduces complex issues to extreme either/or's: *either* liberal ironists *or* liberal metaphysicians; *either* discoverers of truth *or* self-creative makers" (Bernstein 1991: p. 282), *either* transcendence *or* contingency, historicity, etc. Rorty seems to equate transcendence with the ahistorical, the alinguistic, the necessary. For him, it appears, every attempt to speak about transcendence amounts to the foundationalist attempt to escape from history, contingency, and language. Rorty seems to say to theologians: "If classical theology died with metaphysics, then there must be no theology at all" (Dean 1988: p. 20).

But why should the theologian accept this dualism? Certainly it does not follow that just because the notion of an ahistorical, alinguistic, and necessary transcendent Reality cannot be given coherent formulation, that transcendence could not be recast in historicist terms. For some time now William Dean and others have worked on proposals for a genuinely historicist construal of God's reality (see, for example, Dean 1988: pp. 123-144). Dean's more recent reformulation of God as "sacred convention" is especially suggestive: It shows convincingly how a conventionalist construal of the sacred is able to hold together the imaginative, social construction of the God-concept *and* the transcendence of God in a historicist model (Dean 1994: pp. 131-150). Not only is Dean's God-concept thoroughly historical, he is able to push well beyond the forced restrictions created by Rorty's dualism. Further, it seems possible to use Dean's notion of God as sacred convention in support of a *text-mediated* transcendence. Because, for Rorty, *all* reference to transcendence represents an escape from contingency, history, and language, he fails to note this possibility. In other words, transcendence can be re-situated *hermeneutically*. In this way, the reality of God is not a deliverance of universal reason, but, "rather, the supreme figure within a series of texts that invite the reader to think and live alongside their creative mimesis of the world" (Wallace 1993: p. 241). The transcendence of God becomes linked to the capacity of the text to "reveal something 'other'—what William James calls the 'more'—that can support and undergird one's journey to wholeness and selfhood in the midst of disabling pain" (Wallace 1993: p. 249).

Wallace claims that Rorty's unwillingness to countenance "any epiphanic moments where something more or something new is made visible to the interpreter" is a function of his vestigial commitment to *positivist philosophy* (1993: p. 250). Rorty's "strident individualism," says Wallace, expresses his latent attachment (by way of Nietzsche) to the Enlightenment's exigency for throwing off the shackles of authority and convention, and to posit the human subject as the final arbiter of meaning and truth (1993: p. 250). For Rorty, it is, in the final analysis, a question of the *re-location* of authority or power. What Rorty finds unacceptable about thinkers in the Platonic tradition is that, deep down, they needed "to be *guided*, constrained, not left to their own devices" (Rorty 1982: p. xxxix). That is, they felt the need to submit themselves to something "out there" (p. xxxix), call it Nature, or Truth, or God. They all felt the urge, when it was all said and done, to *obey* some ahistorical reality. Truth or Reality, for these thinkers, *confronts* us, *causes* us to see the way things "really are" (compare Rorty 1979: p. 163). Hence they were continually seeking for a criterion deep inside them which will tell them whether they are "in touch" with reality or not, and when they are "in the Truth" (Rorty 1982: p. xxxviii). It is just this *theological* assumption of Philosophers that Rorty wants to cleanse from our vocabulary. But because of Rorty's predilection for Either/Or dualisms, he relocates power entirely in the *self-creative, self-transformative subject*. As a consequence, Rorty seems to have no room in his rhetoric for a genuine "other." As Richard Bernstein observes, in Rorty's Nietzschean, existential moments, "[t]here seems to be no genuine resistance, no otherness . . . to which we must be responsive . . . [O]ur interpretations, our self-creations, seem to be little more than an expression of our idiosyncratic will to power, our will to self-assertion" (Bernstein 1991: p. 247). Bernstein contrasts this attitude with Gadamer's dialogical hermeneutic:

> [F]or Gadamer, when we are engaged in dialogue, whether it be with another partner, a text, or a tradition, there is always something "other" to which we are being responsive, that speaks to us and constrains us. There is a genuine to-and-fro movement that enables us to constitute a "we" that is more than a projection of my own idiosyncratic desires and beliefs. But for Rorty there never seems to be any effective constraints on *me* and *my* interpretations (Bernstein 1991: p. 248).

The either/or dualism of Rorty's brand of historicism makes it difficult for him to incorporate genuine "otherness"; hence, his tone deafness to even a form of text-mediated transcendence. I acknowledge with Mark Wallace that, whether or not one is willing to consider that a text can be "a medium of epiphany" in the life of the reader, initiates in a fundamental "presumption of sympathy" toward the claims to truth of the text (Wallace 1993: p. 239). That is to say, it originates in a *fiduciary* act, in a fragile wager on the possibility that the claims to existence and transcendent truth mediated by the text, are worthy of one's apprenticeship (p. 251). Nevertheless, if my assessment of Rorty on this issue is correct, the theologian could certainly feel at liberty to press beyond the forced either/or strictures of Rorty's historicism.

Rorty's either/or dualism also plays itself out in his attitude toward the *public, rational justification* of rival final vocabularies. A "final vocabulary" is that set of words

> in which we formulate praise of our friends and contempt for our enemies, our long-term projects, our deepest self-doubts and our highest hopes. They are the words in which we tell, sometimes prospectively and sometimes retrospectively, the story of our lives (Rorty 1989: p. 73).

For Rorty, there are no context-transcendent criteria of rationality—no meta-discourse—in terms of which to adjudicate truth-claims of rival final vocabularies. The failure of the search for ahistorical foundations suggests to Rorty that a "circular justification of our practices, a justification which makes one feature of our culture look good by citing still another, or comparing our culture invidiously with others by reference to our own standards, is the only sort of justification we are going to get" (Rorty 1989: p. 57). The absence of ahistorical, transcendental criteria prompts Rorty to draw a radical distinction between *private* and *public* in his liberal society. There is no way to reconcile the individual's idiosyncratic, poetic attempts at self-creation with her obligation to other human beings (Rorty 1989: p. 68). Among these obligations is a quest for solidarity, expressed in the "hope that suffering will be diminished, that the humiliation of human beings by other human beings may cease" (p. xv). But, Rorty tells us, these are "ungroundable desires," since there is no noncircular way to back them up (p. xv). Once again Rorty invokes a "logic of apartheid" (Bernstein 1991: p. 286) positing strict either/or distinctions: *either* ahistorical foundations *or* groundless beliefs; *either* universal criteria *or* local, ethnocentric criteria, *either* solidarity *or* objectivity, *either* strong rational justification *or* groundless liberal hope (Bernstein 1991: p. 288). Rorty's construal eventuates in an "eclipse of the public," an evacuation of rational deliberation from the public space. For Rorty, there seems to be "*no* public space—the space in which human beings come together to *debate* and *argue* with each other" (Bernstein 1991: pp. 284–285). For Bernstein, ironically, Rorty ends up recommending a kind of "fideistic absolutism." He explains:

> If none of our central beliefs can be even minimally rationally warranted, if there is no (non-trivial) way of distinguishing relevant from irrelevant considerations for the beliefs we hold, then it looks as if Rorty is telling us that when doubts are raised about one's final vocabulary the only response that is appropriate is "Here I stand (and I hope you will also stand here)". . . Rorty has cleverly built an unassailable fortress and insulates himself from any criticism, for anyone can enshrine his central convictions in fancy rhetoric, anyone can (if he is imaginative) make his vocabulary "look good" and refuse to give any reasons for holding these beliefs (Bernstein 1991: pp. 278–279).

Rorty's suspicion of any notion of transcendence prompts him to deny *any* possibility of context-transcending criteria. In so doing he flattens out "our notions of reason and truth by removing any air of transcendence from them" (McCarthy 1991: p. 15). But why is it not possible to argue for criteria that are thoroughly historical and contingent, and yet, precisely as regulative ideas, context-transcendent? We noted earlier that there seems to be no *a priori* reason to contrast historicism with transcendence. I believe McCarthy is correct when he calls for a reconstruction of the notion of reason "so that while no longer pretending to a God's eye view, it retains something of its transcendent, regulative, critical force" (1991: p. 27):

> The basic move here is to relocate the tension between the real and the ideal *within* the domain of social practice by showing how communication is organized around idealizing, context-transcending presuppositions. As suppositions that we cannot avoid making when seeking to arrive at mutual understanding, they are effective in structuring communication, but at the same time they are typically counterfactual in ways that point beyond the limits of actual situations (McCarthy 1991: p. 27).

McCarthy goes on to argue coherently how three of these "context-transcending presuppositions"—the accountability of subjects, the objectivity of the world, and the truth of statements—are embodied in social-practical deliberation and thus required for precisely a *pragmatic* rationality (McCarthy 1991: pp. 27–34).

I do not have the space here to articulate what a model of rationality along these lines would look like. However, I have hopefully shown that it is at least *possible* to move beyond Rorty's dualisms, and to advance a theory of rational discourse which is thoroughly historical, fallible, and contingent, and yet, which manages to be truly *public* in the sense of providing the "rational space" (Tracy) in which claims to truth and validity can be adjudicated by the force of the better argument.

And that ought to extend to theologians the invitation to embrace the new historicism fully, yet creatively and critically.

NOTES

1. The assertion that the construct *homo religiosus* underlies Tracy's case for an universal religious dimension is certainly not original with me. Note in this regard the astute analysis by Ronald Thiemann (1985). For a brilliant analysis of Tracy's philosophical anthropology, see the fine study by S. Alan Ray (1987). I draw heavily on Ray's work throughout this paper.

REFERENCES

Alston, William P. 1976. "Two Types of Foundationalism." *Journal of Philosophy* 83/7: pp. 165–185.

Bernstein, Richard J. 1991. *The New Constellation: The Ethical-Political Horizons of Modernity/Postmodernity*. Cambridge, Massachusetts: The MIT Press.

Bonjour, L. 1978. "Can Empirical Knowledge Have A Foundation?" *American Philosophical Quarterly* 15/1: pp. 1–13.

Dean, William. 1986. "The Challenge of the New Historicism." *The Journal of Religion* 66: pp. 261–281.

———. 1988. *History Making History: The New Historicism in American Religious Thought*. New York: State University of New York Press.

———. 1994. *The Religious Critic in American Culture*. New York: State University of New York Press.

Lindbeck, George. 1984. *The Nature of Doctrine: Religion and Theology in a Postliberal Age*. Philadelphia: The Westminster Press.

Magnus, Bernd. 1985. "1. The 'End of Philosophy.'" In *Hermeneutics and Deconstruction* pp. 2–10. Ed. by Hugh J. Silverman and Don Ihde. New York: State University of New York Press.

McCarthy, Thomas. 1991. *Ideals and Illusions: On Reconstruction and Deconstruction in Contemporary Critical Theory.* Cambridge, Massachusetts: The MIT Press.

Ray, S. Alan. 1987. *The Modern Soul: Michel Foucault and the Theological Discourse of Gordon Kaufman and David Tracy*. Philadelphia: Fortress Press.

Rorty, Richard. 1979. *Philosophy and the Mirror of Nature*. New Jersey: Princeton University Press.

———. 1982. *Consequences of Pragmatism*. Minneapolis, Minnesota: University of Minnesota Press.

———. 1989. *Contingency, Irony, and Solidarity*. Cambridge: Cambridge University Press.

———. 1991. *Objectivity, Relativism, and Truth*. Phil. Papers Vol. 1. Cambridge: Cambridge University Press.

Thiemann, Ronald. 1985. *Revelation and Theology: The Gospel as Narrated Promise*. Notre Dame, Indiana: University of Notre Dame Press.

Tracy, David. 1975. *Blessed Rage for Order: The New Pluralism in Theology:* New York: Seabury Press.

———. 1981. *The Analogical Imagination: Christian Theology and the Culture of Pluralism*. London: SCM Press.

———. 1984. "The Role of Theology in Public Life: Some Reflections." *Word & World* IV/3: pp. 230–239.

———. 1987. *Plurality and Ambiguity: Hermeneutics, Religion and Hope*. San Francisco: Harper & Row Publishers.

———. 1992. "Theology, Critical Social Theory, and the Public Realm." In *Habermas, Modernity, and Public Theology* pp. 19–42. Ed. by Don S. Browning and Francis Schüssler Fiorenza. New York: Crossroad.

Wallace, Mark I. 1993. "Ricoeur, Rorty, and the Question of Revelation." In *Meanings in Texts and Actions: Questioning Paul Ricoeur* pp. 234–254. Ed. by David E. Klemm and William Schweiker. Charlottsville and London: University of Virginia Press.

RORTY'S FINAL VOCABULARIES, AND THE POSSIBILITY OF A HISTORICIST METAPHYSICS

Jerome P. Soneson

I.

Thinking about Richard Rorty's recent book, *Contingency, Irony, and Solidarity*,[1] I have been a little surprised to find myself acknowledging that this is one of the most interesting and provocative pieces of religious reflection by a philosopher that I have read in some time. I have not been surprised that it is interesting or provocative but that it is about *religious* matters. I have been surprised by this for two reasons: first, I didn't expect to find distinctively religious reflection from Rorty, given his previous writings; and second, the adjective, "religious," is one from which Rorty has taken great pains to distance himself. I am relatively confident that Rorty would feel uncomfortable with my suggestion that he is becoming a religious (even, perhaps, theological) thinker, one who reflects on the problems and possibilities of the religious dimension of human life. After all, Rorty not only seems to identify himself as fully secular, but he also appears to believe that his own work helps to undermine our most persistent religious temptations. For Rorty, just as for many liberal thinkers of an earlier period, these religious temptations ought to be undermined, for they not only represent intellectual mistakes, but more importantly, they seem to be evil, for they seem to close off the possibility of extending human solidarity and facilitating human creativity.

If this is the case, why do I consider *Contingency, Irony, and Solidarity* to be specifically religious? Precisely because one of the central themes of this book, and certainly the most important theme as far as I can see, has to do with the meaning, significance, function, and possibility of what Rorty calls "final vocabularies." A final vocabulary, Rorty says, is that "set of words" which people

> employ to justify their actions, their beliefs, and their lives. These are the words in which we formulate praise of our friends and contempt for our enemies, our long-term projects, our deepest self-doubts and our

highest hopes. They are the words in which we tell, sometimes prospectively and sometimes retrospectively, the story of our lives (p. 73).

Such a vocabulary is "final," Rorty points out, "in the sense that if doubt is cast on the worth of these words, their user has no noncircular argumentative recourse. Those words are as far as he can go with language; beyond them there is only helpless passivity or a resort to force" (p. 73). What Rorty calls "final vocabularies" seems to me to be very similar to what Paul Tillich identifies as the religious dimension of human existence, our "ultimate concerns," those matters which matter most to us and which therefore give us meaning, purpose and direction in life. They are the concerns for which we get out of the bed in the morning and which make it possible for us to live in meaningful and hopeful ways even in the midst of pain and loss and tragedy.[2]

One of the great values of Rorty's recent book is that it helps to turn the philosophical conversation away from the issue of truth and toward the religious issues of meaning and worth, matters having to do with final vocabularies, with what men and women take to be of ultimate concern in life. In this book, of course, Rorty goes well beyond his position in his earlier work, *Philosophy and the Mirror of Nature*.[3] This previous book consists largely of a criticism and rejection of all philosophical work, past and present, which seeks to discover metaphysical truth. The positive alternative task for philosophical work, he claims in this early work, lies in producing a sense of togetherness by engaging in lively "conversation." In *Contingency, Irony, and Solidarity*, Rorty fills out this early and vague sketch of "conversation" by constructing what he calls a utopian vision of the liberal society. This vision amounts to an imaginative, normative order of social life in which a plurality of final vocabularies would not only flourish but would increasingly promote justice and freedom and diversification. By articulating and enticingly promoting this picture of what he takes to be a future possibility of genuine human meaning and fulfillment, Rorty brings his religious themes into sharp focus, working out for us a captivating version of what theologians call "eschatology."

The particular eschatological vision which Rorty proposes in *Contingency, Irony, and Solidarity* is worthy of much serious consideration. In this paper, however, my focus is upon another but directly related aspect of Rorty's position in this book, namely, his view of metaphysics. This view is puzzling to me because it seems to stand in the way of his attempt to entice others to envision along with him the possibilities of his utopian vision. For his dismissal of all metaphysics, all talk about the nature of the world, undercuts Rorty's own historicist vision of the world in terms of which his utopia could be seen by others as a genuine and viable alternative for their lives, something that could direct them in their conduct. This does not mean that Rorty's critical historicist turn on traditional metaphysics is insignificant; on the contrary, it is valuable precisely because it helps us to focus on the important matters of life, the things that really count, our final vocabularies. Nevertheless, I argue that Rorty does not take his historicist turn far enough. More particularly, my thesis is that Rorty's utopian vision, which is made possible by his historicist turn, would be better served by taking his historicism one step further—by acknowledging the possible meaning and value and function of what I call " historicist metaphysics." Such a metaphysics, I argue, would not violate Rorty's historicist turn but would help to complete it.

II.

For Rorty, of course, the idea of "historicist metaphysics" is an oxymoron, a fundamental contradiction in terms, such as a "round square" or "military intelligence." Indeed, the "historicist turn," he says, "has helped free us, gradually but steadily, from theology and metaphysics—from the temptation to look for an escape from time and chance" (p. xiii). How are we to understand this? What does Rorty mean by historicism, and how and why is it antithetical to metaphysics?

Rorty's interpretation of historicism is based upon what I call a "radical historical perspective." In effect, it consists of an anthropology, a particular interpretation of human nature. Rorty suggests this early on in *Contingency, Irony, and Solidarity* when he notes that historicists

> have denied that there is such a thing as "human nature" or the "deepest level of the self." Their strategy has been to insist that socialization, and thus historical circumstance, goes all the way down—that there is nothing "beneath" socialization or prior to history which is definatory of the human (p. xiii).

This historicist anthropology consists of a negative and a positive claim. The negative claim is that human beings do not share an ahistorical, eternal and unchanging essence which defines them as human, some essential thing which each and every person shares in common regardless of language, culture or historical period. The positive claim is more complex, but at the very least it asserts that humans are plastic in the sense that they are capable of becoming different sorts of persons depending upon the particular language and culture within which they are raised.

This positive claim, of course, does suggest that humans have something in common, but what they have in common is not an ahistorical and identical essence but the ability to be shaped by the historical circumstances of culture. For Rorty, as for many other pragmatists, from James and Dewey and Mead to Quine and Davidson, this shaping is done largely through language, through the process of learning how to talk with and to others round about. By learning language, one comes to share a life with others, understanding what things mean within that culture, what is important, what to hope for, and how best to respond to various circumstances that arise.

This historicist vision, according to Rorty, acknowledges and embraces the radically temporal and contingent character of human life. Who we are, it is believed, is contingent upon the culture into which we are born, a culture which itself has had a changing history of contingent circumstances. This means that an African-American woman raised in the Bronx over the last quarter of a century will be a radically different sort of person than a Virginian farmer during the Revolutionary period or a Roman senator born and raised in a patrician family in Rome during the early Empire.

It is precisely this contingency of human history and language and culture which metaphysicians deny in their interpretations of human nature, according to Rorty. In fact, they seek to escape this contingency by seeking knowledge of a unified and necessary common human essence above and beyond and behind accidental and contingent human history. As Rorty puts it, they believe in "an order beyond time and change which both determines the point of human existence and establishes a hierarchy of responsibilities" (p. xv).

It is helpful to identify several significant assumptions of this metaphysics as Rorty describes it. First, it assumes that the essence of human nature exists apart from language and knowledge, and that knowledge of this essence is a matter of *discovering* what already exists. Valid or true knowledge, therefore, is taken to be a copy of this antecedent essence.

Second, it assumes that this human essence is related to the other matters in one's final vocabulary, all those things having to do with meaning and orientation, things which are taken to be truly real and good and beautiful or truly ugly and painful and evil. All these important things, of course, are understood in the words of the final vocabulary of the culture, and as with the word "human," these words, perhaps because they are taken to be so important, are also taken to refer to real essences out in the world, essences which are also beyond time and change and so can truly stipulate the point of human existence and a hierarchy of human responsibilities (pp. 74–5).

Third, this view of human nature also assumes something about the world as a whole, for the relatedness of unchanging essences implies that the world is itself fundamentally unified, connected in a complex pattern that is complete and finished and unchanging. It is for this reason, no doubt, that one mark of truth is taken to be unity. It is "a sign," Rorty says, "that something *real* has been glimpsed" (p. 96).

Rorty takes historicism to be antithetical to metaphysics, therefore, precisely because historicists affirm the radically historical and contingent character of human life while metaphysicians deny it. Yet the contrast between these two vocabularies is more profound than this, for they involve different ways of engaging the world, of living in the world. The historicist turn, Rorty points out, "helped us substitute Freedom for Truth as the goal of thinking and of social progress" (p. xiii). Among other things, this means that while the aim of metaphysicians is to discover abstract and speculative knowledge of the unchanging truths about human life, historicists, who are sensitive to the contingencies of human life, are able to ask concrete practical questions about what is going on now, and how we might make things better at this particular time in history. In effect, they look in opposite directions: the metaphysician back to antecedent truth, and the historicist forward toward possible solutions of concrete problems facing the self and contemporary society. The metaphors shaping their self-understanding and activity, therefore, are also quite different: for the metaphysician, the operative metaphors are "discovery" and "finding"—discovering antecedent truths—while the central metaphors for the historicist are "creating" and "constructing" and "transforming" and "novelty"—creating new meanings and patterns which enrich and transform human life.

Rorty talks sometimes as if the vocabularies of the metaphysician and the historicist are so incommensurable that it would be silly to argue for the importance of historicism over metaphysics. He suggests that the only thing he can do is redescribe the world in historicist terms in order to help others learn how to speak this language and see its worth (pp. 8–9).

Nevertheless, there are at least two interesting reasons he seems to offer for his own commitment to historicism. First of all, metaphysicians, as Rorty has described them, are insensitive to the contingencies of their own language, the words by which they think about things. He appeals to the work of Donald Davidson to argue that language is not *a medium of expression or representation* of antecedent realities but rather constitutes *a set of tools* which we create in particular historical circumstances for particular contingent purposes (pp. 11–15). Words are things we make up; we don't discover their meanings but we create them for our own practical purposes. Metaphysicians misunderstand language, therefore, when they think that it can be used simply to represent something as such.

The second and more interesting reason is practical. Rorty wants to construct a utopian vision of the liberal society in this book, and he believes his historicism can yield a better vision than is possible by a metaphysician, such as Jürgen Habermas. Rorty's historicist vision of a liberal society allows, he believes, an appropriate and mutually enriching accommodation between the public and the private sides of life. According to Rorty, the public aim of a liberal society is solidarity, and the private aim is freedom for self-creation, the construction of new vocabularies. The public aim has to do with justice and equality and obligations toward others based upon an enlarged understanding of solidarity, of who is included in our community, of whom we count within the category of "us." The private aim has to do with freedom from the constrictions of the past. There can be little doubt that the past imposes constrictions, for if we become who and what we are by learning language created by others, then in learning language we become like others; and when this dominates our lives, we become mere copies of other persons, bound to slavish routinization, to the "crust of convention." A rich and full life, as Rorty sees it, involves more than commitment to justice; it must also allow a "bid for freedom," to use a phrase coined by Whitehead, a bid for novel creation, an attempt to break out of the routine of the past into something fresh. Precisely because we need both the social order of justice and individualizing and novel private purposes, Rorty argues throughout his book that we must refuse to reduce one to the other. It is here, at just this point, that metaphysics constitutes such a problem for Rorty, for it amounts to the reduction of the private side to the public side, even in such a creative philosopher as Habermas. Habermas, Rorty contends, is afraid of the private side, afraid particularly "of the sort of 'romantic' overthrow of established institutions exemplified by Hitler and Mao" (p. 66),[4] and so Habermas denies the private and individualizing impulses and pushes for a vision of democratic society which embodies "universalism," one in which all persons are understood in the same terms, the same final vocabulary.

The real problem with the metaphysical solution to the tension between the public and the private, I take Rorty to be saying, is not simply that it cuts off our bid for freedom but that this cutting off, as it were, undercuts the liberal hope, the continued possibility of solidarity and justice. The private side of life, Rorty argues with some merit, makes the public commitment to solidarity and justice possible and capable of growth because its novel creations, particularly the imaginative narratives it produces, help persons imaginatively identify with others, and so to include within the category of "us" those who previously were seen as "other," as part of "them," as strange and different, as speaking in a foreign vocabulary. In particular, these narratives help us become sensitive to the humiliation others endure and to ways we might be cruel ourselves. In and through narratives, we come to recognize that we share not an eternal and identical essence but "a sense of a common danger" (p. 91), a danger of being humiliated, of being subject to cruelty. It is by imaginative stories created by private fantasy, therefore, that society is capable of what Rorty calls "moral progress . . . in the direction of greater human solidarity," for they improve our "ability to see more and more traditional differences (of tribe, religion, race, customs, and the like) as unimportant when compared with similarities with respect to pain and humiliation" (p. 192). The problem with metaphysics, according to Rorty, is that it cuts the nerve of creativity on the private side of life and so undermines our ability to create narratives which might enhance liberal justice, a type of solidarity which embraces the richness of a growing diversity of final vocabularies. The value of historicism, on the other hand, is that it allows for and encourages the growth of this type of justice.

III.

As we can see, Rorty marshals powerful reasons for his rejection of metaphysics and for embracing historicism. Given his definitions of metaphysics and historicism, it is not difficult to see how and why, from his point of view, the term, "historicist metaphysics," is an oxymoron, a logical impossibility. I agree that metaphysics reduced to Rorty's picture of it is incompatible with historicism. Yet Rorty's picture is not the only possible one; indeed, metaphysics, like everything else, is capable of being cast into a new final vocabulary, helping us see that what might have been taken as metaphysics in the past is capable of being understood and pursued in a quite different way in the present.

In the rest of this paper, I argue for this different historicist understanding of metaphysics. There are three reasons why I think this is important and worthwhile. First, I believe most persons have metaphysical views, views of what they take the world to be like, the sorts of patterns it has and the sorts of values holding sway in that sort of world. It seems to me more effective to attempt to transform people's understanding of metaphysics then to attempt, as Rorty says he does, to change the subject of the conversation altogether. After all, metaphysical ideas, as I have said about the idea of God elsewhere, are very much like cow manure—you can shovel it out the barn all you want, but the damn stuff keeps pouring back in.[5] Second, Rorty's position itself seems to imply certain metaphysical ideas in spite of his persistent denial that he has them and his repeated claims that he wants to undercut the temptation to formulate them. Only by acknowledging our assumed ideas about the world, I would suggest, can they take on a genuinely historicist character, for we can then become critical of them and so make possible their own historical development in conversation with others. Finally, clarifying them from an admittedly historicist position encourages persons to take Rorty's utopian vision more seriously, because it helps them envision a possible world within which that utopia makes sense.

In order to develop my understanding of historicist metaphysics, I would like to take up and discuss important issues in each of these three points.[6] The first point has to do with my conviction that most people have metaphysical assumptions, and that one of the most important things we can do is not to change the conversation entirely but to clarify the historicist character of the assumptions. We can approach the more important issues in this point by discussing one of the central things that bothers Rorty about metaphysics, namely, the assumption that it is possible and good to have a true copy or picture of the way the world really is.

It is important to see that Rorty pictures metaphysics as something done by a dispassionate spectator who attempts to look at things whole and from some neutral and objective perspective, from God's point of view, so to speak (p. 96). Such a perspective assumes, as pointed out earlier, that language is a neutral medium for representing something out there, some timeless essence or pattern unaffected by change, and so language is taken to be a pure means by which subject and object are brought together so that the subject can at last come into genuine contact with the really real. Rorty rightly argues that this perspective misunderstands the language we use to picture the world, and so it is misguided. Among other things, as Dewey so often pointed out, there is no such thing as an entirely disinterested subject who can know something else without affecting it in some way. Indeed, we know the meanings of things only by interacting with them, by doing things for certain purposes and seeing what happens. What we know, consequently, is always historically contingent, involving not simply the metaphors of our particular final vocabularies which prompt and shape our interests; it also involves our historically contingent conduct, what we and others do within particular situations for particular purposes. To know things, therefore, to understand the meanings of things, is not a speculative matter but a practical matter, a matter which we learn in practice and which shapes our expectations and therefore our capacity and tendency to behave in particular ways, guiding our conduct. This does not mean, however, that our knowledge gives us certainty; indeed, one thing we often learn in practice is to expect the possibility of novelty, of something new. In short, we learn we cannot fully anticipate every possibility, and so we learn about the contingency of our language and our understanding and our meanings.

I think it is particularly important to see that some meanings we learn, those having to do with what Rorty calls our "final vocabulary," have a special role in our overall vocabularies. These special meanings have to do with the particular stories which shape our understanding of our place and purpose in the world; they give point to our value judgments and structure to our highest hopes. As such, these meanings function to give order to the rest of our words so that it is possible to see how they are related and therefore how we might get about the world in the most meaningful and fruitful and fulfilling way.

Immanuel Kant makes this point in his first *Critique* when he identifies three of the most important of these special meanings: God, world, and self. He claims these words do not refer to objects out in the world; rather, they are "regulative ideas"—they regulate the way our other ideas are related and ordered. It is possible to argue that Kant believed the regulative order suggested by these ideas might eventually approximate the real order of things some day, but we need not make that conclusion. In a fully historicist fashion, it is possible to claim that these and other regulative ideas are human creations, matters we have constructed in our imaginations (not discovered by reason) for specific purposes, namely, to provide order and meaning and fulfillment in life.

Their value for us, therefore, is not to discover and grasp the really real in our knowledge but to facilitate meaning and orientation and fulfillment in practice, something which is very helpful in a very large and complex and confusing world.

I suggest it is possible to view these special words and meanings of our final vocabulary as *metaphysical*, at least in this sense, that they regulate the patterns which obtain among the words and meanings of our larger vocabulary, specifying the patterns and connections obtaining among them. It is also possible to view them as *historicist*, for they can be understood not to refer to a timeless and final essence or order out in the world but as meanings which are our own creation, which we constructed for purposes of meaning and orientation and fulfillment in life, and which have their meaning in relation to the pressing problems and needs of the present contingent historical situation.

Most men and women presuppose ideas which function in these ways. To be sure, they do not often acknowledge these ideas as historicist; more often, they take them in the sense of Rorty's meaning of metaphysical, believing that they refer to timeless and unchanging essences. Yet I think it is not only possible but helpful to affirm *the regulative function of these ideas* without affirming *the particular way they are often taken*. Indeed, when and to the extent that they are taken to correspond directly to the really real, men and women are reluctant to examine them critically so that they might better orient conduct in the present historical context. Yet precisely because they are meant to serve such a potentially important and useful regulative function for men and women, it would seem most helpful not to dismiss them as simply misguided but to historicize them, to clarify their genuinely historical character and function. The value of this would seem undeniable: it puts men and women in a position to criticize and reconstruct these meanings—to create fresh "vocabularies," to use Rorty's term—in relation to the problems and needs of the present historical context so that conduct might become increasing responsible and fulfilling.

To be sure, taking a historicist attitude toward metaphysical assumptions is not easy. Indeed, it might even be objected that metaphysical ideas cannot be historicized and still function to order understanding and guide action; perhaps, it might be added, this is why Rorty's insists on changing the conversation altogether. It is certainly true that many persons believe that the way they take the world is the way the world really and truly is and has always been and will always be, and so they would powerfully resist adopting a radical historical perspective on their own view of the world. Yet surely such a perspective is no more difficult to adopt than changing the conversation altogether, as Rorty proposes.

Yet something more can be said, for there are at least three reasons why persons might increasingly accept a historical perspective upon their own metaphysical assumptions in spite of initial resistance. First, historical and cultural studies are increasingly impressing upon us the wide variety of ways that men and women have viewed the world, and this has a corrosive effect over time, relativizing the metaphysics of those who take these studies seriously. This side of historical and cultural studies has a negative impact, undercutting the certainty with which so many hold their own metaphysical ideas.

Second, historical and cultural studies also have a positive historicist function, for these studies consider the widely divergent metaphysical views of others within their historical contexts and in terms of *what these views make possible for those who hold them*. Historians and sociologists and anthropologists don't ask whether the metaphysical ideas of others actually correspond to universal and eternal structures of being; rather, they are interested in their cultural meanings, in the consequences which these ideas have for persons in their historical settings—what they make possible, what they draw attention to, what hopes they elicit, what opportunities and problems they present for meaningful response to the great tragedies of life. Such studies, consequently, actually shape a historicist attitude, helping persons understand what is important about these ideas, making it possible to them to take up—to want to take up—a historicist attitude toward their own metaphysical ideas.

A third point follows, for the historicist attitude makes it possible for persons to take responsibility for their own metaphysical ideas, for they can now judge the actual worth of their ideas. Judgment is shifted from correspondence to universal and eternal structures of being—to which humans have never had access anyway—to what such ideas can actually do for them by way of promoting justice and solidarity. This historicist perspective, in fact, liberates women and men to evaluate and reconstruct their own metaphysics in a way never possible before. This freedom to criticize and reconstruct makes the historicist attitude exceedingly attractive for those who are concerned about matters of responsibility and justice, providing potent incentive to accept an historicist attitude toward their own metaphysics.

I have been arguing for the value of clarifying the historicist character of metaphysical assumptions. The second major issue I would like to discuss is that Rorty's own position seems to imply certain metaphysical ideas in spite of his repeated claims that he is changing the subject of the conversation and so is avoiding the temptation to construe things metaphysically. Rorty, indeed, seeks to change the subject of the philosophical conversation, and in fact he is doing something very important for us to the extent that the direction of his conversation leads us away from our desire to take our metaphysical meanings to refer directly to a timeless order of the world. Yet, our felt need for metaphysical ideas does not end with this. For not only do most of us need such assumptions to make our way about in the world, to regulate our meanings and actions, but so does Rorty. Indeed, when Rorty changes the subject and goes on to talk about his liberal utopia, he seems to make certain crucial assumptions about the world.

There are at least three assumptions which Rorty makes. First of all, he seems to assume that the world, like human beings, is plastic, that it is not fixed and final and complete but is historical, open-ended, capable of genuinely novel development. Only in such a world would it seem possible for there to arise a plurality of final vocabularies, each of which is a creation of the human imagination capable of bringing at least private meaning to someone and possibly an enrichment of common public life as well. Rorty wants to make room for these sorts of developments, for freedom to break out of old vocabularies and create new ones. This intention, I suggest, at the very least presupposes that the world allows this and sometimes positively seems to welcome it.

Second, Rorty also seems to assume that the world—at least in the form of other people—is not infinitely plastic to our meanings. Indeed, we are shakers of worlds and makers and remakers of worlds, but there are also limits to how we can conceive the world. After all, our final vocabularies direct us in our conduct—and so we act, guided by these words, and we often find that certain other persons and things react, sometimes favorably and sometimes unfavorably. Rorty assumes this about the world when he recognizes that certain social orders place constraints on our freedom to remake ourselves. Third, Rorty assumes that many of the constraints of the world are capable of being transformed from impediments into the enrichment of life, into dynamic and evolving social orders which increasingly encourage a diversification of new vocabularies, new ways of being human, the flourishing of new self-constructions in and through the creation of new narratives. Certainly not every new vocabulary is valuable; some would be positively dangerous if they ever became public. Yet all vocabularies are valuable, Rorty maintains, to the extent that they are put into narratives which enlarge our imagination, helping us become sensitive to the humiliation of others and to our own forms of cruelty. Such narratives increase our chances of being kind, for they transform strangers into humans, into those we count among the members of our community, fellow sufferers subject to the shared danger of harm by others, and therefore they undermine the possibility that persons will feel the need to act out private purposes which are genuinely harmful to others. The world in short, Rorty assumes, is a place which can grow richer in meaning as difference is transformed by narrative so that the difference, the otherness, the many unique vocabularies, can be sustained and can flourish and proliferate without destroying human life.

Rorty would no doubt object that he holds no such metaphysical assumptions, that his whole effort has been to turn the conversation away from all that, away from looking out there and toward the construction of a utopia, a vision of how we might live a more fruitful life. It is important to see that I am not saying Rorty is assuming something about the world which he secretly believes describes the way the world really is, as if he has been looking out at the world on coffee breaks and has come to these conclusions. My claim, rather, is that these assumptions are best seen as historicist, and what this means, among other things, is that they are not about the world as such but about the most fruitful and fulfilling way in which we can regulate our meanings. They are about the world, to be sure, but only as *we* take it. In this sense, these assumptions are really more about us than about the world. This sort of shift does in fact change the subject of the conversation in a profound way, as Rorty desires, for with this shift we no longer are tempted to ask whether the metaphysical ideas we hold are really true in the sense of correctly corresponding to something out there; instead, we now want to know whether these ideas are the most fruitful ones for our present situation. If and when we follow this shift, then we can also take our metaphysical assumptions as historicist, acknowledging their contingency upon historical circumstances. This shift also makes it possible, therefore, not simply to criticize our assumptions with respect to these circumstances, to how well they regulate our meanings in these circumstances, but also to develop and transform old assumptions and create new ones as historical circumstances change.

The final point I want to make is that it would serve Rorty well, it would help him complete his historicist turn, if he were to acknowledge the historicist metaphysics implicit in his liberal and historicist utopia. In particular, it would help others envision the sort of world in which this utopia would have meaning, one which would also encourage a genuine historicist perspective. Many of us have danced Rorty's historicist turn along with him and some of us have found the need to go one step further. Rorty is inhibited from taking that last step because his definitions of historicism and metaphysics make it difficult for him to see he has assumptions about the world which give point to his utopian vision, a vision he would very much like others to share because be believes it would enrich life. The problem is that most other people have different assumptions about the world, assumptions they will not drop simply by changing the subject, by talking about beautiful utopias. More to the point, because their metaphysical assumptions differ from Rorty's, they will find it very difficult to understand and value his utopia. Such a utopia, of course, becomes just one more castle in the sky, as Dewey would put it, unless it is connected with what really matters to men and women, with how they actually understand their world and live their lives. My suggestion has been that to make this connection we need to change the subject of our conversation not by dropping all talk about metaphysics but by talking more directly about our assumptions of the world, not only to show how and why all metaphysical assumptions can be seen as historicist but how that change of perspective can free men and women to consider alternative views of the world. Historicizing our metaphysics frees us precisely because the concern now is not whether our metaphysical assumptions truly correspond to the really real out there but whether and to what extent they are fruitful for the flourishing of human life. This freedom seems to be the very thing that Rorty is aiming at in his historicist turn. As he puts it, the "historicist turn has helped free us . . . from the temptation to look for an escape from time and chance. It has helped us substitute Freedom for Truth as the goal of thinking and of social progress" (p. xiii). So by recognizing and clarifying his own historicist assumptions, Rorty would be able to complete his historicist turn and make it possible for others at least to understand the sort of world in which his utopia has meaning and the sort of values which it might have in comparison with other final vocabularies, its comparative ability, that is to say, to bring meaning and fulfillment to men and women within the present historical context.

NOTES

1. Richard Rorty, *Contingency, Irony, and Solidarity* (Cambridge: Cambridge University Press, 1989). Page references for citations and quotations from this text will be noted hereafter within parentheses in the body of my paper.

2. See Tillich's excellent phenomenological analysis of the religious dimension of human life in his *Systematic Theology*, Volume One (Chicago: University of Chicago, 1951), pp. 211–30.

3. Richard Rorty, *Philosophy and the Mirror of Nature* (Princeton, NJ: Princeton University Press, 1979).

4. Rorty is not unaware of this danger, and so he spends much time attempting to show how theories which redescribe others in eccentric ways can remain private and so not threaten political liberalism. This is the purpose of Chapters 5 and 6 in *Contingency, Irony, and Solidarity*. Unlike Foucault, Rorty accepts the constraints which modern democratic and liberal societies put on private fantasies, but only to the extent that we are prevented from harming one another. See pages 61–65.

5. See my essay, "Doing Public Theology: John B. Cobb, Jr.'s Reconstruction of the Concepts of 'World' and 'God' in the Context of the Environmental Crisis," *American Journal of Theology and Philosophy* 15/2 (1995) p. 159.

6. For a discussion of my understanding of historicist metaphysics in the work of John Dewey, see my book, *Pragmatism and Pluralism: John Dewey's Significance for Theology* (Minneapolis: Fortress Press, 1993), pp. 161–82. For an excellent example of how historicist metaphysics can be done, see Gordon Kaufman's recent book, *In Face of Mystery: A Constructive Theology* (Cambridge, MA: Harvard University Press, 1993), especially Chapter 18, "Cosmic Visions and Human Meaning," pp. 250–63.

RICHARD RORTY AND THE POSSIBILITY OF THEOLOGY

Everett J. Tarbox, Jr.

Introduction.

> I think that in no country in the civilized world is less attention paid to philosophy than in the United States. The Americans have no philosophical school of their own, and they care but little for all the schools into which Europe is divided.[1]

These words were written over one hundred and fifty years ago. Yet within a generation, "Peirce and James were to baptize a philosophy recognized even in Europe as specifically American, the first American philosophy to name itself: pragmatism."[2] Pragmatism, however, fell from favor by the mid-twentieth century to be seen as a movement in American philosophy that flourished at the turn of the century but which has now been surpassed.[3] In *Philosophical Profiles*, Richard Bernstein observed:

> Despite Dewey's enormous influence in the first quarter of the twentieth century, he was no longer taken seriously as a philosopher. He was viewed as a fuzzy-minded thinker who might have had his heart in the right place, but not his head. Academic professionalism in philosophy had triumphed, and with this triumph not only Dewey but the philosophers associated with the "golden age" of philosophy . . . were marginalized.[4]

The reasons for this shift in thought are complex. However, several factors may be noted. In his excellent historical interpretation of the American philosophical scene, John E. Smith described the shift that took place in professional philosophizing in America since 1930.[5] Philosophers had turned away from Peirce, James, Royce, Dewey, and Whitehead, to embrace British and Continental philosophies. Central to this shift was the great attraction exerted by the several forms of "analytic philosophy" stemming originally from the strong revival of British empiricism at the beginning of the century. The first wave of analytic philosophy that reached America in the 1930s was "logical positivism." The second wave came after 1945, in the form of "ordinary language philosophy."

These two successive waves of "analytic philosophy," Smith observed, gave a quite new orientation to professional philosophy in America. Philosophy in America fell under the domination of British thought to an extent unequaled since the eighteenth century.

Yet there were "pockets of resistance" to these new styles of doing philosophy, although they were clearly on the defensive. One "pocket" was the militant group of neo-Aristotelians at the University of Chicago, especially Robert Hutchins, Mortimer Adler and Richard McKeon, who influenced Rorty's early philosophical development.

This paper is structured in three sections: (1) the correlation of Rorty's personal history and autobiography with his reading of the history of modern Western philosophy, focusing upon the reemergence of pragmatism, (2) Rorty's understanding of religion, and (3) an examination of the possibilities for religion and theology in dialogue with Rorty's philosophy, focusing upon Gordon Kaufman.

I.

Richard Rorty and the "Reemergence of Pragmatism." One of Richard Rorty's major philosophical accomplishments has been his contribution to the retrieval and reemergence of pragmatism in the second half of the twentieth century. Writing at the beginning of the 1980s, Rorty rejects the view that pragmatism is an outdated philosophical movement which had been refuted or bypassed.

> *On my view, James and Dewey were not only waiting at the end of the dialectical road which analytic philosophy traveled, but are waiting at the end of the road which, for example, Foucault and Delleuze are currently traveling* [Italics mine].[6]

Rorty's hermeneutical "retrieval" of the tradition of pragmatism is a redescription or reconstruction of this tradition. As Alasdair MacIntyre observed, a tradition "not only embodies the narrative of an argument, but is only recovered by an argumentative retelling of that narrative which will itself be in conflict with other argumentative retellings."[7] Richard Rorty's retelling exemplifies this approach to pragmatism. His "retelling" of the story in its reconstructive phase focuses on two movements, the analytic philosophy of Quine, the later Wittgenstein, Sellars, and

Davidson, and the Continental philosophies of Nietzsche, Heidegger, and Derrida. This narrative is most clearly developed in his two volumes of Philosophical Papers, *Objectivity, Relativism, and Truth*,[8] in which he discusses themes and figures within analytic philosophy, and *Essays on Heidegger and Others*,[9] in which he discusses Heidegger and Derrida. He sees both post positivistic analytic philosophy and post-Nietzschean European philosophy converging to a single, pragmatist account of inquiry.[10] The history of the analytic philosophical movement is marked by a gradual "pragmaticization" of the original tenets of logical positivism.[11] In a similar fashion, the post-Nietzschean tradition of Franco-German thought is seen to be moving in the direction of the anti-representationalist, pragmatic tradition.[12] For Rorty the pragmatist thinkers were "ahead of their time," anticipating the emerging post-Philosophical culture.[13]

Phase One: From Platonism to Deconstruction. As a thought experiment, I would like to attempt to correlate Rorty's personal and philosophical pilgrimage with his reading of the history of modern Western philosophizing. I am indebted to Professor Don Cupitt, Cambridge University, for this model. In his autobiographical reflections, Cupitt believed that he had found a possible way to correlate the two, autobiography and history, using the insights of the deconstructionists' writings, especially Derrida and Foucault.

> Since the culture is a line of texts whose later members presuppose the earlier ones, and since we are cultural products, then when we produce a text about the individual's spiritual development it cannot help but reflect the larger story in the background. Spiritual biography and autobiography on the one hand, and history of ideas on the other are inevitably going to be modeled on the other and each to influence the other.[14]

I believe this model may be applied to Rorty. His philosophical pilgrimage began from a Platonist perspective. It was only after years of searching that he found his way to pragmatism, a tradition that sees the Platonic tradition as having outlived its usefulness. At this stage he was seeking Philosophy with a capital P![15]

An examination of Rorty's philosophical pilgrimage to pragmatism is very enlightening. In an article published in 1994 he chronicles several of the major steps along the way.[16] Having being born in the home of liberal activist parents, he observed that he grew up knowing that all decent people were, if not Trotskyites, at least socialists. A strong sense of justice and the need of a just social order remains a dominant force in his thought throughout his life, as well as being evident in his major writings on liberal utopias.[17]

During the summer of his fifteenth year Rorty read through Plato, and convinced himself that Socrates was right. "Virtue was knowledge." In Socrates' claim Rorty discovered the two themes which were to dominate his later thought, the desire to hold reality and justice in the same vision. He observed:

> That claim was music in my ears, for I had doubts about my own moral character and a suspicion that my only gifts were intellectual ones. Besides, *Socrates had to be right, for only then could one hold reality and justice in a single vision.* Only if he were right could one hope to be both as good as the best Christians (such as Alyosha in *The Brothers Karamazov*, whom I could not—and still cannot—decide whether to envy or despise) and as learned and clever as Strauss [the teacher who attracted the best of the Chicago students] and his students. So I decided to major in philosophy [Italics mine].[18]

At the University of Chicago, Rorty found that Robert Hutchins, President of the University of Chicago, together with his friends Mortimer Adler and Richard McKeon, had enveloped much of the university in a neo-Aristotelian mystique. "The most frequent target of their sneers was John Dewey's pragmatism."[19] It was vulgar, relativistic and self-refuting.

> As they pointed out over and over again, Dewey had no absolutes. . . . To say that truth is what works is to reduce the quest for truth to the quest for power. Only an appeal to something eternal, absolute, and good—like the God of St. Thomas or the "nature of human beings" described by Aristotle —would permit one to answer the Nazis, to justify one's choice of social democracy over fascism.[20]

Rorty noted that this sounded pretty good to his fifteen year-old ears. Since Dewey was a hero to the people among whom he had grown up, scorning Dewey was a convenient form of adolescent revolt. For Rorty at this stage of his college life the only question was whether this scorn should take a religious or a philosophical form, and how it might be combined with a striving for social justice.

Like many of my classmates at Chicago, I knew lots of T. S. Eliot by heart. I was attracted by Eliot's suggestions that only committed Christians (and perhaps only Anglo-Catholics) could overcome their unhealthy preoccupation with their private obsessions, and so serve their fellow humans with proper humility. But a prideful inability to believe what I was saying when I recited the General Confession *gradually led me to give up on my awkward attempts to get religion*. So I fell back on absolutist philosophy [Italics mine].[21]

Thus Rorty turned to absolutist philosophy. He observed that he very much wanted to be a Platonist. However, problems continued to plague him. He began to worry about what Dewey had called "the quest for certainty" in Platonic thought. Rorty's pilgrimage away from Platonism was gradual. "The more philosophers I read, the clearer it seemed that each of them could carry their views back to first principles which were incompatible with the first principles of their opponents, and that none of them ever got to that fabled place 'beyond hypotheses.'"[22] For Rorty, there seemed nothing like a neutral standpoint from which these alternative first principles could be evaluated. And if there were no such standpoint, then the whole idea of "rational certainty," and the whole Socratic-Platonic idea of replacing passion by reason, seemed not to make much sense.

Rorty's initial disillusionment with Platonism climaxed about the time he left Chicago to study for his Ph.D. at Yale. During his graduate school days at Yale Rorty became more closely acquainted with linguistic philosophy. In the early nineteen-fifties analytical philosophy began to take over American philosophy and began to dominate the most prestigious departments of philosophy in America.

A new sort of graduate education in philosophy was entrenched—one in which Dewey and Whitehead, heroes of the previous generation, were no longer read, in which the history of philosophy was decisively downgraded, and in which the study of logic assumed an importance previously given to the study of languages.[23]

However, Rorty had begun to question the premises of linguistic philosophy, especially the foundations, presuppositions, and metaphors that have tied together the analytic style of philosophizing. Rorty had established his professional credentials by contributing to the discussion of problems that have been in the foreground of contemporary analytic controversies.[24] He had written a number of important papers on such topics as the mind-body problem, incorrigibility, and transcendental arguments, as well as a classic introduction to the collection of readings on the linguistic turn. Yet, at this stage, Rorty's writings began to take a very different turn. Rorty started by discussing problems familiar to analytic philosophers, but the subversive character of his project soon became evident. Richard Bernstein observed:

> Rorty seeks to undermine what he calls the "Cartesian-Lockean-Kantian tradition" which he takes to be the dominant tradition of modern philosophy, and whose legacy is contemporary analytic philosophy. He wants to expose the self-deceptive illusions of foundationalism, epistemology, and such successor disciplines as the philosophy of language and the philosophy of mind. He views his endeavor as a therapeutic one in the spirit of Wittgenstein.[25]

Rorty's transition from Plato to linguistic philosophy to pragmatism was almost complete. His move away from linguistic philosophy was most clearly evident in his "Introduction: Metaphilosophical Difficulties of Linguistic Philosophy."[26] He perceptively argues:

> The history of philosophy is punctuated by revolts against the practices of previous philosophers and by attempts to transform philosophy into a science. . . . In all of these revolts, the aim of the revolutionary is to replace opinion with knowledge. . . . In the past, every such revolution has failed, and always for the same reason. The revolutionaries were found to have presupposed, both in their criticisms of their predecessors and in their directives for the future, the truth of certain substantive and controversial philosophical theses. The new method which each proposed was one which, in good conscience, could be adopted only by those who subscribed to these theses. Every philosophical rebel has tried to be "presuppositionless," but none has succeeded.[27]

It was at this stage that Rorty discovered Continental philosophy. In Hegel, he found a philosopher who had turned away from the knowledge of nature and from the phenomenon of the "New Science" to an historicist self-understanding and self-determination of human beings.[28] Rorty read Hegel's *Phenomenology of Spirit* to be saying: "Granted that philosophy is just a matter of out-redescribing the last philosopher, the cunning of reason can make use even of this sort of competition. It can use it to weave the conceptual fabric of a freer, better, more just society."[29] Rorty reasoned, therefore, that even if there were no such thing as "understanding the world" in the Platonic sense—an understanding from a position outside of time and history—perhaps there was still a social use for his talents, and for the study of philosophy. He concludes that it was the cheerful commitments to irreducible temporality which held the specifically anti-Platonic element in Hegel's work—that seemed so wonderful. Rorty observes:

> About 20 years or so after I decided that the young Hegel's willingness to stop trying for eternity, and just be a child of his time, was the appropriate response to disillusionment with Plato, I found myself being led back to Dewey. Dewey now seemed to me a philosopher who had learned all that Hegel had to teach about how to eschew certainty and eternity, while immunizing himself against pantheism by taking Darwin seriously.[30]

Rorty's rediscovery of Dewey coincided with his first encounter with Derrida. He notes that Derrida led him back to Heidegger, and that he was struck by the resemblances between Dewey's, Wittgenstein's, and Heidegger's criticisms of Cartesianism. "Suddenly things began to come together. I thought I saw a way to blend a criticism of the Cartesian tradition of a quasi-Hegelian historicism of Michel Foucault, Ian Hacking, and Alasdair MacIntyre. I thought that I could fit all these into a quasi-Heideggerian story about the tensions in Plato."[31]

The result was *Philosophy and the Mirror of Nature*.[32] This book, Rorty observes, did not do much for his adolescent ambitions. The topics it treated—the mind-body problem, controversies in the philosophy of language about truth—were remote from his desire to hold reality and justice in the same vision. Rorty concludes:

> But I had gotten back on good terms with Dewey [in *Philosophy and the Mirror of Nature*]; I had articulated my historicist anti-Platonism; I had finally figured out what I thought about the direction and value of current movements in analytic philosophy. But I had not spoken to any of the questions which got me started reading philosophers in the first place. I was no closer to the single vision which, 30 years back, I had gone to college to get.[33]

In *Philosophy and the Mirror of Nature,* Rorty stated that as he began to read the work of Wilfrid Sellers, especially Sellars' attack on the "Myth of the Given," it seemed to him that this attack rendered doubtful the assumptions behind most of modern philosophy.[34] Sellars' attack was reinforced by the influence of Quine. Rorty states:

> I began to take Quine's skeptical approach to the language-fact distinction seriously, and to try to combine Quine's point of view with Sellars's. Since then, I have been trying to isolate more of the assumptions behind the problematic of modern philosophy, in the hope of generalizing and extending Sellars's and Quine's criticisms of traditional empiricism.[35]

The first stage of Rorty's pilgrimage was now completed. Plato had been overcome!

Phase Two: From Deconstruction to Reconstruction. As Rorty tried to figure out what had gone wrong in his quest for a Platonic vision, he gradually decided that the whole idea of holding reality and justice in a single vision had been a mistake—that a pursuit of such a vision had been precisely what led Plato astray.[36] More specifically, he decided that "only religion—only a non-argumentative faith in a surrogate parent who, unlike any real parent, embodied love, power, and justice in equal measure—could do the trick Plato wanted done."[37] Rorty concluded that since he couldn't imagine becoming religious, and indeed had gotten more and more "raucously secularist," the hope of getting a single vision by becoming a philosopher had been a self-deceptive way out. It was at this stage that he decided to write a book about what intellectual life might be like if one could manage to give up the Platonic attempt to hold reality and justice in a single vision.

In the resulting book, *Contingency, Irony and Solidarity,* Rorty argues that there is no need to weave the two strands into one single vision such as had been attempted by Plato and religious thinkers. Rather, one should try to "abjure the temptation" to tie in one's moral responsibilities to other people with one's relation to whatever idiosyncratic things or persons one loves with all one's heart and soul and mind (i.e. Tillich's "ultimate concern"). Rorty concludes that the two strands will, for some people, coincide—as they do in those "lucky Christians" for whom the love of God and of other human beings are inseparable, or revolutionaries who are moved by nothing save the thought of social justice. But they need not coincide, and one should not try too hard to make them do so. Rorty argues that there is nothing sacred about universality which makes the shared automatically better than the unshared. There is no automatic privilege of what you can get everybody to agree to (the universal) over what you cannot (the idiosyncratic). His final conclusion is that there is, in short, not much reason to hope for the sort of single vision that he went to the University of Chicago hoping to get. Yet, one could reconstruct a viable story without this vision. To that task he addressed himself.

Rorty seeks to reconstruct philosophy by telling a story of its history. In the two volumes of his Philosophical Papers, *Objectivity, Relativism, and Truth* and *Essays on Heidegger and Others*, Rorty constructs a narrative in which he develops his major thesis that post-Nietzschean European philosophers [who were assigned places in a conversational sequence which runs from Descartes through Kant and Hegel to Nietzsche and beyond to Heidegger and Derrida][38] and post positivistic analytic philosophers [including Sellars, Quine, Wittgenstein, and Davidson] are converging to a single, pragmatist account of inquiry.[39]

Conclusion: Central Themes in Rorty's Philosophy. Several central themes have now emerged in Rorty's steps toward reconstruction. First, his position is "historistic." As he observed in *Essays on Heidegger and Others*:

> Ever since Hegel . . . historicist thinkers have tried to get beyond this familiar standoff [between the public and private]. They have denied that there is such a thing as "human nature" or the "deepest level of the self." Their strategy has been to insist that socialization and thus historical circumstance, goes all the way down—that there is nothing "beneath" socialization or prior to history which is definatory of the human. . . . This historicist turn has helped free us, gradually but steadily from theology and metaphysics—from the temptation to look for an escape from time and chance. It has helped us substitute Freedom for Truth as the goal of thinking and of social progress.[40]

Second, his position is "naturalistic." In *Objectivity, Relativism, and Truth*, Rorty affirms that the principal motive for writing the two volumes of Philosophical Papers "is the belief that we can still make admirable sense of our lives even if we cease to have what Nagel calls 'an ambition of transcendence.'"[41] Rorty asserts that all taint of dualism must be purged from the philosopher's quest. He states:

I shall define "naturalism" as the view that *anything* might have been otherwise, that there can be no conditionless conditions. Naturalists believe that all explanation is causal explanation of the actual, and that there is no such things as a noncausal condition for possibility.[42]

Rorty asserts that he sees Darwin's naturalism as showing us how to naturalize Hegel—how to hold on to an Hegelian narrative of progress while dispensing with the claim that the real is the rational. "After Darwin, it became increasingly difficult to use the notion of 'experience' in the sense Kant had tried to give it. For Darwin, by making Spirit continuous with Nature, completed the historicizing process which Hegel had begun."[43] We need to switch over from a Cartesian-Kantian picture of intellectual progress as a better and better fit between mind and world to a Darwinian picture of an increasing ability to shape the tools one needed to help the species survive, multiply, and transform itself.[44]

Third, Rorty affirms the "contingency" of humankind. He urges that "we try *not* to want something which stands beyond history and institutions. The fundamental premise of the book [*Contingency, Irony, and Solidarity*] is that a belief can still regulate action, can still be thought worth dying for, among people who are quite aware that this belief is caused by nothing deeper than contingent historical circumstances."[45] This issue will be pursued later.

Fourth, Rorty asserts the priority of language. However, following Davidson, he sees language as part of the behavior of human beings. This "Davidsonian" way of looking at language avoids hypostatizing language in the way in which the Cartesian tradition hypostatized thought. "It lets us see language not as a *tertium quid* between Subject and Object, nor as a medium in which we try to form pictures of reality, but as part of the behavior of human beings."[46] Rorty concludes that attempts to get back behind language to something which "grounds" it, or which it "expresses," or to which it might hope to be "adequate," have not worked.[47]

Finally, Rorty views philosophy as conversation. In the final section of *Philosophy and the Mirror of Nature*, Rorty speaks of "Philosophy in the Conversation of Mankind."[48] He argues that we are well on the way to "seeing *conversation* as the ultimate context within which knowledge is to be understood."[49] His major goal is to insist "that philosopher's" moral concern should be with continuing the conversation of the West, rather than with "insisting upon a place for the traditional problems of modern philosophy within that conversation."[50] Rorty's commitment to "conversation" is evident in his discussion of the trajectories of the history of modern philosophers as discussed earlier.

II.

Rorty's Understanding of Religion: An Example. Rorty's philosophical and personal position on religion appears clearly to be negative. Rorty spells out his alternative non-religious or secular vision in "The Contingency of a Liberal Community."[51] He sees as central the shift from the search for foundations to the attempt at redescription, concluding that this difference is emblematic of the difference between the culture of liberalism and older forms of cultural life.

> In its ideal form, the culture of liberalism would be one which was enlightened, secular, through and through. It would be one in which no trace of divinity remained, either in the form of a divinized world or a divinized self. Such a culture would have no room for the notion that there are nonhuman forces to which human beings should be responsible. It would drop, or drastically reinterpret, not only the idea of holiness, but those of "devotion to truth" and "fulfillment of the deeper needs of the spirit." The process of de-divinization . . . would, ideally, culminate in our no longer being able to see any use for the notion that finite, mortal, contingently existing human beings might derive the meanings of their lives from anything except other finite, mortal, contingently existing human beings. In such a culture, warnings of "relativism," queries whether social institutions had become increasingly "rational" in modern times, and doubts about whether the aims of liberal society were "objective moral values" would seem merely quaint.[52]

He openly affirms that he is both an atheist and a committed secularist. As Freud claimed, we should think of ourselves as just one more among Nature's experiments, not as the culmination of Nature's design.

One of the more interesting discussions of Rorty's personal views of religion is found in his critique of Stephen L. Carter's *The Culture of Disbelief: How American Law and Politics Trivialize Religious Devotion* in his article entitled "Religion as Conversation Stopper."[53] Rorty observes that Carter puts in question what, to atheists like himself, seems the happy Jeffersonian compromise that the Enlightenment reached with religion. Rorty sees this compromise to consist in the privatizing of religion, that is, of keeping it out of what Carter calls "the public square."

The result of this compromise was to make it appear to be in bad taste if one brings religion into discussions of public policy. In contrast, Carter argues for the inclusion of religion in such public dialogue, insisting that its exclusion trivializes religion. Rorty strongly disagreed, observing that atheists such as himself, were doing their best to enforce and extend the Jeffersonian compromise. Rorty suggests that "the claims of religion need, if anything, to be pushed back still further, and that religious believers have no business asking for more public respect than they now receive."[54] Rorty's argument is even more persuasive in the light of the current resurgence of the "Religious Right" in national politics in America.

Rorty's position is rooted in his desire to separate the public and the private, believing that they cannot be held together. He sees the attempt to fuse the public and the private to be central to Plato and to religious visions. Rorty asserts that "contemporary liberal philosophers think that we shall not be able to keep a democratic political community going unless the religious believers remain willing to trade privatization for a guarantee of religious liberty, and Carter gives us no reason to think they are wrong."[55] Further, Rorty criticizes Carter for seeming to think that religious believers' moral convictions are somehow more deeply interwoven with their self-identity than those of atheists with theirs. Carter "seems unwilling to admit that the role of Enlightenment ideology in giving meaning to the lives of atheists is just as great as Christianity's role in giving meaning to his own life."[56] Rorty agrees with Carter that a lot was lost by the transition to the Enlightenment ideology. But he asserts that though much was lost, much was gained.

> In the last analysis, the question about whether the Jeffersonian compromise was worth the price that religious believers are still paying is the question of whether more was gained than was lost. Carter and I may share no premises on the basis of which to argue this question out. But we might perhaps agree that the American public square was enlarged in the course of this century.[57]

III.
Rorty and an Examination of the Possibility of Theology. Like American philosophy, American theology experienced a radical break in the 1930s, when liberalism was challenged by neo-orthodoxy as represented by Barth and Tillich. Neo-orthodoxy swept the American theological seminaries and Divinity Schools. Émigré theologians, like

their colleagues in philosophy, dominated the theological scene. Theologians like the Niebuhrs and Tillich turned to the Continental thinkers for inspiration. "American" theology was isolated in pockets such as the Divinity School of the University of Chicago. John Herman Randall, Jr., writing in 1963, stated that Tillich was "one of the most respected theologians in America, perhaps the thinker who today comes closest to serving as an intellectual spokesman for the more forward-looking and imaginative currents in the very diverse streams of American Protestant thinking."[58] One consequence, as Rorty observed, was the rejection of pragmatism.

> It was as if pragmatism had been crushed between Tillich and Carnap, the upper and the nether millstones. Carnap, with his return to hard-edged empiricism, became the hero of the philosophy professors, but most American intellectuals turned their back on pragmatism and on analytic philosophy simultaneously. They began to look to Tillich, or Sartre, or Marcuse, or some other philosopher who sounded deeper and more intellectually ambitious than the Deweyan anti-ideological liberalism on which they had been reared. Liberalism had come to strike them as, at best, boringly platitudinous, or, at worst, a defensive apologia for the status quo.[59]

Rorty, however, strongly disagrees with this judgment, arguing that pragmatism's "anti-ideological liberalism" is the most valuable tradition of American religious life.

I would like to explore one major theological option which I see as a "possibility" in a post-Rortyian world, that of Gordon Kaufman, of Harvard Divinity School. Kaufman's *In Face of Mystery: A Constructive Theology* is the culmination of his writings on theology as an imaginative construction for over three decades. Central to his theological reconstruction is the recognition of the collapse of traditional Western theology, which became increasingly apparent since the 1960s. This recognition is coupled with his positive conviction that the symbol "God" has functioned in our Western cultural primarily to provide orientation for persons. "God," for Kaufman, indicates the "ultimate point of reference" to which all action, consciousness, and reflection leads.

Gordon Kaufman, however, is convinced that radical theological reconstruction or "revision" is required if theology is to be meaningful for our generation. He asks: "Is it meaningful or useful to speak or think of 'God' at all any more? or is talk about God simply a vestige of earlier stages of culture from which we must seek increasingly to free ourselves?"[60] The first option is, for Kaufman, the only viable one. By the mid-1970s Kaufman had broken completely with the neo-orthodox view of revelation. He observed that the proclamation "God is dead!" makes it clearly apparent that the "neo-orthodox Emperor" had no clothes.[61] It was at this stage of his thought that Kaufman began openly to address the necessity for radical theological revision.

> It is essential for us to recognize that the peculiar logical status of the central concepts with which theology deals demands radical reconception of both the task of theology and the way in which the task is carried out. Theology can no longer conceive of itself as presenting straightforwardly a kind of picture or map of *how things are*—the old schema of God, humankind and the world in their structural relations with each other.[62]

Theologians, Kaufman concludes, have also witnessed a loss of confidence in traditional metaphysical philosophy to provide a foundation or base for theology; this loss was equally true for either rationalist "foundationalism" or empirical "foundationalism." Not only have we witnessed an almost total collapse of the neo-orthodox consensus which had begun in the 1920s and had declined abruptly in the 1960s, we have also witnessed the loss in confidence in metaphysics to provide theology with a foundational base.

Finally, religious experience can no longer be foundational for Kaufman. Religious experience is never the "raw, pre-conceptual, pre-linguistic experience" upon which theologies can be built. Like all our experience, religious experience is a construction or composite.[63] He concluded that "one-dimensional experientialism is, thus, no more feasible in theology than a one-dimensional biblicism."[64]

A new approach, therefore, is needed. One option, for Kaufman, is to explore theology as "conversation." Kaufman asserts: "The best image I know for conceiving what theology ought to be is not, then, the exegesis of sacred texts or the arcane debates of learned intellectuals, nor is it meditation or reflection in the privacy of one's solitude (however important may be the contributions of each of these), but rather *free-flowing, open, and unfettered conversation*" [Italics mine].[65]

In Chapter Five: "Mystery, Theology, and Conversation," in *In Face of Mystery*, he develops his conception of "theology as conversation," along lines paralleling Rorty.

Richard Rorty and the Possibility of Theology   323

> Since theology is principally concerned with what is ultimate mystery—mystery about which no one can be an *authority*, with true or certain answers to the major questions—I suggest that the proper model for conceiving it is not the lecture (monologue); nor is it the text (for example, a book): it is, rather, *conversation*. We are all in this mystery together; and we need to question one another, criticize one another, make suggestions to one another, help one another. . . . It is imperative that the theological conversation be kept open to and inclusive of all human voices.[66]

Central to Kaufman's argument for theology as "conversation" is his suggestion that a major function of religions, and also of theologies, is to represent human beings with visions of the whole of reality.

> Religions (and theologies) provide us with construals of the ultimate mystery within which human life transpires—construals which are sufficiently meaningful and intelligible to enable human beings to come to some significant understandings of themselves in relation to the enigmatic context within which their lives proceed, and which are sufficiently appealing to motivate attempts to live fruitfully and meaningfully within this context.[67]

Based upon this assumption, Kaufman asks several important questions. First, what holistic pattern or picture or concept should the theologian adopt as the "best," "right," or "true" construal of the mystery of things? Second, how is this to be ascertained? And third, through what steps can one best construct such a picture or conception of the whole?

I assume that Rorty would object to Kaufman's quest for a picture or vision of the "whole of reality." This quest for such a vision was Plato's error. For Rorty, there is "no big picture." Rorty, like Wittgenstein, would seek to cure us of the "urge" to seek such a picture.[68] However, Rorty, I think, would approve of Kaufman's method of theology as conversation as a means to achieve his goal, especially since there is no assertion of a privileged position. Kaufman recognizes that there is no "foundation" upon which the theologian can begin her activity of theological construction. "It must never, then, be claimed that the particular choices we are making in our theological construction are the only possible ones, or even the best possible. Our theological moves will necessarily be tentative and problematic."[69]

Kaufman acknowledges the highly questionable character of his theological work, especially the constructive efforts. He also acknowledges that many would question whether such a faith would be sufficient to sustain life. This is especially true since our Western religious and theological traditions have led us to believe that their claims were based on a revelation by "God." Kaufman recognizes that theological construction which at every point acknowledges its problematic and questionable character, while simultaneously inviting a commitment of faith to lead our lives in this particular way, expresses accurately our actual situation as finite beings in a vast enigmatic world. Therefore, every move will be one of faith, yet a faith that engages in a relentless theological criticism of this faith and its symbols.

> Our choice of some particular holistic vision . . . is itself a beginning act of faith, of commitment, to a particular way of seeing the ultimate mystery with which we have to do. Our decision to pursue this particular path rather than that, as we seek to discern and to construct our vision in detail, is a further act of faith. . . . The activity of thinking theologically consists of one step of faith after another, each new step elicited by hope that our movement down the path of theological construction will enable us better to discern the role and place of human life within the mystery that encompasses us.[70]

It is in this context that Kaufman argues for theology as "conversation." He notes that in recent years there has been increasing interest among philosophers and theologians in conversation or dialogue as the proper goal for intellectual activity, instead of the more traditional pursuit of truth. He recognizes Rorty as one of the leaders of this movement.[71] In order to develop his conception of theology as conversation, Kaufman distinguishes between two orders of activities.

> As finite beings we are always engaged in adapting ourselves to one another—that is, we are involved in the activity of continually adjusting the desires, intentions, motivations, actions of each of us to the others round-about. This first-order political activity of continual adaptation to others is carried out, of course, in terms supplied by some frame of orientation, some language and tradition, which provides the patterns of meaning, the ideologies, within which we think and act. Since there is never full agreement, however, on what these ideologies are or should be,

second-order political activities directed toward adjusting our various ways of understanding and thinking to one another are necessary.[72]

For Kaufman theology, when viewed from a sociological point of view, is a second-order political activity, "an activity of adjusting certain of our ideas about human life and the world to those of others, of thinking together about matters of ultimate importance."[73]

Kaufman argues that, if we are to be successful, the theological conversation must be kept open to all interested parties. Considerations of position, prestige, and power must be prevented from dominating this interaction. Christian churches, Kaufman observes, have mistakenly viewed theology as ideology rather than conversation, seeing theology as a body of truths clearly defined and passed on from generations to generations. As a result theology is often perverted into an instrument of domination.[74] In contrast, he asserts that we should view theology as an activity requiring continuous readjustment of the thinking of each of us to all the others with whom we are talking and thinking together.

These traditional authoritarian and hierarchical patterns of religious understanding and theological reflection, for Kaufman, are no longer acceptable today for several reasons. First, they flagrantly violate modern democratic conceptions and ideals. And second, because they seriously compromise the understanding found in religious myths and symbols, as well as in theological doctrines and reflections, mystery is obscured. He argues that it is "human presumptuousness of the highest order for any individuals or groups to make claims to special knowledge on such matters: the concept of mystery . . . levels all human cognitive elites and all religious hierarchies with respect to these profound questions of life and death."[75] Kaufman argues that all such authoritarian moves actually express not the vitality of faith, but its threatening breakdown. "It is necessary to make an authoritarian demand of this sort only when a conceptual frame no longer makes sense of experience, and has thus begun to seem useless or meaningless."[76]

In contrast, Kaufman argues for unrestricted interchange among all interested parties, of unrestricted dialogue among all individuals and groups wishing to pursue such matters. I believe that this extension of the doctrine of the "priesthood of all believers" to all humanity is a significant step forward. For Kaufman this model of theology is democratic, open, and public. It presupposes that one is willing to be but one voice in this developing texture of words and ideas, with no desire to control the entire movement. Such a model encourages criticism and allows all participants to be accepted on equal terms. There is a "level playing field."

Finally, Kaufman asserts that it is important that the theological conversation be kept as open as possible to new and previously unheard voices, such as women, blacks, the poor, "third world" persons, representatives of other religions and secular traditions, etc. "Only thus will we have some chance of coming to grips in a fruitful and redemptive way with the profound mysteries with which life today confronts us."[77]

IV.

Conclusion. Kaufman raises what I see as the crucial problem of his and other postmodern or neo-Enlightenment theologies. Must we believe religious and/or theological symbols such as "God" to be *objective realities*, outside and independent of us, if we are to commit ourselves to them? He asks: "Would it not be idolatrous to commit ourselves to them while knowing them to be simply human imaginative constructs?"[78] In order to answer this question Kaufman distinguishes between three distinct movements or dimensions of human consciousness or awareness of meaning, a distinction influenced by Paul Ricoeur.

> First, there is the *moment* or *sense of naive awareness* in which meaning seems to be simply there, something directly given and to be accepted. In this sort of consciousness our speech about, for example, the value and significance of God and Christ—or of democracy, justice, truth, America, et cetera—is taken to refer to objectively given *realities*, realities which certainly *exist, are there,* realities in terms of which life must be ordered. In most of our unreflective use of such symbols or concepts as these, their meaning is taken in this more or less "objective" way.[79]

For Kaufman, every fundamentalism, religious or secular, lives out of this kind of naive certainty. Unfortunately, it "knows too much," supposing itself to know how thing really are.

The second dimension is the *critical moment* in which our concepts and categories seem in some ways to become questionable and problematic. Kaufman believes that this critical stage is possible because human consciousness is capable of transcending in some degree the meanings within which it lives and of subjecting them to criticism and creative transformation when they do not seem to fit what we are experiencing. He notes:

Sometimes this critical moment becomes sufficiently widespread and powerful to call into question large complexes of cultural meaning—for example, at the time of the destruction of Jerusalem and the exile to Babylon, many wondered whether the covenant with Yahweh had any meaning any longer; with the sophists (and Socrates) in ancient Greece many traditional values were questioned; since the Enlightenment critical attitudes and practices have been deliberately cultivated by some segments of modern culture. In situations like these it becomes apparent to many that, far from being simple representations of "objective realities" with which humans must come to terms, these structures of meaning are human creations; they are cultural artifacts which have grown up in a history and which can be transformed in further history.[80]

Kaufman sees that this conception of meaning has been worked out in modern times by Feuerbach, Marx, Nietzsche, James, Freud, Dewey, Rorty, Foucault, Derrida, and others. He concludes that it has become very influential in the modern Western intellectual world. Ricoeur's "hermeneutics of suspicion" reflects this stage. However, for Kaufman, this stage also "knows too much." In this moment of criticism, one tends to *know* that we can never know how things really are.

I see much of Rorty's small-p philosophy to reflect this second stage. And it is at this point that I see Kaufman disagreeing with Rorty. Kaufman asserts that "it is important to recognize that human beings are not able to live entirely and exclusively within this critical moment or dimension of consciousness."[81] Central to his theological constructive position is the conviction that we can neither think nor act without some accepted conception of the world and of the human place within it. For Kaufman this is our symbolic frame of meaning which gives orientation for our lives. However, two points should be noted. First, Rorty's emphasis on one's "final vocabulary" appears to parallel Kaufman's position. Rorty observes:

> All human beings carry about a set of words which they employ to justify their actions, their beliefs and their lives. These are the words in which we formulate praise of our friends and contempt for our enemies, our long-term projects, our deepest self-doubts and our highest hopes. . . . I call these words a person's "final vocabulary."[82]

Second, Rorty's discussion of Dewey's and Tillich's "God," in which Rorty equates Tillich's "ultimate concern" with Dewey's "God,"[83] seems to parallel Kaufman's position. In analyzing Dewey and Tillich, Rorty views their "God" within a naturalistic context. Central to each man's thought was the belief that the word "God" did not correspond to any "supernatural" object. Rorty's redescription of Tillich's concept of Being is especially interesting. Rorty states: "I take 'Being' to be, in Heidegger and again, derivately, in Tillich, merely 'transcendental German'; for a 'connection of man with the enveloping world.'"[84] Certainly this is true of Kaufman's theological construction as well. Would not Rorty be as generous with Kaufman as he was with Tillich?

This leads Kaufman to the third dimension or stance, which is "rooted in what we shall call a *reflective moment* of consciousness."[85] For Kaufman, this moment includes awareness both that symbolic meaning is indispensable to human life and that every actual structure of meaning is humanly created and must be subjected to criticism, including one's own structure of meaning. He recognizes that this position seems possible only for a few elite intellectuals when formulated this abstractly. However, this is a misunderstanding. "The reflective moment of consciousness is as much a function of the dialectical structure of central idealizing symbols in our language and culture as it is of the degree of sophistication possessed by groups and individuals."[86] Kaufman argues that central idealizing symbols manifest a continual strain toward self-transcendence, and it is this feature that leads them to new experience and to unanticipated possibilities. "Such idealizing symbols manifest their power to a critical consciousness as well as to more naive mentalities."[87]

I find this third moment of consciousness to be crucial to Kaufman's construction. He holds that this moment includes both the awareness that all particular meanings are human constructions and a sense that such symbolic meanings can both draw humans forward and constrain them. He observes that this is the sort of consciousness Paul Ricoeur was alluding when he spoke of a "second naiveté."

> Ricoeur's expression, however, is somewhat misleading, for this reflective moment or stance is anything but naive: it involves a consciousness even more critical, in certain respects, than moment two (the moment of "criticism") which may nihilistically—and thus naively—suppose that humans can live without significant value- and meaning-commitments.[88]

Kaufman concludes that it is out of a stance rooted in this third moment of consciousness, and with the desire to enhance the meaning sensed in that moment, that the constructive work of theology proceeds, in its attempt to put together a religious conceptual frame which can make sense of contemporary experience and life, and to which we today can commit ourselves with integrity. He states:

> It involves commitment both to the meaning of our most profound orienting symbols as well as to the meaningfulness of our activities of criticizing and reconstructing these same symbols in the face of the ultimate mystery of life: in a reflective consciousness of this sort we live out of a trust which enables us to continue acting creatively and constructively even though we do not know with finality who we are or where we are going.... Thus, it is possible to engage in criticism and reconstruction of our conceptual schemes, even while we are living and thinking within them.[89]

With this last position of Kaufman, Rorty is apparently in agreement. Rorty speaks approvingly of Isaiah Berlin's essay in which Berlin quotes Joseph Schumpeter: "To realise the relative validity of one's convictions and yet stand for them unflinchingly, is what distinguishes a civilized man from a barbarian."[90] Berlin observed: "To demand more than this is perhaps a deep and incurable metaphysical need; but to allow it to determine one's practice is a symptom of an equally deep, and more dangerous, moral and political immaturity."[91] Rorty concludes:

> In the jargon I have been developing, Schumpeter's claim that this is the mark of the civilized person translates into the claim that the liberal societies of our century have produced more and more people who are able to recognize the contingency of the vocabulary in which they state their highest hopes—the contingency of their own consciences—and yet have remained faithful to those consciences.[92]

At noted earlier, in his discussion of "solidarity," Rorty asserts that the fundamental premise of his book is "that a belief can still regulate action, can still be thought worth dying for, among people who are quite aware that this belief is caused by nothing deeper than contingent historical circumstance."[93] Herein lies the "possibility" of theology in a post-Rortyian world!

NOTES

1. Alexis de Tocqueville, *Democracy in America* (New York: Vintage, 1945), II, p. 3.

2. John Rajchman, "Philosophy in America," in *Post-Analytic Philosophy*, ed. by John Rajchman and Cornel West (New York: Columbia University Press, 1985), p. ix.

3. Cf. Richard J. Bernstein, *Philosophical Profiles: Essays in a Pragmatic Mode* (Philadelphia: University of Pennsylvania Press, 1986), p. x.

4. *Ibid.*, p. 2. Bernstein noted that Peirce and James were "autodidacts." They were not formally trained as philosophers. Dewey was among the first to receive a Ph.D. in philosophy at the newly founded graduate school at Johns Hopkins.

5. John E. Smith *The Spirit of American Philosophy* (Oxford: Oxford University Press, 1963).

6. Richard Rorty, *Consequences of Pragmatism,* (Minneapolis: University of Minnesota Press, 1982), pp. xvii–xviii.

7. Alasdair MacIntyre, "Epistemological Crises, Dramatic Narrative and the Philosophy of Science," *Monist* Vol. 60 (1977), p. 461. Quoted in Richard J. Bernstein, *The New Constellation: The Ethical Political Horizons of Modernity/Postmodernity* (Cambridge: The MIT Press, 1992), p. 324.

8. Richard Rorty, *Objectivity, Relativism, and Truth: Philosophical Papers Volume 1* (New York: Cambridge University Press, 1991).

9. Richard Rorty, *Essays on Heidegger and Others: Philosophical Papers Volume 2* (New York: Cambridge University Press, 1991).

10. *Ibid.*, p. 3.

11. Cf. *Ibid.*, pp. 11–12, where Rorty asserts that the philosopher whose work seems to him to be the best current statement of a pragmatist position is Donald Davidson.

12. *Ibid.*, p. 2. Rorty notes that despise differences, Nietzsche was as good an anti-Cartesian, antirepresentationalist, and antiessentialist as Dewey.

13. Cf. Rorty, *Consequences of Pragmatism,* pp. xviii ff.

14. Don Cupitt, *Life Lines* (London: SCM Press, 1986), p. 203.

15. Rorty, *Consequences of Pragmatism,* pp. xiv–xv. Cf. p. xlii. "The urge to make philosophy into Philosophy is to make it the search for some final vocabulary, which can somehow be known in advance to be the common core, the truth of, all the other vocabularies which might be advanced in its place. This is the urge which the pragmatist thinks should be repressed, and which a post-Philosophical culture would have succeeded in repressing."

16. Richard Rorty, "Trotsky and the Wild Orchids," which first appeared as an essay in the Winter 1992 issue of *Common Knowledge* and is included in *Wild Orchids and Trotsky: Messages from American Universities,* ed. by Mark Edmundson (New York: Penguin Books, 1993), pp. 29–50.

17. Cf. Richard Rorty, *Contingency, Irony, and Solidarity* (Cambridge: Cambridge University Press, 1989), Part Three: "Cruelty and Solidarity," pp. 141–98. The book was dedicated in memory of six liberals: my parents and grandparents. In Chapter Three: "The Contingency of a Liberal Community," Rorty sketches his picture of a liberal utopia.

18. Rorty, "Trotsky and the Wild Orchids," pp. 37–38.

19. *Ibid.,* p. 36.

20. *Ibid.,* p. 37.

21. *Ibid.,* p. 39.

22. *Ibid.* Cf. Richard J. Bernstein's discussion of "Cartesian Anxiety," in *Beyond Objectivism and Relativism* (Philadelphia: University of Pennsylvania Press, 1985), pp. 16 ff.

23. Rorty, *Consequences of Pragmatism,* pp. 214–15. Rorty noted that, thanks to the postwar baby boom, the sixties and early seventies happened to be the period in which the majority of living American Ph.D.'s in philosophy were educated.

24. Cf. Bernstein, *Philosophical Profiles,* p. 6. Bernstein notes, however, that a close reading of Rorty's early works reveals a "certain marginality."

25. *Ibid.,* p. 7.

26. Richard Rorty, "Introduction," *The Linguistic Turn*, ed. by Richard Rorty (Chicago: The University of Chicago Press, 1967).

27. *Ibid.*, p. 1.

28. Rorty, *Consequences of Pragmatism*, p. 224.

29. Rorty, "Trotsky and the Wild Orchids," p. 39.

30. *Ibid.*, p. 40.

31. *Ibid.*, p. 41.

32. Richard Rorty, *Philosophy and the Mirror of Nature* (Princeton: Princeton University Press, 1979).

33. Rorty, "Trotsky and the Wild Orchids," p.39. Cf. Rorty, *Philosophy and the Mirror of Nature*, p. 5, where Rorty asserts that the three most important philosophers of the twentieth century are Dewey, Heidegger, and Wittgenstein.

34. Rorty, *Philosophy and the Mirror of Nature*, p. xiii. Cf. fn. 9 for the influence of McKeon and Brumbaugh.

35. *Ibid.*

36. Rorty, "Trotsky and the Wild Orchids," p. 39.

37. *Ibid.*

38. Cf. Rorty, *Essays on Heidegger and Others*, pp. 1–2, for Rorty's discussion of his choice of post-Nietzschean philosophers rather than "post modern."

39. *Ibid.*, p. 3. Rorty observed that to see Darwin lying behind both Nietzsche and Dewey helps one see post-Nietzschean European philosophy and post positivistic analytic philosophy converging in pragmatism.

40. *Ibid.*, p. xiii.

41. Rorty, *Objectivity, Relativism, and Truth*, p. 12. He asserts that he is trying to show how a culture without this ambition of "transcendence" is both possible and preferable.

42. Rorty, *Essays on Heidegger and Others*, p. 55.

43. *Ibid.*, p. 53 note 5.

44. *Ibid.*, p. 3.

45. Rorty, *Contingency, Irony, and Solidarity*, p. 189.

46. Rorty, *Consequences of Pragmatism*, p. xviii.

47. *Ibid.*, p. xx.

48. Rorty, *Philosophy and the Mirror of Nature*, pp. 389 ff.

49. *Ibid.*

50. *Ibid.*, p. 394.

51. Rorty, *Contingency, Irony, and Solidarity*.

52. *Ibid.*, p. 45. Rorty claims that his view is well adapted to a liberal polity.

53. Richard Rorty, "Religion as Conversation Stopper," *Common Knowledge*, Vol. III, No. 1, Spring 1994, pp. 1–6.

54. *Ibid.*, p. 2. Rorty observes, ironically, that an uncloseted atheist is unlikely to get elected anywhere in this country.

55. *Ibid.*

56. *Ibid.*, p. 5.

57. *Ibid.*, p. 6. Rorty used the example of Ann Landers's recommendation of masturbation to teenagers living in an age of AIDS. He argued that her ability to send her unpopular view out to tens of millions of readers can be traced back to the trickle-down effects of liberal philosophy, and to the Enlightenment suggestion that we privatize religion without trivializing it.

58. John Herman Randall, Jr., "Philosophy and Religion," *The Great Ideas Today: 1963*, ed. by Robert M. Hutchins and Mortimer J. Adler (Chicago: Encyclopædia Britannica, Inc., 1963), p. 261.

59. Rorty, *Objectivity, Relativism, and Truth*, p. 64.

60. Gordon D. Kaufman, *An Essay on Theological Method* (Missoula MT: Scholars Press, 1979), p. ix.

61. Gordon D. Kaufman, *God the Problem* (Cambridge: Harvard University Press, 1972), p. 226.

62. Kaufman, *An Essay on Theological Method*, p. 28.

63. Cf. *Ibid.*, pp. 4–8

64. Kaufman, *In Face of Mystery*, p. 23.

65. *Ibid.*, p. 66.

66. *Ibid.*, p. 64.

67. *Ibid.*, p. 62.

68. Cf. Rorty, *Contingency, Irony, and Solidarity*, p. 46 where Rorty argues that a liberal society should aim at curing us of our "deep metaphysical need."

69. Kaufman, *In Face of Mystery*, p. 62.

70. *Ibid.*, pp. 63–64.

71. *Ibid.*, p. 467. In footnote 6 Kaufman refers to Rorty's *Philosophy and the Mirror of Nature* and *Consequences of Pragmatism*.

72. *Ibid.*, p. 64.

73. *Ibid.*

74. Cf. *Ibid.*, pp. 64–65, where Kaufman notes that traditional Christian conceptions of religious truth have grown up in a context of fundamentally authoritarian relationships.

75. *Ibid.*, pp. 65–66.

76. *Ibid.*, p. 48.

77. *Ibid.*, p. 69.

78. *Ibid.*, p. 52.

79. *Ibid.*

80. *Ibid.*, pp. 52–53.

81. *Ibid.*, p. 53.

82. Rorty, *Contingency, Irony, and Solidarity*, p. 73. For Rorty such a vocabulary is final in the sense that if doubt is cast on the worth of these words, their user has no noncircular argumentative recourse. One has radical and continuing doubts about one's final vocabulary.

83. Cf. Rorty, *Objectivity, Relativism, and Truth*, p. 69 where Rorty equates Tillich's "ultimate concern" and Dewey's "God." He told his students that they should treat Dewey and Tillich as saying the same thing to different audiences.

84. *Ibid.*, p. 74.

85. Kaufman, *In Face of Mystery*, p. 53.

86. *Ibid.*

87. *Ibid.*, p. 54.

88. *Ibid.*

89. *Ibid.*, p. 55.

90. Rorty, *Contingency, Irony, and Solidarity*, p. 46. Cf. Isaiah Berlin, *Four Essays on Liberty* (Oxford: Oxford University Press, 1969).

91. Berlin, *Four Essays on Liberty*, p. 172.

92. *Ibid.*

93 *Ibid.*, p. 189.

THE FUNCTION OF RELIGION IN CULTURE:
A Hiatus in the Liberal Pragmatic View of Culture and Religion[1]

Henk M. Vroom

I.

Every culture includes not only ways of answering human needs and desires but also systems for solving problems arising from shortages, limitations, or contradictory and even objectionable desires. Social institutions, such as the legislature, judiciary, and the economic system, as well as philosophies of life and religious and moral traditions, function in the process of dealing with that which is objectionable. In our cultures we need—and have—conceptions about which desires are worthwhile or superficial, which are to be rejected, or even immoral, which ideals are important and which are doubtful, and which obligations are primary and which are secondary; such conceptions are interwoven with conceptions of the good life.[2]

Cultures contain what I would call *hermeneutical traditions* in which the abstract conceptions and formulations of obligations, virtues, and norms are elaborated, applied in various circumstances, and balanced over against one another. Only through such elaborate *hermeneutical traditions* can general norms and broad ideals (e.g., a world at peace) acquire and hold meaning for our concrete daily existence, both in private life and in the public square. Not only does a culture need values and norms but it also needs, if such values and norms are to be concrete, *hermeneutical traditions*. The thesis of this contribution is that religious and secular world view traditions are the most important *hermeneutical traditions* in the formation of the heart of a culture. I will show what role a view of life plays in human existence and describe how religion "functions" as (part of) the hermeneutical apparatus in relation to both our self-understanding as human beings and the context in which we live. This theory on the relation between culture and religion should also be tested in empirical research, which investigates the sources of ideals, values and norms, their appropriation and application in varying circumstances. In this contribution I describe my view on "culture and religion" and its implications for the role of religious traditions in societal life. I will develop my argument in discussion with liberal ideas, in view of the extensive influence they exercise in the political atmosphere of North America and northwestern Europe, and refer specifically to the works of Richard Rorty, who has become one of the foremost spokesmen of the liberal pragmatic tradition.

The most important characteristic of general norms, values, and ideals is their *relative independence* of the concrete situations in which we live. Wishes, norms and ideals exist by virtue of the difference between what is and what is not. Wishes and ideals presuppose an idea of a situation other than that in which we are thrown and in which we have to live, to adapt or not adapt, to make choices or to acquiesce.[3]

Norms have a higher status than wishes and ideals. When Rorty remarks that "The only things that are really evident to us are our own desires,"[4] one should take into account that we have to select and judge our wishes. Often we postpone the fulfilment of some wishes in order to be able to realize other desires which we feel to be more important. Many of our spontaneous desires are left unsatisfied so that room can be left for the realisation of more important and broader ideals. The daily collision of our wishes and desires turns life into a continuous process of weighing and judging them over against one another. We have to decide whom to consider as "our own": *whose* desires really count and *which* desires really matter? We evaluate *our* and *their* desires as well as the ideals for our lives in the light of norms, values, and broader ideals. Functioning in the background is an anthropology in which human beings are considered to be equal in certain respects.[5]

Norms presuppose that we are able to compare what is with what is not and with what should be. Sometimes we are conscious of a different situation than that which we have realized, or we know of an alternative which we could have realized. In such a case we evaluate what we have done or not done in the light of a norm or broader ideal. In whatever way we explain the origin of norms, they are, as a matter of fact, not simply given along with what actually is.

The question thus arises as to the status and nature of norms and values. Because they have relative independence with respect to changing situations and our desires and wishes, norms have been sought in general ideas and universal rules. Such an approach, with reference to either the idea of the good, the categorical imperative, or the greatest happiness for the greatest number, remains necessarily abstract and vague.[6] In order to make them concrete and meaningful in practical life, we need *hermeneutical traditions* with balances and the application of norms and values for *interpreting* human existence in the light of broad ideals. Rorty rightly accentuates that feelings and attitudes are more powerful than obligations. The question is how attitudes (like compassion) and right feelings are formed by traditions.[7]

In this context Rorty rejects the search for generally valid methods of reasoning and definitive speculative truths. In his view, a debate of an ethico-political nature is important, centering on the question of "what purposes are worth bothering to fulfil, which are more worthwhile than others, rather than which purposes the nature of humanity or of reality obliges us to have."[8] This reflection on purposes inevitably stands in the context of conflicting interests and often of struggles between groups and classes, such as those between people in power ("oil men") and those who are terrorised because they lack this power, or those threatened by starvation, or between the underclass of modern Western societies and the better situated who are able to hold their own.[9] Rorty rightly points out that today's big problems cannot possibly be solved either by pure science or by philosophy. For our rescue we must trust ourselves to "the poets and the engineers, the people who produce startling new projects for achieving the greatest happiness for the greatest number."[10] However with respect to the engineers we have to take into consideration that they serve large industries which employ psychologists to stimulate our ideas about what we need and even create new desires which they can fulfil against payment. Therefore wisdom requires us to evaluate the proposals and economic projects of engineers. Truly new insights have to be found by poets—and perhaps by a few others. Thus we can understand why Rorty elsewhere abandons the engineers and leaves this task to the poets. His move from classical philosophical thinking to novelists and poets is remarkable and important.[11] They are the people who produce new ideas; on our situation they throw a different light than that which most of us— civilians, politicians, captains of industry—tend to take for granted.

We may notice how classical such a turn to poets, dreamers, and seers is. In the Hindu tradition authority has been given to seers who have seen what is beyond ordinary sight. In the European Middle Ages songs and plays dealt with virtues and vices. Ancient Jewish culture foretold that sons and daughters would prophesy, old men would dream dreams, and young men would see visions. An unknown poet sang of a servant who would succeed where others had failed.[12] For Heidegger poets give voice to a new language which announces new developments in Being and even brings them about: "die Sprache spricht."[13] However, some dreamers have also dreamed of the *Übermensch*, the values of an elite class or caste, or a supreme nation. Poems and dreams cannot be taken at face value either.[14]

Rorty also indicates the ultimate limit of morality: "cruelty is the worst thing we do,"[15] an insight which is not specifically liberal. But this lowest limit of morality also needs explanation: when is behaviour cruel? For whom are we responsible? How serious is unintended, indirect cruelty? We can never transcend the processes of concretisation and of weighing various evils. A kind of hermeneutics for everyday practice is needed here as well.

Inevitably, ideals are a long way from our desires. The really powerful ideas of a good or better life are full of *imagination*; they are visions, dreams, sometimes protests and frequently imaginative pictures of a good world: everybody under her fig tree. These imaginations are not abstract formulas and concepts; their real nature is poetic, exemplary and paradigmatic.[16]

Choices and decisions as to what to do and what to leave undone are as characteristic of human existence as obligations and prohibitions. We have many wishes, springing from our physiological constitution, such as the need for shelter, food, and sex, from social reality, like the desire for cooperation so we can be protected from the forces of nature, disaster and enemies, and from our psychological make-up, like the fear of accidents, violence, and the longing for friendship, acknowledgement, and acceptance.[17] Within the diversity of societies our needs have been shaped in various forms; they have been modeled according to cultural schematisms—the reason for the great variety of ways of the preparation of food, marriage customs, social structures and architectural styles.[18] Cultural pluralism is an undeniable fact, which cannot be overcome by any philosophical scheme because every philosophical school or political theory adds another way of ordering beliefs and desires. A final vocabulary from which we could judge all cultural, philosophical and religious paradigms does not exist, as Rorty rightly states. In his opinion, a pure experience of "true" reality, the laying bare of a "true self," a pure life, or a real "I" is impossible. The only things that do exist are the many paradigms or final vocabularies, which are engaged in a hopefully peaceful rhetorical struggle for influence.[19]

Rorty acknowledges that it is important to "keep our web of beliefs and desires coherent."[20] In ever-changing situations we hope that others will say anything that can help us to do so. Indeed, it is very important to note that desires and beliefs are interwoven. On the basis of our ideas of the good life we select desires worthy of pursuit and reject those we must suppress. Attractive ideals of the good life are brought to the fore by poets, seers, and prophets. Only ideals can help us to solve conflicts of duties and rights.[21]

Traditions pass on such images of the good life. Such traditions exist in a close intermingling of cultural and religious components. In all their complexity and dynamics they help us to make choices between desires and wishes, to balance our own desires over against those of others, and to judge our acts and desires in the light of broader and more far-reaching ideals and norms. They do this by drawing images of the good life, not only for individuals but also for the community as a whole.

For this reason a strict liberal separation of the public and the private sphere cannot be maintained.[22] Also, the public good depends on ideas of the good life. Ideas of the good life transcend the private sphere. They are imaginative, expressed in symbols, utopias and eschatological myths. The very idea of the possibility of the separation of private and public is part of one world view but not of others; it is not a neutral stance at all but one view among others, and a mistaken one.

II.

The problematic distinction between the public and the private sphere has its origin in the acknowledgement of the pluralism of world views. From the sixteenth century on especially, Western philosophy has claimed to be an able arbiter amidst the diversity of (secular and) religious world view traditions. Typical of the postmodern phase is that philosophy has been forced to resign this function. Because ideas of the good life are necessary for all choices between desires, wishes and longing, society is fully dependent upon world view traditions. Pluralism demands that in a critical dialogue we have to discern what is really important. The solution for religious pluralism is not a neutral public square, but a conscious, well-organised critical dialogue.[23] Only through a sympathetic *and* critical exchange of views of what is really and legitimately desirable can peace, coherence, and solidarity be maintained in our societies. Room for individuals to live their specific ways of life and the need for a common responsibility for one another should be brought into balance very carefully—and that cannot be done by neglecting world view traditions.

In what follows I will show how world view traditions and religious traditions especially are complex and dynamic hermeneutic configurations which function by helping people to discern feelings, desires and obligations, to legitimise and appropriate them partly or to show ways to change or to channel them. They mediate between abstract and distant ideals of the good life and the concrete practice of our lives. Religion and culture are interwoven.[24]

I will make one comment. Even if this paper describes how religion works, this does not imply a naturalistic view of religion. I think that religion has a real influence on human life because it both fulfils a strong need *and* touches upon a deeper and broader reality which cannot be experienced empirically. For this very reason religion can also be effectively misused.

In choosing what we do and which needs we fulfil we do not function as *tabula rasa*. We have been formed by cultural traditions—for better or for worse. We even know that behind the things we say and are conscious of we are determined by hidden emotions and desires. Since Freud it has become evident that many of our wishes are unconscious and that all kinds of hidden motives are covered by what we think and say. Since Marx we also know that a cultural edifice can be a façade covering a cruel struggle for power and wealth. Therefore, the question arises as to whether we can take our desires as a point of departure, and even whether they are as clear as Rorty claims. Should they not be purified, curtailed, and thus judged and criticised? In a complex society the questions start at the point where we have to explain what is cruel, undesirable, illegitimate, at the point where our will needs to guide our desires, and where we have to choose among the many obligations and wishes we have to take into account. Since Marx, Nietzsche, and Freud, since the Holocaust and Vietnam, and in view of the continuing destruction of the rain forests and nature in general we cannot be satisfied with Rorty's confession, which we have already quoted: "The only things that are really evident to us are our own desires." Our deepest wishes are not as evident as he claims—and they are also suspect.[25] We are frequently mistaken in our real motives; we do not discern the real situation but only our perception of it, and we often overlook aspects of reality that are less pleasant to us. In other words, there are many things we will not see and cannot see as they really are. Clear insight into our real situation is not the rule. Religious traditions nearly always give two reasons for this phenomenon: attachment and ignorance.[26] Because we are attached to our interests, sympathies and antipathies, our primary desires—be they good, wrong, or ambiguous—we do not judge our ends and desires purely and cannot bring them easily into harmony with the needs and desires of others.

However much political freedom we may have, in our inner lives we are not free.[27] We do not distinguish clearly between primary and secondary ends and often do not discern our real interests. Therefore, our insights in relation to purposes and desires are suspect. They have to be purified of false undertones and scrutinized by clear judgment. We thus cannot let ourselves be inspired by the dreams of the poets or retire to our private lives but have to look for guidance in the wisdom of other generations and the people who have gathered insights and passed them on through the generations: the world view traditions.

III.

Traditions help people distinguish between good and wrong desires. Some world view traditions are secular, but most are religious. I will concentrate on religious traditions, since they have a much more elaborate "hermeneutical apparatus," but much will apply also to secular world view traditions. Religious traditions are *historical-hermeneutical processes* in which life itself on the one hand and the cumulative insights of the tradition (the "traditum") on the other are explained. The actual, living tradition mediates between (1) human existence, (2) the *traditum*/tradition, and (3) the contexts in which we live.

Religious traditions are not primarily doctrinal systems; in a way they are not wholes or systems at all. Just as the term culture stands for a melting pot of subcultures, and subculture for a melting pot of sub-subcultures, a religious tradition is a melting pot of subtraditions in exchange with other world view traditions, scientific theories, the cultural fashions of the day and urgent tasks. Cultural and religious vocabularies are dynamic; they are not "wholes" nor final vocabularies. As far as I can see, such final vocabularies in the sense which Rorty means do not exist at all; they are not wholes but dynamic configurations of basic insights, allowing for the possibility of dialogue, mutual critique, various unexpected overlappings and developments.[28] We can see this more clearly when we look into the way in which religion functions.

Religious traditions are ways of life. They comprise (1) narratives, (2) practices, (3) holy scriptures, (4) effective histories of the (re-)interpretation and application of these scriptures, (5) organizational structures in one form or another, (6) summaries and introductions in their views, (7) moral admonitions, and (8) a number of basic insights.

In traditions stories are primary. Stories interpret human existence and evoke attitudes.[29] Different kinds of stories have different functions.[30] Myths tell about the origin and goal of existence: narratives about creation, consummation, *kalpas*, or the chain of interrelated beings. Grand narratives are the narratives about "the history" by which individuals and groups are embedded in comprehensive meaningful "entities" (the history of progress, of the white race, of a special people, or the relation between somebody's reincarnations, of the compassionate preaching of the Buddha). Other stories concern the good way of life directly. The measuring stick will usually be placed higher than most of us can jump: stories about saints, examples like Martin Luther King, Jr. ("I have a dream"), Mother Theresa and Gandhi. Again, other stories interpret norms; the biblical story of the good Samaritan is the "concrete definition" of neighbourly love, not an abstract formula. It is a story to live by, an evoking, paradigmatic narrative.[31] Some stories mediate between a distant future, like the Last Judgment, and our daily life, like the story of the five wise and five foolish virgins. Narratives have a "plot." They help us to do the right thing in baffling situations in which our many emotions, obligations and desires bewilder us. They do not work by only prescribing commandments but primarily by showing human beings in all their troubles, shortcomings and limitations, their good and bad choices, giving way to desires and temptations (e.g., David and Bathsheba) and their entanglement in hopeless situations. The primary sources of such narratives are religious traditions, folk traditions (e.g., Robin Hood) and only secondarily individual poets, authors and filmmakers.

Typical for religious traditions is that human existence in these stories is related to transcendence, be it *brahman, rita,* the *dharma, tao* or God. Narratives about experiences are primary in the ideas of transcendence which people have as well. In our experience *shunyata* ("Emptiness") becomes present through the preaching of the Buddha and through what Zen masters say about it, especially about the path to Enlightenment and the instructions for meditation. Preaching, such as the famous First Sermon of the Buddha, is an interpretation of human existence *and* a report of somebody's experience. The stories of the many experiences, rather than philosophical speculations, which people had with the reality of God are primary.[32] The imaginative pictures that are passed on in narratives have affective, cognitive, and moral sides. Traditions live on in the stories of the Talmud, Hassidic tales, *hadith* of the Prophet, the stories about Jesus and the apostles, the martyrs and the great examples like Francis of Assisi, Luther, and John XXIII, in the volumes with the conversations of the Buddha, the Mahabharata and a great many Puranas. Myths, legends, historic tales—together with rituals they form the heart of religious traditions. Christianity also is not a doctrine or speculation about

God but a cumulative tradition of narratives about experiences of life, especially in relation to an unexpected reality which has been called "I am who I am," and the story of Jesus who has discerned the deepest desires and needs of fellow human beings.

The reason why religious narratives are not easily accessible lies in the two barriers which hinder us from acquiring real insight: attachment and ignorance. In hermeneutics it can be defended that every understanding of texts requires a sympathetic, yielding movement of the reader. This comprises not only the trust that the text has an understandable meaning (Gadamer's *Vorgriff der Volkommenheit*[33]) but also the idea that we can learn something from the text.[34] In reading these texts we have to open ourselves to new insights and be willing to be criticised. Religious texts almost always have a tense relationship with our daily life and culture as it "normally seems to be." Not all our wishes, desires, and ideals are acceptable to religious traditions. They try to help people find a good way to live; religious traditions are paths rather than doctrinal systems. They help us to look with other eyes. Therefore, they not only inform us about real life (like "the chain of causality") but also exhort us to improve our lives and adopt another attitude ("But I say to you . . ."). They intend to change our lives, to *transform* us, as it has been expressed, from ego-directedness to reality-directedness.[35]

The stories of the tradition pass on insight into wrong ways of living, objectionable desires and valuable ways of life. Many stories are imaginative construals of the good life amidst many temptations, especially of egoism and group egoism. For many people the appropriation of these insights requires a change in their lives, often also a re-interpretation of a philosophy of life (compared with what is usual in our cultures). In this sense religious traditions go against the grain.[36] Thus, in the Hindu tradition the gurus try to help people attain inner deepening and purity, and in the Jewish tradition the prophets oppose injustice and neglect—also cruelties which had not been perceived so clearly before.

Religious traditions have organisational forms in which insights and ways of life are passed on. In many cases these organisations are structured in relatively loose ways, but sometimes they are tightly structured. Within traditions rites are central. The forms these rites may take may be contextually influenced by the culture. The force of a ritual lies in the repetition of stories and central insights and the practices of a group of people. Through repetition the patterns are internalized. The transformation of ideas of the good life and a world view is brought about by rituals in which adherents of a tradition participate.

Traditions are not static entities. In rituals not only is human existence (re-)interpreted, but the "tradition" itself is re-interpreted and applied as well.[37] A living tradition relates the *traditum* with the context; religious leaders underline insights which are relevant under certain circumstances and relate them to other insights. In this way the "effective history" (*Wirkungsgeschichte*) of religious texts is a continuous process of re-interpretation and application. Rituals form the heart of this hermeneutical history. The analyses of Gadamer and Ricoeur concerning the passing on of a tradition and the application of the meaning of texts have to be radicalised in religious hermeneutics. Because these texts are canonical and have authority, they are passed on carefully; the "effective history" is dealt with very consciously.

In the rituals of religious traditions which have holy scriptures, their central parts are recited and explained. The explanation itself is the application *and* adaptation of the "tradition" to the context. What is explained is what is important and central; insights from the tradition are related to the situation, accentuated and internalised.

Such an interpretation of the *traditum* by a part of the tradition can be called a *scheme of interpretation*: a dynamic configuration of insights and usages with which a religious group explains and actualises its holy scriptures. A scheme of interpretation mediates between the texts and the contextual re-interpretations within a religious community. An example of this is the way in which many Protestant churches have opened their offices to women, whereas according to Paul women are not allowed to speak in the services. The explicit acknowledgement of the role of the religious community in the re-interpretation and application of the scriptures can be found in the Jewish distinction between scriptural and oral traditions and the Catholic attribution of authority to church tradition.[38] One function of rituals is the accentuation of central insights and rules for living. In the next section I will return to the nature of central insights.

Rites comprise texts, symbolic acts in which faith is internalised and beliefs are made visible, as in the eucharist and baptism as well as in meditation sessions, sacrifices, communal meals, religious festivals, and pilgrimages. Their function is to re-interpret human existence and to make clear positive and negative desires and ideals.[39] In the long run a change of attitude is effected in the believers, often for the better, sometimes for the worse. Group rituals are accompanied by rituals in the family and personal habits such as personal prayer and meditation. In this way religious traditions pass on their insights and ways of living within groups of people whom they help to distinguish between good and bad desires and personal ideals.

The insights of religious traditions do not exist primarily in formulas. For a good understanding of the nature of religious insights it is important to realize that it is characteristic that believers have to search for the right words to express what they believe carefully and understandably. This phenomenon can be understood as follows. In faith experience is primary. These experiences relate to the ways in which people are conscious of themselves, the world, other beings, and transcendence. Traditions cherish some basic experiences (e.g. of contingency, responsibility, finiteness, being part of a larger whole) and interpret them by a series of basic insights, which are evoked by religious symbols, rituals, and meditation.[40] For example, in the Abrahamic religions the finite world is seen as meaningful; a basic insight states that the world is created, which does not entail a theory of how the world has been made but that the world has a Maker and has been created on purpose. The experience of the world as a mixture of good and evil has been expressed in some traditions in terms of sin and guilt and in terms of the brokenness of existence. These insights relate to some attitudes which help to experience the world as meaningful and at the same time ambiguous and to see human beings as responsible for their choices. Religious faith comprises a number of such basic insights which cohere in a rather complicated system—and not in a clear and fully coherent theory about God, human beings, and the world. The explanation of the different basic insights in the various traditions usually gives way to many nuances. In the narratives especially they are expressed in a variety of ways, with more nuances than philosophers and scientist like. To give some examples, the book of Genesis in the Tanakh and the Bible contains two creation narratives and one on the fall. At the basis of these stories are deep reflections on the relation between God, good and evil, human responsibility and finitude. Scholastic theology has frequently discarded these nuances, just like the critique of religion by many unbelievers who dismiss religious narratives and symbols because of their poetic, symbolic, and sometimes paradoxical character. Through the modernist requirements of clear and distinct formulation of insights in propositions people began to neglect the evocative and poetic language of religion. However, it is precisely the shortcomings of modernist theories that have been criticised aptly by authors like Heidegger, Gadamer, and Rorty as well.

Because a religion is a dynamic configuration of quite a number of basic insights a continuous exchange and dialogue with other traditions and insights, in a culture is possible: when one conviction is under discussion, the whole "building" of somebody's belief does not automatically fall apart.[41]

Personally, I think that those who direct our attention to new and also forgotten insights which have been articulated in poetic language, oughtnot forego religious traditions and their wisdoms. As a liberal philosopher, Rorty directs our attention to poets and other people who break through the views of life which have developed in society. They show things as they are, the cruelty and injustice, but also the courage, the dedication and wisdom of some, both the ugly and the beautiful events. We need not only the poets and filmmakers but also communities with centuries-old experiences which bring to mind deeper insights and help us to distinguish between our desires: which are valid, wrong, or dangerous. Every culture is in need of organisational forms in which wisdom is passed on. Wisdom consists in insights into life, i.e., deep, basic insights, which are interwoven with moral intuitions and ideals. Everybody has such insights. If we prefer to place the measuring stick somewhat higher than the prevention of cruelty, we need larger ideals. Moral rules have a weak foundation and in the long run cannot bear the burden of breaking with egoism. I suppose that the small number of books of poetry and even television soaps with their large audience are not apt ways of re-directing our lives. Politicians frequently refer to the educational system, which should acquaint children with norms and values. Until this century, religious traditions were almost always entrusted with the task of shaping our lives and helping us to improve them. When we remember the enormous problems that face our cultures, I am afraid that we are forced to admit that the liberal view of culture is lacking. We cannot abandon our ideals, the interpretation of our needs and desires to the private sphere alone. A culture is in need of *hermeneutical world view traditions* which help people to discern what is worthwhile, to internalise insights and re-direct their lives in a broader perspective. Happily enough, a truly postmodern view of culture allows the possibility of acknowledging the role of narratives, dreams, religious symbols and rituals. Reflection on the way in which world view traditions can find new forms in a pluralist society is urgently needed. Because not all narratives, "sentimental stories," and insights are right and worthwhile, a critical, public dialogue

The Function of Religion in Culture 349

should also be stimulated and organized.[42] But it has to be acknowledged, first of all, that world view traditions are at the heart of societies and therefore more than a private affair. Liberal and pragmatic philosophers should integrate not only hermeneutical philosophy but also *religious hermeneutics* into their thought.

NOTES

1. I would like to thank Dr. Henry Jansen for the correction of my English text. The article will be published in Dutch as chapter 1 in my *Religie als ziel van de cultuur* (Zoetermeer: Meinema, 1996).

2. Cf. P. Ricoeur, *Oneself as Another*, tr. Kathleen Blamey (Chicago: University of Chicago Press, 1992), p. 170.

3. Cf. M. Heidegger, *Sein und Zeit*, 11th ed. (Tübingen: Niemeyer, 1967), p. 135 (*"Geworfenheit"* and *"Faktizität"*). While Heidegger stresses the inevitability of making choices, the *content*, i.e., notions of a better and a good life, is also important.

4. R. Rorty, *Essays on Heidegger and Others*, Philosophical Papers I and II (Cambridge: Cambridge University Press, 1991), II, p. 29.

5. Cf. my "Brede en smalle gelijkheid," in: R. Kranenborg and W. Stoker, eds., *Religie en (on)gelijkheid in een pluriforme samenleving* (Apeldoorn: Garant, 1995), on the divergent religious anthropologies with their differing interpretations of equality and the abstract character of the idea of equality when isolated from the network of beliefs and practices. In his valuation of the individual, Rorty is indebted to Jewish, Christian, and humanistic values and ideas.

6. Cf. Rorty, *Papers* II, p. 54; *Contingency*, p. 192 f.

7. Cf. Rorty, "Rechten van de mens, rationaliteit en sentimentaliteit," in: *Richard Rorty*, pp. 15–34, 27 f.

8. Rorty, *Papers* I, p. 110; cf. Rorty, *Philosophy and the Mirror of Nature* (Oxford: Blackwell, 1980), pp. 17–128.

9. R. Rorty, *Papers* II, pp. 25 f.

10. R. Rorty, *Papers* II, p. 26.

11. Cf. R. Rorty, *Contingency, Irony and Solidarity* (Cambridge: Cambridge University Press, 1989), chs. 5, 7–9.

12. Joel 2:28 f.; Isaiah 42:1–7; 49:1–7; 50:4–11; 52:13–53:12.

13. Cf. Rorty, *Papers* II, p. 34. M. Heidegger, "Brief über den "Humanismus"," in: Heidegger, *Wegmarken* (Frankfurt a.M.: Kloostermann, 1967), p. 158 (and elsewhere): "*Sprache ist lichtend-verbergende Ankunft des Seins selbst.*"

14. See M.-H. Parizeau, "Individuele narrativiteit en identiteit: Rorty over de ethiek van het goede leven," in: G. Hottois *et al.*, eds., *Richard Rorty: Ironie, politiek en postmodernisme* (Antwerpen: Hadewijch, 1994), pp. 79–93, 89.

15. Rorty, *Contingency*, pp. 146, 65, *passim*.

16. Cf. the extensive literature on narratives and their meaning for morality, world views, and human identity, e.g., Johan Verstreaten, "Narrativity and Hermeneutics in Applied Ethics," *Ethical Perspectives* 1 (1994): 51–70; Garrett Green, *Imagining God: Theology and the Religious Imagination* (San Francisco: Harper and Row, 1989); Paul Brockelman, *The Inside Story: A Narrative Approach to Religious Understanding and Truth* (Albany: State University of NY Press, 1992); Paul Ricoeur, "Life in Quest of Narrative" and "Narrative Identity" in: D. Wood ed., *On Paul Ricoeur, Narrative and Interpretation* (London/New York: Routledge, 1991), pp. 20–33, 188–200; J.M. Bernstein, "Grand Narratives," in: *On Paul Ricoeur: Narrative and Interpretation*, pp. 102–23.

17. Cf. J. Habermas, *Erkenntnis und Interesse* (Frankfurt a.M.: Suhrkamp, 1968) on technical, social and "critical" interests.

18. Cf. e.g., Melville J. Herskovits, *Man and its Works: The Science of Cultural Anthropology* (New York: Alfred Knopf, 1949).

19. R. Rorty, *Contingency*, pp. 90 f., 108 f., *passim*.

20. R. Rorty, *Contingency*, p. 185; Rorty, "Rechten," p. 18.

21. Cf. L. Bégin, "Rechten ernstig of ironisch nemen?" in: *Richard Rorty*, pp. 202–20, 214–6; see also J.M. Bernstein, "Grand narratives," p. 111.

22. Rorty makes a strong distinction between the private and the public atmospheres. Cf. *Contingency*, pp. 83, 194, *passim*. A critical discussion of this issue in relation to the discussion on public philosophy can be found in R.J. Mouw and S. Griffioen, *Pluralism and Horizons* (Grand Rapids: Eerdmans, 1993), pp. 162–64.

23. See my *No Other Gods: Christianity in Dialogue with Buddhism, Hinduism and Islam*, tr. Lucy Jansen (Grand Rapids: Eerdmans, 1996) for examples of such a dialogue; see also Mouw and Griffioen, *Pluralism*, pp. 104 f. on dialogue.

24. Cf. my "Religious Hermeneutics, Culture and Narrative," *Studies in Interreligious Dialogue* 4 (1994): pp. 189–213. Definitions of the concepts of culture, religion and value are supplied here.

25. In *Papers* II, p. 29 Rorty makes an epistomelogical point; my objection has an epistemological and an ethical point as well.

26. Cf. my *Religions and the Truth*, tr. J. Rebel (Grand Rapids: Eerdmans, 1989) pp. 305–07, *passim*.

27. On the one hand, from the point of view of religious epistemology Rorty's notion that freedom takes care of truth is true, but (because of the inner lack of freedom) naive on the other. Cf. Rorty, *Contingency*, pp. 66 f., 84, 176 ("If we take care of freedom, truth can take care of itself"). The development of freedom is intertwined with the development of truth and *vice versa*. It is both that we need to be free to see the truth and that the truth makes us free. See my *Religions and the Truth*, *passim*.

28. Cf. my *Religions and the Truth*, ch. 12.

29. Cf. Rorty, "Rechten," pp. 30 f.

30. Cf. my "Religious Hermeneutics," pp. 195–210.

31. Luke 10:25–37, perhaps the nicest example of what Rorty calls a sentimental story, cf. "Rechten," pp. 30 f.

32. Cf. Henry Jansen, *Relationality and the Concept of God* (Amsterdam: Rodopi, 1995) pp. 214–32; cf. my *Religions and the Truth*, ch. 10.

33. H.-G. Gadamer, *Wahrheit und Methode*, 2nd. ed. (Tübingen: Mohr, 1965), pp. 277 f.

34. In some cases we learn about the subject matter of the text (the *"Sache"* in Karl Barth's, Gadamer's and G. Ebeling's hermeneutics), sometimes about the wrong views of the author. But when we read we are always involved in one way or another. Cf. Heidegger, *Sein und Zeit*, p. 150.

35. Cf. J. Hick, *An Interpretation of Religion* (Houndmills: Macmillan, 1989) pp. 36–55, *passim*.

36. Therefore they are not only re-descriptions of life, as Rorty says (*Contingency*, p. 80); in divergent ways they contend with what seems to be normal. The possibility of critical dialogue is given with the fact that our awareness and experience is *not* embedded *equally* in the web of our language games. Rorty himself acknowledges a point outside of that web of language and interpretation: "pain is non-linguistic" (*Contingency*, p. 94). Actually, there are more experiences like this and all kinds of gradations of "interwovenness" in cultures, languages, and world views. Apparently, not all experiences are "interpreted," and they are not "interpreted" equally strongly or in equal ways. Some negative or positive basic experiences break through our views—otherwise changes could not occur. See Christa W. Anbeek, *Denken over de dood* (Kampen: Kok, 1994), especially chs. 1 and 5, *passim*.

37. On what follows cf. Wilfred C. Smith, *The Meaning and End of Religion* (New York, 1962), *What is Scripture?* (London: SCM, 1993); and, e.g., the Roman Catholic declaration on divine revelation, *Dei Verbum*, of the Second Vatican Council. A description of the role of a scheme of interpretation is given in my "Scripture Read and Interpreted," *Calvin Theological Journal* 28 (1993): pp. 352–71.

38. E.E. Urbach, *The Sages—Their Concepts and Beliefs*, tr. I. Abrahams, 2nd ed. (Jerusalem: 1979) I, pp. 286 ff.

39. An attempt at a more concrete description of such an re-interpretation through liturgical texts (concerning death) can be found in my "Religion als Deutung des Todes," in: G. Oberhammer ed., *Im Tod gewinnt der Mensch sein Selbst. Das*

Phänomen des Todes in asiatischer und abendländischer Religionstradition (Vienna: ÖAdW, 1995), pp. 252–72.

40. See my *Religions and the Truth*, pp. 321–29, 340f. Cf. Anbeek, *Denken* (Kampen: Kok, 1994), especially pp. 7–45.

41. See my "Syncretism and Dialogue: A Philosophical Analysis", in: J.D. Gort *et al.*, *Dialogue and Syncretism* (Amsterdam: Rodopi / Grand Rapids: Eerdmans 1989), pp. 26–35.

42. Such a dialogue is also needed because our own being is dialogical, see C. Taylor, "The Politics of Recognition," in: Charles Taylor *et al.*, *Multiculturalism* (Princeton: Princeton University Press, 1994), pp. 25–73, 32 f. See also, H.J.M. Hermans and H.J.G. Kempen, *The Dialogical Self* (San Diego: Academic Press, 1993), especially chs. 3 and 5.

IV. Other Themes

FINITE IS ALL RIGHT!
Confessions Of A Slow Learner[1]

Donald A. Crosby

I once came into possession of a mobile, comprised of varied and delicate objects suspended from rods of uneven lengths and a maze of strings, all in the most delicate equipoise and beauty. I hung it from the ceiling of my study with a thumbtack and thereafter would sit and watch it in fascination as it swung about, its parts darting to and fro with every breath of current. It was like a little world of its own, with its own distinctive dynamism and character, its own frail elegance. I came in one morning expecting once again to admire the mobile's floating delicacy, only to be astonished to find it crumpled on the floor! The thumbtack had gradually prised loose from the gypsum board ceiling, and the splendid little world was no more.

As I reflect on my life and thought in my mid twenties when I graduated from Princeton Theological Seminary and became, for a brief time, a Presbyterian minister, I recall that the universe seemed to me much like the endlessly fascinating mobile. For me the universe hung, as it were, from the heavens, its supports reaching beyond the murky clouds and distant stars to its point of origin and ultimate support. Everything flowed from and found its meaning in this final reference point, this Cosmic Thumbtack in the sky. Without it, nothing could exist and nothing would make sense. The panoplied systems of nature, history, and culture, of philosophy, art, science, morality, and religion hung from this absolute point, what I and others in my culture had learned to reverence as "God."

And were this absolute, all-sustaining God to be taken away, then everything would collapse. Nature would become cold and inscrutable, and the saga of human history would sink into a meaningless muddle. Individual life would lose all aim and purpose. I was unable at that time to entertain the possibility of the self-sufficiency of the finite world or the intrinsic, non-derivative worth and importance of any of its aspects. It either flowed from and found its meaning in the absoluteness of God, or it lay in ruin.

My mood at that time was an acute case of what Friedrich Schleiermacher called "a sense and taste for the infinite,"[2] an infinite before whose dazzling radiance all things finite must pale into insignificance. I yearned for the absolute on which I could absolutely depend. And the fervent "search for absolutes" (to use Paul Tillich's phrase[3]) that characterized this time of my life—absolutes in ethics, epistemology, metaphysics, and, especially, religion that could witness to the reality of an absolute God—was unrelenting. Nothing temporal, contingent, or conditioned would do.

My *ethics* assumed the absoluteness of moral laws anchored in unchanging divine decrees. Without God, I was convinced that morality would dissolve into brutal egoism or vapid relativism. In *epistemology*, I was a realist, and a rather uncritical one at that. As the product of God's absolute intelligence and wisdom, the world is eminently knowable, and God has created us with ability to know it. Its structures and kinds are "out there," objectively present and awaiting discovery. Our task as knowers is to learn how adequately to picture or represent these preexisting traits of a divinely ordered world. We are greatly assisted in this process, I then believed, by a definitive revelation in the Holy Scriptures of God's nature, the character and goal of his creation, and his purpose for human life. My *metaphysics* was dualistic and God-centered. I believed that a vast spiritual realm lies beyond the material world, and that the human soul transcends its bodily context just as an immaterial, purely spiritual God—in whose image we are made—radically transcends the world he has created. We are not so much in the world as above it or over against it, and we are destined for an everlasting spiritual life that has no need of the trappings of earthly existence.

Religion was inconceivable without a theism that assumes the total self-sufficiency of God. While the world depends radically on God for its existence moment by moment, God has no need of the world. That he cares for it at all, or even that he had bothered to create it in the first place, is an inexplicable gift of his grace. And since both the goodness and power of God are absolute—as shown compellingly in the conquest of sin and death in the resurrection of Christ—we can be confident of their triumph over all forces of destruction and evil, whether in ourselves or in nature. From God's standpoint, nothing is uncertain, ambiguous, or precarious—however much it may seem so to us. The world rests serenely "in his hands." Finally, human beings, with their debilitating condition of sin, stand in need of a radical transformation of heart and life that only a God of absolute power and goodness can provide.

Finite is All Right! 359

This preoccupation with absolutes in my twenties, and a profound aversion to giving final importance to anything finite or relative (which I viewed then as the essence of idolatry) was deeply ingrained by my religious upbringing in conservative Presbyterian churches of my Deep South hometown (Pensacola, Florida), in the Presbyterian college I attended (Davidson, in North Carolina), and in Princeton Theological Seminary, where it was reinforced by intensive study of classical theologians such as Augustine and John Calvin, and of neo-orthodox theologians such as Karl Barth, Emil Brunner, and Reinhold Niebuhr. The last three were unrelenting in their criticisms of liberal theology. Had I been exposed in the seminary to knowledgeable and sympathetic interpretations of this theological tradition, I might have been able to embark sooner than I did on the "escape from absolutes"[4] that began in my late twenties and has continued to the present. But since I was not, I had to find my own way.

As I look back through the nearly forty years from that time to this, I can acknowledge the content of that young person's beliefs and even register the obviousness and conviction with which they were held. But I cannot identify with that person. He is a stranger to me, an exotic object of wonder rather than a familiar and intimate friend. I respect his outlook, but I cannot imagine that it was ever my own.

From where I now stand, the Cosmic Thumbtack has long since been prised loose from the sky. I no longer believe in a God or in absolutes of any kind to which ultimate appeal can or need be made. But the universe for me has not collapsed or become pointless and alien. Instead, I have gradually learned to accept and even to reverence the entwined dependencies of a world of which I and all other finite beings are an integral part, a world that is itself finite through and through. And I no longer believe that this finite world has, or has need of, any sort of ground or support beyond itself. Thus I have undergone what can only be described in retrospect as an "experience of conversion." It was not an overnight conversion; in fact, it was slow and incremental, stretching over many years. But the change of outlook it finally produced was radical. I will try to describe some of the experiences and reflections that helped to bring about this change.

I was minister for three years of a small Presbyterian church near Wilmington, Delaware. During this time I also completed a master's degree in American church history at Princeton Theological Seminary. With an undergraduate and two graduate degrees now under my belt, I realized how strongly committed I was to academic pursuits, so I decided to change my career to teaching in a college or university. I applied to graduate programs in Religion and chose the program jointly sponsored by Union Theological Seminary and Columbia University, in New York City.

During my work for the doctorate, I began the move away from an earlier absolutism toward the realization that "finite is all right." This change, from that time to the present, has turned primarily on one basic intellectual principle and two supporting principles. I call them "the big E and the two p's" (no, this is not the name of a musical trio!). I did not become aware of these principles and their implications all at once, but only slowly, and even more slowly did they become incorporated firmly into my life. The basic principle is *empiricism*, not the narrow, merely sensate empiricism of Enlightenment philosophy, but a more comprehensive type closely akin to what William James dubbed "radical empiricism." The two supporting principles are *processism* and *pluralism*.

I shall explain the meaning I attribute to these three principles in turn, indicating in what contexts and for what reasons I came to identify with each of them over the years. I shall also say something about how I came to see their relations to one another, with particular emphasis on relations of the other two principles to the most basic one, empiricism. Most importantly, I shall indicate how the principles freed me from my fixation on absolutes and convinced me that the finite is *all* we have and all we *need* to have.

I.

I was already sympathetic to a kind of empiricism in my teens through my upbringing in evangelical, pietistic churches that gave great stress to firsthand experience of the presence and power of God. Christianity, we were taught, was to be lived, not merely analyzed or professed. As Evangelicals say today, Christians were to "walk the talk," putting their faith into practice, especially moral practice, and anticipating confirmation of its truth in its continuing ability to address the needs, challenges, and responsibilities of everyday life. Genuine religion was thus claimed to be thoroughly experiential. However, the idea that experience might *disconfirm* teachings of the Bible or the church was never seriously entertained. It was an empiricism of confirmation only, not of possible falsification. We were to trust experience when it supported the faith, but not when it might call that faith into question. The qualified, one-sided character of this so-called empiricism I later recognized and rejected, but the principle of empiricism itself stayed with me. And it helped to transform my outlook on the world.

Like pietistic religion and the moral outlook and practice it required, music had also been a critical part of my life since my earliest years. I had a high soprano voice as a child and was given voice lessons by people who developed and encouraged love of music. When my voice changed, I continued to sing in glee clubs and choirs in high school, college, and seminary. As a result, I was exposed to many types of music and developed an ardent appreciation for its Orphic powers. Later I came to regard the very existence of music as important experiential evidence against my earlier dualistic view of the relations of body and mind. That we can be so powerfully stirred in spirit by mere physical vibrations and rhythms helped to make me aware that we are intimately related to our bodies and, through them, to the material world, in ways that dualism cannot explain. One way I came to symbolize this intimacy of relation to myself was by reflecting on the striking fact that mundane materials such as horsehair and sheep intestines, and the woods of maple, pine, and silver fir, can be assembled into a violin, an instrument whose soaring notes evoke experiences of compelling beauty and significance.

Steeped as I was, then, in religious, aesthetic, and moral dimensions of experience, I was early on an unwitting "radical empiricist," in at least two senses of that term. First, it never occurred to me to restrict or reduce significant experience to the supposed simple data of the five senses that play such a dominant role in the epistemological theories of John Locke, George Berkeley, and David Hume. As fundamental as sensate experience is, I recognized the importance of other kinds of experience as well and regarded them as important in their own right. Second, I was convinced that basic beliefs and commitments informing one's life must be continually brought to the test of experience comprehensively conceived. In cases of conflict between beliefs and experience, beliefs should give way to experience and not the other way around. I do not think I ever bought into the tacit assumption of my early religious teachers that the central beliefs of Christianity could only be confirmed, never refuted, by experience. I was confident in my twenties and early thirties that these teachings would continue to be confirmed but did not dismiss out of hand their possible refutation.

The wider conception of experience and its crucial role for thought were reinforced and made vivid for me especially by the study of two thinkers while at Union-Columbia: Alfred North Whitehead and Horace Bushnell. I first encountered Whitehead in an introductory course on his metaphysics taught at Union Seminary by Daniel Day Williams. It was a case of love at first sight! Williams was a superb teacher, and Whitehead's thought captivated me as soon as I began to study it. It continues to instruct me, even though I am now critical of certain of its aspects, especially those relating to Whitehead's concept of God and some that now seem to me suspiciously rationalistic rather than empirical.[5]

Whitehead's repeated emphasis on experience as the focus of philosophical thought made a deep impression on me when I first came across it. I especially liked the analogy he draws in Part One of *Process and Reality* between philosophical reflection and the flight of an airplane.[6] Metaphysical discovery, he tells us, starts out from the ground of particular observations, then ascends into the thin air of a scheme of tentative generalizations suggested to the imagination by those observations, and finally comes back to the ground again, there to test empirically the adequacy of its generalizations. And metaphysics, in his view, has nothing to do with putative truths that might be claimed to lie *beyond* experience but only with "description of the generalities which apply to all the details of practice," or with a "system of general ideas in terms of which every element of our experience can be interpreted."[7]

I also warmly endorsed Whitehead's contention that we should expand beyond ordinary sensate experience our vision of the types of experience philosophical inquiry must take fully into account. I learned that his catalogue of such relevant experience includes aesthetic, moral, and religious experience; experience of causal efficacy and the "withness" of the body; experience of memory and anticipation; experience of aim, purpose, and freedom; experience of organic unity with nature and fellow human beings; and other intimations, feelings, and modes of awareness— however vague or ill-defined—that give context and meaning to the five senses and are regular components of the concreteness of daily life. A fundamental task of philosophy, according to Whitehead, is to keep all these experiences constantly in view, lest we neglect part of what philosophical systems must seek to interpret and understand. This claim means for him that philosophers must resort to stratagems of poets and other artists, boldly exploiting imaginative powers of language in order to evoke and encompass such experiences.[8] What is lost in clarity and distinctness by his appeal to a greatly widened idea of experience, I was convinced then and am convinced today, is amply compensated for by what is gained in adequacy and importance.

On the suggestion of Joseph Blau, whose course on American philosophy I savored at Columbia, I decided to write my dissertation on

Finite is All Right! 363

Horace Bushnell's theory of language, analyzing it in the context of other nineteenth-century speculations about language, especially in the United States; investigating the theological and methodological uses to which Bushnell put it; and reflecting critically on the storm of controversy it, and the theological conclusions he based on it, generated among his theological peers in New England.[9] The subtitle of the dissertation, "An Historical and Philosophical Study," helps to explain why this was an ideal topic for me, blending my earlier interest in American church history with an ever-increasing fascination with philosophy.

A side benefit of this dissertation project was my being exposed to and influenced by Bushnell's own brand of empiricism. Three traits of it are particularly important. The first is that he refused to rely uncritically on Scripture, tradition, or authority for religious truth but sought to determine, by searching reflections on his own experience and that of others, renewed meanings that Christian teachings might have for himself, his parishoners, and his society. In consequence, he was a highly original thinker who devised imaginative ways of reinterpreting old ideas and showing how they could be made relevant to the demands of life in turbulent, rapidly changing America at mid-century. Second, he was convinced that the function and worth of any religious teachings, including those of the Bible itself, are eminently practical and consist in contributions the teachings make to the transformation of life and character. Only when this "instrumental"[10] end is kept squarely in mind can the significance of religious teachings be properly understood. Finally, for Bushnell, there are depths and dimensions of experience that reach far beyond the five senses, and the vivid symbolism and imagery of religious language are required to bring these aspects of experience into awareness in ways that straightforward literal assertions cannot. Excessive literalism and exclusive attention to logical reasoning that pays no heed to the exuberant poetic qualities of religious language are thus grave mistakes in theological thinking. Bushnell, like Whitehead, was committed to a comprehensive vision of experience and linguistic expression in which the roles of feeling and imagination are given prominent place.

The seeds were well planted, then, early in my life and then in my Union-Columbia years, for my later discovery of the radical empiricism of William James. A number of years after I began teaching at Colorado State University,[11] I began to use James's *Essays in Radical Empiricism* and *A Pluralistic Universe* in an undergraduate metaphysics course that is a regular part of my assigned teaching. Still later, I twice team-taught a course with Wayne Viney, a colleague from the Department of

Psychology, for graduate students in our two departments on "The Psychology and Philosophy of William James." As I read and reread the writings of James and interacted with the students in these two courses, the contours of his empiricism became clearer, and I was brought gradually under its sway. My experiences in these courses are examples of how, throughout my academic career, my intellectual development and the research projects accompanying it have been steadily influenced by my teaching.[12]

In addition to the two traits of empiricism I have already discussed, both of which are also emphasized by James (the primacy of experience and a comprehensive view of the relevant types of experience), four more traits are stressed in James's writings and have become aspects of my own empiricism. Two of these remaining traits relate to metaphysical pluralism,[13] which, because of limitations of space, I will not be able to discuss in this essay. Since the other two can be associated with epistemological pluralism, which I am here calling the principle of pluralism, I shall defer discussion of them to the section devoted to that principle. Right now I want to say something in a preliminary way—anticipating these discussions to come—about ways in which the principle of empiricism has contributed to my growing conviction, not only that there is no warrant for believing in absolutes, but that there is no need for them.

A starting point for my discovery of ways in which the principle of empiricism leads to this conclusion was my inquiries into the thought of the two Protestant theologians Søren Kierkegaard and Paul Tillich. I avidly read most of Kierkegaard's writings on my own while at Princeton Seminary, and I made extensive use of Tillich later, both in the philosophy of religion class I taught at Colorado State University and in my book *Interpretive Theories of Religion*.[14] Kierkegaard claims that religious truth is "subjectivity." Years later I expressed what I thought this affirmation means to Kierkegaard and what it had come to mean to me, saying that religious truth "is realized . . . only when it is incorporated into the concrete life of the individual and becomes for that individual, not abstract doctrines generally conceived, but the specific truth of that individual's personal existence, in all its stubborn particularity."[15] From Tillich's functional theory of religion as ultimate concern about the ultimate, I learned to distinguish between what people might unthinkingly assume their religion to be and what it might turn out, upon analysis, actually to be in their lives. Both thinkers insist on complete honesty in such matters.

What, then, was the truth of my own subjectivity or concrete particularity? What, in fact, functioned in my own life as an ultimate concern, and did anything really function in this way? These questions stuck in my mind and eventually prompted me first to reexamine my own experience and then to reconsider implications of the concept of experience itself.[16]

When I turned to my own experience in my mid-thirties, I discovered two things. First, I realized that the God in whom I had long believed was not for me an experienced reality. The traditional idea of God had now come to seem incurably incoherent, inadequate, and narrow, the vestige of another era that was out of touch with my own day-to-day life and the scientifically informed world in which I lived. Not even the finite God of process theology spoke to me with any genuine religious meaning.[17]

Second, I became aware that my most basic yearning was not to go to heaven and be with God when I died, or even to commune in the present with an absolute, all-sustaining Being. Nor did I seek strength and forgiveness from on high. Instead, I yearned to learn how to be fully and responsibly at home in the natural world of which I now realized myself to be an integral part, and to do so in the limited time allotted to me as an earthly creature that, like all others, comes into being and passes away. I gradually came to understand that this aspiration can be a profoundly religious path in its own right, completely this-worldly though it be, and that it can provide challenges and meanings enough for a lifetime.

These two discoveries about my own personal experience led to reflections on the general character of experience and what can be learned from it. From those reflections I drew three more important conclusions. First, as Stephen David Ross puts it in a recent book, experience is "inexhaustibly open and modifiable,"[18] as are all reasonings based upon it. There are no finalities or unassailable certainties here, whether of reason or revelation, fact or value, but only tentative probabilities. Second, all the entities disclosed by experience are finite and intertwined, and the whole system of such entities appears to be entirely self-sustaining. Experience gives no credible evidence for, and provides formidable evidence against, some ultimate, unlimited source from which everything must derive or on which it must depend.

Third, as I thought about the general character of experience, I found no justification in it for a belief that I had long held but never before subjected to analysis. The belief is that the highest and most valuable kind of reality or state of being is one which is beyond limitation, relationality, or dependence, including subjection to space and time. Once I questioned this assumption, I saw that it betrays a blind unwillingness to give credit to the wonderous world in which we live, the interdependent, ever-changing, multifarious world disclosed to us on every hand by experience. There are plenty of lasting, satisfying, compelling values in this world and no requirement that they be subordinated to putative values of a transfinite realm.

Thus an honest assessment of my own personal experience and of the general concept of experience seemed to leave no room for absolutes of any kind. And despite seductive claims to the contrary through centuries of our religious and philosophical traditions, I concluded that the limitations of finite, earthbound existence do not desperately cry out for resolution and release but can be positively and even enthusiastically affirmed.[19] With these conclusions stemming from the principle of empiricism in mind, we can now turn to the two supporting principles of processism and pluralism. These principles will help to flesh out what has already been said and to show in more detail how and why I have come to affirm the sufficiency of the finite for thought and life.

II.

When I was at Princeton Seminary, I remember seeing the movie *The Bridges at Toko-Ri*. It is about the pilot of a navy fighter-bomber in the Korean War who dreads the assignment, which he knows will soon come, to attack some strategically placed bridges that are heavily fortified with anti-aircraft guns. The assignment finally does come, and in one of the bombing runs his plane is hit. He drops from the sky and is barely able to make an emergency landing in an open field. After fleeing to a ditch, he is quickly surrounded by enemy soldiers. A navy helicopter comes to his aid but is disabled by small arms fire when it lands. In the brief battle that ensues he, the helicopter pilot, and the helicopter crewman are killed.

I was deeply moved by this film, and as I walked home in the night I thought about its symbolism, or at least what it seemed to symbolize to me. The confident vigor of our lives, like the spiraling splendor of the sleek fighter-bomber against the sky, will soon be brought crashing to earth by relentless death. The downed pilot in the field fought with the puny means at his disposal to fend off his death, just as we all do, but none of us can finally succeed. The film brought to mind a verse from the familiar hymn, "Our God, Our Help in Ages Past," which we often sang in the seminary chapel.

Time, like an ever-rolling stream,
Bears all its sons away;
They fly forgotten, as a dream
Dies at the opening day.

These seemed like gloomy words to me, for I was convinced that if there is no hope of life beyond death, then the death of human beings must be regarded as irremediably tragic and evil. I was reassured, however, by the final verse of the hymn and could pray in its words to the God in whom I then fervently believed,

Be Thou our Guard while life shall last,
And our eternal Home.[20]

But what if there is no eternal God and no eternal home? What if the onrush of time eventually sweeps away everything that lies in its way? What if change is the name of the game, and there is no other game around? Are these ideas not reasons for despair? I used to think so, but I no longer do. I no longer do because I came to realize that my unconscious and therefore unanalyzed bias in favor of the eternal, the unchanging, and the static has no basis in experience and little else to commend it. Not only do we never experience the fixed and unchanging, it is doubtful that we would respond positively to it if we did. Our lives thrive on risk and uncertainty. Unending quietude and rest, with nothing challenging or new, would soon grow dull. We are creatures of time, not of eternity. Take us out of the river of time, and we would suffocate like fish out of water. I was later to reflect at some length on this insight in a section of my book *The Specter of the Absurd*.[21]

Part of what helped me to come to terms with the inevitability of temporal change and the necessary endings, including that of death, it brings in its train was my encounter with process philosophy during my doctoral studies. In Whitehead's version of this philosophy, the "category of the ultimate" is the principle that asserts the interdependence of continuity and novelty, order and change, throughout the universe. For him, the category applies even to God—if not to God's abstract "primordial nature" at least to the concrete fullness of God's being. Just as continuity or relative endurance provides the necessary basis for introductions of novelty, so the transformations of novelty will eventually override all existing continuity or order. It is "by reason of transition [the flow of time]," he writes, that "'the actual world' is always a relative term. . . ."[22] Whitehead took this outlook to mean that even the fundamental laws of this present "cosmic epoch" will eventually be eroded away and replaced with other laws by the inexorable workings of novelty.

When I later came to study the works of Henri Bergson, in connection with the course on process metaphysics I regularly taught, I found this same insistence on the pervasive inevitability of process and change. I came to appreciate how much Bergson influenced Whitehead's own thought as well as that of William James. Acknowledgment of his pivotal idea of *durée* is, for Bergson, acceptance "of a reality that creates itself gradually,"[23] of the "duration which gnaws on things, and leaves on them the mark of its tooth."[24] Such acknowledgment means recognizing "[r]eal duration" as "that in which each form flows out of previous forms, while adding to them something new."[25] Nothing stands out more clearly in experience, Bergson teaches, than that the "flux of time is the reality itself . . . "[26] At this point, the principle of empiricism and that of processism come together.

My work in the thought of John Dewey reinforced the principle of processism in my understanding of the world. Dewey flatly announces that "every existence is an event," an event with a beginning and an ending.[27] Dewey goes on to protest "[t]he isolation of structure from the changes whose stable ordering it is," arguing that this renders structure "mysterious . . . a kind of ghostly queerness."[28] For similar reasons, I was to realize, Whitehead, James, and Bergson reject the hoary concept of an unchanging substance with a superficial overlay of accidental changes, first formulated by Aristotle, and all the other heavy prejudice of the Western philosophical tradition that assumes a metaphysical priority of permanence over change.

Since our lives are immersed in time, and time includes novelty as well as continuity, the future is to a significant extent open and unpredictable. This ineluctable openness of the future means that we have no way of knowing whether present beliefs that seem certain and unassailable will seem so in the future. The principle of processism guards in this way against intellectual hubris, the illusion that there are necessary and universal truths that must hold for all time, and that we know or can know what those truths are.

Moreover, our only access to the past is through reports and memory, both of which are selective, leaving out as much if not far more than they include, and both of which have been discovered, in numerous cases, to have been notoriously unreliable. Even the present has its limitations, so far as knowledge goes, for no sooner do I think, "This is the present," than the moment of awareness recedes into the past. But with its built-in limitations of past, present, and future knowledge, life in time also allows room for critical and innovative ways of thinking and believing, so that we are not simply stuck in thought patterns of the past, doomed to prolong them endlessly into the future.

The upshot is that we are bounded by time both epistemologically and metaphysically, epistemologically in the manner just shown, and metaphysically because all the things we cherish, including our own lives and the lives of those we love, must someday come to an end. This brute fact of life has its undeniably tragic side, as when we experience drastic setbacks in our plans, or when our own lives or those of loved ones are taken from us prematurely. But it also has its positive side; it makes way for new projects, new hopes, new achievements—if not by us, then by others who will come after us. Time, with its beginnings and endings, its intrusions of transformative novelty, thus militates against inertia and stagnation, the bland sameness of uninterrupted continuity. It makes possible the evolution of biological species that has led to our presence on earth. The tenacious gnawings of time are evidence of finitude, but it is a finitude in which old things are set aside in order that new things may take their place. When you think about it, this is not an altogether bad tradeoff. Over the years, I have thought often about it and learned to affirm it as generally good. Moreover, I can imagine no meaningful alternative to it for creatures like ourselves whose every passing moment of experience witnesses to the ineradicably temporal character of our lives and of the universe in which we live.

III.

The principle of pluralism, like that of processism, has epistemological and metaphysical aspects, but for purposes of this essay I shall refer to it only with regard to its epistemological aspect. My first confrontation with epistemological pluralism—though I had not yet learned to call it that—was in the thought of Bushnell. Bushnell's pluralism depends, to a significant degree, on his sense of the majesty and mystery of God, and of the elusive intimations of religious experience. This attitude coincided nicely with my own absolutistic assumptions at that time, so I was readily able to affirm Bushnell's pluralism, not realizing that it would soon contribute to an undermining of those same assumptions.

"Christian comprehensiveness" is the name Bushnell gives to his pluralism. I summarized it in my dissertation by saying that it means "a generous comprehension of religious differences, the necessity of taking into account all attempted expressions of Christian truth, and not just those of one's own denomination or religious persuasion. Only in this way . . . could one even begin to apprehend the many-sided truth of the Christian symbolism."[29] Bushnell holds that clarity and consistency in Christian discourse are not so important as adequacy. We should therefore not only tolerate but actively affirm such a plethora of angles of vision on the Christian tradition as to generate ample appreciation for its scope and complexity. We should welcome multiple facetings of Christian truth that need to be held in the mind for the sake of their collective breadth of insight, even though they cannot be reduced to an entirely coherent, logical system. Each doctrine or creed by itself, as well as each particular theologian's way of thinking, viewed apart from their intimate relations to the wealth of often widely varying images, symbols, conceptualizations, and assertions in the Bible and throughout the history of Christian thought, is for Bushnell a "thimble measure of truth,"[30] a tiny sampling of unfathomable depths.

It was not long before I began to realize that his idea of pluralistic inclusiveness could and should be extended beyond the Christian tradition to the other religious traditions I was studying as part of my doctoral work, thus greatly broadening and challenging my conception of religious truth. Convinced "neo-orthodox" thinker that I was, still bearing strongly the imprint of my conservative education at Princeton Seminary, I was being brought subtlety but steadily, partly by Bushnell's tutelage, under the spell of a liberal way of thinking that would characterize my later thought and life. This way of thinking is aptly characterized by Daniel Day Williams as "the position that truth can be attained only through a never-ending process of criticism and experiment. It is the willingness to understand many points of view."[31]

Why should we try to understand many points of view? It is because their very existence calls our own point of view into question, suggesting at least the distinct possibility of its being partial and incomplete, requiring supplementation from other perspectives. Why are there so many different points of view? It is not just because of a perverse unwillingness on the part of others to recognize the obvious truth of our own perspective. Rather it is because the experienced world in all its multiple dimensions—like the complexity of Christian teachings as envisioned by Bushnell—is so inordinately hard to comprehend and that there are so many possible and inherently plausible ways of trying to comprehend it.

Are there not some foundational, timeless, universally applicable truths which we can discover and on whose basis we can adjudicate among these contending points of view? The answer is that no satisfactory set of them has ever been discovered and that, given our in-principle inability to know how things will look in the future (here the principle of processism comes into play), we could have no way to be finally sure about such truths even if we thought we had them in hand. We cannot escape the limitations of our historical situation.

What, then, about divine revelation? Can that not safeguard us against error? The difficulty with this approach, of course, is that there are many putatively definitive revelations in the religions of the world, and these do not agree with one another. Such revelations are both historically and culturally situated. Moreover, a revelation is truly that only if it *reveals*, that is, casts convincing light on the world and the lives of human beings. But that can be determined only by ongoing personal reflection and experience, not by mere appeals to authority. These are conclusions to which I was eventually led. They show the need for a principle of pluralism in epistemology and make painfully evident the finitude of all our claims to knowledge. In matters religious, for example, we cannot help but be heretics with respect to positions that differ fundamentally from ours, just as those positions will seem heretical or wrong-headed from our own point of view. Let me sketch a few of the ways in which these conclusions became increasingly apparent to me.

One of these was in my years of teaching courses in philosophy and religion. In teaching the history of philosophy, for example, or a course on Western religions, it was necessary for me to help students to understand how a philosophical or religious system looks from the inside, from the point of view of those who believe in it and live by it. And this meant showing as clearly and convincingly as possible how their own belief systems might be challenged by these alternative perspectives, and encouraging them to think about how they could respond to those perspectives. Such teaching was thus a kind of exercise in pluralistic epistemology, and I could not help being myself influenced by it.

Moreover, in a course in philosophy of religion, which I set up in the 1960s and 1970s in a deliberately comparative way rather than focusing just on Christianity or Western theism, one of the tasks I undertook was to try to formulate a set of criteria of religious truth. Drawing from such texts as William A. Christian's *Meaning and Truth in Religion* and Ninian Smart's *Reasons and Faiths*,[32] I did compile an extensive list of such criteria. When I invited the students to apply these criteria to the various world religions we had brought under philosophical scrutiny, they made the surprising discovery that each, in its own specific ways, measures up convincingly to the criteria. And this was the case even though the religions were saying very different things about the world. We carefully noted that this discovery did not mean that these religions were necessarily all *equally* true; that would mean another conclusion, one requiring different analysis. But the fact that, by all available criteria, they were all in some sense true, meant that no one religious tradition could simply take for granted the absolute truth of its own claims, especially if those claims included an assertion of its *exclusive* truth. This set the students thinking, and it set me thinking as well.

Some time in the 1970s I did a reading course with several students on the nature of truth. Among other things, we read Roger Trigg's *Reason and Commitment* and Nelson Goodman's *Languages of Art*.[33] Trigg is a staunch defender of traditional realism and of the correspondence theory of truth. Goodman is an equally staunch critic of those same notions, a critic whose powerful arguments cannot be ignored. Goodman and Thomas Kuhn[34] were my introduction to constructionism, with its notion of a possible plurality of plausible, well-reasoned ways of viewing the world (or "ways of worldmaking," as Goodman put it in a later work[35]). For Goodman and Kuhn, it is useless to talk of the world as it "really is" and then to construe our claims as referring to that world. Contrary to Trigg, who contends that "[w]hat reality is like and how we conceive it are always separate questions,"[36] both Goodman and Kuhn see these questions as one and the same.

In other words, the world is as we conceive it; that is the only world we ever have. And since there are different ways of conceiving it, it follows that there are different worlds. The worlds of Aristotelian and Newtonian science, for example, are different from the world of Einsteinian science. And the world of a great painter or poet is not the same world as that of a physicist. Neither Kuhn nor Goodman goes so far as to claim that these different conceptions are completely arbitrary. There are important criteria for distinguishing wildly implausible worldviews from ones that can be rationally defended. But these multiple worlds cannot be reduced, on the basis of such criteria, to a single way the world "really" is, nor can they be graded in terms of their degrees of approximation to such a world.

The insight with which Goodman and Kuhn are operating was brought home to me one evening when I was a participant in a public debate on the existence of God. I had been asked to make a case for atheism, and I did my dead-level best to do so, drawing on the standard arguments and some of my own that I had developed for the students in

Finite is All Right! 373

my class on introduction to philosophy, where we had focused on the existence of God as one of our topics. When I had finished presenting the arguments, a faculty member from the College of Engineering stood up in the back of the room and said, "Young man, God exists as an absolute fact, whether you recognize his existence or not!" To this I replied, "My task here is the only one we could possibly undertake as finite human beings: to ask whether we have *sufficient reason to believe* in the existence of such a God." This response collapses truth into the available means of justification, refusing to see the two as separate issues. And in doing so, it concurs with the reasoning of Kuhn and Goodman.

But are not truth and justification separate? Could something not be true but unjustified, or false but justified, at given times? Is there not a nature of things to which our claims are finally responsible? This question vexed me until I came across Richard Rorty's observation, in *Philosophy and the Mirror of Nature*, that, although truth and justification are distinguished syntactically in our language, this is not a distinction that carries any philosophical weight because there is no meaningful way to explicate the notion of "theory-independent truth."[37] Once we have done everything we can with available evidence and argument, there is nothing left over to worry about. As I noted in *The Specter of the Absurd*, had René Descartes realized this, there would have been no introduction, in his *Meditations on First Philosophy*, of the possibility of an all-deceiving demon. The demon symbolizes the pernicious but highly seductive notion in the history of philosophy of an antecedent, in-itself world to which beliefs, if true, must correspond.[38]

Another phase of my adoption of the principle of pluralism was the influence of my readings of works of James and Dewey. I spoke earlier of two traits of James's radical empiricism that relate to a pluralistic epistemology. The first of these is his allegation that distinctions between subject and object, knower and known, are made wholly within the field of experience, meaning that experience does not *presuppose* a subjective experiencer. Thus James rejects the subjectivist turn of early modern philosophy and avoids problems attendant upon mind-body dualism. Some time after reading and reflecting on the writings of James, I read Dewey's *Experience and Nature*, in which he convincingly argues for this aspect of radical empiricism, with acknowledged indebtedness to James. "Among and within" the occurrences of experience, he writes, "not outside of them or underlying them, are those events which are denominated selves." Dewey also rejects the assumption that "experience by its very nature is owned by some one; and that the ownership is such in kind that everything about experience is affected by a private and exclusive quality."[39] For neither James nor Dewey, then, is there an assumed primacy of solitary self-awareness from which we must precariously infer the existence and character of an external world.

But this trait of radical empiricism also means that the concept of a world existing in-itself, entirely independently of the self's experiences and beliefs, must be called into question. And, of course, James does call it into question, affirming instead another trait of his radical empiricism, namely, that "experience and reality come to the same thing."[40] This statement implies, among other things, that the experienced (or experienceable) world is the only world with which we can or need be concerned. Dewey chimes in with James on this point, arguing that truth as well as value are outcomes of directed inquiries into ongoing experience, not into some kind of single-ordered, wholly determinate world "out there" to which veridical claims must correspond. He thus takes issue as much with a supposed in-itself world existing replete with meanings, although prior to inquiry or interpretation, as with a supposed in-itself self that must struggle somehow, in its ineluctable privacy and from its solitary ruminations, to build bridges to the prior meanings of that world.[41] For both, then, it is the world of experience and of pragmatic interpretations of that experience with which we have solely to deal. There is no inaccessible thing-in-itself for which we must futilely yearn or that can give ammunition to philosophical skepticism. But it is also the case for both that no wedge can be driven between truth and the available means of justification, between the way the world is and outcomes of our directed inquiries into experience.[42]

Do these outcomes always agree? It is well known that they do not. James and Dewey lay strong emphasis on the role of hypothetical conceptualizations of experience in giving meaning to that experience, and on the selectivity, incompleteness, and fallibility—and hence, the predictable variability—of all such presumed meanings. James contrasts the "aboriginal confusion"[43] of relatively uninterpreted experience with our conceptualizations of it. These conceptualizations are like stepping-stones in a turbulent stream, he suggests in one place.[44] With them we can wade through the stream, but only at the price of neglecting much of its overbrimming fullness. Moreover, there are other stepping-stones we could have chosen which might have gotten us through the stream (or other parts of it) in markedly different ways. No escape can be found from such selectivity and plurality of visions. As James says, "[t]here is no possible point of view from which the world can appear as an absolutely single fact."[45]

For his part, Dewey notes that the contexts of meaning from which we must begin our quests for knowledge are not objects in the world "given to us defined, classified, and labeled," but social traditions, practices, and modes of expression.[46] As is well known, such contexts of meaning vary—and often vary widely—with differences of cultures and historical periods. He also notes that all claims to knowledge involve "something selected for a purpose," in some particular context of inquiry or with reference to some particular set of problems. And he warns us of the folly of viewing these selective claims as the whole truth.[47] When something is selected, something else is perforce left out, meaning not only that knowledge is always doomed to be incomplete, but also that ample room is allowed for different selective emphases and for the illuminations they may well provide.

Finally, Dewey reminds us that the general principles, rules, and hypotheses of pragmatic thinking are only instrumental pointers to a primary experience that never stands still but is always relentlessly underway, endlessly churning out events whose evanescent, unrepeatable, spontaneous character makes them resistant to containment within abstract conceptualizations and predictions. Because poets are keenly aware of this limitation of rational thinking and want to bring home to us the concreteness and elusive volatility of lived experience, they are, says Dewey, "the true metaphysicians of nature."[48] But poetry is notably idiosyncratic; no two great poets are alike in their visions of the world, showing, once again, that experience not only admits of but requires for its comprehension a radical pluralism of perspectives. Dewey properly concludes that "there is no rest for the thinker, save in the *process* of thinking."[49] Here the principle of pluralism and the principle of processism join hands.

And here we have dinned into us once more the humbling fact that the finite—relating in this case to the domain of knowledge—is all that we have or can ever expect to have. But we are also made aware of how much refreshment, enrichment, and enlightenment can result from a frank acknowledgment of the finitude of all claims to knowledge, even those that might seem most compelling and convincing to us at a given time, and from a consequent willingness to learn from other points of view.

In the latter part of the 1980s and the early part of the 1990s I was able, by drawing on the work of Stephen David Ross, John B. Cobb, Jr., Fred D'Agostino,[50] and others, to develop an understanding of epistemological pluralism that could be clearly contrasted with epistemological relativism. I was never tempted to relativism but always sought in my adoption of pluralism to argue for what I call "convictional openness." Here many things may go, but not anything goes. And we can be faithful to our own convictions while yet continually allowing them to be challenged and criticized by the convictions of others. I outlined the spirit and approach of such pluralism in a key part of my book *The Specter of the Absurd*, published in 1988, and set forth a model of a pluralistic epistemology as it relates to ethics and politics in a paper presented in Ahmedabad, India, in 1991, at the ninth international social philosophy conference.[51]

IV.

In this autobiographical sketch, I have tried to show how the three principles of empiricism, processism, and pluralism have conspired to convince me that "finite is all right" and to allow me to be comfortable with the idea that there is no absolute Thumbtack in the sky on which everything must depend or to which ultimate appeal must be made. The imagery of the mobile has given way to another, quite different symbolism. This is a wall-hanging from Thailand that my wife and I bought each other for Christmas a few years ago. Unlike the mobile, which directs attention upward to its single point of origin and support, this work directs our gaze earthward to a system of diverse insects, animals, and birds, surrounded by flowering plants and fruitful trees, all intermingled with rivers, lakes, and sky. A panoply of color and delight to the eye, the wall-hanging symbolizes experience of a universe that is sublime in its interwoven, ever-evolving finitude and never ceases to evoke admiration and awe. It is a universe of which we are privileged to be a part.

NOTES

1. I am grateful to Pamela Aydelott for her detailed critical reading of an earlier version of this essay. What is presented here complements an earlier autobiographical sketch, "From God to Nature: A Personal Odyssey," *Religious Humanism*, 25/3 (Summer 1991), pp. 107–116. Each annual meeting of the Highlands Institute for American

Finite is All Right! 377

Religious Thought features as intellectual autobiography by a member of the Institute. The present essay was the autobiography for the meeting in 1995.

2. Friedrich Schleiermacher, *On Religion: Speeches to Its Cultured Despisers*, trans. John Oman (New York, NY: Harper Torchbooks, 1958), p. 39.

3. Paul Tillich, *My Search for Absolutes* (New York, NY: Simon and Schuster, 1969).

4. I might have entitled this intellectual autobiography "My Escape from Absolutes," in deliberate contrast with Tillich's title *My Search for Absolutes*, but "Finite is All Right!" captures better what I regard as the *positive* direction of my thought since my late twenties.

5. See Donald A. Crosby, "Whitehead's God and the Dilemma of Pure Possibility," in *God, Values, and Empiricism: Issues in Philosophical Theology*, ed. Creighton Peden and Larry E. Axel (Macon, GA: Mercer University Press, 1989), pp. 33–41; and "God as Ground of Value: A Neo-Whiteheadian Revision," *American Journal of Theology and Philosophy*, 13/1 (January, 1992), pp. 37–52. I spent a profitable sabbatical year at Yale University in 1971–1972, in which, among other things, I sat in on a graduate course on Whitehead taught by William A. Christian, Sr.

6. Alfred North Whitehead, *Process and Reality: An Essay in Cosmology*, Corrected Edition, ed. David Ray Griffin and Donald W. Sherburne (New York, NY: The Free Press, 1978), p. 5.

7. *Ibid.*, pp. 13, 3.

8. *Ibid.*, pp. 4, 11. For more detail on this aspect of Whitehead's thought, see Donald A. Crosby, "Whitehead on the Metaphysical Employment of Language," *Process Studies*, I/1 (Spring, 1971), pp. 38–54.

9. Horace Bushnell (1802–1876) was a Congregational minister, theologian, and prolific author whose provocative preaching and writing did much to stimulate a new era of liberal thought in Protestant theology in America in the second half of the nineteenth century and on into the early twentieth century. An excellent recent biography is Robert L. Edwards, *Of Singular Genius, of Singular Grace: A Biography of Horace Bushnell* (Cleveland, OH: The Pilgrim Press, 1992).

10. Horace Bushnell, *God in Christ* (New York: Charles Scribner's Sons, 1903), p. 175; *Christ in Theology* (Hartford: Brown and Parsons, 1851), pp. 163–165. See also Donald A. Crosby, *Horace Bushnell's Theory of Language: In the Context of Other Nineteenth-Century Philosophies of Language* (The Hague and Paris: Mouton, 1975), pp. 216–218.

11. I came to Colorado State University in 1965, after teaching for three years at Centre College, in Danville, Kentucky. At Centre, I was the sole philosopher as well as a teacher in religious studies and was assigned eight different courses (and new preparations, since I had never taught before) in my first two years. I think I learned as much from that demanding and invigorating experience as I did from my doctoral studies. But of course the doctoral studies made the diverse teaching possible.

12. Two other examples are especially worth citing. My book, *Interpretive Theories of Religion* (The Hague: Mouton, 1981), grew out of my teaching an upper-level class in philosophy of religion, where we puzzled about the nature of religion. And my *The Specter of the Absurd: Sources and Criticisms of Modern Nihilism* (Albany, NY: State University of New York Press, 1988) was stimulated by teaching a course on "Nihilism and the Modern Age." I taught both of these courses for several years prior to writing the books.

13. These two traits are that relations are as real in experience as things related, and that these experienced relations include both internal and external, or conjunctive and disjunctive, relations. The first trait guards against the strong nominalistic tendencies of British Empiricism, and the second allows for an irreducible multiplicity of specific entities and occurrences which also exhibit complex patterns of interrelatedness. For a description of all six traits of radical empiricism in James's thought, see Donald A. Crosby and Wayne Viney, "Toward a Psychology That Is Radically Empirical: Recapturing the Vision of William James," in *Reinterpreting the Legacy of William James*, ed. Margaret E. Donnelly (Washington, D.C.: American Psychological Association, 1992), pp. 101–117; see also my "Experience as Reality: The Ecological Metaphysics of William James," in *Religious Experience and Ecological Responsibility*, ed. Donald A. Crosby and Charley D. Hardwick (New York, NY: Peter Lang, 1996, pp. 67–87).

14. Donald A. Crosby, *Interpretive Theories of Religion* (The Hague: Mouton, 1981). I also used some of Tillich's books at various times in my course on nihilism.

15. Crosby, *The Specter of the Absurd,* p. 415, n.12. Kierkegaard talks about truth as subjectivity in his *Concluding Unscientific Postscript;* see *Kierkegaard's Concluding*

Unscientific Postscript, ed. and trans. David S. Swenson and Walter Lowrie (Princeton, NJ: Princeton University Press, 1944), esp. pt. II, ch. 2

16. This kind of self-reflection was also greatly stimulated for me by Whitehead's *Religion in the Making* (New York, NY: The Macmillan Company, 1925), where Whitehead stresses the importance of personal reflection on the meaning of one's life and contrasts a relatively taken-for-granted "communal" type of religious outlook with one that continues to be critically analyzed on the basis of each particular individual's ongoing thought and experience. See my "Religion and Solitariness," in *Explorations in Whitehead's Philosophy*, ed. Lewis S. Ford and George L. Kline (New York, NY: Fordham University Press, 1983), pp. 149–169.

17. This was my *experiential* reaction to process theology, despite the fact that I came to admire it *intellectually* for avoiding the traditional problem of evil by refusing to attribute omnipotence to God and for allowing God to be immanent in the world rather than, as in classical theism, radically transcending the world and having no need of it, but inexplicably interacting with it. For more detail on the process of, and reasons for, my abandoning belief in God, see my "From God to Nature: A Personal Odyssey."

18. Stephen David Ross, *The Limits of Language* (New York, NY: Fordham University Press, 1994), p. 84.

19. Unwillingness or inability to affirm these limitations, together with the realization that there is no plausible way to transcend them, helps to explain the nihilistic mood that has swept through Western culture since at least the second half of the nineteenth century. This nihilism can be concisely defined as "despair of the finite."

20. "Our God, Our Help in Ages Past," by Isaac Watts (1719), based on Psalm 90. This is Hymn 111 in *The Hymnbook*, published by several Presbyterian denominations and the Reformed Church in America (Richmond, VA: John Ribble, 1955), p. 105.

21. See Crosby, *The Specter of the Absurd*, ch. 6, sec. 3.

22. Whitehead, *Process and Reality*, p. 211.

23. Henri Bergson, *Creative Evolution*, trans. Arthur Mitchell (London, U.K.: Macmillan and Company, 1919), p. 374.

24. *Ibid.*, p. 48.

25. *Ibid.*, pp. 382–383.

27. John Dewey, *Experience and Nature*, 2nd ed. (New York, NY: Dover Publications, 1958), p. 71.

28. *Ibid.*, p. 72.

29. Crosby, *Horace Bushnell's Theory of Language*, p. 286.

30. Bushnell, *Christ in Theology*, pp. 54–55. For discussions of Bushnell's idea of Christian comprehensiveness and its relations to his language theory, see Crosby, *Horace Bushnell's Theory of Language*, pp. 32–37, 265–267. See also *Horace Bushnell*, ed. H. Shelton Smith (New York: Oxford University Press, 1965), pp. 106–108. Bushnell presents the basic principles of the idea in his essay "Christian Comprehensiveness," published in *New Englander*, VI (1848). An excerpt of the essay is contained in the Smith volume, pp. 108–126.

31. Daniel Day Williams, *The Andover Liberals*, (New York: Kings Crown Press, 1941), p. 64. I quoted this statement on the last page of my doctoral dissertation and then later in the book based on it, because it captures so well the liberal spirit that Bushnell brought to his times, a spirit much at odds with the narrow authoritarian outlook of most of his theological peers. See my *Horace Bushnell's Theory of Language*, p. 286.

32. William A. Christian, Sr., *Meaning and Truth in Religion* (Princeton, NJ: Princeton University Press, 1964); Ninian Smart, *Reasons and Faiths: An Investigation of Religious Discourse, Christian and Non-Christian* (London: Routledge and Kegan Paul, 1958).

33. Roger Trigg, *Reason and Commitment* (Cambridge: Cambridge University Press, 1973); Nelson Goodman, *Languages of Art: An Approach to a Theory of Symbols* (Indianapolis, IN: Bobbs-Merrill Company, 1968).

34. Thomas S. Kuhn, *The Structure of Scientific Revolutions*, 2nd ed., enlarged (Chicago, IL: University of Chicago Press, 1970).

35. Nelson Goodman, *Ways of Worldmaking* (Indianapolis, IN: Hackett Publishing Company, 1988). First published in 1978.

36. Trigg, *Reason and Commitment*, p. 168.

37. Richard Rorty, *Philosophy and the Mirror of Nature* (Princeton, NJ: Princeton University Press, 1980), pp. 280–281.

38. See Crosby, *The Specter of the Absurd*, pp. 183–185. Here I make use of O.K. Bouwsma's intriguing essay "Descartes' Evil Genius," in Alexander Sesonske and Noel Fleming, eds., *Meta-Meditations: Studies in Descartes* (Belmont, CA: Wadsworth Publishing Company, 1966), pp. 26–36. Bouwsma's essay was first published in 1949.

39. Dewey, *Experience and Nature*, pp. 232, 231. See also pp. 231–235, 8–12. The reference to James is on page 8.

40. William James, *Essays in Radical Empiricism* and *A Pluralistic Universe*, 2 vols. in 1 (New York: Peter Smith, 1967), I, p. 59. I explain and defend this statement in "Experience as Reality: The Ecological Metaphysics of William James."

41. Dewey, *Experience and Nature*, pp. 9–10, 29.

42. Against Jeffrey Stout, who argues for the critical importance, especially in the domain of moral discourse, of drawing a sharp distinction between truth and justification, I defend James's conflation of the two in "Was William James a Closet Nihilist?" *Ultimate Reality and Meaning*, 16/1–2 (March, June 1993), pp. 141–148.

43. James, *Essays in Radical Empiricism* and *A Pluralistic Universe*, II, p. 232.

44. See *Ibid.*, p. 272, for a suggestion of this imagery of the stepping-stones and the stream. Conceptual or discursive forms enable us "to jump over life instead of wading through it," James says, in talking about Henri Bergson's point that concepts, though useful for practical life, frequently have the effect of distracting attention from fundamental aspects of experience.

45. William James, *The Will to Believe* (Cambridge, MA: Harvard University Press, 1979), p. 6.

46. Dewey, *Experience and Nature*, pp. 219, 169–173.

47. *Ibid.*, p. 30.

48. *Ibid.*, pp. 116–117.

49. *Ibid.*, p. 118.

50. The book of Stephen David Ross that influenced my understanding of pluralism is his *Perspective in Whitehead's Metaphysics* (Albany, NY: State University of New York Press, 1983). Two books of John B. Cobb, Jr. were also influential in this regard: *Christ in a Pluralistic Age* (Philadelphia, PA: The Westminster Press, 1975) and *Beyond Dialogue: Toward a Mutual Transformation of Christianity and Buddhism* (Philadelphia, PA: Fortress Press, 1982). My thinking was also clarified by Fred D'Agostino, "Ethical Pluralism and the Role of Opposition in Democratic Politics," *Monist*, 73/3 (July 1990), pp. 437–457.

51. Donald A. Crosby, "Civilization and Its Dissents: Moral Pluralism and Political Order," *Journal of Social Philosophy*, 23/2 (Fall 1992), pp. 111–126. A slightly condensed version of this essay is contained in *Freedom, Dharma, and Rights*, ed. Creighton Peden and Yeager Hudson (Lewiston, NY: The Edwin Mellen Press, 1993), pp. 101–115.

THE PLACE OF THE "SACRED":
A Critical Response To Edward Farley's
Good And Evil

Charley D. Hardwick

In this paper I want to respond critically to Edward Farley's *Good and Evil*.[1] Subtitled "Interpreting a Human Condition," this work draws on the Biblical heritage to articulate an understanding of human evil and good. This richly textured theological anthropology[2] is as fine a work in philosophical theology as has been produced by an American in recent decades. Already notable for such names as Brunner, Tillich, Bultmann, Niebuhr, Ricoeur, Pannenberg, and others, theological anthropology is probably the field distinguished by the most significant achievements of twentieth century theology. This work by Farley certainly deserves standing in this company. My purpose, however, is not simply to describe Farley's work but to use it as the background for my own theological response; therefore, I preface my analysis of Farley with some introductory comments about my own views.

I.

The Context for Engaging Farley's *Good and Evil*. My encounter with Farley arises from my constructive theological work in *Events of Grace*.[3] In this book I defend a naturalist version of Christian theology. Its background is set by my reading of the two-hundred-year history of liberal theology. Far more deeply than any other religious tradition, liberal theology has articulated what I take to be the central religious and theological issue of our time: how are we to understand ourselves religiously and theologically in light of the modern world-view of the natural sciences? So understood, liberal theology is far from finished, for all of the traditions from which we take our beginnings religiously are premodern. They are deeply mythological, even archaic, or they are articulated philosophically in terms that are today highly problematic. These issues are so deep that our problems are often simply to know how to frame the right questions. The heritage of liberal theology is, therefore, broadly revisionary, imposing a revision not merely of this or that doctrine but of the very meaning of religion itself as it is available to fully modern sensibilities.

Events of Grace argues that this revisionary mandate requires a theological appropriation of naturalism, that the world-view imposed by the natural sciences requires commitment to the truth of philosophical naturalism. The twentieth century has, of course, seen numerous religious naturalists, in particular among thinkers from the Chicago school. In my opinion, however, most of them are only half-hearted naturalists, nostalgically retaining archaic and mythological elements from the religious traditions while ostensibly re-clothing them in naturalistic garb.

To state the demands of a more austere naturalism straightforwardly, I argue that naturalism requires surrender of three basic religious tenets that still appear not only among classical and revisionary theists but among many of these half-hearted naturalists themselves. These tenets are: (1) any version of a personal God, (2) any version of cosmic or ontologically intrinsic teleology (or final causality), and (3) any conservation of value, except over brief cosmic epochs.[4] The exclusion of these tenets works its force negatively by disallowing any theological position that depends on or implies any of them.[5] An ostensibly religious naturalism that fails to meet these negative criteria has, in effect, blinked before the austere demands of the world-view of natural science and cannot really claim to be naturalist at all. The chief culprit among these three tenets is not the one about a personal God but the one about teleology. Many so-called theological naturalists, for instance, adopt William James or process categories because these positions permit them to maintain a cosmic teleology, without which they believe—in my mind erroneously and nostalgically—that the metaphysical outlook would be so bleak as not to support any religious self-understanding at all.

I realize that the position I am defending is enormously complex and is open to considerable dispute. I use it here not to settle these issues but to frame the challenge. The challenge posed by the liberal agenda is properly foundational and deeply revisionary: how are to we rethink the nature of religion and the resources of our religious traditions in the light of the challenge of modernity? Addressing it naturalistically already places severe constraints around any possible answer, and this is even more the case with a truly austere naturalism that must operate with the exclusions mentioned above.

In *Events of Grace*, I address this revisionary challenge by defending three methodological conditions for a naturalist theology.

Farley's work becomes interesting from the viewpoint of these conditions. The first condition involves radicalizing Bultmann's demythologizing proposal. The positive side of his proposal demands that all religious and theological terms be interpreted existentially. I argue that we must take this proposal with complete seriousness. The mythological, cosmic, and metaphysical contents of traditional religion which conflict so profoundly with the terms of modern affirmation can be overcome if we can understand their meaning entirely in terms of modes of human existing. This "reductionist" program requires a second, even more controversial condition: the ultimacy terms which religion always involves must be reconceived valuationally rather than ontologically. Theologians and philosophers too readily assume, I argue, that the meaning of religious terms are locked down finally by reference to the ontological conditions of things entire (being-itself, the ground of all being, God as ground and source of being and order, etc.). It is, of course, precisely those ontological conditions that naturalism challenges. If the ultimate ontological conditions of things entire are as naturalists conceive,[6] then the solace traditional religionists have sought in ultimate metaphysical conditions is deeply undermined. But if religion can be rethought entirely in valuational terms, then religious meaning can be detached from cosmic or metaphysical conditions. I argue that an exhaustively existentialist conception of religious meaning entails precisely such a valuational conception of religion.

A truly naturalist *theology* requires a third condition. We must be able to show that there is a situation of human distortion, evil, or sin that legitimates Christianity's claims about redemption. It must be possible, that is, to give a *phenomenologically transparent* account of the human condition that warrants the notion of sin (and thereby warrants a notion of liberation, deliverance, or redemption). By "phenomenologically transparent," I mean that a naturalist theology must give an account of the human condition that does not beg the question by depending on hermeneutically opaque theological terms. Drawing on standard contemporary interpretations of sin from Bultmann, Reinhold Niebuhr, and Tillich, I show that such accounts are phenomenologically transparent in the requisite sense. I then argue that an account of "grace" can be given on naturalist terms, and this makes possible a naturalistic account of redemption. The naturalist theology that I defend thus requires a radically anthropological starting point.

This anthropological starting point of *Events of Grace* is what makes an engagement with Farley so enticing. *Good and Evil* does in effect develop a phenomenologically transparent account of the human condition by showing how the Judaeo-Christian paradigm interprets the human condition of bondage and liberation.[7] Furthermore, as with *Events of Grace*, Farley makes this conception of sin turn on a notion of *idolatry* that he interprets in a fashion that is itself phenomenologically transparent. Formally and phenomenologically, therefore, there is a striking parallel between Farley's *Good and Evil* and *Events of Grace*. Furthermore, Farley is aware of the critical problems in identifying and appropriating the Biblical paradigm in a modern intellectual setting. Though he does not use the terminology, in effect he articulates a demythologized version of the Biblical paradigm.[8] Farley is thus formally close to *Events of Grace* in both his phenomenologically neutral account of sin and his theological paradigm. Because of these parallels, the points where he departs from naturalism are especially noteworthy. These are not merely points at which he and I disagree but exactly the points where the revisionary problems about the nature of religion I mentioned above are raised systematically. For both of us, the issue is how, starting from phenomenologically transparent accounts of the human condition, we locate the "place" of the sacred in human experience.

II.

Farley's Account of the Human Condition. Farley terms his account of the human condition a reflective ontology. In this respect, it parallels the anthropological starting point of *Events of Grace*, though in contrast to my use of Heidegger, he draws more widely from the entire phenomenological literature. Both approaches are ontological because they attempt to identify the structural (rather than contingent) features definitive of human reality.[9] "Being" here does not, however, identify "a static or timeless essence [of something] . . . but its characteristic powers or ways of existing in the typical and extended situation of that thing" (p. xix). It is a *reflective* ontology because this "being" is not immediately or experimentally apparent but becomes evident only in "ways of thinking that embody modes of experience and practical interests" (p. xix).

Taking it ontologically in this sense, Farley divides human reality into three spheres: the interhuman, the social, and the agential (the sphere of agency), though he emphasizes that they can be separated only conceptually and are in fact interrelational and co-dependent.[10] The significance of this division should already be apparent. Most philosophical anthropologies are dualistic, dividing the human between the individual (i.e., the agential) and the social. Not only does Farley insist upon a third sphere, the interhuman or the sphere of face-to-face relations, but he gives this sphere a certain primacy (cf. p. 46). This third sphere has received far less intense philosophical scrutiny (and has even tended to be overlooked entirely) because its independent reality is hard to identify; it has therefore been easy simply to generate "being-together in relation" (p. 33) out of the other spheres or to reduce it to them.

Ultimately, however, the agential sphere is more important for the development of Farley's argument. This sphere, which Farley terms "personal being" (and which is ordinarily presented simply as the individual in opposition to the social), has a more complex and more fully elaborated structure than the other two. Its immediate character is that of self-transcending personal agency, which Farley elaborates with a splendid discussion of human temporality derived from Husserl's phenomenology of internal time consciousness. Here Farley nicely develops the now classical phenomenological argument for how "meaning" in its distinctively human sense arises through the temporal structure of personal being. Human existence, that is, is defined ontologically not by timeless essences but by powers of agential action that are constantly realized through meanings; the very *being* of human being is constituted by meanings that arise out of a temporal structure. In this existential/phenomenological sense, agential personal being is defined by historicity.

But Farley also wants to emphasize that personal historical being is both embodied and impassioned (or passional). So, in addition to delineating the agential's specific self-transcending structure, he expands this sphere with discussions of its biological (or embodied) character and of agency's impassioned (or "interested") background. This element of the passions in the embodied character of personal agency becomes the guiding feature in the structure of good and evil, not just in reference to personal being but in relation to the other two spheres as well. Farley thus defines human nature as *impassioned existential freedom*, in effect challenging the role of reason in classical discussions of human nature. He appropriates a central strand in modern thought that has reversed the classical hegemony of reason over desire and replaced it with claims that reason's function arises from and serves desire, interest or passion (p. 97 f.).

The passions are not, however, simply "miscellaneous aggregates of interests" (p. 99). They are structured by comprehensive passions that orient more specific desires organized under them. Farley defines three such *elemental passions*: (1) the passion for subjectivity oriented to personal being as "the passion of the agent for its survival and the well-being of its own agency" (p. 99); (2) the passion for the interhuman by which personal being, however individualized, is nevertheless "structured by a passion for interhuman confirmation and fulfillment" (p. 99); and (3) the passion for reality that arises from our vulnerabilities which require that we negotiate with a world independent of us.

This brief, schematic view of Farley's description of human reality shows how complex his anthropology becomes. There are three spheres of human reality, and the third (personal being) has three dimensions (personal being itself as self-transcending historicity, its biological embodiment, and the passions that guide it). Furthermore, the elemental passions are themselves threefold. Since, as we shall see, these passions are basic to the origin of evil, each of them becomes a source of corruption and therefore requires its own separate delineation. Human ontology thus has seven points through which the human condition can be corrupted and distorted: the three spheres (the interhuman, the social, and personal being), the biological dimension of personal being, and the three elemental passions. Each of these, in turn, is correlated with its own structure of redemption. Because each of these points has its own phenomenological integrity (that is also intertwined with the others), the fullness of the human condition becomes extremely complex.

Farley's description of the human condition is so rich that I cannot possibly reconstruct his entire account of sin and redemption here. Instead I want to concentrate on the theological categories by which he interprets sin and redemption. Since we both start from a phenomenologically transparent account of the human condition, what will be significant for each of us will be (1) how we introduce (or find) religious content in the phenomenology and (2) what categories we use to construe this phenomenology theologically.

III.

Evil and Good in Farley's Account. Farley identifies evil and good in the human condition through categories correlated with the three spheres of human reality. In relation to personal being, evil and good are named, respectively, as "idolatry" and "being-founded" (to be explained below), in relation to the interhuman evil and good are "alienation" and "communion," and in relation to the social they are "subjugation" and "theonomous sociality." Although "idolatry" is the name for evil only in one sphere, the elemental passions are so central to the *origin* of evil that "idolatry" attains a certain primacy in the origin of all forms of human evil, if not necessarily in the specific role evil plays in each sphere.[11] We must pay special attention, therefore, to the relationship between the elemental passions and the origins of evil.

The notion of tragedy is crucial for Farley's conception of the human condition. Each sphere is exposed to specific vulnerabilities. Personal being, for instance, is subject to the contingencies of life that make us anxious about the preservation of our subjectivity. The interhuman is vulnerable to loss and also to what Farley terms "benign alienations" that arise from the irreducible otherness of autonomous beings in face-to-face relations (p. 44 f.). Quoting Farley, we can conclude that the

> most general feature of [the] human condition is its tragic character. The term *tragic* refers to a situation in which the conditions of well-being require and are interdependent with situations of limitation, frustration, challenge, and suffering. Human condition is not tragic simply because suffering is an aspect of it but because sufferings of various sorts are necessary conditions of creativity, affection, the experience of beauty, etc (p. 29).[12]

At the same time, the tragic is not evil (or does not constitute the nature of evil) just because it is tragic. For Farley, one of the most significant advances in the history of religions was the separation by the Biblical faiths of evil and its origins from the tragic (p. 125 f).[13] This separation gives force to the notion of sin. It also permits sin to be understood as a corruption of a basic human reality, thereby authorizing notions of bondage to a condition that is a basic distortion of fundamental potentials (p. 124). Farley emphasizes that this separation also permits conceptions of redemption that are not merely returns to an earlier ideal state but achievements of fundamentally new human possibilities.

The elemental passions have an inherently tragic structure.[14] Unlike specific desires, the elemental passions are open-ended and never permit complete satisfaction. Though specific interests can achieve satisfaction, these are never entirely sufficient given the structure of the elemental passions. We seek not merely affection and recognition from face-to-face relations, but unconditional acceptance without the potential for loss. We seek not merely security but an "invulnerable subjectivity" (p. 110) and a significance for our own agency beyond any threat of annihilation. There is always a gap between the unconditional referent of the elemental passions and their momentary satisfactions. These passions have a horizon, therefore, that always reaches beyond any specific entities that provide their momentary satisfactions (p. 112).

I shall bypass Farley's rich, highly nuanced account of how idolatry arises from this tragic structure of the elemental passions (pp. 130–135), but the basic idea is as follows. Idolatry originates from existential postures that attempt to suppress our vulnerability and transform its inescapability into something accidental or contingent. Idolatry seeks to collapse the indeterminate horizon of the elemental passions into mundane goods that are treated as ultimate "securerers." To quote Farley,

> . . . we move to free ourselves from intolerable discontent. We insist on a secured subjectivity, a finally satisfying face, a final enrichment of knowledge and experience. Guided by the conviction that because tragic finitude as contingent can be defeated, we move to defeat it. . . . Driven by this insistence, we . . . move through our times and places alert to anything that might fill our existentially hungry maws. What is it that solves the problem? A hunger that must be fed is never choosy. It settles for anything whatever, and this means what it can in fact find and what holds some promise of solving its problem (p. 133).

Of course, more comprehensive ends appear less vulnerable and promise more, so, though anything can and has served to fill the gap between desire and fulfillment, the perennial candidates are "religions, sciences, nations, social movements, comprehensive interpretive schemes, . . . value-preserving institutions, and even revolutions" (p. 133).

Idolatry changes the relationship both to mundane goods and to the horizon of the elemental passions. Mundane goods must serve roles that take them beyond their capacity to satisfy straightforwardly, and, though the collapse of the horizon does not eliminate the structure of the elemental passions, it does establish a new set of expectations and fears (p. 134 f.). From these "the specific acts and postures of evil are born" (135). The outcome is a corruption of the structure of personal being that Farley terms a "diminishment of agential freedom" (p. 135), where by "freedom" he means not merely the capacity to choose but "the power by which agents are able to actualize themselves toward their well-being." Freedom is "that about the agent that shapes desire and sets its direction" (p. 136). Idolatry distorts and reduces these powers by narrowing the ways we engage the world, experience meanings, and enter face to face relations (p. 136 f.).

Taking freedom as the condition of well-being, the Biblical paradigm views this condition as deeply corrupted by the dynamics of idolatry. Redemption will refer, then, to the way these dynamics are broken. The Biblical paradigm was articulated with judicial and monarchical metaphors of guilt and acquittal. Farley powerfully analyzes the problems associated with these metaphors and argues that the paradigm can be stated independently of them. This critique is one element in what I call the "phenomenological transparency" of his account.

For these reasons, Farley replaces the classical notion of "justification" with the notion of *being-founded* (p. 144). The elemental passions are a striving *through* mundane goods toward a horizon that will fulfill them. Idolatry and evil originate out of the desperate discontent that collapses this horizon into goods at hand; idolatry, in other words, seeks *founding* through goods at hand. Evil arises out of a kind of weakness which amounts to an incapacity to tolerate unsecured existence (p. 144). The alternative to idolatry, therefore—the very meaning of redemption or salvation—will be a founding at the very limits of the elemental passions, at their horizon. Keeping the horizon open, it will "secure" in a fashion that holds open precisely our finitude, our unsecured existence. The horizon does not itself found, however, since it refers simply to the structure of the elemental passions. What founds is "something" met *at the horizon* (since the horizon is not collapsed) in "the form of an actual presence" (p. 144). This presence Farley terms the sacred.

It is important to recognize that "being-founded" and "the sacred as an actual presence" occur in existence or in lived experience. These terms do not refer to metaphysical theories about God, a World Ground, or an Absolute, though such theories may interpret them. Being-founded as an actual presence nicely captures the notion of "event" which is the conceptual heart of *Events of Grace*, and Farley's account has the virtue, to this point at least, of remaining phenomenologically neutral about the conceptual content of *what* presences. Because being-founded occurs at the level of existence, its reality cannot be demonstrated but only testified to by communities that have experienced "the breaking of the stranglehold of idolatry" (p. 144). As Farley notes,

> In the old texts of Hebrew religion, being-founded occurs in connection with political conflicts, formal symbolic traditions, and radical critical interpretations. What we cannot do is discover in these texts pristine incidents of being-founded in individuals that are so

compellingly real and public that they mediate our own founding. *Human agents experience being-founded in conjunction with community-mediated exposures of the dynamics of idolatry.* Being-founded is, thus, not a discrete apprehension that chases away a worried and insecure world-view but a participation in a historical milieu that existentially mediates the . . . horizon as a sacred presence (p. 145, my italics).

Farley articulates the content of being-founded through the notion of courage in what I consider the most powerful rethinking of "redemption" or "salvation" in contemporary theology. The very nature of being-founded, given the "horizonal" structure of the elemental passions, must leave the passions open and not displace finite vulnerability. It must be "a way of existing as fragile and vulnerable amidst the sufferings and tragic incompatibilities of the world" (p. 146). It is appropriately termed courage because it continues to resist finite limit and vulnerability with an underlying openness to and acceptance of them.[15] Being-founded makes possible an open, courageous, and joyous affirmation of being in the midst of finite vulnerabilities that are not denied.

The existential posture of courage has three elements: relativizing, consent, and risk of being (pp. 146–150). Sacred presencing *relativizes* goods at hand by removing their superordinate valuation (that is, by resisting the collapse of the horizon of the elemental passions), thereby permitting them to be experienced simply as the goods they are. This relativizing makes possible a *consent to being* that Farley argues is the equivalent of the classical notion of the goodness of creation.[16] In contrast to postures of resignation, it is an openness to the "total complex of reality" (p. 149) as sufficient for affirmative well-being, despite continuing limitation, incompatibility, and vulnerability. Finally, *risk of being* refers to how being-founded carries one beyond the fearful, self-protective postures that define normality (even its non-idolatrous form) and opens to a venturing exposure to the world. Being-founded, like all the forms of redemption, thus does not restore the structures to an original form but makes possible richer, more creative existential modes. With each form of redemption, Farley tries to show how natural, self-protective egocentricity is transcended—not by self-denial but by finding one's fullness of being in a self-forgetfulness that amounts to a kind of natural grace. With "risk of being," our normal reluctance to risk ourselves in the perilous situations of being is displaced by a kind of openness: "Once the self is founded by the presence of the sacred, it is not turned away from the world (and in refusal) but turned toward the world as a venturing of

The Place of the "Sacred"   393

the self amidst the perils of the world.... [W]hile this may include situations and acts of physical courage, the attitude of risk of being applies to any and all the ways the self exists in the world" (p. 150).

IV.
The Place of the Sacred in Farley's Account. We now have enough of Farley's argument to turn to a critical response. Structurally idolatry and being-founded are associated only with the sphere of personal being. Farley therefore develops the notions about sin and redemption first in relation to the specific form of personal being (corrupted historicity) (pp. 154–170), then in relation to the three elemental passions associated with personal being (pp. 171–210), and finally with the biological dimension of personal being as embodied existence (pp. 211–230). He goes on to develop specific conceptions of sin and redemption in relation to the other two spheres, the interhuman (pp. 231–250) and the social (pp. 251–280). I have indicated, however, that given the centrality of the passions in his conception of human reality, idolatry and being-founded play a more central role than a linear description of his organization suggests.

Earlier I emphasized the phenomenological transparency of Farley's descriptive categories, a quality of Farley's work that is important for my anthropological starting point. To repeat, by phenomenological transparency I mean an account of a corrupted human condition and of the possibility of its redemption that does not rely descriptively on any phenomenologically opaque theological terms. This is necessary for my position because anti-naturalist theological terms that are introduced into the phenomenology from the outset will defeat the possibility of a naturalist rendering. For numerous reasons, I believe a naturalist theology should be attractive to many Christians and is certainly a theological option that needs renewed attention today. Its possibility, however, requires that a large part of the Christian or Biblical paradigm be patient to a naturalist rendering, hence the phenomenologically neutral starting point on which I insist. Farley is no naturalist, but I have presented enough of his position to show how much of his interpretation of the human condition is phenomenologically neutral in the requisite sense. This conclusion is supported by Farley's own reflectively critical attempt to render the Christian paradigm in a fully modern form.

I have intentionally described the origins of sin and being-founded to highlight the phenomenological neutrality of Farley's position. In doing this I have, however, neglected certain categories that drive his phenomenology. A crucial issue for my approach to theology will be how the theologically relevant categories arise in the phenomenology. It will now become evident, I believe, that the real issue here is not one of description but of naming. There is very little to question in Farley's wonderfully rich and nuanced description. But there is an issue in precisely what he names at the crucial junctures in his phenomenology. It is precisely at these joints that Farley's phenomenology needs to be challenged.

I shall do this by questioning a series of names or identifiers Farley uses. These are: eternal horizon, chaos, sacred presence as grounded in the totality of things, creativity as an aesthetic category, and the personal character of founding presence. What is striking in all these cases is how clichéd his adoption of these categories is and how grating they seem as identifiers for what appears phenomenologically. At just these points I believe Farley fails to be phenomenologically innocent enough; he fails, that is, just to look and instead uncritically adopts too much from the paradigm he is trying to rethink. The "names" I have mentioned, however, are not innocent at all but at each point drive his analysis through crucial conceptual transitions. My purpose in challenging these names is not at this point to replace them naturalistically but simply to suggest that the phenomenology itself can be left open for another, perhaps naturalist, naming of the place of the sacred.

I have described the elemental passions, idolatry, and being-founded so as to highlight their phenomenological neutrality. My account varies slightly, however, from Farley's. His approach to the elemental passions initially supports phenomenological neutrality: "Because the passions desire through the relative realizations at hand in the world" their referent "is not an entity in the world system but the horizon of entities and resources . . . As such this referent cannot coincide with any finite entity of the world system or the world system as a whole" (p. 112). This seems exactly right. But how should we now describe this horizon? Note the abrupt and undefended move that Farley makes at this point: "Because no finite resource fulfills the passions, their referent is an infinite resource, an *eternal* horizon" (p. 112). Farley continues throughout to use the term, "eternal horizon," to name this structure. This is an entirely unwarranted identification. In whatever fashion we do name this horizon, phenomenologically the last thing it is is "eternal." In terms of its immediate character in lived experience it is neither outside of time nor everlasting, for nothing of this sort *can* appear in the phenomenology of finite experience. Phenomenologically, the most to which we are entitled would seem to be some such label as "infinite" or "unconditioned" or simply "indeterminate." And even then, such labels can serve only as markers for the inherently unsatisfied passions, not to name any specific content of the horizon. But "eternity" has no appropriateness to the experience at all. Farley himself acknowledges that God cannot be the specific referent at the "eternal horizon" of the elemental passions because this horizon is indeterminate (p. 112). At the same time, the structure of the passions is not unrelated to God, for "the eternal horizon of the passions is not simply a nothingness but is whatever would fulfill the passions" (p. 113). At this point in a phenomenology, however, this use of "God" is purely formal and leaves entirely open *what* it is that would found an existing defined by elemental passions. Of course, once founding, or "God," or the "sacred" is on the scene, then one might, retrospectively, present arguments that any candidate for founding *must be an eternal being*. But *that* claim requires independent arguments and cannot be read into the phenomenology from the outset without begging the question. One can only conclude, therefore, that Farley is in fact reading something into the phenomenology that is phenomenologically unwarranted and is basically an uncritical assumption about the content of the Biblical paradigm.

Another phenomenologically questionable identifier is what Farley calls "chaos." He uses this term to name the referent for what, existentially, we fear. Thus, for instance, he says:

> Informed by [our] yearnings and their discontents, our self-awareness is constituted by the question of the world but it receives no answer.... This is not to say that there is no meaning in the totality of things. It only says that such meaning is not itself contained in the act of existing. Thus, hiding at the heart of things appears to be chaos. And this is the one situation we human beings seem incapable of accepting. Because of the intensity of the passions and their discontents, we find this situation intolerable (p. 133 f.).

Again, Farley's phenomenology seems exactly right, but I question whether what we encounter here at the limits of our yearning and discontent is properly identified *in lived experience* (or existentially) as chaos.[17] The opposite of "chaos" is "order," and it is not "order" for which we yearn existentially but "founding."[18] This notion does not beg theological questions as does "eternal horizon," but it is phenomenologically opaque and, I believe, inappropriate.[19] I call attention to it because Farley uses it so frequently to move his analysis forward.

The point to note is how phenomenologically careful one must be at just these points.

Another theologically innocent example is Farley's appeal to aesthetic categories to articulate both the courage that arises from being-founded and the redemption of the interhuman sphere. As with any modern theology, Farley recognizes the necessity to develop alternative root metaphors to the monarchical one that dominates the Biblical narratives. Identifying *creativity* with either the creation of or the response to beauty, he suggests "an aesthetic or creativity metaphor" (p. 143). He then argues that redeemed historicity which the courage of being-founded makes possible is fundamentally an aesthetic openness to being in its particularities. He also argues that the redemptions both of the passions for the interhuman and of the violations of that sphere arise from the "beauty" of the other's face.

This issue is very tricky. The problem, in my opinion, is that there is a kind of phenomenological "clang" in using aesthetic metaphors to name the existential postures which Farley so effectively describes. Aesthetic categories may be appropriate identifiers for the content of some relations to the world and to other persons. But surely it is a mistake to subsume all postures of creativity under them. The creativity metaphor may provide a good alternative to the monarchical one, but it is incorrect, I believe, to collapse this metaphor solely into claims about aesthetic content. Part of the problem lies in Farley's attempt to define beauty in terms of a fit between form and function (see pp. 166 ff.). This definition is perhaps adequate for the aesthetic realm. But the notions of "form" and "fit" (though not "function") are so vague that they can be used to cover too much, too many "fits" of "form" to "function" that are not aesthetic at all. So, though Farley is correct to speak of a kind of "existential creativity" (p. 167) that arises from being-founded, he is wrong—and wrong phenomenologically, I think—to identify this solely with aesthetic categories, and especially wrong to claim that it is the beauty of the face that ultimately draws us into redeemed relations with others.

Not so theologically innocent are the last two of Farley's identifiers. Note that Farley's name for what "founds," "sacred presence," is phenomenologically neutral, simply a name, that is, for a fact of experience. Yet Farley assumes that the "whence" of this founding can only be the ground of all being (see, e.g., pp. 144, 250). Based on a variety of sources, including the moral recognition of the face in the old Hebrew texts and the form of reconciliation in the sphere of the interhuman, he also simply assumes that this ground of all being must be personal. The following is his most direct statement of this dual theme:

> [B]ecause that which founds, unlike goods at hand, is able to found, it is the center, power, and meaning of being and thus is that on which we and all goods at hand depend. What happens in founding is that the desired eternal horizon is disclosed as the transmundane power and meaning of being which is both good and personal (p. 151).

Speaking of the sacred as an actual presence that "founds," he claims that "if the presence addresses the passion of the interhuman, it would seem to be in some sense a personal other" (p. 151).

Now, whatever theological history supports these positions, they are not phenomenologically warranted by the descriptions Farley himself provides. At these points he seems simply to read into his phenomenology a largely clichéd set of labels he unreflectively draws from an unreconstructed theological background—a background that it is admittedly difficult to evade. There is a very large gap between the phenomenological evidence of a being-founded in an actual "presencing" and the assumption that the source of such "presencing" is a transmundane ground of all being. Farley inadvertently admits such a distinction by occasionally speaking simply of the "divine ground of all *goods*" (p. 164). Here (with Wieman) I simply point out that we can identify the divine with the source of good and with creativity without identifying it with the ground of all being.

Whether this source must be a personal being is very intricate, as Farley himself recognizes (cf., p. 151). In the history of the Biblical religions, there is certainly an intimate connection between the recognition of the claims of the face and the attribution of personality to God, and any Christian theology, including a naturalist one, must account for this dimension of the personal. But the attribution of personality to God is so metaphysically problematic that today one should no longer assume that metaphysical personality is the only way to connect the divine with the sphere of the personal. God can be the ground of the personal (including its redemption) without being metaphysically personal him/herself—as Wieman so powerfully showed.

My point here, however, is simply to hold open the phenomenology of reconciliation in the interhuman sphere. Farley's claim, quoted above, that "if [sacred] presence addresses the passion of the interhuman, it would seem to be in some sense a personal other" (p. 151) is not phenomenologically evident. The courage and the openness to all things made possible by "being-founded" can account for reconciliation of interpersonal violations without its source being itself personal. In a sensitive discussion of reconciliation through forgiveness, Farley comes close to admitting as much. "Relation begins to be redeemed," he says, "when being-founded transforms the corrupted existentials and reciprocities of individuals" (p. 250). Exactly so! How does this come about? Here Farley maintains precisely the phenomenological transparency for which I call: "How does [communion or agapic relation] originate? Since redemption occurs from the presence of the sacred, the question is as unanswerable in the sphere of the interhuman as it is in the sphere of agents. No one has access to the way in which the sacred is present in the creaturely. Even the most literal and immediate Christological discourses do not explicate that immediacy" (pp. 249, cf., 247). This conforms exactly to the argument I make in *Events of Grace*. There, following Bultmann, I argue that the transcendence of God is not ontological at all but refers to the indisposability of creative transformation. We are founded in and through events ("sacred presence") that are events of grace precisely because they transcend our ability to dispose over them.

Let me conclude by pointing out again why these issues of phenomenological neutrality or transparency are so basic. A naturalist theology that conforms to the naturalism we otherwise assume so widely throughout modern life is possible only if we can conceive religion valuationally rather than ontologically. We must free ourselves from the almost reflexive assumption of religionists that religious meaning is tolerable only if some sense of the ground or totality of all being supports it. The reason is that in becoming naturalists, we accept assumptions about the ground or totality of things that *do not* support the religious meanings our traditions seem to assume. But if in fact those meanings were solely valuational all along, then we can separate our ontology from our religion. We can form our world-view according to the best metaphysical canons we can conceive, all the while that we settle the issue of religious meaning on other terms. To do this, however, we must sustain an openness to precisely what the phenomenology of our religious heritage discloses. This is why I want to endorse almost everything that Farley says about the structure of good and evil in the Christian paradigm except his naming of the place of the sacred.

NOTES

1. Edward Farley, *Good and Evil: Interpreting a Human Condition* (Minneapolis: Fortress Press, 1990). Hereinafter direct references to this work will appear in the text.

2. Farley recognizes that his effort is both narrower and broader than a strict "theological anthropology." Nevertheless, using the term loosely, it is entirely appropriate to describe his endeavor and the use I make of it. See Farley, p. xvi, n. 4.

3. Charley D. Hardwick, *Events of Grace: Naturalism, Existentialism, and Theology* (Cambridge: Cambridge University Press, 1996).

4. See *Events of Grace*, pp. 5–18, and Charley D. Hardwick, "Theological Naturalism and the Nature of Religion: On Not Begging the Question," *ZYGON: Journal of Science and Religion*, Vol. 22, No. 1 (March 1987).

5. Theologians who explicitly deny naturalism would, I believe, agree with this position.

6. This is entirely irrespective of the *metaphysical* problems even naturalists must continue to find in those conditions. As Robert Neville has pointed out, for instance, none of the modern "internalist" cosmological models (naturalisms generally as well as Hegelianism and process thought) can account either for the universe's large scale ordered structure or for the specific ontological givenness of particulars within that order. Cf., Neville, *A Theology Primer* (Albany: State University of New York Press, 1991), p. 34 f. I certainly would not want to deny the mystery these issues raise. It is not evident, however, (1) how an appeal to a creator God "solves" these mysteries (except in an ad hoc fashion) or (2) how even if an appeal to God did solve them *metaphysically*, this solution would necessarily have any *religious* significance or interest.

7. See p. 139 f. for a close approximation by Farley to what I have termed "phenomenological transparency" or "neutrality."

8. Farley articulates the Biblical paradigm in two contexts. In both he is sensitive to modern critical problems with Biblical categories. The first context is the classical Biblical/theological account of sin where Farley identifies seven features, three of which can be extracted and reformulated, two of which are precritical, containing "cosmological elements that cannot survive the impact of modern sciences and modes of

thought" (p. 125), and two which are theologically problematic in their own right (pp. 124–130). (The two precritical features are the comprehensive cosmological narrative which assumes an origin of sin both in a single specific historical event involving a single pair of human beings and in a transhistorical cosmic event and the notion of a biological propagation of sin. The two theologically inappropriate features are the dominance of a monarchical metaphor in the comprehensive narrative and the suppression of any notion of the tragic in the origin of sin.) The second context is the domination of themes of redemption by monarchical and legal metaphors that led to the undue influence of judicial metaphors of reward and punishment (hence, for instance, Christological models emphasizing Christ's satisfaction) (pp. 140–144).

9. It pertains to "perduring features that constitute the being of something in its region or situation" (p. xix).

10. For instance, Farley's division dictates that intersubjectivity be identified within the sphere of the interhuman. But agents are constituted at least in part by participation in the interhuman, so intersubjectivity could also be located in the sphere of agency (see pp. 29, 36 f.).

11. Farley is not entirely clear about whether idolatry is a separate structure of evil or is basic and underlies all the others. Formally he identifies idolatry only with the sphere of personal agency and names it as one source of evil among others. Yet, the centrality of the passions in his account, his insistence on the interrelatedness of the spheres, and his actual account of the origin of evil in the other two spheres (the interhuman and the social) seem to attribute priority to the role of the elemental passions (and thus idolatry) in the origin of all forms of evil. A careful reading will also show, I believe, that despite his description of the dynamics of evil in the two spheres of the interhuman and the social *once it has arisen*, he is less effective and indeed is somewhat obscure in comprehending its origin in these spheres apart from the dynamics of idolatry as it arises in the sphere of personal being. On the other hand, his account of source or origin in the latter sphere is very strong. (In several instances, Farley comes close to acknowledging this interpretation; see p. 135, and for "reconciliation" in the sphere of the interhuman, pp. 247 f., and 270 in relation to the social.)

12. The first sentence is italicized in Farley's text as is the italics in the text as quoted.

13. As Farley says about religious orientations that do not make this separation or do not make it as decisively: "The evil we are up against is the world system itself, the very existence and character of imperiled finitude, the very structure of the self and its self–

presence" (p. 125). In a very astute observation, Farley notes that the separation of the tragic from evil was made possible by the way in which the Hebrews recognized something about the experience of the face (Emmanuel Levinas) in the sphere of the interhuman that permitted them to appreciate how acts of individual and social violation can have consequences that accumulate in history and are the sources of enormous suffering but are not simply identifiable with conditions of tragic limitation (p. 126). Note how Farley's extrapolation of the separation of the origin of evil from the tragic here is an instance of "phenomenological transparency" I have insisted upon—even though in its actual historical development among the Hebrews it may have originated in a quite mythological theocentricism.)

14. Farley insightfully develops the notion of a "timbre of discontent" that informs the background of lived experience and arises from this tragic structure (or the frustration of the elemental passions), and he connects it with the notion of "anxiety" that has played such a significant role in existentialist thought since Kierkegaard (cf., p. 123 f.). He also distinguishes this timbre of discontent from intellectualized views that come to terms with it (p. 131 f.). As he says: ". . . the intolerable sneaks past world-views, methods of criticism, and metaphysical speculations. For it is *human passionate existence, not the intellect*, that cannot accept its own ultimate nonsignificance" (p. 132, my italics).

15. *Events of Grace* uses the notions of "openness to the future" and "trust in being" to articulate the same content. It also argues that the doctrine of redemption is prior to the doctrine of creation in the sense that it is redemption that restores the goodness of creation—where these notions are interpreted existentially to mean that the transformation of faith restores our capacity to *affirm* the goodness of being as a gift of being.

16. In the classical tradition, under the doctrine of creation, this theme appears as the goodness of being and is associated with the view that evil is essentially privational. "Because of this essential goodness of being, the most formal feature of evil is a reality's departure from itself, a distortion of what is in itself real, valid, or beautiful" (p. 147). At the same time, largely missing from the classical tradition is an exploration of how the goodness of being is correlated with a way of existing in the world. With the striking exception of Jonathan Edwards, it failed, in other words, "to thematize the virtue implied by the goodness of being and the privational character of evil" (p. 147). Farley's striking notions of courage, and, especially, consent, seek to redress this imbalance (see pp. 146–150).

17. Farley correctly emphasizes that the "chaos" encountered here is not the intellectual concept of ultimate chaos (p. 132) but a negativity "contained *in the act of existing*" (p. 131, my italics). This existential emphasis makes the notion of chaos even less plausible.

18. Heidegger's analysis of anxiety seems far more phenomenologically and existentially adequate here. What appears phenomenologically in the "nothing" which anxiety encounters is not disorder (chaos) but precisely a kind of order: the *obtrusiveness* of the world as "world," before the bottomless unanswerability of which our response is "uncanniness" in the sense of unsettledness and homelessness (*Unheimlichkeit*). Cf., Martin Heidegger, *Being and Time*, trans. J. Macquarrie and J. Robinson (London: SCM Press, Ltd., 1962), pp. 230–233. Before this experience we do seek a kind of order, namely, security or "founding," but this is not in reaction to chaos.

19. For instance, though "consent" does consent to "suffering" and "tragic incompatibilities," I question that it consents to chaos (p. 149). Chaos in this sense is rarely, if at all, in lived experience.

THE MINIMALIST CRITIQUE OF RADICAL MONOTHEISM
A Reconsideration of Transcendence

Thomas D. Parker

With the publication of Jerome A. Stone's *The Minimalist Vision of Transcendence, A Naturalist Philosophy of Religion* (SUNY Press, 1992), the discussions about radial monotheism have taken a new and promising turn. The Nietzschean dilemma of either the God of monotheism or the loss of transcendent meaning and power is rejected in favor of a much more nuanced analysis of the options for philosophy of religion. Religious naturalism, Stone maintains, drawing on the sources of American religious empiricism, nourishes important aspects of transcendence within human experience without affirming an ontologically superior transcendent One. The loss of the God of monotheism need not mean the loss of all transcendent meaning and power, nor the wholesale rejection of religious insights that come from the monotheistic traditions. In fact it may be the reverse in our secular age. Stone argues that with ontological reticence (minimalism) there can be a recognition and response (openness) to real resources and challenging ideals which transcend the situation and promote creative transformation. This paper pursues this claim.

I.

Stone's discussion of transcendence without monotheism is an extension of the conversation begun by H. Richard Niebuhr and continued in our time by Gordon D. Kaufman and James M. Gustafson (among others). In *Radical Monotheism and Western Culture* (Harper and Row, 1960), Niebuhr proposed an analysis of human faith in God which distinguished radical monotheism from two other types of faith: social faith, or henotheism, and pluralistic faith, or polytheism. In henotheistic faith the center of value is One among the many, while in polytheism there are many centers of value that call forth confidence and loyalty from moral persons. In radical monotheism, however, there is one center of value, the

One beyond the many, as he put it, transcending everything else that properly calls forth that confidence and loyalty he called "faith."

Niebuhr's refusal to separate "God" and "faith" follows the old Protestant linkage of the two, as he acknowledges.[1] This has the virtue of focusing on faith in God as it actually exists, but makes it impossible for him to consider theism as a conceptual problem in itself. Apart from faith, the concept "God" is merely an empty placeholder for something else. While moral persons may direct their faith to many centers of value or causes, a center of value *ex hypothesi* is a center of value for someone or some community. When God or the gods are taken as value centers for human confidence and loyalty, the question of their ontological status is postponed, and the question of their meaning and function is brought to the fore (pp. 22-3).

The concept of the center of value for responsible selves is the critical underpinning of Niebuhr's treatment of radical monotheism.[2] Value is given in the relation of beings to each other and to their wider context. The "good" for anything is multidimensional, embracing objective, internal, and connectional relations. It is *good-for-ness*, assisting each thing in the realization of its potential. A relation is "right" when the potentiality for being good-for each other is realized.

Every relation has a context in reference to which interpretations of values refer. This is a "center of value," that good in relation to which all other goods are judged to be good and all right relations right. Implicitly or explicitly moral persons recognize such centers in their decisions and actions (pp. 109-10). When persons or communities have two or more competing centers, they are divided within themselves. When one value is dominant over all others, the relation is distorted. Moral maturity comes when all valued relationships are unified through reference to an embracing center of value. Changing the terms, an overarching good present in every relation valorizes every particular good within it.

Faith in God is a moral relation to that center of value in which confidence is placed and to which loyalty is given. If there are plural centers, it is a polytheistic form of faith, and persons or communities are divided within themselves (pp. 29-30). If there is one dominant center among others, it is a henotheistic form of faith, and persons or communities are united within themselves but divided from each other (pp. 25-28). If there is one center of value, it is a monotheistic form of faith, and persons or communities are united in confidence and loyalty to a universal god. But monotheism can be problematic if it is not radical, for it can fund imperialisms of every sort, as a particularly aggressive form of henotheism. Niebuhr thinks that this is a far more prevalent form of faith than the radical monotheism he espouses.

Radical monotheism is, by contrast, faith in "the One beyond all the many," a center of value which lends every value its meaning and power but is not one of them. Niebuhr calls it the "principle of being itself" (p. 32), a code-word for the source of all being which sustains every existence as "worthy in being." This is a faith with a universal intention: confidence in the whole and loyalty to every existent for the sake of that One which sustains and transcends all. Love of enemies as well as friends and giving each thing its due in the context in which it exists are examples of the universal moral imperative of radical monotheism (p. 34).

The unification of all things and relations through their relation to the One transcending them as their source and end includes the faithful self or community of selves. While henotheism unifies life, it does so in opposition to other centers of value. Humanism, vitalism, and naturalism are taken by Niebuhr as examples of such henotheisms (pp. 35–7). Each offers a valuable critique of the narrowness of communal faiths, but does so "by excluding some realm of being from the sphere of value." Radical monotheism by contrast unifies life inclusively, without setting up oppositions between concrete centers of value.

Radical monotheism does not assert "there is a God," as if it had special knowledge of an ontologically supreme being, but rather that "Being is God,"[3] and every existent is equally grounded in God and is good. The term *being* is not essential although it has a history in Western monotheistic thought. God refers rather to the mystery of being, the source and abyss of all things, "the last shadowy and vague reality, the secret of existence by virtue of which things come into being, are what they are, and pass away"; this "reality, this nature of things, abides when all else passes" (p. 122). This is the supreme reality with which we must reckon, though we do not know what it is.

Why then has faith attached itself to this abysmal reality, to have confidence in it and be loyal to its cause, the cause of all things without exclusion? Niebuhr gives three considerations, one negative and two positive. First, although humans are constituted to live by centers of value, none exists universally or can be an object of universal faith; our gods have limited competence and cannot save us from "meaningless existence." Moreover, all our gods are divisive, setting us against ourselves personally and socially. If that were not enough, all gods are finite, all causes fail, and all sources of sustenance give out; none is worthy of that confidence and loyalty which human responsibility requires.

Those who are disillusioned by little faiths and little gods have few choices, it seems. Since morally responsible persons do in fact have centers of value by which they live and act, there will be some center for confidence and cause for loyalty. But if all such centers are finally unable to sustain a universal faith, the choice is between arbitrarily chosen centers (henotheism) and the source and end of all things (radical monotheism). Niebuhr concludes that faith in this "last power" is "the end of the road for faith" (p. 125), which I take to mean that the dialectic of disillusionment and confidence stops here.[4] Reason cannot go further.

But second, certain historical persons and traditions have incarnated this faith in a way that transforms restricted faiths into universal faith. It is a historically available option, although no one is coerced into choosing it. Third, for those persons and communities which do follow the road of faith to its end, there are important consequences, Niebuhr argues. Although everything is relativized (nothing is God), everything has value which elicits reverence (nothing is not of God) (pp. 37; cf. 52). Cognitively and morally the world is opened up for fruitful inquiry and recognition of the values embedded in every relation. Radical monotheism engenders a vision of the world in which all things are unified in being and in worth ("the universal love of all being" in God [p. 126]).

II.

For the minimalist, the problem of faith in our time is not that its contemporary forms are either polytheistic or henotheistic rather than monotheistic, with the problematic consequences Niebuhr (and others) noticed. It is rather that the secular mind-set has closed itself to experiences of transcendence altogether, and the resources of criticism and renewal they make possible (p. 1). While the religious traditions of the West historically nurtured such experiences, in the secularized world now dominant such traditions have lost much power, although some of their insights could still be helpful in developing a secular openness to transcendent resources and challenges. In this situation Stone proposes an understanding of "this-worldly" transcendence to guide in "the recovery of openness to criticism and transformation."[5] It may be that a minimalist vision can provide a way to nourish the sense of transcendence in a secular world without resorting to a "doubtful maximal model."

The basic question the minialist asks is "what sort of reality there is corresponding to our idea of God" (p. 10). The answer can be briefly stated in theoretical language: "the transcendent is a collection of all situationally transcendent resources and continually challenging ideals we experience" (p. 11). The form of Stone's minimalism is in the grand tradition of *a posteriori* arguments for the existence of God. These arguments generate a theoretical concept of what, in devotional language, "all persons call God" (Aquinas). Yet there is an important difference: the minimalist concept is an empirical generalization rather than a transcendental presupposition. We experience "situationally transcendent resources" and "continually challenging ideals" in a way we do not experience a first cause or first intelligence.

Stone recommends this minimalist position with five clarifications. First, this model makes no "extravagant" claims such as the theistic traditions make concerning God's radical superiority in being and worth to any finite thing. By asserting less, its assertions gain certainty as being more supportable. Thus, God is defined as a set of actual and possible experiences of transcendence, not a doubtful ontologically supreme ultimate. This first clarification is the key to the proposal (cf. p. 202).

Second, a separation is made between real and ideal aspects of transcendence, in contrast to maximal models which unify them. We experience them differently, and, with no certain grounds for asserting their ultimate unity, each can be given its full expression without a background theory that emphasizes one or the other, or assimilates them to a third. Third, it follows that minimalism is a pluralism: the transcendent is a set of resources or ideals rather than a unity in itself.

Fourth, relinquishing ultimacy, minimalism gives no guarantee of the ultimate efficacy of the resources or attainment of the ideals. The only claim is that they are really there in some experienced situations, not that outcomes are sure. In fact, every such transcendent factor is ambiguous; it is only with reference to its power for good that it appears as a grace or a challenge (p. 15). This accords with our experience. Last, even if there is a transcendent "unity, ultimacy, and intelligent purposiveness" beyond our experience, Stone sees no way of asserting this in a public, responsible way (p. 13).[6]

Why then use the term "transcendence" used by so many others with a different meaning? Stone distinguishes the traditional concept from the experience because, in every situation, there can be unexpected and uncontrolled resources for good and worthy ideals which surpass what is actualized and offer continual challenge. These resources and ideals are functionally transcendent, not ontologically so. They are "greater in power and worth, being and value, than things or events in the world as normally experienced" (p. 21). Under different conditions, the same resources or ideals would simply be naturally known factors in the situation to be taken as unproblematic. It is the limitation of the situation as known which underlies the sense of otherness that constitutes the experience of transcendence. Since our experience of reality is that of an indeterminable complexity, and no situation is closed off from others, this situational transcendence is potentially characteristic of any conceivable experienced situation. It is what Dewey would call a "generic trait" of existence. Thus, by focusing on actual transcendent factors, the secularization of life actually can nourish the sense of transcendence rather than stultify it.

Stone calls minimalism a philosophy of openness.[7] To live according to this interpretation of transcendence is to live open to resources and ideals that can transform the situation for good, but which come to us as extra-situational gifts and judgments. Thus minimalism encourages openness to the unknown, gratitude for resources, and commitment to ideals that exceed our attainments. It is this openness, rather than the concept of God, which characterizes minimalism and is its preeminent practical consequence. Thus the meaning of transcendence is the openness to which it leads, and vice-versa.

Why then use the symbol "God" to refer to a collection of natural factors which are relatively transcendent in situations as perceived? Stone gives a carefully nuanced reply to this question. "Transcendence" is not the dictionary definition of God in the West, but is enough like it in its function as a real resource and challenge to warrant the extension of the term. Whether or not one chooses to use "God" to symbolize this interpretation of transcendence is a matter of "personal choice and context" (p. 18), not of intellectual necessity. With reference to a statement by B. Loomer to the effect that in our traditions "God" symbolizes ultimate values and meanings with an absolute claim of our loyalty, Stone argues that it is appropriate to use "God" for "the sum of the worthy and creatively challenging aspects of the world" which elicit "a primacy of trust and a priority in our commitments" (p. 19). Stone does not depend on the associations of rhetoric to carry the point, however, for at the end of the day it is not the term "God" but the attitude of openness to the transcendent minimally understood that is the important point.

The positive case for the minimalist model involves several strands of argument. First is the question of empirical fit as it is found to be exemplified (or not) in "the major types of religion" and how well it fares in critical discussions of scholars in the field (p. 25). Stone believes it fares very well; the triad of gift, demand, and sense of otherness is reiterated in many religious forms across the globe and is affirmed by many religious thinkers. Second, it is recommended by the restraint it shows in refusing to overextend its claims on reality; it is all too easy to indulge in metaphysical imagination in the face of the lack of any consensus on these matters (p. 31). Third, it does retain a notion of the transcendent so as to nourish experiences of it within the limits of reticence and cultivate openness to as yet unrealized value. By thematizing secular experiences, Stone argues, minimalism persuades us that "inner-worldly transcendence is real" (p. 32), and so addresses the loss of transcendence in our time.[8]

The minimalist focus on *experiences* of transcendent resources and ideals rather than on the experience of ultimacy emphasized by radical monotheism is underwritten by what Stone calls "a generous empiricism" (Chap. 4, pp. 111–167). The American philosophical tradition of radical empiricism provides minimalism with a way of including the sense of otherness in perceptions of real resources and imaginations of worthy ideals. Several aspects of this tradition are pertinent to reflection on religious experience.[9] Moreover, since radical empiricism and pragmatism can fund no metaphysical concept of an ultimate reality apart from concrete realities, this tradition in philosophy supports the reticence minimalism advocates.

To summarize the minimalist critique of radical monotheism, four objections are to be noticed. First, the circumstances of secularity favor a this-worldly transcendence thematizing actual experiences of transcendence. An ontologically supreme ultimate is a distraction if not simply a block to the openness to real transcendence an all too self-enclosed culture needs. Since radical monotheists make the same points about the nature of secularization and the need of our time, but with a different prescription, the issue is joined.

Second, naturalism has won out in the argument with theism since it makes fewer unwarrantable propositions about ultimate reality. As the minimalist reads it, the history of theistic discussion is not favorable for theism, while naturalism is able to sustain the values of religious awareness and moral commitment without being burdened by inarguable metaphysical assumptions. Since prominent radical monotheists agree with much of the criticism of theism without dismissing it, and nevertheless mount arguments against aspects of naturalism; this issue is also in debate.

Third, minimalism has a more highly nuanced empirical interpretation of human experience. Without denying the power of generalizations to bundle together different kinds of experience and different dimensions of things (as in Stone's "set" of resources and challenges read as grace and judgment) within limiting concepts such as unity and totality, minimalism focuses on actual experienced realities; it refuses to reify the referent of such theoretical concepts and locate them on the other side of an ontological divide. It is a thoroughgoing nominalism. By contrast, radical monotheism must supplement its empirical references with a speculative argument in order to justify its ontological realism. A minimalist awaits justification of such arguments as legitimate in relation to available evidence with reticence. In the meantime, there is confidence in the experiences of transcendence as realities by which human beings live gratefully and faithfully.

Fourth, minimalism has no need to "complete the picture" by relating transcendence to whatever there is the way radical monotheism must. The divine is the set of creative resources and worthwhile ideals which nourish what is good and direct persons toward the most fulfilling existence possible under the circumstances. Factors in the situation which do not work for good are not the divine, no matter how transcendent (unexpected or uncontrollable) they are. Transcendence is a larger frame than "God" or the divine. Radical monotheism's use of "God" to refer to the largest frame of reality, and not just to those factors which we judge functional, must face the issue of the goodness of God in a way the minimalist does not.

III.

In Stone's book, the two radical monotheists most often discussed are Langdon Gilkey and Gordon D. Kaufman. Since the book was published, Kaufman has written *In Face of Mystery: A Constructive Theology* (Harvard Univ. Press, 1993) in which the argument for radical monotheism has been pursued with some attention to the kind of criticism Stone gives. Additionally the Niebuhr legacy has been given new statement by James M. Gustafson in an earlier volume, *Ethics From a Theocentric Perspective, Vol. I, Theology and Ethics* (The University of Chicago Press, 1981). Since Gustafson's work closely engages aspects of the minimalist position while remaining firmly monotheist—Reformed monotheist at that!—his work addresses the four critical issues raised by Stone in the course of arguing for a theocentric ethics. While Stone has responded to Kaufman,[10] questioning the model of agency and the unity of being and value in Kaufman's God-construct, he has not to my knowledge engaged Gustafson, who shares his bias toward the empirical though not his (default) ontological pluralism.

The first critical issue is the character of the environment within which the question of transcendence or God is raised. In contrast to Stone, Gustafson does not interpret the challenge of the contemporary situation according to the narrative of secularization. In fact, the word *secular* is scarcely found in his work.[11] Rather, the distinguishing mark of our culture is its anthropocentrism, where the human is not only the indispensable context of all knowledge, morals, and aesthetic appreciation, but the center and measure of everything else. The so-called secular is neither more nor less anthropocentric than religion and the religious traditions. Human beings measure, they are not the measure (p. 82); what is called for is a theological tradition which turns from the human to "that which is objective in relation to human subjects, the limits, demands, principles and boundaries within which human life can find its good as well" (p. 84). As Kaufman has it, everything human beings do is anthropic, but not everything is anthropomorphic nor need our attitudes be anthropocentric.

Three characteristics of our cultural situation predominate. First, there is the greatly extended range of human control over the conditions of life for the sake of human security and well-being (pp. 3–8). Although this does not assuage our insecurity, it greatly enhances human responsibility and the temptation to various centrisms. Second, there is the inescapable finitude of everything which limits success and, serendipitously, undermines even our best efforts (pp. 8–16). Even if we are not sure about God, he contends, we are sure we are not God, for there is no overcoming the "fundamental conditions of human finitude" (p. 14). Third, there is functional religion and philosophy (pp. 16–31) whose utilitarianism is largely unchallenged. Even theology, which should have known better, has often abandoned the sense of mystery without and within for norms and ends that serve our (supposed) species self-interest. Nor is ethics any better off, although the best theology and ethics (e.g., H.R. Niebuhr) has elements of protest against self-interested functionalism.

This assessment of the challenge of our times differs from that of Stone's minimalist. It is not clear how this-worldly transcendence would help; it could simply be a further expression of the problem Gustafson surfaces, the endemic anthropocentrism of our time (and most other times he knows anything about). As Gustafson sees it, the problem is not this versus another world; it is failure of moral and religious vision to see the human in its tragic circumstances. Without this global vision, human interests and values are fundamentally distorted (pp. 82–5). His recommendation on behalf of theocentricity follows from this premise. The shift of focus from the human to that which is "objective" to the human, to the cosmological, material, biological, and social structures which form the matrix of humanity, leads to a recognition of the "power and ordering of life in nature and history" which sustains and limits humanity, demanding recognition and "consent" as a basis for responsible ethics.[12] Any view of transcendence which underwrites anthropocentrism is unacceptable for our time.

The second critical issue is the relation of naturalism to theism, with the recommendation of ontological "reticence" to postulates of an "ontologically supreme ultimate," as Stone puts it. The doubtful complexities of traditional or revisionist theism actually hinder rather than help support a philosophy of openness to transcendence. Surprisingly, Gustafson does not argue the ontological issue at all as Kaufman does. He frames the issue in terms of the appropriateness of radical monotheism for human faith in opposition to endemic and destructive anthropocentrism. The metaphysics of traditional theism that trouble the minimalist is simply by-passed the way the minimalist also bypasses it. But he also bypasses metaphysical naturalism; such hypotheses are unneeded.[13] The phennomenological-descriptive mode of argument has no interest in supporting either side of the argument between naturalism with theism.

In place of a metaphysical or (pure) phenomenological argument for God, Gustafson offers observations about religion and God with empirical roots.[14] Human life is lived in the context of powers which "bear down and sustain it," enabling and limiting it at the same time. Our experience is experience of "an other," other things and persons external to us (p. 128), apart from which we cannot live at all. The task of human flourishing requires us intellectually to know, morally to interact with, and affectively to engage this complex environment. It is the source of the principles and boundaries which shape our ends. However far its reach, reflection begins with the brute terms of existence, biological and social, in its effort to interpret the conditions of human life and promote its well-being.

Religious affections and actions ("piety") embody such interpretations of this basic situation. The senses of dependence, gratitude, obligation, remorse, possibility, and direction construe an attitude of engagement with these "others." Religious cultures provide metaphors that nourish and express the meanings germane in these senses, and foster social cooperation aligned with these senses. Theological reflections construe the meanings authorized by a religious culture, to elaborate them and indicate their significance for a wide range of questions and challenges (p. 229). While religions vary in their symbolism and theologies in their concepts (e.g., nontheisms, monotheisms, and polytheisms), all share a sense of the portentous reality of that which is beyond human control or proof. The "religious consciousness" moves beyond the "secular" at this point, whether or not the concept of God or the divine is used (p. 135). For those associated with a religious tradition, this step is overt, unconcealed. In monotheism, respect and reverence for *an* Other is close-coupled with experiences of others and of "otherness." There is no persuasive argument for this move; it simply emerges from hearts and minds nurtured in monotheistic piety "to *see* experiences of diverse others as various manifestations of the *Other*" (p. 136).

Monotheism is a complex phenomenon, with multiple sources of nourishment in the wider experiences of persons and communities over time. It brings into a unity (p. 206) diverse objects of experience. It is a piety before it is a theory, and the theory rests on the piety rather than vice-versa. As a piety, it organizes "putatively non-religious experiences" (e.g., nature, history, culture, society, and the self) into "warrants for affirming the reality of an ultimate power that orders and sustains the world" (p. 207).[15]

The monotheistic construal of the world indeed raises questions of justification similar to the questions at stake in the older discussion of theism and naturalism. Gustafson believes there are and can be no successful arguments for (or against) a "powerful Other" in the abstract; abstracts are vindicated by reference to concrete experiences they elucidate, generalize, and apply. Yet because religious belief, as any belief, has an "objective pole," it is subject to "reality checks" (p. 128) such as accuracy of information about objects to which responses are given, seriousness of consequences, and effective action, rational coherence, etc. argued in a public venue (pp. 158–9).

Such reality checks do not require a speculative concept of a divine something, reifying it and then trying to see if it is "out there." Rather, the close relation between experienced "powers" and an "ultimate Power," or "others" and "an Other" discerned within it, serves to focus attention on the particularity of objects and relations. The only access we have to the "powerful Other" is through the actual "powers" and "others" with which we have to deal. For this, the special sciences are required and such cosmological generalizations as knit them together, as well as the affectivities of piety and the religious symbols that give them social form. The discernment of an ultimate unity serves to heighten the importance of diversity in all its interconnectedness in contrast to generalizations which unite by excluding concreteness. Thus Gustafson's rhetoric slips easily between "powers" of God and the "power" of God.

The third critical issue is the minimalist focus on experiences of transcendence rather than on the global frame of such experiences. The minimalist needs no speculative hypotheses about the unity or directionality of the cosmic historical process (Kaufman) in order to locate, interpret, and celebrate experiences of this-worldly transcendence. They stand on their own ground. Gustafson agrees, though with important reservations. Stone mentions typical instances of transcendence capable of a minimalist interpretation and religious thematization.[16] These are situations in which persons can be open to "more" than their previous understandings and experiences had led them to expect, and are engaged affectively as well as intellectually and morally.

Like the minimalist, Gustafson argues that experience is always experience of an other-than-self (p. 128); there is an objective aspect. Knowledge of the divine power is always mediated through engagement with particular powers. But these are not always immediately known in personal experience; human experience cannot be limited to the idiosyncratic. There are indeed experiences of dependence on the life-support systems of the natural and social world, for example; the breakdown of these systems shocks us into recognition of how much we take for granted (p. 130). These and others (pp. 131 ff.) evoke religious responses, including the sense of God (pp. 197 ff.). But equally important are the arenas of experience in the larger sense, human experience collectively, of being in a world of nature, history, culture, society, and of selfhood (pp. 209 ff.). Empiricism is limited if its focus is exclusively on personal dimensions of experience. Referring to James, Gustafson reiterates that what makes any response religious, however, is neither personal affect, belief, commitment, (etc.) nor special environments, but the ultimate object. The danger is to sever the immediate and the ultimate object or to identify them indiscriminantly.

That said, Gustafson has strong reservations about focusing on experiences of transcendence which might serve to strengthen instrumental pieties (pp. 20-1). Apart from "consent to the divine governance" in nature and the ordered human relationships, experiences with religious significance may only deepen destructive anthropocentrism. Thus there is a need to reflect critically about universality (p. 151) in order to critique particularities and parochialisms and to relate God or the divine to global as well as local issues. "Efforts to overcome the boundaries of our communities, or to extend membership in them, cannot and ought not to be demeaned"(p. 127). Neither in ethics nor theology can reflective thought be reticent about the global implications of an empirically based piety. Although Gustafson doesn't join Kaufman in constructing a historical metaphysics to ground his assertions about God, he does agree that any worthy construction of God in our time must take global realities into account and not disconnect God and the whole of reality to which we owe responsible consent.

The fourth critical issue follows from this: the scope of reference for the divine grace and judgment. When transcendence or the divine ("God") refers to those transcendent resources and ideals which work for good in particular cases, there is no need to "complete the picture" by any kind of theodicy which connects the divine to what is tragic, destructive, or dysfunctional in the larger sense. The divine is unequivocally good (worthy and constructive), though the world is not (Stone). By contrast, the radical monotheist must see "God" or the divine in relation to all that is without exception: each individual thing in its particularity has a relation to God. Gustafson's vision of the powers of God "bearing down on us" and sustaining us in a basically tragic (if beautiful and bountiful) world is a global hypothesis about the determinants of human existence as such. If the world is ambiguous with respect to human good, so is the relation of humanity to God.[17] By the same token if this ambiguous world is the matrix of all worthy ideals and beautiful forms we know, so is the ordering power of God.

If Stone's minimalist wishes to advocate such ideals as that of the universal community (pp. 87 ff.) or care for others as brothers and sisters that takes account of their intrinsic worth rather than merely their use (impartially?) (pp. 97 ff.), an all-embracing environment joining being and value is implied, so that each has to do in principle with all the others who have come to be within the same prodigal conditions. It is no accident that radical monotheists (such as Gustafson, Kaufman, and others in the Niebuhr tradition) have understood such ideals as implicates of their theocentrism. The maxim of Gustafson's ethics is an abstract statement of the same point: act toward others according to *their* relation to God. The impartiality and unconditionality of that maxim grows directly from "the consent to being" which drives radical monotheism. It can even foster the odd ethic of the love of enemies! While it may be "completing the picture," this nascent universalism puts in question the strategy of limiting religious responses to creative qualities, to worthy ideals, in short, to a highly partial reading of the experienced world. Gustafson's advocacy of theocentrism in contrast to anthropocentrism lives from a refusal to do just this. But if the only experiences of transcendence that count are the positive, upbuilding ones, it is hard to see that the ethical outcome can ever be a truly universal community, critical care of others as brothers and sisters, or heartfelt pluralistic vision. Something will always have to be excluded for the best of reasons.

IV.

At the end of the matter, both minimalist and radical monotheist reject the dichotomy of *either* transcendence and openness *or* a metaphysically constructed theism in favor of a more empirically oriented set of observations and reflections. Stone's positive appreciation for aspects of radical monotheism (i.e. the importance of ultimacy and the ideal of the universal community) joins Gustafson's hesitancy to thematize them extensively beyond the portentous reality symbolized by affectively grounded religious traditions.

That said, the discussion between them raises important questions for further reflections on the meaning and function of transcendence in human life in the world. One question is surely the assessment of the situation within which the discussion is carried forth; whether our problematic is secularism or anthropocentrism (or something else) makes a difference. The same is true for the issue between naturalism and theism; if this is no longer a significant issue religiously or morally, discussions about experiences of transcendence and the object(s) intended by such experiences can proceed in quite new ways.

Another question is the relation of the global frame of experience to the concrete wholeness of it; if experiences do not stand alone, as radical empiricists always insisted, the global questions cannot be finessed in discussions of transcendence or the divine through generalizations about experienc*es*. Assumptions about the unity, contingency, and directionality (or lack of them) of the world matter. Although this concerns Kaufman more overtly than either Stone or Gustafson, their work raises the subject to prominence.

The Minimalist Critique of Radical Monotheism 417

Lastly, there is the matter of impartiality in valuing whatever is, irrespective of its appearing right or good to some local perspective or other. Should God or the divine be conceived in relation to the whole of reality or simply to those aspects and experiences of the whole judged to be superior in value or fundamental in import (i.e., the "creative event" rather than "created things")? Or will such centrisms inevitably distort our judgment and destroy critical openness to the fecund complexity of the world?

As an appendix to this discussion of transcendence and radical theocentrism, I notice the assumption that we can use the tradition-bound term "God" for whatever we decide is the base-line of experienced reality, in hopes that its associations of reverence, gratitude, and loyalty will travel with it to its new location in the conceptual cosmos. Yet, when "God" no longer means that which evoked the desirable affects, why assume the new referent will continue to elicit them?

NOTES

1. "Theology must attend to the God of faith if it is to understand faith no less than it must attend to faith in God if it is to understand God" (p. 11). In the essay "Faith in Gods and in God" (1943) Niebuhr states that in this context the problem of God appears "as an eminently practical problem, a problem of human existence and destiny, of the meaning of human life in general and of the life of self and its community in particular" (pp. 115–16).

2. See esp. the essay "The Center of Value" (1952), reprinted in *Radical Monotheism*, pp. 100–113. In *The Responsible Self* (Harper and Row, 1963), responsibility is taken as "the idea of an agent's action as response to an action upon him in accordance with his interpretation of the latter action and with his expectation of response to his response; and all of this in a continuing community of agents" (p. 65). Such responses are not mere accidental episodes, but "part of a larger pattern" (p. 77) in relation to which the self is a self. This is the "third" (p. 79) that accompanies responsible action between selves, something which is of value because it is a condition of our life together. This "third" is a transcendent reference (pp. 83–4). In Niebuhr's ethics the overarching value is the universal community embracing all particular communities.

3. "... or, better, that the principle of being, the source of all things and the power by which they exist, is good, as good for them and good to them. It is relied on to give and conserve worth to all that issues from it. What otherwise, in distrust and suspicion, is regarded as fate or destiny or blind will or chance is now trusted. It is God" (p. 38).

4. Niebuhr refers in the text to A. N. Whitehead's *Religion in the Making* (1926), where the development of religion is found in the "transition from God the Void, to God the Enemy to God the Companion" (quoted pp. 123–4).

5. *Minimalist Vision*, 3. Stone sees his work as complementary to work done within religious communities by those who are reconstructing the idea of God as the "Archimedean point of transcendence" rather than an obstacle to it.

6. Stone's negative arguments against a supreme ontological ultimate all hang on this judgment. See pp. 28–30 for a summary of "negative arguments": 1) empirical justification fails, 2) the history of ontological (read transcendental) arguments gives no basis for affirming them, 3) "there is no immediate awareness of the Unconditioned" (p. 30), and 4) religious authority is undermined by historical contingency.

7. Cf. Chap. III, "The Ethics of Openness" (pp. 83–110): "*we should adopt and continually nurture a stance of critical openness and commitment*" (p. 83). The first principle of this ethics is the discernment of worth, cherishing of value, and "sensitive appreciation" (Meland) of the qualities creative of good in any situation. Since every situation is constituted by transactions (Dewey), such good is neither objective nor subjective but relational, and includes the entire gamut of value: intellectual, moral, and aesthetic.

8. Stone has in mind common experiences such as openness to transforming joy and suffering in the midst of extremity, courage in spite of finitude, and especially courage to act in the midst of uncertainty. The continually challenging goals found in science, the moral life, and the arts constitute a further common experience (pp. 33–40).

9. Briefly stated, radical empiricism furnishes a broadened interpretation of experience that includes both focus and field, nurturing a widened understanding of perception which Stone calls "sensitive discernment" (pp. 112 ff.). It also emphasizes the transactional nature of experience in which organic participation is primary and selective conceptualization subsequent. Stone calls this "transactional realism" (pp. 127 ff.). Moreover radical empiricism (at its best) recognizes that all experience is historically situated, with inquiry itself being part of a series of interpretations,

The Minimalist Critique of Radical Monotheism 419

influenced by and influencing cultural and social environments. Stone calls for a self-critical empiricism (pp. 42 ff.). Finally, radical empiricism re-funds language of the directly had, vague, affectively tinged and value laden aspects of experience. Stone connects the conceptual language of inquiry to the language of symbol, parable, and metaphor which gives expression to these aspects; the contrast is between what he calls a language of "transparency" and that of "translucency," rather than between two types of experience (p. 158). Experience remains whole; the contrasts are within, not between, experiences.

10. "How Far Can Kaufman Go Toward Naturalism? The Divine Plurality as a Test" in *New Essays in Religious Naturalism*, W. Creighton Peden and Larry E. Axel, eds., (Macon, GA: Mercer University Press, 1993), pp. 226–234.

11. In this, Gustafson and Kaufman are similar. For Kaufman, it is not the construct of secularization that provides the challenge to rethink constructs of God, but the emerging global culture, and the challenge of finding a universal community amidst the conflicting communities when transportation, communication, and capital formation are globalized, and when wars spill over national and cultural boundaries. Our situation is characterized by an emerging single history (*Mystery*, pp. 119–122) demanding a global consciousness (p. 133). The classic narrative of secularization is swallowed up by the old-new narrative of historicization ("the world process of which we all are part") (p. 137). A "modern secular faith" (p. 433) takes this new world picture into account as it reconstructs the idea of God.

12. Although this vision does not require a leveling of humans and everything else to a common value, "it does require that man as a species, individuals as persons, and human communities be redescribed in relation to other aspects of nature, to powers beyond their control, to a destiny which is not in human hands, and to a termination which...will be without us" (p. 109). "The proper orientation is not primarily toward self but toward God - to the honoring of God, and to the ordering of life in relation to what can be discerned of the divine ordering" (p. 110). What can be discerned is our best scientific and moral knowledge of the way things are.

13. It will be remembered that Niebuhr as well as Gustafson after him (but not Kaufman), focused on the meaning of radical monotheism for human faith, and was also reticent to put metaphysically fixed concepts alongside the idea of God as source and end of all things. Niebuhr's use of "Being" in contrast to beings is best understood in the context of discussion at the time, shaped as it was by early twentieth century European philosophies, rather than as a critically developed concept. It is adjunct to his

phenomenology of faith, I believe, rather than central to it. It depends particularly on the discussions surrounding Tillich's idea of God as "being-itself," and thus appears in the later rather than the earlier, more pivotal, work, "Faith in Gods and in God."

14. For the following see esp. "The Priority of Experience," (pp. 5 ff.) Gustafson believes there is no coercive argument from particulars to a powerful Other. What can be done is "to show descriptively how, given affectivity and the ways in which it is engendered not only by common experience but also by participation in a religious tradition, the religious tradition provides warrants and symbols for moving from particular experiences to the experience of responding to an ultimate power" (p. 196).

15. "The order of experience, if I am correct, is not a sense of the powers of God ordering nature, but experiences of the natural world that evoke affectivities that can be religiously significant. The intellectual construal of the theological significance of the objects that evoke the affectivities and of the affectivities themselves is a further step in the discussion. . . . The ultimate power that sustains us and bears down upon us is experienced through particular objects, events, and powers that sustain us, threaten our interest, create conditions for human action, or evoke awe and respect" (p. 209). For Gustafson's interpretation of piety, see pp. 195–204 and compare pp. 163–178 for his borrowings from the Reformed theological tradition.

16. Resources of renewal that are uncoerced and unexpected are indicated on pp. 34–40. *In extremis*, persons with appreciative awareness can become aware of their limits and the resources for good beyond their doing, engaging them with due sorrow and joy; in the face of contingency, they can act with courage accepting the terms of life as a gift and a challenge to grow, and in opportune times, they may with courage seize the moment because of recognition of hitherto unnoticed resources. Continually challenging goals meet us in the search for values in science, art, moral life, and social responsibility. The minimalist needs no "ontologically ultimate correlate" to achieve openness in these kinds of situation.

17. "Piety stands in awe of the powers that bear down on us and sustain us; it does not trust them to fulfill all our perceptions of human good. Piety in the presence of such powers can be expressed in fear as well as gratitude" (p. 272).

ON LISTENING TO INDIGENOUS PEOPLES AND NEO-PAGANS:
Obstacles to Appropriating the Older Ways

Jerome A. Stone

Many religious people wish to engage in dialogue with other religious viewpoints. However, this is usually done with what are often called the "high religions." I propose also engaging in dialogue with the old ways, the religions of primary or indigenous peoples. Furthermore, since I understand dialogue to be a two-way street, I find one of the best opening moves is to ask what we can learn from the dialogue partner. As Delwin Brown affirms in expounding Gadamer, "Dialogue is questioning and questioning is being opened by, opening, and keeping open the possibilities that the past presents."[1] What I am doing is opening further the boundaries of the usable past.

This proposal takes focus from the recent rise of what can be called neo-paganism, particularly by some people who believe that women's spirituality should leave traditional monotheism behind and by an overlapping group, those interested in pre-patriarchal and neolithic or native American contributions to environmental philosophy.[2]

The dominant ideas of Western culture are a mix, uneasy at times, of themes derived from scientific-industrial modernism and of monotheism. I assume a general familiarity of my readers with this mix. I will focus on particular obstacles to learning from the older traditions, obstacles arising from their violation of the major assumptions of both scientific modernism and monontheism. This paper seeks to address these obstacles.

One way of addressing these obstacles is to point out that the distinction between Western culture and older ways is usually exaggerated. A second way is to rethink the superiority of humans. Third, the older ways are not simply pre-scientific. We need to recognize that the issues are far more complex than that. We shall need to deepen our understanding of gender, of ritual, of our embodidness. We shall need to discover the value of multiple images of time.

Above all we should drop the question of which religion is true, or better or superior. Instead we should focus on what we can learn from each other, in this case, the older religions or cultures. We should stop reifying a religion or a culture as if it had a permanent essence or clearly defined necessary and sufficient conditions for membership, with boundaries that cannot be crossed.

A sub-theme of my treatment is to show in particular how my own brand of religious naturalism approaches these issues. In case anyone is interested in this view, out of curiosity or a sense of the adequacy of religious naturalism, I will indicate the direction which could be taken. However, I wish to speak in more general terms to a wider audience, modernists, reluctant post-modernists, eager post-modernists, and people with a foot in more than one paradigm or culture, in short, anyone who will listen. Hence, religious naturalism will be a minor point in this essay.[3]

A second minor theme is that there are some values in the dominant Western paradigm which could be retained. All cultures have their values and can contribute to the rich tapestry of the council of all beings. All cultures need to be approached with a difficult mix of appreciation and suspicion. Especially we need to be appreciative and suspicious of our own culture as well as of the Other. No one is sufficient for this task, of course, but let us begin.

A personal word is in order. I was raised and later received training in liberal Protestant Christianity and absorbed a deep-seated rejection of idolatry, a rejection so deep-seated that it involved the feeling of abhorrence. Worship of the one God is, after all, the first commandment. Furthermore, and this is important, as I matured and became self-reflective, I discovered that my feelings were rooted as much in Enlightenment as in Christian sensibilities.

At the same time I have developed a growing appreciation of Greek myths and of traditional African and native American, specifically Lakota, Dineh, and Hopi ways. Furthermore my work in Schelling's philosophy of mythology and in the pluralistic, even polytheistic, possibilities of religious naturalism have given me an interest in the possibility of learning from polytheism. Indeed my entire writing has been partly motivated by a desire to overcome the arrogance of a Eurocentric outlook. Recently I have also been deeply interested in pagan retrievals in women's spirituality. In this paper, rather than concentrate on any one of these sources, I would like to be reflexive and look in general at the questions that arise when we try to learn from the spiritual ways of indigenous peoples or their contemporary advocates.

I have decided to retain the word "pagan," at least by using "neo-pagan." This is in part because it resonates with some of the explorations of women's spirituality. Also, since it historically has derogatory connotations, it points to the necessity of confronting honestly the obstacles in the way of appropriating insights from the indigenous religions.

I.

Focusing the question. A common question is, "Which religion is true?" or "Which religion shall I follow or join?" In a way these are questions with a monotheistic background, assuming that there is one true God and one true religion. One does not think of being a Jew and simultaneously a Christian religiously. One is either a Christian or a Moslem. On the other hand there is no difficulty in following Taoist, Confucian and Buddhist ways, since the exclusivity of monotheism is not operative in the typical Chinese outlook. In many ways these are also modern questions in that they recognize a variety of outlooks, assume that one of them is correct or more correct, and that a person has some autonomy in recognizing truth or giving commitment. Presupposed here are the principles of identity and noncontradiction. Of any two outlooks, if one is true the other must be false, and also there is a distinction between them, so that one cannot adopt both at the same time. Boundaries between positions can be crossed, but the boundaries are not permeable. The outlook or religion has become reified. One is either a Christian or not, a believer or not. These assumptions are not always made clearly nor held by all thinkers that can be called modern. Nevertheless, these presuppositions are typical of the modernist period.

I suggest changing the question or refocusing it. Instead of "Which is the true religion?" let us ask, "What can we learn from another religion?" This starts without the assumption that either my religion or another is better. It does assume that it is possible and desirable to learn from another. Note also that this question does not commit one to relativism. It does not assume that there is no truth or dimension that is better or more adequate. It does assume that truth, goodness, or adequacy is not one's possession. It also assumes that we can learn.

For this discussion I wish to focus the question further, by asking "What can we learn from the religions of very old or indigenous peoples?" This directs attention away from the high religions, which are often presumed to be the really important religions. For a monotheist or a modernist, especially an evolutionary modernist, such a focus can be seem radical. On the other hand, there are bits of nostalgia floating around about the past, often romanticized as a pagan past, a non-credal, perhaps erotic, environmentally cozy past.

To try to learn from the old ways is to free oneself radically from the usual approaches to religion in the West in the past three centuries. Usually one or more of the monotheistic religions is taken as a baseline and a person tends to focus religious reflection around accepting or rejecting them. One could take a defensive attitude, a reconstructive approach, or a radical rejection, but for Western thinkers it is usually one or more of the monotheistic traditions from which a person starts and which is either accepted, revised, or rejected. Usually a person does not go back earlier than her own tradition. A person seldom is concerned about a pre-Biblical period, however defined.

"Free-lance" spirituality. Recently some people have become "free-lancers" in religion, trying various things from other religions. The term "spirituality" owes part of its popularity to this mood, as opposed to the seeming restrictions of "a religion." This approach has an upside and a downside. The upside of this is that there is a freedom and even creativity which can come from this approach. The downside is that to oppose spirituality to a religion can cut a person off from the discipline, support and challenge of a tradition. It is easier to reject a tradition than to engage in the hard task of learning its counter-themes, minority strands and resources for self-criticism and the equally hard task of personal critical appropriation. Such simplistic rejection also renders one vulnerable to a similar lack of critical engagement with other traditions, learning the multiplicities and self-critical resources within the other.

My concern here is not to reject those who adopt a spirituality unattached to an historical religion, but rather to point out that such an approach does not provide a short-cut to spiritual development.

II.

Many Gods. One major obstacle to be faced is that indigenous people often have many Gods. This can be horrifying both to monotheistic and to enlightenment sensibilities.

The pluralism of paganism should not be overstated. There is a tension between the plurality of the Gods and their unity. To some extent the One God and the many Gods are partly fluid concepts. Joseph Mbiti, for example, has argued that it is inappropriate to characterize traditional African religions as polytheistic, since above the many Gods there is a highest God. It is common in the Hindu world to refer to the various deities as manifestations of the one ultimate reality. The Lakota seer Black Elk also was quite clear that the various Gods are, in some sense, one God.[4]

If the plurality of the Gods should not be emphasized, neither should the unity of the God of monotheism. Officially the monotheists stress one God, yet popular piety in at least some branches of Christianity seems functionally akin to polytheism. The petition of the aid of angels and saints in popular Roman Catholicism seem to be quite similar to the invocation of gods and deified heroes in traditional Africa. And in both Catholic and Protestant churches the prayers to Jesus seem remarkably akin to the bhakti personal devotion to Lord Krishna. At the farthest end of unmitigated monotheism, in Judaism, Islam and sometimes Christianity, the Shekinah, the Qu'ran, a Jesus seem to function as subordinate divine agents or powers. If the monotheist wishes to make a clear distinction between God and lesser agents or powers, then why cannot the supposed polytheist make a similar distinction between the supreme deity and lesser divine powers? Perhaps there is a distinction between a focus on one and on many divine powers, but the contrast between monotheism and polytheism is not as stark and as definite as the monotheists have claimed.

Religious naturalism, as I understand it, suggests that the key category to be used in thinking about religion, at least in European languages, is the sacred or perhaps the divine, rather than God. The sacred is a quality of events, processes or experiences and can denote powers and agents that transcend the ordinary or the surface. God is sacred. So are the Gods. So also are certain natural events and processes. The sacred, like any quality, may take different hues in its diverse instantiations and yet has some unity among its diversity. Thus one assumes from the start that there is diversity as well as unity in the sacred. This proposal fits well with the writer's own religious naturalism, yet it can be taken as a point of discussion for traditional and for revisionary theists. Perhaps the many Goddesses and Gods of the primary peoples are the same as the angels of monotheism. In many ways they function the same way. They have power, more or less specific functions, and sometimes may be petitioned. A crucial difference between Gods and angels is that angels are clearly servants of the one high God. However when the Gods are seen as manifestations of the high God, their role is similar to that of servants. On the other hand, if you take the view of religious naturalism, the Gods are loci of the sacred in its diverse aspects, while God or the Divine is the unified aspect of the sacred.

Monotheism gives philosophical coherence to the world. If there is a single creator, governor, and redeemer, then there is a unity and integrity to the cosmos. The many gods of paganism seem to be constantly fighting. However, this is a narrow reading of the stories of the Gods. Only in some religious narratives, as in Homer and Hesiod, is the realm of the Gods characterized by strife. This is not the picture we receive from the stories of many of the native peoples of the earth. Indeed, this may be a factor of the struggle between the Trojans and the Hellenes or perhaps between the earlier Goddess religion and the later conquering tribes with their patriarchal ways. Besides, if we want to see a picture of strife, we need look no further than the warlike Yahweh of the premonarchical times. Again, the pictures of the pagans and of the one true God are overdrawn.

However, the world has varying degrees of unity and disunity (following William James and some recent ecologists, it does seem to be a patchwork). If one takes the suggestion that the Gods of the early peoples can be assimilated to the angels of the monotheists, then the one God can be seen as governing the multiple servants of the High God. On the other hand, if one takes the more radical speculation of my own religious naturalism, the world is a mosaic, and we do not need a unifying principle beyond the mosaic itself. In any case, we need not reject the religious paths of the primary peoples just because they seem to have many Gods and Goddesses.

The Goddess. Many of the current attempts at reviving the old ways include the return of the Goddess.

Perhaps it would help to know the position from which I have started. My feeling has always been that the divine transcends gender, that God is neither male nor female. This seems fundamental. However, I have been listening to feminist reflection on religion and have tried to be open to what seems to be creative movements. It seems that the gender neutrality of the divine is not the last word in the matter.

If indeed there are strong elements of patriarchy in the images and institutions of religion, and I believe there are, then a stance of neutrality leaves this bias unchallenged and reinforces it by leaving it unchallenged.

We do use symbols, images and metaphors for the divine. Surely images of Mother, Sister and Feminine Lover are just as appropriate for the divine as images of Father, Brother and Masculine Lover. Further, these symbols are as inadequate and need to be transcended as do any symbols. We are probably at the moment of Kairos when these female symbols can be received and need to be used.

If the divine is a quality, as I have suggested, then it can be a quality of the physical and, indeed, of the sexual. Perhaps one of the reasons for some of our personal and cultural neuroses is that we separate sex and religion, that we do not combine prayer and our love lives.

As a religious naturalist I have a strong sense of the inadequacy of all religious symbols. Nevertheless, they have a place, and a very important place, in both our cultural and our personal lives. She who is speaks and bodies forth with power today.

Bodies and spirits. Some of us find it difficult to believe in unembodied spirits. That would be superstition. Others of us find it hard to believe that bodies could be gods. That would be sheer idolatry.

However, suppose that our major religious category is not "god" or "spirit," but "the sacred" or "the divine." As a quality or adjective, there is much less of a problem in conceiving of a material organism or process as having a divine quality. Further, if there are spirits, one or more of them might be divine also.[5]

Furthermore, correlative to the sacred is "veneration," rather than "worship." In official Roman Catholic theology a person is allowed to have worship (*latria*) only for God, but to have veneration (*dulia*) for the saints. A monotheist has trouble worshipping more than one God or worshipping anything with a body. However, "veneration" of a tree does not detract from worship of God. Veneration need not be exclusive nor anti-material.

Animal deities. Some of the old ways had theriomorphic deities. When encountered this can be a further stumbling block to a serious encounter with the primary religions. In addition to the issue of idolatry, that is, of identifying God with a finite existent, and the apparent trapping of the spiritual within the physical, we have the additional factor that animals have generally been considered to be inferior to humans, often with a focus on inferior rationality or morality.

Two comments can be made. In the first place serious thought should be given to the alleged inferiority of animals. Clearly animals are different. Indeed, each species is different from all of the others. In many respects, difference, not inferiority, is the category which should be employed. An ascription of inferiority can easily lead to a justification for domination and mistreatment. To be sure, animals are inferior to us in many ways, but this is an aspect of difference. By the same token, we are inferior to animals in other ways.

Where two species or individuals differ, one species or individual may be said to be superior in respect to the difference. I am larger than the male Northern Cardinal in the horse chestnut tree, and he can call more clearly and beautifully. I am superior in size, and he is superior in song. For this type of superiority "difference" is a better term. Furthermore, for any superiority on the part of one species, there is often a corresponding superiority on the other. I can camouflage myself to hide from or make weapons to kill my enemies. However, the cardinal can warn his enemies off or can fly from them. It is a trade-off. Neither of us is clearly superior in relation to our enemies, except possibly for a moral superiority in the cardinal in that he will not kill his enemy.

To be sure, we are more rational than animals. Possibly. Rationality is a complex notion involving several intellectual skills. For example, our thinking is probably more plastic or variable, allowing for more novelty than that of other animals, but this strength has a corresponding weakness. Plasticity allows the possibility of error. To focus on morality, we are capable of more freely chosen or habitual moral behavior than most other animals, but at the same time are capable of more immoral behavior.

The second comment is that most indigenous people do not identify the one monotheistic God with an animal. Often the animal or plant is a manifestation of a God or of the Divine in general. There is a difference between identity and manifestation. The general comments on the relation of "spirit" and "body" hold here.

Finally, religious naturalism suggests that the old ways can best be appropriated not as the worship of many Gods in nature, but as the veneration of and reception to the divine quality of some or all aspects of the rest of the natural world.

Prescientific modes of thought. The religious ways of the primary peoples are often rejected as basically prescientific. This is a complex question and I can only sketch some tentative solutions. These issues should not be sidestepped, however.

In the first place many apparently unscientific practices of the primary peoples achieve results which are not explainable with current scientific theories, but scientific theories could in principle be developed to account for them. Many healing practices, herbalism and acupuncture for example, have a high rate of success, as far as we can tell from the evidence. Some of the cures or mitigations are not fully understood by current scientific knowledge, but we can envision the direction research could take and the fair possibility of achieving such understanding. The cures seem legitimate. We have here cases of scientific thought not yet caught up with the facts. No major revolution in our understanding of science will probably be indicated by successful pursuit of scientific investigation in these areas.

More difficult are cases, such as shamanism, which do seem to run counter to our scientific notions. Here there is a genuine tension between pulls in opposing directions. On the one hand it is well to give up a naive notion of the superiority of science as a closed system, especially with the corollary relegation of other cultures to the limbo of inferior intellect. On the other hand there are values to the pursuit of intelligence and careful evidence which we neglect at our peril. Some of Aldo Leopold's most significant environmental insights came as the result of his careful attention to the facts as he could best discern them.[6]

It is very important to understand that scientific theories are extrapolations from observations and experiments. Unconsidered variables may very well make the theories inapplicable to regions not yet observed. My own scientific understanding does not encourage me to anticipate that I could be visited by animals or birds in the flesh if I waited on a mountain for a vision. However, it would be foolish of me to maintain that such a visit would not occur. Vertebrates have greater awareness of us and are ready to communicate on more levels than Western moderns often are prone to credit.

In addition much occurs in dreams. It would be foolish to dismiss all dreams as subjective in the sense of arbitrary and unsubstantiated. I have come to enough insight and resolution of conflicts in my dreams not to dismiss their significance automatically. Further, when a wolf appears to my student, while I do not think that either a physical wolf or a spirit of wolf (defining spirit narrowly) visited her, it would be narrow-minded of me to say that the cultural and experiential materials which wolves supply had no objective bearing on her vision. Indeed, viewed generously, it was the spirit of the wolf that came to her.

Finally, the old ways should not be taken as simply either pro- or anti-scientific. The issues are far more complex. We can, at certain times, say that in our best judgment a cognitive judgment can be reached on scientific grounds. For example, I find it reasonable to affirm that levitation does not occur. However, I would not immediately ostracize a Hindu philosopher who assumed it was a matter of course. And if I found Jesus walking the streets, I would look for the mirrors or at least into my psyche. Having made such judgments, we need to remember that thoughtful and rational people, operating from different epistemic principles, could arrive at different judgments. While holding fast to our judgments, if need be, we need not automatically cast them out into the limbo of intellectual darkness.

Time. It is customary to distinguish the Biblical and later Western outlooks from other worldviews by distinguishing between a linear as opposed to a cyclical view of time or history. Indeed this distinction goes back at least to Augustine. The linear view of time has, of course, been secularized in the modern view of progress and in the Marxist dialectic of history. These linear views are usually accompanied with the assumption of the superiority of the linear view as supporting a forward-looking dynamism.

Perhaps it is time to take a new look at the cyclical view. There is much routine and repetition in our daily lives. The linear view treats this as drudgery, chores to be finished, perhaps derogated as women's work or for the janitors or clerical staff, so that the rest of us can get on with the real work. Changing images will not bring new life to maintenance or nurturance functions, but a linear view of time can easily exacerbate their drudgery. One problem with a linear view is that when a forward movement is frustrated, everything that leads up to it seems pointless. Also the present seems to have its value only from the future.[7]

Much of our life is a dynamic movement among myriad things. It is inevitable that much of our work will be cyclical or nearly so. Some of it is very repetitious, like washing dishes or driving to work. Some of it is quasi-cyclical, as in exercise or rest or in correcting a personal or social pendulum swing. Much of this is the yin-yang restoration of a balance or a different tack in a forward movement. None of this is *ipso facto* meaningless.

Many primary peoples give great importance to the practice of the dance and to the dance as a major image for life. In a dance there is value in both the repetition and the innovation, in both dancing alone, as couples, or in a group. The dance can help give significance to both the individual and the group. It makes reconciliation as important as competition. Normally there are no winners in a dance. For a bioregionalist view a dance celebrates place, not journey.

The dance is not the only appropriate metaphor. Conflict and decay are realities, as well as boredom and frustration, loneliness and despair. There is a need for hope as well as for repetition. We need a plurality of metaphors for life. But surely in our time there is a need to restore the significance of the view that when a forward movement is frustrated, everything that leads up to it is not pointless. The present has a value of its own which does not derive from the future. The dying infant has its value.[8]

Sacred Places. To recapture the spirit of the Older ways, we shall need a sense of sacred places: trees, rocks, prairies, rivers and mountains. Part of the problem is that we do not wish to tie down the sacred to one place. If God is everywhere, we say, then God cannot be localized. On the other hand, we build sanctuaries where we expect and often do have a sense of the presence of the divine. If we can go to special places, built by humans, which are designated as sacred, surely we can go to special places, shaped naturally, which are recognized as sacred. Indeed, the human and the natural can cooperate, as when tradition or an act of consecration acknowledge the sacred place. There is a strong monothesitic tradition of cutting down the sacred groves. What we need is to realize that to have a sense of sacred place is not tree worship, in the sense of confusing the one Creator with a plant, but is rather the acknowledgment of the awesome, of the overriding and overwhelming. To recover some of the meaningfulness of the primal traditions we need to rethink the notion of sacred place. For a religious naturalist it is not hard to recover the notion of sacred place. The religious naturalist is, to begin with, open to sacred qualities of some experiences. Sometimes this sacred dimension will be especially evoked by the qualities of a special location. For a theist there can be Beth-els, places associated with epiphanies. There is no theoretical reason, if the sacred dimension of life is recognized, for the sacredness of certain places not to be recognized by theists or religious naturalists.

When the sacred is recognized there is a very strong motive to preserve, even defend it. For this reason the recognition and also the nurture of these experiences have a key place in the recovery of an appreciative stance towards the special places of this world.

Gary Snyder has a word of wisdom about sacred places. We have lost much. Some places we can once again find to be sacred ground if we slow down, walk and listen. However, we may have to wait until the places speak to us. Our ears are weak. But if we wait some of these places may yet name themselves to us.[9]

There is a danger of idolatry, of course. The Nazis sacralized place, blood and soil. However, monotheists can idolize the finite as well as neo-pagans.

Ritual. Dolores LaChapelle has given thoughtful attention to reestablishing ritual. Ed McGaa Eagle Man, has devoted much care to making the essentials of Lakota ceremony available to white audiences.[10]

Some of these rituals are obstacles to observers. Sometimes a person of one tradition can find rituals from another heritage to be alien. Sometimes a person from the Enlightenment or a puritan tradition will disdain ritual in principle. However, the rituals of nature are no more of an obstacle than any set of rituals. As we come to recognize the importance of ritual in human life the importance of the work of people like LaChapelle and McGaa will become more appreciated.

III.

Should we appropriate? There is a very serious objection to this entire project of learning from old ways. It has come from a variety of sources and it is often presented in a very thoughtful manner. The general drift is that it is disrespectful of native peoples to treat their ideas as "resources." Also, when an idea is taken from one culture it loses its meaning when set in a new context. "Cultural cannibalism" is what Greta Gaard calls it.

Particular mention may be made of Greta Gaard's objection to the use of native American ideas by ecofeminists. A similar objection is made by Ward Churchill of the American Indian Movement to appropriations by environmentalists of native ideas and rituals. Gerald Larson in similar fashion inveighs against mining Asian traditions for environmental thinking.[11]

My response to these objections is first that seeking to learn from another is most respectful. It is a recognition that one has something to learn and that the other has important insights which need to be explored. To be sure, such learning can be done arrogantly or flippantly. However, the danger of abuse does not mean that you should not do it.

In the second place, the thing to do is to admit that we are transforming these ideas. We are not "going native." Rather we are developing new ways, hopefully, creative ways. There is much precedent for one culture to learn from another. Chinese, Korean, Japanese, Indonesian, modern African, Arabic, Jewish, European, Plains Indian, indeed, most cultures have learned from other cultures and, in so doing, transformed what they learned, often in creative ways.

There are understandable historical reasons for the self-imposed cultural provincialism, including the frequent temptation to ethnocentrism. My proposal is that we overcome this provincialism, not because the Others are right and we are wrong, but because we all have much to learn from each other.

Postscript

The particular religious outlook which I have developed, and even propose for public consideration, is a kind of religious naturalism. I want to make it clear that listening to the old way does not require religious naturalism. However, I am a religious naturalist, and I do have an obligation to my listeners to help them locate the place from where I listen.

There are a variety of religious naturalisms. Although an adequate theoretical definition is not easy, we can say that most religious naturalisms involve a denial and an affirmation. Negatively there is a rejection, tentative in my case, of a transcendent deity. Part of the difficulty in making this rejection precise is that some sophisticated articulations of theism have a strong sense of the indwelling of God in the natural world so that a simple rejection of supernaturalism will not suffice. Positively, most religious naturalisms acknowledge a sacred aspect of this world to which a religious attitude is appropriate. Perhaps you could be cautious and say that there are aspects of this world which are sufficiently analogous to what has traditionally been called "sacred" that attitudes of recognition, of gratitude, of being dumbfounded, or some similar attitudes towards these aspects can be called religious in a broad sense.

My own version of religious naturalism I have dubbed a "minimalist vision of the transcendent." I have elaborated this in a book of the same title, especially the first chapter. In explaining it a useful term is "sacred." There are occasions which many people would call sacred. There is not so much a common essence to these experiences, but rather a cluster, a family of experiences. My pluralism suggests that rather than "*the* Sacred" lurking behind these occasions, we may appropriately use an adjective like "sacred" to describe them. There is no clear boundary around the sacred, but rather an extended family whose border-line cases may cause frustration to those who wish for necessary and sufficient marks for the proper denotation of this term.

If it is any help to the reader, I trace my spiritual genealogy back at least as far as Spinoza. My general world view owes much to American pragmatism and process thought, although without the unique, ontologically supreme (supreme even in relatedness and temporality) being or process of the latter. Definitely this is not a mechanistic world-view. It is not necessarily a materialistic world view, either, although the overlap is so close to a dynamic-relational materialism that it is virtually a materialism, a half-sister at least. More recently I have been moving towards John Dewey's religious naturalism, although with a deeper appreciation of the nurturing matrix of specific religious traditions. Lesser known thinkers who have also strongly influenced my own brand of naturalism are the Chicago thinkers Henry Nelson Wieman, Bernard Meland and Bernard Loomer. Those interested may consult relevant passages in my *The Minimalist Vision of Transcendence*, Volume Two of the forthcoming, *The Chicago School of Theology—Pioneers in Religious Inquiry*, which I am coediting, and my article "Bernard Meland on the New Formative Imagery of Our Time" in *Zygon*, Vol. 30 (September, 1995).

NOTES

1. My understanding of dialogue has been deepened by my reading of Gadamer. See Delwin Brown, *Boundaries of Our Habitations: Tradition and Theological Construction* (Albany: State University of New York Press, 1994), p. 37; Hans-Georg Gadamer, *Truth and Method*, 2nd, rev. ed., trans. by Joel Weinsheimer and Donald G. Marshall (New York: The Continuum Publishing Company, 1994), esp. pp. 265–380; Jerome A. Stone, *The Minimalist Vision of Transcendence: A Naturalist Philosophy of Religion* (Albany: State University of New York Press, 1992), chap. 4.

2. Writings about the recovery of older or the creation of new traditions in women's spirituality are too numerous to begin to list. My own reading has been influenced by the essays in Part IV of *Womanspirit Rising: A Feminist Reader in Religion*, ed. by Carol P. Christ and Judith Plaskow (New York: Harper Collins Publishers, 1979, 1992); Elinor W. Gadon, *The Once and Future Goddess: A Symbol of Our Time* (San Francisco: Harper & Row Publishers, 1989); Starhawk, "Power, Authority, and Mystery: Ecofeminism and Earth-based Spirituality," in *Reweaving the World: The Emergence of Ecofeminism*, ed. by Irene Diamond and Gloria Feman Orenstein (San Francisco: Sierra Club Books, 1990), pp. 75–86; Charlene Spretnak, *Lost Goddesses of Early Greece: A Collection of Pre-Hellenic Myths* (Boston: Beacon Press, 1981 (1978)); Spretnak, *States of Grace: The Recovery of Meaning in the Postmodern Age* (San Francisco: Harper Collins Publishers, 1991), chaps. 1, 5, 6 and Appendices.

Appreciative criticism from a woman who seeks to revision the Christian traditions can be found in Rosemary Radford Ruether, *Sexism and God-Talk: Toward a Feminist Theology* (Boston: Beacon Press, 1993 (1983)) and *Gaia and God: An Ecofeminist Theology of Earth Healing* (San Francisco: Harper Collins, Publishers, 1992), pp. 144–155.

3. Jerome A. Stone, "Broadening Care, Discerning Worth: The Environmental Contributions of Minimalist Religious Naturalism," *Process Studies*, Vol. 22, No. 4 (Winter 1993), pp. 194–203; "Caring For the Web of Life: Towards a Public Ecotheology," *Religious Experience and Ecological Responsibility*, ed. by Donald A. Crosby and Charley D. Hardwick, (New York: Peter Lang, 1996).

4. John Mbiti, *Concepts of God in Africa*, (New York: Praeger Publishing Company, 1970).

5. See Paula Gunn Allen, "The Woman I Love is a Planet," in Diamond and Orenstein, *Reweaving the World*, p. 56.

6. See Sandra Harding, *The Science Question in Feminism* (Ithaca, NY: Cornell University Press, 1986); "The Method Question," *Hypatia*, Vol. 2 (Fall, 1987), pp. 19–35; "Is Science Multicultural? Challenges, Resources, Opportunities, Uncertainties" in David Theo Goldberg, ed., *Multiclturalism: A Reader* (London: Blackwell's, 1995); and Lynn Hankinson Nelson, *Who Knows: From Quine to a Feminist Empiricism* (Philadelphia: Temple University Press, 1990), esp. the Introduction and chap. 6. Nelson wishes to develop a theory of evidence within a holistic epistemology. I find her work to be a helpful antidote to the neo-pragmatists who throw out a theory of evidence along with the notions of foundations of evidence and epistemic privilege.

7. For a thoughtful position on how a cyclical view of time has a stronger pragmatic adequacy than the religious and the widespread secular apocalyptic versions of the linear view, see Starhawk, in Carol P. Christ and Judith Plaskow, *Womanspirit Rising*, p. 78

8. For comments on dance, see "The Ceremonial Motion of Indian Time: Long Ago, So Far," in *The Sacred Hoop: Recovering the Feminine in American Indian Traditions* (Boston: Beacon Press, 1986), pp. 147–154, Dolores LaChapelle, *Sacred Land, Sacred Sex, Rapture of the Deep* (Durango, CO: Kivaki Press, 1988), Gary Snyder, "The Same Old Song and Dance," in *The Practice of the Wild* (San Francisco: North Point Press, 1990), pp. 48–53.

9. Gary Snyder, *op. cit.*, "Good, Wild, Sacred," pp. 78–96.

10. Dolores LaChapelle, *op. cit.*; Ed McGaa Eagle Man, *Mother Earth Spirituality: Native American Paths to Healing Ourselves and Our World* (San Francisco: Harper Collins Publishers, 1990), and *Rainbow Tribe: Ordinary People Journeying on the Red Road* (San Francisco: Harper Collins Publishers, 1992). See also Allen, *op. cit.*, Sam Gill, *Native American Religious Action: A Performance Approach to Religion* (Columbia: University of South Carolina Press, 1987); Starhawk, p. 77, *op. cit.*

11. Churchill Ward, "Another Dry White Season," *Z Magazine* 6 (October 10, 1993), pp. 43–48; Gaard, Greta. "Ecofeminism and Native American Cultures: Pushing the Limits of Cultural Impoverishment?" in *Ecofeminism: Women, Animals, Nature*, ed. by Greta Gaard (Philadelphia: Temple University Press, 1993), pp. 295–314; Larson, Gerald James. "'Conceptual Resources' in South Asia for 'Environmental Ethics,'" in *Nature in Asian Traditions of Thought: Essays in Environmental Philosophy*, ed. by J. Baird Callicott and Roger T. Ames, (Albany: State University of New York Press, 1989), pp. 267–278; reprinted in *Environmental Ethics: Divergence and Convergence*, ed. by Susan J. Armstrong and Richard G. Botzler (New York: McGraw-Hill, 1993).

GORDON KAUFMAN AS A LIBERAL THEOLOGIAN:
An Aesthetic Appraisal

Edgar A. Towne

In the current political and theological situation the term "liberal" has acquired a pejorative connotation. In both *milieux*—political and theological—distinct pejorative connotations are allowed to stand for the complex array of meanings this term has acquired historically in each context. In the United States of America both the Democratic Party and the mainstream churches are struggling to overcome the destructive effects of these connotations upon their reputations as liberals. To characterize a perspective by the "L-word" in this situation, is to anticipate scoring points against that perspective.

An aesthetic perspective brings public discussion into a softer focus because it considers the *process* of coming to conviction as well as the *conversation* among diverse convictions. Liberal convictions are still vital in the mainstream churches as well as in the nation. It would be unreasonable to expect the discussion in the churches to be entirely free of the polemics characteristic of public discussion that center in the distinction between "liberal" and "conservative." After all, churches are human associations with their own politics; and they utilize the resources of the culture as they participate as "citizens" in our constitutional democracy. Both nation and churches can benefit from clarification of the meaning of "liberal" in these contexts, and from an aesthetic appraisal of theological constructions that might rightfully bear this name. Such an appraisal offers new ways to appreciate not only how we differ, but also why we differ.

Among other things, an aesthetic perspective keeps prominently in view the embodied quality of lived experience, characteristic of radical empiricism, and it attends to the recursive agility of the human mind and imagination that enables those constructions that are products of what Paul Tillich called the moral, cultural, and religious functions of life. Gordon D. Kaufman's theology is an appropriate object of study because his commitments are liberal and modernist while at the same time his focus on "imaginative construction" suggests postliberal and postmodern sensibilities that he, nevertheless, seems unable fully to embrace.

In the first part of this paper I will discuss the liberal perspective in the political and religious contexts, and I will identify "autonomy" as an indispensable element of liberalism significant for the Christian witness and for the nation's "general welfare." In the second part I will show how "modernism" as historicism is an enduring legacy of liberalism when chastened by a postmodern mood. In the third part I will attempt to show further the contribution an aesthetic perspective can make to theological understanding.

I.

As a cultural legacy of the modern period, liberalism is by all accounts a complex phenomenon. Claude Welch has observed the ambiguities of the term.[1] It might connote a spirit of inquiry, a program of action, a complex of ideas. Criticism may focus on one or more of these meanings. A complex of ideas (liberty, equality before the law, an open society, tolerance, morality) led to a program of action (the revolution and the Constitution) in America. Undoubtedly, the ethos described by Immanuel Kant as "Enlightenment" informed the work of the founding fathers.

Kant wrote, "Enlightenment is man's exodus from his self-incurred tutelage. Tutelage is the inability to use one's understanding without the guidance of another person . . . 'Dare to know' (*sapere aude*)! Have the courage to use your own understanding; this is the motto of the Enlightenment."[2] Undoubtedly, too, this sentiment has informed liberal theology as its defining principle, the principle of *autonomy*, which permits a non-alienated respect for tradition. Presently, in the United States this principle is under pressure by theologians and sociologists, who construe it to be an appeal to the *individual* bereft of relations to a past or to a community and its texts. On the terrain of public discourse, flattened by dichotomizing polemics, this construal impugns the moral integrity of the liberal voice in politics and theology by obscuring its rootedness in the ethos of our culture, in the community we share. Michael L. Westmoreland-White, for example, documents the rootedness of the human rights ethos in the biblical tradition and the synthesis of Free Church Puritan teaching with Enlightenment liberalism.[3]

William Earnest Hocking reminds us the liberal ethos has its roots in the notion of the "free man" in Greece and Rome, able to devote his time to pursuits of his own choosing, including public life, and the life of inquiry, "free, *liber*, then free in his manners, then free in his giving, then free in his way of thinking." In the course of development in western Europe, the moral imagination extended the notion.

> .... liberalism is disposed to spread liberty: it is the free man demanding his freedom for every man, on the assumption that every man is inwardly free, in the primary sense of freedom, or capable of becoming so. Liberalism is the belief that all men are potential liberals, and the program for realizing this potency.[4]

Hocking provides a perceptive discussion of the paradoxes of liberalism: "shall the liberal be liberal also to the illiberal? If its principle is universal, it must be. But on the other hand the opposition is not prevented by its own principles from moving to annihilate liberalism."[5] This paradox makes a critically-adequate construal of liberalism much needed in the present situation, for the ruthlessness of terrorism threatens to subvert the liberal ethos.

Voices calling for civility in our public discourse are appealing on the ground of this liberal ethos. So Richard Rorty points out that our duty is not to establish a methodological and epistemological foundation for religious or political claims, but "to talk to each other, to converse about our views of the world, to use persuasion rather than force, to be tolerant of diversity, to be contritely fallibilist."[6] Rorty provides a valuable public service when he defends the Enlightenment hopes that created the Western democracies, who need not claim—he says they *were* not claiming—that theirs is a way of life "objectively" superior to all others.[7] And while he acknowledges that the vision behind our way of life has an ethical base, he points out that loyalty to our own traditions is "morality enough," that we need be "responsible only to [our] own traditions, and not to the moral law as well."[8] This argument resembles the way George Lindbeck suggests the postmodern mood encourages attention to the texts that shape forms of life, and it is "rhetorical force rooted in forms of life that gives [Homer's gods and the physicist's quarks] different cognitive status."[9] The liberal vision of the rule of law under the Constitution, its text, *is a form of life* whose status as such is obscured and its voice crowded out by partisan voices, both political and theological, that misrepresent it or subject it (and morality) to a theological or epistemological hegemony.[10]

Gordon Kaufman shows he shares this liberal vision when he suggests his model of theology is "democratic, open, and public," a conversation where "all participants are accepted on equal terms," and

> ... each wishes to contribute whatever possible from the richness of experience and the perspective on life which has come to him or her, and will be listened to respectfully and attentively; all expect to learn from the others through appropriating with appreciation what they have to offer, and through opening themselves willingly to probing questions and sharp criticism.[11]

He showed this also when he repudiated what he considered his foundationalist treatment of revelation in earlier work. As is well-known, he came to view theology as a human work, its concepts a kind of imaginative construction.

> ... these concepts have been created and developed in and through human processes of reflection on life and interpretation of experience. It is only because some persons at certain times and places found it useful and meaningful and perhaps even necessary to speak of "God's revelation," in order to make sense of the life and history which they were undergoing, that these terms and concepts were developed and employed within the human sphere at all.[12]

These citations show Kaufman is a liberal as Bernard E. Meland has characterized liberalism's defining trait as "a will to be liberated from the coercion of external controls and a consequent concern with inner motivation"; theologically liberalism is "a form of religious thought that establishes religious inquiry on the basis of a norm other than the authority of a tradition."[13] These are authentic commitments of liberalism, not to be repudiated. Other matters such as programs of action, complexes of ideas (including *accounts* of ethical and theological construction, and of the authority of traditions and texts) are negotiable. But it is the claim of liberalism, at least in the biblical and Christian context, that autonomy is the necessary condition of both faith and ethics.

II.

Bernard E. Meland distinguished three stages in the development of theological liberalism, the period of rationalism or the Enlightenment, romanticism, and modernism opening out upon a period of "renewal of concern with the major themes of the Christian faith, following from a critique of certain historical liberal presuppositions."[14] Each of these periods produced liberal theologies whose constructions came to be criticized.

The *rational stage* in theological liberalism followed upon two centuries of fratricidal religious strife in which Europe's population was decimated by war and plague. The search for "universal truths" of religion not only responded to the Baconian view of science and the increasing awareness of non-western faiths, but it also was a practical intellectual strategy designed to mitigate theological strife among the religions. Ironically, 19th and 20th century fundamentalism continues to espouse this early liberal commitment to truth in propositional form, which in the modern period was well-calculated to precipitate the modernist-fundamentalist controversies. During the *romantic stage* in theological liberalism attention shifted to religious experience both as a way to do justice to diverse religious identities as objects of study and as a type of apologetic. Here the rational-universal theme was combined with the experiential with the expectation that the individual, who as a locus of authority (and since Kant of the "a priori categories of understanding," and since Schleiermacher of the "feeling of absolute dependence") could with the aid of faith know God, if not in a publicly-demonstrable way, at least in "passionate subjectivity" (Kierkegaard) or moral action.

During the *modern stage* of theological liberalism the sense of the historical situatedness of all human inquiry was acknowledged to mean not only that experience makes its contribution to a person's knowledge, but also that the social and cultural situation, including language, influences that knowledge and even that experience. It is the recognition of this historical relativity, and the success of the natural sciences, that makes liberals also *modernists*. This meant to the inquiring liberal mind that purported knowledge in any age would itself be informed by the historical legacy bequeathed it by its past—linguistic forms, world-picture, dominant images. This meant that the "texts" or "classics" of a religious tradition and their truth-claims were not only shapers of religious identity, but also could be examined for the way these claims showed the influence of their cultural situation. Here, of course, the principle of autonomy might be expected to clash with traditional claims for the authority of those texts. The modernist, therefore, is the person who welcomes this insight into past and present knowledge—including his or her own.

The theological work of Gordon Kaufman, of course, exhibits this modernist sensibility; for he not only welcomes the legacy of the natural sciences whose methods are devised in the name of the autonomous critical mind (albeit in conversation and community), and whose knowledge is intended to be revisable by those methods; but he also construes his own theological vision with the assistance of that knowledge. This is, presumably, one aspect of what he means by "imaginative construction." So he says in *In Face of Mystery*:

> God is not thought of as some being outside the world but rather as a particular form of creativity and ordering going on within the world, namely that serendipitous ordering which has given rise (among other things) to the evolution of life on planet Earth and the emergence of human beings, and which continues to sustain us and to move us toward a more profound humanization.[15]

Notice this liberal-modernist sensibility exploits the reflexive quality of mind by which the self is able to be aware of his or herself (in this case) believing. This is a form of what Meland called the liberal interest in "inner motivation." The mind, of course, is also able to distinguish religious faith from theological reflection (in general or upon faith), lived experience from its construal by philosophy or theology.[16] The former is "concrete," the latter "abstract," and the concrete *contains* the abstract. In identifying God with one or more aspects of "the world," which for him is also a construction, Kaufman shows that he *intends* the reality of God in a significant sense other than that of its intention or connotation as a mental construct. It seems reasonable to assume for purposes of our inquiry that this *intention* contributes to the capacity of the concept-symbol "God" to perform its relativizing, orienting, and humanizing function for human individuals and communities, as Kaufman affirms. As Shirley Jackson Case and Shailer Mathews made clear,[17] people who have believed in God in other historical periods have also intended the reality of God *in some sense that communicated an efficacy in their life.*

The Chicago liberals also realized that in any particular historical period conflicting "knowledges" could be identified, manifest with varying degrees of tolerance or conflict. This meant they construed the so-called "essence" of Christian faith to be a matter of life, not a matter of language only. They regarded life as a practical task informed by the language of faith. Doctrine was a part of life as an abstract element of life, which is concrete. They made this recursive move, but the fundamentalists, who remained on the linguistic level, did not. Consequently, they regarded the liberals as heretics. However, these liberals regarded themselves as "orthodox," in their reformulation of doctrine.[18] Another way to put this point is to say that the fundamentalists were unable to appreciate the "kernel-husk" metaphor so popular among liberals. Adolf Harnack spoke of the "phenomena" associated with the Christian gospel as he enlarged upon the historical dimensions of his effort to identify the gospel as the Christian norm, an effort he said would help "us to grasp what is essential in the phenomena, and to distinguish kernel and husk."[19] By means of this metaphor and its more abstract counterpart, the distinction between content and form, modernist liberals defended their integrity as Christians, if they did not succeed in proving their orthodoxy. So it was no surprise to them, though it greatly pained them, to be at the center of the fundamentalist-modernist conflict.[20]

The dynamics of the "conversation" represented by this controversy are not unlike those of the conversation we are now having, and the challenge is to prevent a reversion to the divergent premises of the old conflict that never met in conversation because they passed on different planes. William J. Hynes pointed out the "psychogenetic" dimension of Case's functionalism, his concern with the "dynamic human dimension," the "inner impulse" of religious faith as lived, which implicitly appealed to the elemental level of human experience as embodied.[21] This meant that the kernel-husk metaphor could function (when it did so) dynamically, and so *spontaneously*, to mediate a perceived dissonance or discontinuity in religious belief. The co-existence of diverse knowledges is consistent with this. Religious belief gains in "plausibility" the more it is coherent with other knowledge, as the modernist-historicist principle implies. The autonomy principle, as we have seen, divests traditions and texts of any *intrinsic* authority claimed for them. But it does not require the repudiation of tradition as such; so the resolution of discontinuity is a matter of continued participation in a religious community. The Chicago School theologians' work implied that here, too, spontaneity may be involved in the mediation. This mediation might be effected dynamically in the believer's life by a metaphoric process. The effect of this is to construe the world to be more *open* than modernism in its over-confident moods would concede. While every knowledge is influenced by cultural and linguistic forms, that influence does not constitute control in such a way that they or new knowledge compel belief or unbelief. They anticipated the current recognition of co-existing diversities in human communities (the "other"), co-existing communities near and far ("multiculturalism"), in sum "pluralism." New and old styles co-existing together in architecture and the arts and in modes of thought forced this dogmatic modernism into a repentant mood and a greater openness to the novel, the incongruent, the dissonant, the many. This sensibility is what is designated by *postmodernism*. Bernard M. Loomer's discussion of the "stature" and ambiguity of God expresses this theme in a way not without pathos, even for liberals.[22]

In sharing modernist sensibilities Gordon Kaufman embraces the liberal ideal of autonomy. "*Act! Take responsibility for yourselves!*" he writes, ". . . *so as to sustain and strengthen the moral fabric!*"[23] Nevertheless, he considers a failure to adopt a postmodern, constructivist understanding of our historicity "arbitrary and authoritarian" from the perspective of "the common experience and understanding of life and culture which have become pervasive in modernity."[24] Modernity requires the faiths "to reconsider the symbolic structures within and through which they have grasped and interpreted human life . . ."[25] The dogmatic tone here requires those of us in conversation with Kaufman about theological construction to examine modernist *versus* postmodernist views of the influence of language and world-picture upon dissonance and discontinuity in belief. Likewise, his work needs examination in view of the spontaneity in belief just discussed. For, as we have seen, it is the element of spontaneity that accounts for diversity. These are distinct questions that can be discussed in a postmodern mood without foreclosing or founding epistemologies.

I would suggest that attention to this spontaneity in relation to construction can help us comprehend why it is difficult to hear one another adequately in the theological conversation, how and why we differ. For example, Robert Neville, in saying that "[t]he most significantly 'liberal' of Kaufman's claims is that theology is not intended to refer to independent realities such as God" and that he "abandons naive religious realism,"[26] presupposes a notion of the independent reality of God that he associates with orthodoxy and implies liberalism cannot affirm. Kaufman, of course, does intend the independent reality of God. William Placher, however, grasps Kaufman's intention, but he also complains of his functionalism that, as players in a good basketball game create something beyond themselves, "[a]nalogously, Kaufman sees no need 'to think in terms of some "cosmic person" out there somewhere'; his God lies in the mystery of the cosmic process itself."[27] Neither Neville nor Placher has given an account of their own believing that discloses how they resolve dissonance and discontinuity, if they can. Their own believing is out of sight, and on the face of their criticism here they cement linguistic form and content together as fundamentalism does. Kaufman's believing is in sight, and he gives an account of his believing—the *spontaneity* of his faith in the same God and the same Christ they worship.

By contrast, seemingly, radical empiricists like Jerome Stone can carry on a conversation with Kaufman on the level of *controlled construction* questioning not the appropriateness of his construal of "God" to the Christian norm, but the adequacy of his characterization of that in the natural order which enables "specific experiences of unexpected and unmanageable resources and healing."[28] While the Christian norm is claimed to require a metaphysics compatible with a God whose unity is personal, Stone favors Kaufman's construal of that unity as a regulative ideal. He prefers to construe "God" or "the divine" to refer to what is common to a plurality of "situationally transcendent" experiences of grace and mystery beyond our control "in sanctuary and bedroom, in terror and joy, in sacrament and prayer, in guilt and reconciliation, in forest and on sidewalks."[29] To observe the ways these two different types of conversation partners disagree with Kaufman is to see not only their differing attitude toward confessional authorities (which risks becoming a renewed modernist conflict of two dogmatisms), but also that confessionalists as well as radical empiricists are called upon in this conversation to give an account of their believing also. Of course they may not consider such a project coherent with their perspective. However, Kaufman's account of his own beliefs implies *he* is able to give an account of *their* beliefs in terms of his because he is claiming that *all* religions involve imaginative construction. And he would have to offer a construal that could be credible *to them, taking their premises into the account.* To my knowledge he has not done this. I suggest it is because he has overlooked spontaneity in construction on the first-order level of religious experience and the role of mythic and metaphorical imagination in this construction. Here Kaufman resists postmodern insights.

III.

An aesthetic perspective, of course, is implicit in the perspective of radical empiricism, which attends the testimony of the body as well of the mind, of perception as well as sensation, given both in lived experience and forms of inquiry. A self-conscious *aesthetic* approach is able to attend to this construction by focusing on five aspects of theological work: (1) imaginative construction in both lived experience and theological work, (2) spontaneity as well as control, (3) recursiveness of consciousness, (4) patterns in image and process, (5) texture and sensuousness in image and process. The first two aspects are involved as Kaufman's indebtedness to Immanuel Kant is often noted. It can be said, with Walter Capps, that Kaufman's treatment of the imagination is formal and dependent on the

First Critique, resistant to the more material interests of the Third Critique.[30] This means that while he is often involved in discussions of metaphor, he is less interested in the way metaphors bear meaning *spontaneously* in use, but more interested in using them in *controlled* construction of concepts (and symbols) in theological (human) work. Radical empiricism, with its interest in lived experience and the use of language and image on a first-order level, admits into the discussion the "voice" of the body and its contribution to spontaneity in living. Kaufman has not attended to what Kant called the "spontaneous syntheses of the Imagination" (apprehension, reproduction, recognition in a concept) that occur on a pre-reflective level of experience.[31] What Kaufman seems not to take into account—though he seems to realize it—is that imaginative construction occurs in lived experience on the first-order level in a spontaneous way.

For in *In Face of Mystery* he concedes an element of spontaneity when he approves the Christian view that faith is a gift, and when he says the "small increments of faithing" do not involve "purely intellectual activity."[32] He also locates the "ground" of *both* secular and Christian faith in what Meland called our elemental creaturehood. "[A]ll our musings and thinking and reflecting, our intentions and our deliberate acts, are grounded in and emerge out of and are the expression of these deeper levels of our being."[33] Of course, Kaufman denies we have knowledge of the pre-reflective levels of experience. Still, he has acknowledged here their influence upon our believing. And at the least, he says, "attitudes or postures of selves and communities such as faith and trust and love are *evoked* from us; they cannot be understood as simply and straightforwardly under our control, the direct expression of our own free decisions."[34] Were he to have thought in terms of a phenomenology of faith, of "non-conscious processes" rather than "subconscious ideas,"[35] Kaufman might have been more willing to find room for an element of naïveté in second and third order theological reflection.

For Kaufman what Paul Ricoeur called "second naïveté" is not possible under the conditions of cognitive dissonance. His discussion of the three "moments of awareness of meaning" in *In Face of Mystery* is in effect a phenomenology.[36] While it cannot be addressed fully here, in this discussion Kaufman quite rightly says, "both know too much: the moment of naïveté supposes itself to know how things really are; the moment of criticism knows that we can never know this."[37] What he needs to add is that the moment of criticism is limited in its knowledge in another way; it cannot know that claims to know what we cannot know are false either.

(This could be called a "postmodern" comment.) No doubt he intends his reference to mystery to cover this. On the conceptual level there is no "room" for naïveté and spontaneity, only room for an act of freedom, a commitment to trust one's concept/symbols as one is constructing them. On the elemental level of dynamic process, however, images, concepts, symbols, metaphors, analogies can be *construed* to contribute to a trust, commitment, even surrender to the realities they so fallibly signify. There is room on the level of process because that is concrete and the level of conceptualization is abstract; and, of course, this construal is a conceptual aspect of the process. There is no violation of the principle of autonomy in this construal because of the recursive and cybernetic elements of human consciousness. Autonomy in inquiry, therefore, can have access to the power of both the *logos* and the *mythos,* as Meland has employed these terms.

Naïveté is a spontaneity mediated by the body as well as thought. It is an element in the *power* of religious symbols. The point I am making has been made by Wayne Proudfoot in a careful discussion of both Kaufman and Lindbeck, seeking to show that *both* employ a strategy from the romantic stage of liberalism that seeks to protect God-talk from conflict with nonreligious statements. This strategy, of course, violates the historicist commitments of modernist liberalism. Proudfoot's analysis of Kaufman, however, is surely not wholly correct; for we have observed Kaufman's modernist commitment, and can observe it also when he says that in orienting, relativizing, and humanizing our idea of God "can perform these functions properly only when it is significantly interconnected with our (implicit and explicit) understandings of humanity and the world."[38] But Proudfoot is surely correct when he says, "This Kantian point [that our concepts and even perception are products of the human mind and its history] is not widely disputed; but that all of our concepts are human constructions does not imply that they are subject to self-conscious choice and alteration in the way that Kaufman suggests."[39] Construction occurs on the first-order level of discourse spontaneously enabling the truth-claims implicit in religious conviction to be articulated with an efficacy in lived experience, shaping a way of life. "Those claims," Proudfoot says, "provide the authority and force by which religious concepts and beliefs are able to provide a framework for orientation, critical leverage, and foci for devotion."[40] It is in this region of spontaneity that the function of images, metaphors, myths should be considered; there is a *poesis*—a making—that occurs on every level of religious discourse and the body always has its influence.

Kaufman neglects the role played by the body in theological construction. So he does not attend to primary processes except as they are in awareness. But his work in this area deserves further scrutiny.[41] For he implicates these primary processes when he writes, "the values and meanings, to which symbols of this sort call us, continue to shine through them even when we are aware that every version of them is limited and inadequate."[42] To attend appreciatively to the testimony of the body, all elements of the human sensorium, is to take an "aesthetic" perspective in the classical sense. It promises a fuller account of the influence of analogy and metaphor upon patterns and texture in image and process, which in turn contribute their efficacy to the spontaneous impulses of faith and commitment. Liberalism need not fear this fuller account.

NOTES

1. Claude Welch, *Protestant Thought in the Nineteenth Century: Volume 2, 1870–1914* (New Haven: Yale University Press, 1985), p. 222.

2. Translated and cited by Claude Welch in *Protestant Thought in the Nineteenth Century: Volume I, 1799–1870* (New Haven: Yale University Press, 1972), p. 32.

3. Michael L. Westmoreland-White, "Setting the Record Straight: Christian Faith, Human Rights, and the Enlightenment," *The Annual of the Society of Christian Ethics* (1995), pp. 75–96. Both "liberal" and "conservative" convictions are documented in mainstream churches as well as in the nation: Robert Wuthnow, *The Restructuring of American Religion* (Princeton: Princeton University Press, 1988). Poll data disclose these terms are meaningful to persons they characterize: Robert Wuthnow, "Seeking Common Ground between Evangelicals and Mainline Churches," an address to the Indiana Office of Campus Ministries at Christian Theological Seminary, April 21, 1993. He expressed his disapproval of the term, "culture wars," and its associated premise that an "insuperable metaphysical gulf" separates conservatives and liberals. Asserting there is no evidence for this claim, he attributed the conflict to "media and interest-group accounts of these controversies themselves" (pp. 3, 5–6). See James Davison Hunter, *Culture Wars: The Struggle to Define America* (New York: Basic Books, 1991).

4. William Earnest Hocking, "The Meaning of Liberalism" in David E. Roberts and Henry Pitney Van Dusen, eds., *Liberal Theology An Appraisal: Essays in Honor of Eugene William Lyman* (New York: Charles Scribner's Sons, 1942), pp. 47–49.

5. *Ibid.*, p. 49. In the present context, of course, all "men" means all men and women.

6. Richard Rorty, *Objectivity, Relativism, and Truth: Philosophical Papers, I* (Cambridge, UK: Cambridge University Press, 1991), p. 67.

7. *Ibid.*, p. 34.

8. *Ibid.*, pp. 24, 199 for these citations respectively. In our present context, of course, morality is made an issue by the so-called religious right. Since a universe of moral discourse is created by "conversation," it would not be inconsistent for pragmatists and radical empiricists to employ the language of ethics and morality in public discourse. Their challenge is to employ moral and religious language persuasively consistent with their own epistemological commitments.

9. George A. Lindbeck, "The Church's Mission to a Postmodern Culture," chapter 3 in *Postmodern Theology: Christian Faith in a Pluralist World*, ed. Frederic B. Burnham (San Francisco: Harper and Row, 1989), p. 51.

10. I have treated this matter in "The Future of Biblical Authority: Implications for Public Policy Issues," chapter 5 in *Conservative Moderate Liberal: The Biblical Authority Debate*, ed. Charles R. Blaisdell (St. Louis: CBP Press, 1990), pp. 119–36.

11. Gordon D. Kaufman, *In Face of Mystery: A Constructive Theology*, (Cambridge, MA: Harvard University Press, 1993), p. 67.

12. Gordon D. Kaufman, *An Essay on Theological Method* (Missoula: Scholars Press, rev. ed., 1979), p. 2. He was critical of his work in *Systematic Theology: A Historicist Perspective* (New York: Charles Scribner's Sons, 1968) as foundationalist, though his view of this work as a representation of the "Christian categorical scheme" is more appreciative.

13. Bernard E. Meland, "Liberalism, Theological," *Encyclopedia Britannica*, vol. 13 (Fourteenth Edition, 1968), pp. 1020–22.

14. *Ibid.*, pp. 1021–22. Meland is referring here to neo-orthodoxy, a perspective which he appreciated and to which he devoted much attention.

15. Kaufman, *In Face of Mystery*, p. 346.

16. Kaufman distinguishes three orders of theology in *An Essay on Theological Method*, pp. 37–41.

17. I have briefly documented this in "God and the Chicago School in the Theology of Bernard E. Meland," *American Journal of Theology and Philosophy*, 10 (January, 1989), pp. 5–9.

18. Bernard M. Reardon, ed., *Liberal Protestantism* (Stanford: Stanford University Press, 1968), pp. 9–11. It is easier to characterize liberalism as a spirit of inquiry and autonomy, as I have done here following Claude Welch and W. E. Hocking, than it is in terms of its content and program. Along with Reardon, William R. Hutchison, *The Modernist Impulse in American Protestantism* (Cambridge, MA: Harvard University Press, 1976) focuses on content. In the nature of the case, this will have the tendency to make orthodox formulations normative irrespective of their ability to "communicate reality." This is not so prominent in *American Protestant Thought in the Liberal Era*, ed. William R. Hutchison (Lanham, NY: University Press of America, 1968), pp. 1–16.

19. Adolf Harnack, *What Is Christianity*, trans. Thomas Bailey Saunders, (New York: Harper Torchbooks, 1957), p. 12.

20. I have discussed this conflict in "A 'Singleminded' Theologian: George Burman Foster at Chicago," *Foundations: A Baptist Journal of History and Theology*, 20 (1977), pp. 36–59, 163–80.

21. William J. Hynes, *Shirley Jackson Case and the Chicago School: The Socio-Historical Method* (Chico, CA: Scholars Press, 1981). For these terms see pp. 43, 63, 105 respectively. An influential critique of the rationalist tendency to reduce religious faiths to the abstraction, "religions," is Wilfred Cantwell Smith, *The Meaning and End of Religion* (San Francisco: Harper and Row, 1978).

22. Bernard M. Loomer, "The Size of God," *American Journal of Theology and Philosophy*, 8 (January & May, 1987), pp. 20–51. A helpful account of postmodernism in its diverse forms is Michael W. Messmer, "Making Sense of/with Postmodernism," *Soundings*, 68 (1985), pp. 404–26.

23. Kaufman, *In Face of Mystery*, pp. 202, 203, italics are Kaufman's. In a postmodern way he speaks of "a cybernetic complexification within action which results from growing consciousness of the conditions required for responsible human life to be sustained." One may compare Heinz von Foerster's "Act always so as to increase [sic] the number of choices" in "On Constructing a Reality" in *The Invented Reality: Contributions to Constructivism*, ed. Paul Watzlawick (New York: W.W. Norton and Company, 1984), p. 60.

24. Kaufman, *In Face of Mystery*, p. 110.

25. *Ibid.*, p. 123.

26. Robert C. Neville, Review of *In Face of Mystery*, in *American Journal of Theology and Philosophy*, 15 (1994), p. 327.

27. William C. Placher, "Thinking our way to the ultimate mystery" (review), *Christian Century* (May 19–26, 1993), pp. 558–59.

28. Jerome A. Stone, *The Minimalist Vision of Transcendence: A Naturalist Philosophy of Religion* (Albany: State University of New York Press, 1992), p. 209.

29. Jerome A. Stone, "How Far Can Kaufman Go Towards Naturalism? The Divine Plurality as a Test," in *New Essays in Religious Naturalism*, eds. W. Creighton Peden and Larry E. Axel (Macon: Mercer University Press, 1993), p. 231.

30. Walter H. Capps, "Theology as Art Form," *Journal of the American Academy of Religion*, 50 (1982), pp. 93–96. I have treated an aesthetic perspective more fully in "Imaginative Construction in Theology: An Aesthetic Approach" (unpublished paper, 1990, revised 1995), 48 pp.

31. Immanuel Kant, *Critique of Pure Reason*, discussed in the "Transcendental Deduction," A95–A110. Norman Kemp Smith, trans., *Immanuel Kant's Critique of Pure Reason* (London: Macmillan and Co., Ltd., 1958), pp. 129–138.

32. Kaufman, *In Face of Mystery*, pp. 447–48. In this passage he makes clear he is not proposing a phenomenology of faith.

33. *Ibid.*, p. 434.

34. *Ibid.*, p. 447, italics are Kaufman's.

35. The terms are from Norman Kemp Smith, *A Commentary on Kant's Critique of Pure Reason* (London: Macmillan and Co., 1930), p. 273. Postmodern criticism has been attentive to the dynamics of unconscious process.

36. Kaufman, *In Face of Mystery*, pp. 52ff. Compare *An Essay on Theological Method*, chapter 3.

37. Kaufman, *In Face of Mystery*, p. 55.

38. Kaufman, *In Face of Mystery*, p. 452.

39. Wayne Proudfoot, "*Regulae fidei* and Regulative Idea: Two Contemporary Theological Strategies," in *Theology at the End of Modernity: Essays in Honor of Gordon D. Kaufman*, ed. Sheila Greeve Davaney (Philadelphia: Trinity Press International, 1991), p. 108.

40. *Ibid.*, p. 111.

41. Cf. Kaufman, *In Face of Mystery*, pp. 448, and 341 where he refers to the "symbolic patterns" operative in human subjectivity. Resources include: Paula M. Cooey, *Religious Imagination and the Body: A Feminist Analysis* (New York: Oxford University Press, 1994); and Mark Johnson, *The Body in the Mind: The Bodily Basis of Meaning, Imagination, and Reason* (Chicago: University of Chicago Press, 1987).

42. *Ibid.*, p. 54. "Thus, it is possible to engage in criticism and reconstruction of our conceptual schemes, even while we are living and thinking within them" (p. 55). Here Kaufman acknowledges the point I made in a review of *Theology for a Nuclear Age* in *Encounter*, 47 (1986), p. 76.

WHY DO WE MAKE THOSE CHOICES?
Some Reflections On Faith, Pluralism and Commitment

J. Wentzel van Huyssteen

> When a question is raised about the authority or dispensability of the idea of God or of an ultimate point of reference, . . . functional criteria alone will not serve to establish it in such a way as to enable it to fulfill those functions and to provide an object of loyalty and a critical perspective.
> . . . Theology must somehow reconstitute itself as genuine inquiry.
> (Proudfoot, 1991: p. 113)

Those of us who work in philosophical theology, and who believe that this mode of reflection does have some legitimate interdisciplinary status, are faced with a complex, if not bewildering set of questions: what, from an epistemological point of view, is the status of an ultimate religious commitment and thus of one's preferred faith or religion? Are there "real" or "true" religious experiences as opposed to "false" ones? How, and why, do some of us hang on to some form of faith in a postmodern age, and what happens to the problem of religious certainty in a postmodern context that celebrates pluralism? Can theology, as a reflection on religious experience, indeed claim to be a credible partner in the postmodern conversation, and if so, what will the effect of this conversation be on theology's claim to some form of credible knowledge? And last but not least, how does all of this relate to the shaping of other modes of inquiry, especially scientific knowledge, which often still seems to go unchallenged as the ultimate paradigm of human rationality?

Those of us who are concerned with these difficult questions, and especially with establishing theology as a genuine mode of inquiry, should realize that the most important point to this challenge will be the reconstruction of theological reflection as a mode of reflection with a legitimate interdisciplinary location. At the heart of this reconstruction of theology's interdisciplinary location, we find the quest for the epistemic and non-epistemic values that shape the rationality of religious/theological, and of scientific reflection. I also believe that in this interdisciplinary quest for the values that shape the rationality of theological and scientific reflection, at least two points have already been clearly established through a positive and constructive appropriation of the postmodern critique of foundationalist epistemology: first, when postmodernism is constructively seen as an ongoing and relentless critical return to the questions raised by modernity, and not just in radical opposition to modern thought, it shows itself best in the ongoing interrogation of our foundationalist assumptions, and thus as part of the to-and-fro movement between the modern and the postmodern elements of our various modes of intellectual inquiry (what we could broadly call the experience of knowing). Second, based on this imperative to always return to our assumptions with critical and responsible judgment, it seems to be highly implausible and certainly premature to claim that all arguments about epistemology belong to the "preliminaries," which as such (along with modernity) are now passe and thus, when jettisoned, will free us finally to "do" theology in terms of its own internal "logic." The epistemological task of reflecting on the epistemic and non-epistemic values that shape the rationality of theology and of science is therefore never done. This also seems to be the main reason why Calvin Schrag has recently claimed that postmodernism has not been able to deal with the issue of rationality in any adequate sense at all (cf. Schrag 1992: p. 155).

We all know today that the failure of foundationalism also was the failure of all forms of objectivist justification as handed down by the classic model of rationality. But both the extremes, an objectivist foundationalism and a relativist or subjectivist nonfoundationalism, reflect the inability of our intellectual culture to unite personal experience and personal conviction with some form of intersubjective rational justification (cf. M. Harvey 1994). I have recently argued for the retrieval of the experiential dimension of personal, responsible judgment as a truly *postfoundationalist* move to unite personal conviction with some form of plausible, rational evaluation or justification through communally shared expertise (cf. van Huyssteen 1996). Because of the shared resources of rationality between our various modes of human knowing, this fallibilist alternative to the opposites of foundationalist and nonfoundationalist models of rationality appears as a promising and viable option for both theological and scientific reflection.

I have also argued before that all religious (and certainly all theological) language always reflects the structure of our interpreted experience (cf. van Huyssteen 1993: pp. 253–265). In science too our concepts and theories can be seen as products of an interaction in which nature and ourselves play a formative role. The personal dimension of this relational knowledge does not at all take away from its validity and objectivity, which is warranted by a communally shared expertise. Our search for legitimate knowledge in fact always takes place within the social context of a community, and individuals who share a certain expertise make up this community and help, challenge, critique and confirm one another. If we relate to our world epistemically through the mediation of interpreted experience, our attempts to locate theology in the ongoing and evolving interdisciplinary discussion acquire new depth and meaning. It also brings us a few steps closer to answering Wayne Proudfoot's challenge to somehow reconstitute theology as genuine inquiry (cf. Proudfoot 1991: p. 113).

I.

From Fideism to Postfoundationalism. Part of the problem of the shaping of rationality in theological reflection is precisely the fact that religious experience may often seem to be immediate and noninferential, while in reality it never is independent of concepts, beliefs and practices. And if we always relate to our world epistemically through the mediation of interpreted experience, then our experience will always be theory-laden and tradition-specific. With this the profound and comprehensive ramifications of a religious commitment becomes clear: the criteria for identifying a specific form of religious consciousness as such will always include not only a reference to a whole framework or network of concepts, but also to a specific belief about how the experience is to be explained (cf. Proudfoot 1985: p. 14). This, however, will have important implications for any postfoundationalist critique of theological assumptions. Precisely because all religious experience is intentional or transactional (cf. Stone 1992: p. 130), it is always already interpreted in terms of the pre-existing patterns of the belief-systems we are already committed to. This then is the necessary tension we must hang on to: language gives us access to experience, while experience in turn predetermines linguistic expression. This is also the reason why the impact of a religious experience can best be accounted for by the fact that the criteria for identifying an experience as religious is always going to include reference to a very specific explanatory claim (cf. Proudfoot 1985: p. 216). Thus it is also revealed why religious beliefs and faith commitments will always already include in themselves important values and value-judgments which shape the rationality of theological reflection.

From this some important conclusions have to be drawn. Not only are religious beliefs and practices interpretations of our experiences which as such again become objects of interpretation; as interpretations of our experiences, religious beliefs also assume explanatory roles (cf. Proudfoot 1985: p. 41). In a postfoundationalist model of rationality, hermeneutics and epistemology will therefore always go together very closely. To say, therefore, that there is no such thing as an uninterpreted experience, is to say that all observation is theory-laden, and that again is to assume a concept of interpretation that reaches deep into the pragmatic, cognitive and evaluative dimensions of a postfoundationalist epistemology. Proudfoot says it well: our tacit theories and hypotheses have already played a constructive role in the perceptual judgments that make up our experience (1985: p. 61). To say, therefore, that experience is always interpreted, is to say that all our experience assumes particular concepts, beliefs, hypotheses, i.e., judgment skills about ourselves and the way we relate to our world through theological and scientific reflection.

The distinguishing mark of *religious* experience in this sense would therefore be the individual's judgment that the experience, and the beliefs that constitute the experience, can only be accounted for in religious terms. Why anybody would identify an experience as a religious experience could of course be explained in many ways, e.g., historically, psychologically, culturally or epistemologically. But what is to be explained here, is *why* we understand what happens to us in religious terms, and this requires the evaluation of the commitments and the tacit value-judgments we bring to our experiences, as well as contextual conditions, and the network of concepts, theories and beliefs that may support the plausibility of our judgments to identify our experiences in religious terms in the first place. Our judgments about the causes of our respective experiences therefore account for the difference between one of us having a religious experience and the other not (cf. Proudfoot 1985: p. 231). In this sense an explanatory commitment is always embedded in the criteria we use to judge or identify an experience as religious. An interest in explanations, and the value-judgements we bring to them, are therefore not alien elements illegitimately introduced into the study of religious experience: those of us who identify our experiences in religious terms are seeking the best available explanations for what is happening to us.

Thus, once more, the rationality of the quest for intelligibility in theological reflection is revealed, and along with that the fact that through the crucial epistemic skill of responsible critical judgment, theological reflection too may claim reasons for specific theory choice through an ongoing process of problem-solving. Locating theological reflection within the context of interdisciplinary reflection is possible especially because religion and science, within the context of our typically Western culture at least, are both part of the same interrelated intellectual conceptual structure. This explains why modes of critical thought that are at home in contemporary science, contemporary culture and in common sense, should indeed have a bearing on our assessment of the plausibility or rationality of religious belief. Foundationalist as well as nonfoundationalist attempts to deal with the justification of theory choice in philosophical theology have typically resulted, on the one hand, in inferential procedures that completely lose the experiential basis of religious reflection or, on the other hand, in nonfoundationalist attempts to evade the issue of the justification of religious belief altogether. This fideist view that religious beliefs are commitments which as such cannot be justified, has become especially popular in some forms of contemporary postmodern and postliberal theologies.

Some philosophers of religion relate much of the current fideism in philosophy of religion and in philosophical theology directly to Wittgenstein's celebrated notion of language games, which as forms of life cannot and need never be justified (cf. Frankenberry 1987: p. 11 f.). Fideism, as a blind, uncritical commitment to a set of beliefs, could of course be at the heart of both foundationalist and nonfoundationalist models of rationality. What happens in the fideistic move, however, is that an ultimate faith commitment in, for instance, the Christian God, is first isolated in a very definite protective strategy, and then equated to a commitment to a very specific set of foundational beliefs. Often, however, fideism and nonfoundationalism also collapse into one another when, for instance, religion, morality or science would each claim to have internal criteria of intelligibility peculiar only to itself. The fideist move where any account of religious faith, practices or experiences is nonfoundationally restricted to the perspective, worldview, beliefs and judgments of the subject alone, is thus equally revealed as a protective strategy (cf. Proudfoot 1985: p. 197), where the subject's own experience and explanation is never contested, and the need for transcommunal or intersubjective evaluation is never taken seriously.

Certainly the most serious limitation of any fideist epistemology, however, is its complete inability or explain why we choose some viewpoints, some language games or networks of belief over others, and why we believe that some in fact offer better and more plausible explanations than others. This not only brings us back to the crucial epistemic role of critical judgment in all human cognition, but also clearly suggests the need for some form of transcommunal or intersubjective criteria in theological reflection. There is obviously more to the matter of using religious language than just understanding and adopting the internal workings of some specialized linguistic system that is not answerable to anything or anybody outside itself (cf. Frankenberry 1987: p. 13). There obviously also is more to the making of commitments than just being embedded in forms of life that never can be questioned.

Religious language and theological theories are human conventions, and as such are closely interwoven with the way we relate epistemically to our world through the mediation of interpreted experience. As such they are the results of creative intellectual construction, and along with the commitments they serve to express, they should be examined and critiqued too. If this does not happen, fideist epistemologies will be misused as ideological shelters and protective strategies for immunizing religious beliefs and theological theories from critical examination, refutation or revision. Nancy Frankenberry goes even further and states that the work of some fideists is dominated by the same conservative attitudes which also characterizes some forms of evangelical Christianity: in the end, both groups embed their arguments in assumptions that reinforce dogmatism and serve to insulate from criticism precisely those already established standards, frameworks or activities that have come to be the most controversial in society (1987: p. 13). Thanks to the work of both Frankenberry and Proudfoot, it has also become abundantly clear what kind of protective strategies are invoked when appeals are made to direct or immediate religious experiences. The fact that appeals to immediate religious experiences, and therefore also appeals to self-authenticating notions of divine revelation, have become almost universally suspect, does not, however, take away from the serious problems created for theology by our claim that (like in science) we have no access to uninterpreted experiences. Does this mean, for instance, that we can never have direct experiences of God, but only experiences interpreted in a theistic manner?

It seems that Jerome Stone was right: in a sense one's concept of experience will indeed entail one's concept of meaning, which in turn will determine one's concept of religious cognition (Stone 1992). So why do some of us choose for more or less traditional forms of Christian faith, others for minimalist visions of transcendence, and still others for naturalism or constructive historicism? First of all, it has hopefully now become clear that, because of the nature and implications of interpreted experience, no general epistemological account can ever be given of the way in which we make these choices, and why a transcendent possibility may, for some at least, become a plausible experienced reality. A postfoundationalist model of rationality does, however, leave us an important epistemic opening: we can pragmatically point to the fact that throughout history, and in various cultures (including our own) human beings have found it helpful, if not necessary, to make room for a religious interpretation of the natural dimensions of our world and ourselves. This then is what we mean by the experiential accountability of religious faith: some of us judge it to be fruitful, within specific cultural contexts and the ongoing dynamic flow of traditions, to view the nature of this religious awareness as based in a relational interaction between humans and God (cf. Gill 1981: p. 122). Our commitment to God thus would arise not only *from* experience, but in a very specific sense also *for* experience, i.e. for making optimal sense of our experience within the concrete contexts of specific evolving traditions.

This postfoundationalist choice for the relational quality of religious experience thus opens up the possibility of interpreting religiously the way which we believe God comes to us in and through the manifold of our experiences of nature, persons, ideas, emotions, places, things, and events. And because of this religious quest for ultimate meaning, each dimension and context of our experience may contain within itself not just a potential element of minimalist transcendence, but an element of mystery, which when responded to, may be plausibly said to carry with it the potential for divine disclosure. It is also the element of mystery in all religious reflection that has often led to claims that theology and the sciences, if not in conflict, should at least be seen as incommensurably different paradigms from one another. This element of mystery, when followed by a religious commitment, does indeed again seem to force theology out of the shared domain of interdisciplinary discussion and now confronts us with the serious question: are deep and personal religious convictions radically opposed to, and different from other forms of knowledge, and does this again imply a radical and incommensurable difference between scientific and theological rationality? The postfoundationalist notion of rationality for which I have argued above claims, of course, the exact opposite: we should be able to enter the pluralist, interdisciplinary conversation with our full personal convictions and at the same time be theoretically empowered to step beyond the limitations and boundaries of our own contexts or forms of life. How do we, however, in this discussion justify the pragmatic move of choosing for or against a commitment, a theory, a model, a tradition?

II.

Tradition, Commitment and Pluralism. To try to answer this question adequately, I now want to take the ramifications of the fact that we relate to our world epistemically only through the medium of interpreted experience one step further by exploring what it might mean that our interpreted experience is always contextual and as such determined (epistemically and non-epistemically) by living and evolving traditions. We saw earlier that responsible judgments and problem-solving theory choices ultimately constitute the true nature of rational reflection. This implies that not just our rational beliefs, but also any plausible notion of problem-solving progress, are therefore located within the context of living, changing and developing traditions. Any time we choose to modify or replace a theory with another theory, that change is progressive if and only if the later version is a better problem-solver than its predecessor (cf. van Huyssteen 1989: pp. 172 ff.). The real meaning of intellectual growth is then found (in fallibilist terms) in our ability to find good enough reasons for choosing one theory or framework of ideas above another. Larry Laudan also convincingly argued that it is these more general, global theories, rather than only the more specific ones, which turn out to be our primary tools for understanding and appraising progressive theory choices (cf. Laudan 1977: p. 71 f.). These comprehensive or global frameworks of theories, because of the interpreted nature of all human cognition, form an essential part of the structure of all forms of human cognition. Kuhn called them paradigms, Lakatos called them research programs, and Laudan calls them research traditions. These research traditions are complex and comprehensive frameworks and when carefully analysed always reveal a network of conceptual, theoretical, instrumental and metaphysical commitments that give the research tradition its particular identity.

No postfoundationalist notion of rationality would ever claim that these broader traditions, unlike specific theories, are in any way directly testable or justifiable. This does not mean, however, that they are outside the problem-solving process. Because a progressive or successful research tradition leads one, through its component theories, to the adequate solution of an increasing range of empirical and conceptual problems, the tradition itself could claim a very specific form of theoretical and experiential adequacy. The degree of this adequacy, of course, tells us nothing about the truth or falsity of the tradition itself (cf. Laudan 1977: p. 82), but rather points to pragmatic criteria for choosing (through responsible judgment) between frameworks of thought, frameworks that may in reality be very different from one another. We thus saw that the role of critical judgment in all cognition not only implies a distinctly pragmatic move, but also enables us to retain the idea of intersubjective rational appraisal and the idea of progress in a clearly postmodernist and postfoundationalist way.

Research traditions, like all traditions, are historical creatures (cf. D. Brown 1994: pp. 24 ff.). As such they are created and articulated within a particular intellectual milieu, and like all other historical institutions, they wax and wane (cf. Laudan 1977: p. 95). We saw earlier that in both theology and in other modes of knowledge, we relate to our worlds epistemically through the medium of interpreted experience. This interpretation of experience, however, always takes place within the comprehensive context of living and evolving traditions, and these traditions are epistemically constituted by broader paradigms or research traditions. Because of their historical nature, research traditions in all modes of human knowledge can change and evolve through either the internal modification of some of its specific theories, or through a change of some of its most basic core elements. Larry Laudan correctly points out that Kuhn's famous notion of a "conversion" or paradigmatic revolution from one paradigm to another (cf. Kuhn 1970: pp. 92 ff.) can most probably be better described as a natural evolution within and between research traditions. Traditions, however, not only imply ongoing change and evolution, they also exhibit continuity. In this sense Delwin Brown is right in maintaining that in any adequate theory of traditions, continuity and change would be primary categories (D. Brown 1994: p. 24 f.).

To understand what continuity and change might mean in the dynamic of evolving traditions, Laudan (like Lakatos) suggests that certain elements of a research tradition are sacrosanct and can therefore not be rejected without repudiation of the tradition itself. Unlike Lakatos, however, Laudan insists that what is normally seen as sacrosanct in traditions can indeed change with time (cf. Laudan 1977: p. 99). This not only reveals again the radical historical nature of all research traditions, but also that intellectual and scientific revolutions take place, not necessarily through complete shifts, but through the ongoing integration and the grafting of research traditions.

This now takes us back again to a problem which, while exceedingly difficult for theology to deal with, has become impossible to ignore if we want to move beyond both the epistemological extremes of foundationalism and nonfoundationalism: are we ultimately, and fideistically, the prisoners of our research traditions and commitments? And if not, why do we choose to commit ourselves (often passionately) to only certain traditions, theories, viewpoints? In trying to answer these complex and challenging questions, I will argue that, first, we should be able to enter the pluralist, interdisciplinary conversation between research traditions with our full personal convictions, while at the same time stepping beyond the strict boundaries of our own intellectual contexts. And, second, we can indeed in interdisciplinary discussion justify our choices for or against a specific research tradition. As we saw earlier, the fact that broader research traditions can as such never be directly tested or justified, does not mean that they are outside the problem-solving process.

III.

A Christian voice in a pluralist conversation? An intriguing attempt to move beyond the objectivism of foundationalism and the radical relativism of nonfoundationalism, and to identify a distinctly Christian voice in the contemporary pluralist American culture, is found in an argument put forward by William C. Placher (1989). Thanks to its confusing and unfortunate title, this book starts out on the wrong foot, and *Unapologetic Theology* indeed seems to suggest that an "assertive" and esoteric Christian theology, not caring about the rules of responsible conversation, might turn out to be the only way to speak "Christianly" today. The most important reason for this confusion is, however, not so much the book's title, as Placher's claim that Christians ought to speak in their own distinct voice without worrying about finding philosophical "foundations" for their claims (cf. Placher 1989: p. 13).

Placher wants Christians to be both authentic partners in the pluralist conversation between diverse research traditions, and also to remain faithful to their own vision of things for reasons internal to the Christian faith. However, when Placher begins to argue against theology's intellectual isolation and hopes for making "wider connections while still speaking faithfully in one's own voice" (cf. 1989: p. 13), he has already moved beyond any nonfoundationalist "unapologetic theology" into what I have consistently called the third option of a postfoundationalist rationality. In our pluralist and often fragmented postmodern culture, an adequate Christian apologetics could hardly still be about just adopting and assimilating the language and assumptions of our culture (cf. Placher 1989: p. 11 f.). On the contrary, good apologetics today is precisely about finding an authentic and committed voice in a pluralist conversation. In fact, for Placher too Christians have reasons internal to their own tradition for seeking out members of *other* traditions for serious dialogue (cf. 1989: p. 116).

Although Placher's initial anti-philosophical remarks remain puzzling and unfortunate, it should not detract from the fact that he seriously engages with contemporary theology, philosophy and science, and thereby inadvertently clears the way for a postfoundational epistemology in theology. By now proposing authentic interdisciplinary conversation as a model for meaningful interaction between theology and culture, theology and science, theology and philosophy, and between different research traditions in theology, Placher already moves beyond his own self-confessed postliberal leanings (cf. 1989: p. 20). This is eminently clear from the structure of this work which is developed exactly around the specific implications which an interdisciplinary conversation will have for the relation between religion and science, for the dialogue with different research traditions and other religions, and (last but not least) for theological method.

By locating theology in the heart of the interdisciplinary conversation, Placher wants to develop a theological "middle ground" by moving beyond various forms of (nonfoundationalist) relativisms like the Wittgensteinian fideists' image of cultures as self-contained worlds that never interact and postliberalism's theological isolationism. Because of theology's interdisciplinary location, conversation now becomes possible even in the absence of any claims to universal rules. For Placher a genuine conversation involves conversation partners who come to the conversation with all their beliefs, prejudices, and presuppositions intact. In developing this interactionist position, Placher's viewpoint (although he never explores these possibilities) now reveals remarkable epistemological similarities to what earlier I identified as a postfoundationalist notion of rationality. Even with widely divergent viewpoints, we do share similar resources of human rationality, and because of these epistemological overlaps there may be an overlap of beliefs that may provide a place or common ground for a particular conversation to begin (cf. Placher 1989: p. 106).

In his recent *Boundaries of our Habitations: Tradition and Theological Construction*, Delwin Brown also takes up some of these issues and proposes a constructive historicism where theology retrieves its trans-contextual obligation precisely by being the caregiver of tradition (1994: pp. 111–155). Seeing tradition as the matrix of creative theological reflection may help us to develop a form of theological thinking that would be both culturally and religiously more effective, by achieving an integration of inheritance and imagination in theological reflection that is as adequate as possible. The central theme of Brown's book thus develops around an exploration of the idea that tradition is one type of cultural strategy, one way of negotiating chaos and order, or (as I would put it) one way of facilitating responsible critical judgment in our theory choices.

Both William Placher's (1989) and Delwin Brown's (1994) views on trans-contextual conversation and evaluation will be significantly strengthened when supported by the kind of postfoundationalist epistemology I have outlined above, which also has close affinities with what religious epistemologist Andy F. Sanders has recently called "traditionalist fallibilism" (1995). I would put it as follows: we begin our conversations by bringing our fallible views and judgments to those who traditionally make up our epistemic communities (the "experts"). In a postfoundationalist evaluation of the beliefs, opinions and viewpoints that hold our commitments, the epistemic movement thus goes from individual judgment to expert, communal evaluation to intersubjective conversation. Because each judgment, and each rhetorical argument always takes place in some community, and each community has a particular tradition and history, the broader research tradition(s) in which communities are embedded will now epistemically shape (but not completely determine) the questions one asks, the assumptions one can make, and the arguments one will find persuasive. For theology this interdisciplinary location not only opens the way to genuine conversation, but also reveals a judgment about how theology should be done and the criteria to which theological claims should be obligated. Delwin Brown puts a similar conclusion succinctly: Theology, even specifically Christian theology, is answerable to canons of critical inquiry defensible within the various arenas of our common discourse, and not merely within those that are Christian (cf. D. Brown 1994: p. 4 f.).

The fact that there are no more foundationalist, universal, cross-cultural or interreligious rules for theology does not therefore necessarily mean that all criteria are now always going to be strictly local or exclusively contextual. If none of our criteria were to be acceptable beyond the boundaries of a research tradition, the giving of rational reasons beyond the boundaries of any tradition would be impossible (cf. D. Brown 1994: p. 6). The crucial problem for a theology located in interdisciplinary conversation therefore remains the following: is it at all possible to make sensible and rational choices between different viewpoints and alternative research traditions? At this point Larry Laudan's admonition to scientists and theologians comes to mind: unless we can somehow articulate criteria for choice between research traditions, we neither have a theory of rationality, nor a theory of what progressive growth in knowledge should be (cf. Laudan 1977: p. 106). In theology, like in other forms of inquiry, providing warrants for our views thus becomes a cross-contextual obligation (cf. D. Brown 1994: p. 6 f.).

The postmodern challenge always to critique our own assumptions certainly means that there are no universal standards of rationality against which we can measure other beliefs or research traditions. The fact that we lack a clear and "objective" criterion for judging the experiential adequacy or problem-solving ability of one tradition over another, does not, however, leave us with a radical relativism, or even with an easy pluralism. Our ability to make rational judgments and share them with various and different epistemic communities also means that we are able to communicate with one another meaningfully through conversation, deliberation and evaluation. Sharing our views and judgments with those inside and outside our epistemic communities can therefore lead to a truly postfoundationalist conversation, which we should enter not just to persuade, but also to learn from. In Placher's terms: such a style of inquiry can provide a way of thinking about rationality that respects authentic pluralism—it does not force us all to share the same assumptions, but it finds ways we can talk with one another and criticize our traditions while standing in them. In this sense genuine pluralism ought to allow for conversations between people who may enter the conversation for very different reasons (Placher 1989: p. 117). This means that, even if we lack universal rules for rationality, and even if we can never judge the reasonableness of statements and beliefs in isolation from their cultural or disciplinary contexts, we can still meaningfully engage in cross-contextual evaluation and conversation and give the best available cognitive, evaluative or pragmatic reasons for the responsible choices we hope to make.

REFERENCES

Barbour, Ian G. 1974. *Myths, Models and Paradigms: A Comparative Study in Science and Religion.* New York: Harper and Row.

———. 1990. *Religion in and Age of Science.* San Francisco: Harper and Row.

Bartley, William W. 1964. *The Retreat to Commitment.* London: Chatto and Windus.

Brown, Delwin. 1994. *Boundaries of our Habitations: Tradition and Theological Construction.* New York: SUNY.

Brown, Harold. 1990. *Rationality.* London/New York: Routledge.

Frankenberry, Nancy. 1987. *Religion and Radical Empiricism.* Albany: SUNY.

Gill, Jerry H. 1981. *On Knowing God.* Philadelphia: The Westminster Press.

Harvey, Michael G. 1994. *Personal Conviction and Rational Justification.* Unpublished paper for a Ph.D. Seminar on "Theology and Rationality" at Princeton Theological Seminary.

Johnson, Elizabeth A. 1993. *She Who Is.* New York: Crossroad.

Jones, Stanton. 1994. "A Constructive Relationship for Religion with the Science and Profession of Psychology: Perhaps the Boldest Model Yet." *American Psychologist* 49 (3).

Kuhn, Thomas S. 1970. *The Structure of Scientific Revolutions.* Chicago: University of Chicago Press.

Laudan, Larry. 1977. *Progress and its Problems: Towards a Theory of Scientific Growth.* London: Routledge and Kegan Paul.

Merleau-Ponty, Maurice. 1962. *Phenomenology of Perception.* London: Routledge and Kegan Paul.

Murphy, Nancy. 1990. *Theology in an Age of Scientific Reasoning.* Ithaca: Cornell University Press.

Placher, William C. 1989. *Unapologetic Theology: A Christian Voice in a Pluralist Conversation.* Louisville: Westminster/John Knox.

Polkinghorne, John. 1991. *Reason and Reality.* Philadelphia: Trinity Press International.

Proudfoot, Wayne. 1985. *Religious Experience.* Berkeley: University of California Press

———. 1991. "*Regulae fidei* and Regulative Idea: Two Contemporary Theological Strategies." In: Sheila Greeve Davaney (Ed.), *Theology at the End of Modernity: Essays in Honor of Gordon Kaufman.* Philadelphia: Trinity Press International.

Rolston, Holmes. 1987. *Science and Religion: A Critical Survey.* New York: Random House.

Rottschaeffer, William A. 1985. "Religious Cognition as Interpreted Experience: An Examination of Ian Barbour's Comparison of the Epistemic Structures of Science and Religion." *Zygon: Journal of Religion and Science* 20 (3).

Sanders, Andy. 1995. "Traditionalism, Fallibilism and Theological Relativism." Forthcoming in *Nederlands Theologisch Tijdschrift.*

Schrag, Calvin O. 1992. *The Resources of Rationality: A Response to the Postmodern Challenge.* Bloomington/Indianapolis: Indiana University Press.

Stoeger, William R., SJ. 1988. "Contemporary Cosmology and Its Implications for the Science-Religion Dialogue," in Robert J. Russell, William R. Stoeger, SJ, George Koyne, SJ, (Eds.): *Physics, Philosophy and Theology: A Common Quest for Understanding.* Vatican City State: Vatican Observatory.

Stone, Jerome A. 1992. *A Minimalist Vision of Transcendence: A Naturalist Philosophy of Religion.* Albany: SUNY.

Trigg, Roger. 1977. *Reason and Commitment.* Cambridge: University Press.

Van Huyssteen, J. Wentzel. 1987. *The Realism of The Text.* Pretoria: UNISA

———. 1989. *Theology and the Justification of Faith: Constructing Theories in Systematic Theology.* Grand Rapids: Wm. Eerdmans.

———. 1993. "Critical Realism and God: Can there be Faith after Foundationalism?" In: *Intellektueel in Konteks: Opstelle vir Hennie Rossouw.* A.A. van Niekerk (Ed.). Pretoria: HSRC Publishers.

———. 1996 *The Shaping of Rationality in Religion and Science.* [Forthcoming]

ABOUT THE AUTHORS

Victor Anderson (Ph.D. Princeton University) is Assistant Professor of Christian Ethics at Vanderbilt Divinity School. He is the author of *Beyond Ontological Blackness: An Essay in African American Religious and Cultural Criticism* (1995), and *Pragmatic Theology: Negotiating the Intersections of An American Philosophy of Religion and Public Theology* (Forthcoming).

J. Harley Chapman (Ph.D. University of Chicago) is Professor of Philosophy and Humanities, and Dean of the Liberal Arts Division at William Rainey Harper College. He is the author of *Jung's Three Theories of Religious Experience* and co-editor of a forthcoming volume of critical studies in the thought of Robert Neville.

Donald A. Crosby (Ph.D. Columbia University) is Professor of Philosophy at Colorado State University, Fort Collins, Colorado. In addition to articles in professional journals, he is the author of *Horace Bushnell's Theory of Language: In the Context of Other Nineteenth-Century Philosophies of Language* (1975), *Interpretive Theories of Religion* (1981), and *The Specter of the Absurd: Sources and Criticisms of Modern Nihilism* (1988). His current interests lie mainly in the fields of American philosophy, process metaphysics, and the philosophy of nature.

Sheila Davaney is Associate Professor of Theology at Iliff School of Theology, Denver, Colorado. She is the author of *Divine Power: A Study in Karl Barth and Charles Hartshorne*, and the editor of *Theology at the End of Modernity* and *Feminism and Process Thought*. She is also the co-editor of two forthcoming volumes, the first with Dwight Hopkins entitled *Changing Conversations: Religious Reflection and Cultural Analysis* (Routledge, 1996); and the second with Rebecca Chopp on feminist theology and the role of theory (Fortress, 1997). She has written widely on feminist issues. Her current research is on pragmatism and theology. She is presently chair of the Theology and Religious Reflection Section of the American Academy of Religion, serves on the Board of Directors of the AAR, the Committee on Regions, and the Long Range

Planning and Development Committee of the AAR. She is Secretary of the Rocky Mountains-Great Plains Region of the AAR.

Mary Doak is a Ph.D. candidate in The Divinity School at The University of Chicago, where she is working on a dissertation on the contributions of narrative to an American public theology. She also teaches in the philosophy department at North Park College.

Warren Frisina (Ph.D., University of Chicago) is currently the Associate Executive Director of the American Academy of Religion and Assistant Professor in the Department of Religion at Emory University. His writings include articles on American pragmatism, process philosophy, and Chinese philosophy.

David L. Hall (Ph.D. Yale University) is Professor of Philosophy at the University of Texas at El Paso. His first three books dealt with the philosophy of culture: *The Civilization of Experience* (1973), *The Uncertain Phoenix* (1982), and *Eros and Irony* (1982). He has also written three works on comparative Chinese and Western thought with Roger Ames of the University of Hawai'i: *Thinking Though Confucius* (1987), *Anticipating China* (1995), and *Thinking From the Han* (1997). In addition, Hall has published a work entitled *Richard Rorty—Prophet and Poet of the New Pragmatism* (1994), and *The Arimaspian Eye*, a philosophical novel (1992).

Fred W. Hallberg is an Associate Professor of Philosophy at the University of Northern Iowa, where he has taught philosophy and humanities since 1967. He received his B.A. (1958) from the University of Minnesota, and after two years in the U.S. Army, returned to the University of Minnesota to complete his M.A. (1963) and Ph.D. (1969) in philosophy. While at UNI he completed an M.S. in Counseling Psychology at Iowa State University and 100 hours of training in Gestalt psychotheraphy at the PCM Institute of Oak Brook, Illinois.

Charley Hardwick (Ph.D. Yale University) is Professor of Religious Studies at The American University in Washington, D.C. In addition to articles in professional journals, he is the author of *Faith and Objectivity: Fritz Buri and the Hermeneutical Foundations of a Radical Theology*, *Religious Truth in the Absence of God*, and *Events of Grace*. A recipient of Danforth, Guggenheim, American Council of Learned Societies, and

About the Authors

The Society for Values in Higher Education fellowships, he also served as editor of the American Academy of Religion "Aids to the Study of Religion" and "Studies in Religion" monograph series.

Yeager Hudson (Ph.D., Boston University) Charles A. Dana Professor of Philosophy, Colby College. Books authored: *Philosophy of Religion*; *Emerson and Tagore: The Poet as Philosopher*. Books edited: *Philosophy of Religion: Selected Readings*; *Rending and Renewing the Social Order*. Books co-edited: *The Social Power of Ideas*; *The Bill of Rights: Bicentennial Reflections*; *Terrorism, Justice and Social Values*; *Revolution, Violence and Equality*; *Communitarianism, Liberalism, and Social Responsibility*; *Freedom, Dharma and Rights*.

Jennifer Jesse is a Ph.D. candidate at the University of Chicago Divinity School in the field of Religion and Literature. She is writing her dissertation on the religious thought of William Blake.

Henry Samuel Levinson is Professor and Head of Religious Studies at UNC Greensboro. He is the author of many essays, articles and reviews, and *Santayana, Pragmatism, and the Spiritual Life* (1992), *The Religious Investigations of William James* (19981) and *Science, Metaphysics, and the Chance of Salvation* (1978). He is currently writing a book about Judaism, politics and philosophy, from his pragmatic Jewish American point of view.

Robert C. Neville is Professor of Philosophy, Religion, and Theology at Boston University where he is also Dean of the School of Theology. He is past president of the American Academy of Religion, the Metaphysical Society of America, and the International Society of Chinese Philosophy. Among his books are *A Theology Primer*; *The Tao and the Daimon*; *God the Creator: On the Transcendence and Presence of God*; *Reconstruction of Thinking*; *Recovery of the Measure: Interpretation and Nature*; *Behind the Masks of God*; *Eternity and Time's Flow*, and *Normative Cultures*.

Mason Olds (Ph.D. Brown University) is Professor of Religion and Philosophy at Springfield College and editor of the journal *Religious Humanism*. In addition to numerous articles in professional journals, he is the author of *Religious Humanism in America: Dietrich, Reese, and*

Potter and of *Story: The Language of Faith*, and is the editor of *What If The World Went Humanist?* (Ten Addresses by John H. Dietrich).

Thomas D. Parker (Ph.D. Princeton Theological Seminary) is Cyrus H. McCormick Professor in Systematic Theology at McCormick Theological Seminary in Chicago. He is co-editor of *Christian Theology. A Case Method Approach* and of *Peace, War and God's Justice*, and the author of many articles and reviews. He was a recipient of a Rockefeller Brothers Doctoral Fellowship in Religion and of an Association of Theological Schools Faculty Fellowship for post-doctoral research in questions of theology and aesthetics at the University of Munich.

Hendrik R. Pieterse, M.div., is currently associate pastor at First United Methodist Church in Tullahoma, Tennessee. He is a D.Phil. candidate at the University of Port Elizabeth, Port Elizabeth, South Africa. His dissertation is entitled, *The Revisionist Theology of David Tracy: A Postmodern Challenge*.

Wayne Proudfoot (Ph.D., Harvard) is Professor of Religion at Columbia University and the author of *God and the Self* and of *Religious Experience*. He is currently working on a book on pragmatism and American religious thought.

J. Wesley Robbins (Ph.D. University of Chicago Divinity School) is Professor of Philosophy at Indiana University South Bend. He has published widely in a number of journals on topics in the philosophy of religion, ethics, and religion and science.

Richard Rorty is University Professor of Humanities at the University of Virginia. He previously taught at Wellesley College and Princeton University. His books include *Philosophy and the Mirror of Nature; Contingency, Irony and Solidarity; Consequences of Pragmatism*, and *Objectivity, Relativism and Truth*. He is a graduate of the University of Chicago and received his Ph. D. from Yale University. He has held Guggenheim and MacArthur fellowships.

Jerome P. Soneson (Ph.D., Harvard University) is Associate Professor of Religion at the University of Northern Iowa. His recent book, *Pragmatism and Pluralism: John Dewey's Significance for Theology*, argues for the

About the Authors

value of pragmatic historicism as a method and perspective adequate for addressing pressing problems in theology.

Jerome A. Stone (Ph.D., University of Chicago) is Professor of Philosophy at William Rainey Harper College. In addition to articles in professional journals, he is the author of *The Minimalist Vision of Transcendence: A Neo-naturalist Philosophy of Religion*.

Everett J. Tarbox, Jr. is Professor of Humanities at Indiana State University. He is a graduate of Texas Tech University (B.A.), Southwestern Baptist Theological Seminary (B.D., Th.D.), and the University of Chicago (M.A., Ph.D.). He is the author of scholarly articles focusing upon the writings of Ludwig Wittgenstein, William James, and Donald Cupitt.

Edgar A. Towne is Professor of Theology, Emeritus, at Christian Theological Seminary. He is a graduate of the College of Wooster (B.A.), Pittsburgh Theological Seminary (M.Div.), The University of Chicago (M.A., Ph.D.). He has published widely in journals and is a past president of the American Theological Society (Midwest Division), 1986–87.

J. Wentzel van Huyssteen, originally from South Africa, is Princeton Theological Seminary's first James I. McCord Professor of Theology and Science. He has research degrees in Philosophy (M.A.) and Philosophical Theology (D.Th.) and is the author of several books and numerous articles. His book *Theology and the Justification of Faith* (1989) was awarded the Andrew Murray Prize, as well as the Venter Prize for Academic Excellence. Since moving to Princeton in 1992, he has won three Templeton Awards for his work in theology and Science.

Henk M. Vroom is Professor of Philosophy of Religion at the faculties of Theology and Philosophy of the Vrije Universiteit at Amsterdam. His fields of special interest are theological hermeneutics, interreligious dialogue and theory of religion. He has published widely on these subjects in journals, is author of six books, and is co-editor of nine volumes, most recently of *Human Rights and Religious Values*, eds. A. An-Na'im, *et al.*, *Religions and the Truth*, and *No Other Gods*.

American Liberal Religious Thought

This series is devoted to monographs and collections of essays that explore historically and develop constructively the tradition of American liberal religious thought in the context of its ongoing relations with other forms of thought, especially those of American philosophy. Themes pertinent to the "Chicago School" of theology and to naturalism in American theology and philosophy figure prominently in the religious liberalism focused on in these volumes. The sponsor of the series is the Highlands Institute for American Religious Thought, a community of productive scholars with diverse religious and philosophical perspectives that has its headquarters in Highlands, North Carolina.

Peter Lang Publishing
Acquisitions Department
275 Seventh Ave., 28th Floor
New York, NY 10001